NATIONHOOD AND
NATIONALISM IN FRANCE

TITLES OF RELATED INTEREST

*Cities and Social Change in Early
Modern France*
edited by Philip Benedict

*The French Revolution 1787–1799: From the storming
of the Bastille to Napoleon*
Albert Soboul

European Society 1500–1700
Henry Kamen

A Social History of Nineteenth-Century France
Roger Price

Henry IV King of France
David Buisseret

Themes in Modern European History 1830–1890
Edited by Bruce Waller

*Fascists and Conservatives: The radical right and the
establishment in twentieth-century Europe*
Edited by Martin Blinkhorn

*The First Imperial Age: European overseas
expansion c. 1400–1715*
G. V. Scammell

NATIONHOOD AND NATIONALISM IN FRANCE
From Boulangism to the Great War
1889–1918

Edited by
ROBERT TOMBS

HarperCollins*Academic*
An imprint of HarperCollins*Publishers*

© Robert Tombs 1991

This book is copyright under the Berne Convention. No reproduction without permission. All rights reserved.

The author asserts the moral right to be identified as the author of this work.

Published by
HarperCollins*Academic*

77–85 Fulham Palace Road
Hammersmith
London W6 8JB
UK

10 East 53rd Street
New York, NY 10022
USA

First published in 1991

British Library Cataloguing in Publication Data

Nationhood and nationalism in France.
I. Tombs, Robert
320.50944

ISBN 0–04–445742–1

Library of Congress Cataloging in Publication Data

A catalog record for this book is available on request

Typeset in 10 on 12 point Garamond
Printed in Great Britain by The University Press, Cambridge

Contents

Acknowledgements	page	ix
Preface		xi

PART 1 Sentiment and ideology

Introduction
Robert Tombs — 3

1 Gauls versus Franks: conflict and nationalism
Eugen Weber — 8

2 The political culture of nationalism
Zeev Sternhell — 22

3 Nationalist responses to the revolution
Christian Amalvi — 39

4 Families and fatherlands: the lost provinces and the case of Captain Dreyfus
Michael Burns — 50

5 Joan of Arc between right and left
Gerd Krumeich — 63

6 Words and images of nationhood
Pierre Sorlin — 74

7 The national sentiment of soldiers during the Great War
Stéphane Audoin-Rouzeau — 89

PART 2 Nationalism and politics

Introduction
Albert Vaiciulenas — 103

8 Royalists and the politics of nationalism
William D. Irvine — 108

9 The nationalists of Meurthe-et-Moselle, 1888–1912
William Serman — 121

Contents

10 Nationalists and Bonapartists 136
    Bernard Ménager

11 The Jeunesse Antisémite et Nationaliste, 1894–1904 147
    Bertrand Joly

12 Parisian white-collar employees and nationalism in
    the *belle époque* 159
    Lenard R. Berlanstein

13 *La république et la patrie*: the radicals' nationalism
    under attack 168
    Judith F. Stone

14 Dividing and uniting: sports societies and
    nationalism, 1870–1914 182
    Pierre Arnaud

15 Exploring the sexual politics of republican nationalism 195
    Karen Offen

16 Social defence and conservative regeneration:
    the national revival, 1900–14 210
    Philip Nord

PART 3 Policy in the era of nationalism

Introduction 231
David Stevenson

17 The army and the *appel au soldat*, 1874–89 238
    Jean-Charles Jauffret

18 The school battalions in the east, 1882–92:
    reasons for failure 248
    Gérard Canini

19 Patriotism, politics and policy in
    the Foreign Ministry, 1880–1914 255
    John Keiger

20 Strategic independence and security of communications:
    the undersea telegraph cables 267
    Jean-Claude Allain

List of contributors 279

Index 282

Acknowledgements

This book stems from a conference held at St John's College, Cambridge, in April 1989. I should like to thank the Master and Fellows for their financial generosity, which made it possible, and for their hospitality, which made it agreeable. Valuable financial assistance was also given by the French Cultural Delegation in Cambridge, the British Academy, and the Cambridge History Faculty. Professor Philippe Levillain kindly handled much of the administrative work involved in bringing over the French participants. The publishers, represented principally by Jane Harris-Matthews, were both encouraging and understanding. Special thanks are due to Meg Sanders, who translated the French contributions so lucidly.

Preface

The theme of 'nation' has been central in French political thought and practice since the revolution. For the revolutionaries, the nation replaced the king as the source of political legitimacy; the will of the nation was the justification for their acts. From the beginning, this concept was a domestic political weapon and so it always remained: opponents were attacked as enemies of the nation. The revolutionary wars brought out xenophobic aspects, exalting the uniqueness of the French nation as the embodiment of progress, and justifying its conquests as acts of liberation.[1] The return of the Bourbon monarchy in 1814 and again in 1815 'in the baggage train of the Allies' renewed the domestic political potency of the national theme, by associating the ultraroyalist party with the nation's foreign enemies. Moreover, as Eugen Weber recalls below, aristocrats were alleged to be descendants of the conquering Franks who had for centuries oppressed the Gauls. Hence the overthrow of the Bourbon monarchy in 1830 was hailed as a 'national revolution' and revenge for Waterloo.

Throughout the next two decades the national theme continued to be played in many contexts – for example, hostility to foreign goods or foreign workers could be justified as the defence of *le travail national* against the depredations of the English or the Jews – but was always founded on the assertion that the true interests of the nation were being neglected or betrayed by decadent anti-national elements within the body politic, and by governments that were toadying to these or to foreign pressures. During the 1840s, the most vehement accusers were Bonapartists, left-wing liberals (the Centre-Gauche and Gauche Dynastique groups), republicans and socialists, and their principal targets were the bourgeoisie – caricatured as 'les satisfaits', 'les ventrus', 'gros, gras et bêtes' – and the 'bourgeois monarchy' of Louis Philippe. They were endlessly accused of creating an atomized and decadent society by putting selfish material interests before the honour and greatness of the nation and its historic mission: in Michelet's words, 'c'est l'égoisme pur du calculateur sans patrie'.[2] 'We shall first bring down the enemy within, and then we shall deal with the enemies without,' wrote a liberal in 1840, encapsulating the classic nationalist programme.[3] The supporters of these attacks were broadly speaking the whole political left (though often echoed by the legitimist right), but with different degrees of virulence between the parliamentary opposition such as Thiers, Tocqueville, or Barrot, and

Preface

more radical elements, republicans such as Quinet or Michelet (discussed below by Zeev Sternhell), socialists such as Cabet, Buchez, or Considérant, and Bonapartists such as Carrel. The former wished to harness national feeling to push the regime in a more bellicose and hence more popular direction, but with the intention of saving it from its own weaknesses; the latter hoped to destroy it, and with it the political and social order in France and Europe, if necessary in a new, and this time victorious, revolutionary war of national liberation.

The revolution of 1848, like that of 1830, was suffused with national fervour and seemed about to precipitate the long-expected Armaggedon; but as had been the case after 1830, the new regime drew back from the abyss. It was eventually Napoleon III who began to put the 'national' programme into effect, with major wars in the Crimea and Italy that did indeed appear to reverse the consequences of Waterloo, and gave the regime a prestige and popularity that none of its predecessors since 1815 had attained. This was surely a major reason why in the 1860s the national ardour of republicans and liberals became muted: the pugnacity that they had long advocated had proved to be a rod for their backs by strengthening their common political enemy, Napoleon III.

The defeat of 1870 and the fall of the empire awakened national fervour, but also inflamed old divisions. According to the left, the war had been lost in spite of heroic republican resistance by the folly and egoism of a right willing, as in the past, to betray the nation for the sake of its own material interests. According to the right, the republicans, as in the past, had seized the opportunity of national disaster to promote revolution. The civil war of 1871 was the most violent expression of this division. It still coloured the struggle between royalism and republicanism during the 1870s, when the royalist de Broglie could accuse the republicans of truckling to Bismarck as eighteenth-century Poles truckled to Catherine, while the republican Gambetta could assert that no Catholic could truly be a patriot. Irvine shows below that similar accusations were still being made in the 1880s.

After 1870, the country was bombarded as never before with patriotic exhortation, in part in reaction to defeat, in part in an attempt by the new republic to create a legitimating secular ideology, in part as a means for the enemies of the republic to modernize and widen their own political appeal as traditional loyalties waned. The effectiveness of this barrage – in so far as it was effective (a question considered below by Pierre Sorlin and Stéphane Audoin-Rouzeau) – was made possible by the process of social and cultural integration which, in Eugen Weber's phrase, was making peasants into Frenchmen. It burst, as later chapters relate, not only into party politics and state policy making, but also into such areas as sport and the women's movement.

Distinct from the ubiquitous theme of nationhood, however, and yet in a symbiotic relationship with it, were the variegated political ideologies which made up the 'new nationalism' – 'a nationalism of dissatisfaction, of tension and of protest'[4] – which erupted on to the political scene during the 1880s in the form of Boulangism. It displayed its novel character by basing its appeal principally on the nationalistic rhetoric long associated with the left and yet forming a political alliance with the right. At first this was merely opportunistic complicity, but by the turn of the century, a true if unstable compound of ideas and values emerged.

Lively debate continues about the essential nature and significance of this 'new nationalism'. Most historians would agree that it was related to urbanization, the spread of literacy and all that is conveniently summed up as 'mass society', and hence was paralleled by political movements elsewhere in Europe.[5] Most would probably agree that it is also (though it has proved difficult to show precisely how) connected with the widespread economic stagnation of the 1880s, and so is in this sense too paralleled elsewhere.[6] Similarly, there are links with the intellectual critique of liberalism, positivism and Marxism in Italy, Germany and other parts of Europe. Yet general analyses do not, of course, explain why France was the birthplace of this new ideological and political formula, and at this precise moment.

Specific to France in the 1880s was its political flux: the country seemed to be 'up for grabs' as old-style royalism was moribund, but the new republic itself seemed to be running on to the rocks, with liberal 'opportunist' republicanism attempting to monopolize power and yet proving unable to meet society's needs. Hence, liberal values themselves were exposed to attack in France (and to some extent in Italy) because of their political predominance. Moreover, there was an unusually acute – though ironically very longstanding – sensitivity to symptoms of decadence, materialism and demoralization, and an equally longstanding and familiar nationalist rhetoric with which to denounce political and social inadequacies. Many historians believe that there is no significant comparison between the left-wing nationalism of the first half of the century and that of the 1880s and 1890s, the former being universalist and revolutionary, and the latter exclusive and reactionary. On the other hand, as suggested above, the domestic political use of nationalism was strikingly similar in both cases. Zeev Sternhell further argues below that there were, even in the earlier form of nationalism, ideas linking it with the later. All this helped to create the French manifestation of the 'new nationalism'.

In the unstable nationalist alliance of the 1880s, monarchists provided the money and the big battalions of voters.[7] Left-wing elements provided urban activism and, more important, a language that seemed attractive and modern: it is mainly this that makes the phenomenon important for historians. This cynical collusion, if it never became a love match, at least turned into a durable liaison. Partly this was through the falling away of lukewarm or scrupulous elements after the first flush of enthusiasm

Preface

over Boulanger, leaving only the desperate and determined. Partly it was the Dreyfus Affair that confirmed the alliance of the different nationalist tendencies, and marked them off definitely from the pragmatists and moderates. From that time onwards, whatever their differences of theory, the republican nationalist Déroulède did not scruple to associate with anti-semitic riff-raff, as Bertrand Joly shows below.

A fundamental debate concerns the essential nature of the nationalist amalgam. Zeev Sternhell[8] has stressed the importance of the left-wing element, which made it, he argues, a radical proto-fascist national socialism, 'the beginning of modern politics in France', indeed the origin of the revolutionary phenomenon of fascism. Other historians deny such importance to left-wing participation even in the seemingly radical Boulangist movement, which, they argue, was essentially repackaged conservatism.[9] This debate reflects a quite different understanding of the nature of politics, and of the importance of ideas as opposed to concrete forces. In practice, it can be argued, the political manifestations of nationalism tended to ally with conservatism and support conservative interests. But nationalism, Sternhell replies below, was not only a political movement, but also a cultural explosion, which retained an enormous subversive potential despite the failures of political enterprises directly inspired by it: after 1902 'the Parti Nationaliste appeared to be dead but nationalism had never been so much alive' (below, p. 26). The debate is complicated by the ambiguity of 'conservatism': when that term was a euphemism for the monarchist right, it had ceased as early as the 1870s to be conservative in the sense of defending the established order. As Thiers had stressed in 1872, 'The Republic exists, it is the legal government of the country: to want anything else would be a new revolution, and the most fearsome of all'. Daniel Halévy wrote many years ago of the Comte de Chambord's tacit rejection of the throne that it was

> in its way a revolutionary act, which destroyed one of the most solid supports of the old governing classes. . . . Through [that act] the French monarchy left this earth to become legend and myth. It would have, in that form, strange and ardent awakenings.[10]

Nationalism – revolutionary in its ambition to destroy the 'bourgeois' republic, and reactionary in its repudiation of political and social equality – was, among other things, one of these awakenings.

This book examines three major aspects of the problem. Part 1 takes up the complexities of the national culture within which the ideology of nationalism existed, and also explores the extent of its diffusion. Part 2 concerns political expressions of nationalism and its impact on other movements. Part 3 looks at significant areas of state policy and the effects of nationalistic concerns on them.

Preface

These chapters reflect the latest thinking and research of many of the leading international historians in a field opened up by the pioneering work of Girardet, Weber and Sternhell.[11] They show how important a force in French life was 'nationhood' in all its ramifications, and hence contribute to our understanding of the history of France and, more broadly, the development of the most enduringly virulent of modern ideologies.

NOTES

1. On the development of these ideas, see Gérard Fritz, *L'Idée du peuple en France du XVIIe au XIXe siècle* (Strasbourg: Presses Universitaires de Strasbourg, 1988), pp. 70–1 ff.
2. Quoted in Tzvetan Todorov, *Nous et les autres: La réflexion française sur la diversité humaine* (Paris: Seuil, 1989), p. 237.
3. Léon Faucher, *Biographie et correspondances* (2nd edn, Paris: Guillaumin, 1875), vol. 1, p. 96.
4. Raoul Girardet, *Le Nationalisme français* (Paris: Seuil, 1983), p. 276 (my translation).
5. The links between urban society and nationalism are well described by Ernest Gellner, *Nations and Nationalism* (Oxford: Basil Blackwell, 1983).
6. See Jacques Néré, 'La Crise industrielle de 1882 et le mouvement boulangiste', doctoral thesis, University of Paris, 1959. Norman Stone, *Europe Transformed* (London: Fontana, 1983), makes a brave attempt at a general explanation of European politics along these lines.
7. See Philippe Levillain, *Boulanger, fossoyeur de la monarchie* (Paris: Flammarion, 1982) and William D. Irvine, *The Boulanger Affair Reconsidered: Royalism, Boulangism and the Origins of the Radical Right in France* (New York: Oxford University Press, 1988).
8. In *La Droite révolutionnaire 1885–1914: Les origines françaises du fascisme* (Paris: Seuil, 1978; and new edn, 1984). The controversy surrounding this and his other work is discussed by Antonio Costa Pinto, 'Fascist ideology revisited: Zeev Sternhell and his critics', *European History Quarterly*, vol. 16 (1986), pp. 465–83.
9. An argument put strongly in Irvine's recent expert dissection of Boulangist politics, *The Boulanger Affair*.
10. *La Fin des notables* (Paris: Livre de Poche, 1972), p. 26 (my translation).
11. Raoul Girardet, *Le Nationalisme français*; Eugen Weber, *The Nationalist Revival in France, 1905–14* (Berkeley, Calif.: University of California Press, 1959); *Action Française: Royalism and Reaction in Twentieth-Century France* (Stanford, Calif.: Stanford University Press, 1962) and *Peasants into Frenchmen: The Modernization of Rural France 1870–1914* (London: Chatto & Windus, 1977); and Zeev Sternhell, *Maurice Barrès et le Nationalisme français* (new paperback edn, Brussels: Complexe, 1985), *La Droite révolutionnaire*, and *Neither Right nor Left: Fascist Ideology in France* (Berkeley, Calif.: University of California Press, 1986). It was a privilege to have all three present during our discussions, and I am grateful to them for having presided over some of the sessions.

PART 1

Sentiment and ideology

Introduction

Robert Tombs

We agreed, in our discussions in Cambridge, that it was desirable and necessary to make a clear distinction between the sentiment of nationhood and the ideology of nationalism. The former was compatible with a wide range of social, political and intellectual positions, from royalist to socialist. The latter promoted the values and interests of the nation to a position of primacy, subordinating or even excluding from consideration other loyalties or beliefs.

Yet to make the distinction between sentiment and ideology was and is no simple matter. Obviously, even the seemingly most apolitical sense of nationhood is based on an ideology, for the nation itself is an ideological construct: as Maurras said, 'there is naturally no France'.[1] That thing to which one feels a sense of belonging has been created and its characteristics and its boundaries defined (or invented), not only in geographical but also in cultural and often racial terms. Eugen Weber discusses some examples below. Furthermore, the language of nationhood was so widespread and prominent among practically all parties that, as Pierre Sorlin suggests, it was difficult for avowed nationalists to distinguish themselves clearly from everyone else, at least in terms that the man on the Clichy omnibus could understand.

The problem of comprehension was not confined to the politically unsophisticated, for the intellectual components of nationalist ideology – what Raoul Girardet has called 'the nationalism of the "nationalists"'[2] – were on one hand diverse and even contradictory; and on the other hand, many of them were shared with opponents professing what one might call 'the nationalism of the non-nationalists'. In their chapters, Eugen Weber, Christian Amalvi and Gerd Krumeich analyse some of the diverse historical references that nationalists of various tendencies held to, and which also overlapped with those of the 'non-nationalists'.

As Eugen Weber explains, theories of national origins could be used to promote division or reconciliation. The Frankish invasion was for long – certainly from the 1790s at least to the 1870s – a metaphor widely used to explain the origins of class divisions between the nobility, descended from the conquering Franks, and the common people, descended from the vanquished Gauls. Class conflict and revolution were therefore seen as stemming from racial conflict – a concept that could be used to aggravate or alternatively to evade present realities. For moderate republicans such as Henri Martin, the history of Gauls and Franks could become a message of 'national unity and integration' by showing that the modern French nation was the fruit of the fortunate historic intermingling of races and civilizations, with conflict relegated to the distant past. During the stresses of the 1880s and 1890s, there was a need to define again what the nation was, and Vercingétorix and Joan of Arc were elements in a mythology that could be used either to include or to exclude.

The towering event in the national mythology was the revolution, traditionally the benchmark of right and left. But as Christian Amalvi shows, nationalists held fundamentally opposing views of it. While one pole, that of Maurras and his followers, repudiated the whole revolution as evil, and another pole round Drumont reviled it as the harbinger of Jewish capitalism, the most dynamic element of the nationalist alliance, Déroulède and his Ligue des Patriotes, and its most prominent intellectual, Barrès, eulogized the revolution as the inspiration of energy. Even those whom Amalvi dubs 'ordinary nationalists', those crypto-monarchists who saw in nationalism a way to revive a mouldering cause, accepted the militaristic aspects of the revolution as part of the national saga. The great left/right fissure in the French ideological tradition, therefore, ran through the middle of the nationalist party.

The same polyvalence of national themes can be seen in two great symbolic figures of the time. The first was historical, Joan of Arc, whose nineteenth-century interpretations are minutely examined by Gerd Krumeich. The second was contemporary, Alfred Dreyfus, whose family and personal history are reconstituted by Michael Burns. Joan, merely a cypher for earlier generations of royalist historians, was rediscovered as a popular national heroine by the left – men such as Michelet and Quicherat – in the 1840s, as part of a populist national saga which, as Weber shows us, included Vercingétorix and the Gauls as earlier resisters of foreign oppression. It was the left who began to celebrate Joan as a daughter of the people, a proto-nationalist 'betrayed by the king and burnt by the Church'. But from the 1860s onwards the church itself adopted a similar view of Joan as popular heroine, the symbol of a rival *Catholic* nationalism, combining love of France with religious devotion. Both these versions could claim some legitimacy, and Krumeich rejects the facile view that their exponents were mere manipulators of mythology. In the long run, it was the Catholic version that tended to prevail, being able to base itself on an older Catholic-nationalistic tradition. Hence, Joan's statue in Paris became (and remained) a place for nationalist rallies from Action Française to Le Pen. We see, then, that the same myth was disputed by opposing political forces.

An even greater irony is brought out by Michael Burns: Dreyfus, the nationalists' hate figure, had led the life of a nationalist paragon.

Introduction

Having left Alsace out of loyalty to France, he had devoted himself, just as much as the most passionate of Déroulède's Ligueurs, to preparing for *la revanche*. For Dreyfus, just as for Barrès who execrated him, the French nation represented a supreme spiritual value: 'Above all human passions, above all human error, there is the Fatherland... and it will be my supreme judge' (below, p. 56). This, surely, is an expression of the ideology of nationalism, and not merely the sentiment of nationhood.

Dreyfus and Barrès might be taken to embody what Zeev Sternhell argues were two strands within the French nationalist tradition: the one individualist, universalist, rationalist and democratic; the other particularist, organicist and racialist. It has often been assumed that these two strands corresponded to the political left and right respectively (and hence the common description of nationalism moving from left to right in the late nineteenth century). But Sternhell argues that the two strands were always linked, even within the works of the same writers such as Michelet, one of the prophets of the romantic 'left-wing' nationalism of the mid-nineteenth century, in which both universalistic liberal and anti-individualist deterministic ideas coexist.[3] What was new about the 'new nationalist' ideology of the end of the century, says Sternhell, was that it avowedly gave primacy to what had previously been partially concealed: 'By definition [it] denied the validity of any universal and absolute moral norm: truth, law, justice only existed in order to serve the needs of the collectivity' (below, p. 37). It was in these ideas, he argues, that the radical significance of nationalism lay, and he further suggests that the nationalists had 'a chance of success only as long as they remained true to their leftist and populist origins'. Another view, however, would be that it was the absence of an opportunity to practise successful leftist and populist politics that forced them into a compromise – the fate of would-be revolutionaries lacking a revolutionary situation – with conservatives. From this fate they, unlike the Italian and German fascists, fortunately lacked the opportunity or the strength to escape as long as the Third Republic lasted.

A different set of problems is raised by Pierre Sorlin and Stéphane Audoin-Rouzeau: how, and to what extent, did both the sentiment of nationhood and the ideology of nationalism reach the mass of the population, and how deeply did it influence their everyday thoughts and feelings? Both approach the problem in very different ways, and yet reach a number of suggestively complementary conclusions. Sorlin makes a bold and controversial attempt to gauge the extent to which the very language of nationalism was capable of being understood by a nonpolitical audience in the late nineteenth and early twentieth centuries, and also whether the use of language in nonpolitical contexts reflects the political preoccupations of the time. He also examines national themes and symbols in popular imagery. He concludes that although there was in common circulation vocabulary and imagery connected with what we have termed 'the sentiment of nationhood', it was very difficult for nationalists to get across their distinctive message: linguistically, there was 'no room' for them. It was suggested earlier that nationalism fed on the sentiment of nationhood; but it may be that, as far as mass appeal was concerned, it tended to be swallowed up by it. As Stone, Offen, Arnaud and Nord show later in the book, republican varieties of 'quasi-nationalism' were still very much alive. Hence, the distinctive message of *the nationalism of the nationalists* failed to get across clearly to a mass audience. In Sorlin's words, 'the conceptual context [may have been] particularly unsuited not to the elaboration of a doctrine but to its circulation' (p. 83).

Audoin-Rouzeau analyses the writings of soldiers in the trenches during the Great War. He finds that nationalist themes are scarcely present, with the possible exception of an emotional tie to the earth in which the dead lay buried – a sentiment which may be a reflection of Barrèsian nationalism, but which in any case seems to be expressed mainly by the more educated soldiers. The author finds that even the language with which the schools of the Third Republic tried to inculcate a sentiment of nationhood is present only very selectively. He further suggests that, far from being a creation of the end of the century, the sentiment of nationhood that helped to hold the army of 1914–18 together had much older foundations.

The findings of Sorlin and Audoin-Rouzeau prompt a further reflection. This gap in understanding between the minority on whom nationalist ideas made an impact, and the mass of the population for whom more familiar themes (such as religion or duty) had greater significance, gives a further perspective on the mutual need of radicals and monarchists for an alliance under the nationalist banner. The radical nationalists stood to gain the popular constituency still clinging to the monarchists, who conversely were attracted by the former's intellectual prestige and dynamic populism.

What, then, was 'the nationalism of the nationalists'? The meeting of two Utopianisms, one revolutionary, the other traditionalist, which for all their seemingly irreconcilable differences of belief, aspiration and history, and of the heterogeneous sociological composition and interests of their constituencies, shared common denominators: a long-ingrained detestation of the 'bourgeois' political order founded on individualism, utilitarianism and all that Benjamin Constant had termed 'la liberté des modernes'; and a consequent yearning for various notions of a purified, united, organic society. Together they formed one side in the conflict between pluralists and their enemies which, Raoul Girardet suggests,[4] has been a fundamental ideological and political divide during the past two centuries, but which does not coincide with the familiar division of right and left.

NOTES

1. Quoted by Christian Amalvi, below p. 41.
2. *Le Nationalisme français* (new edn, Paris: Seuil, 1983), p. 16.
3. Michelet's contradictions are rigorously analysed by Tzvetan Todorov, in *Nous et les autres: La réflexion française sur la diversité humaine* (Paris: Seuil, 1989).
4. *Mythes et mythologies politiques* (Paris: Seuil, 1986), p. 143.

1

Gauls versus Franks: conflict and nationalism

Eugen Weber

In the beginning was the conflict. This chapter is about conflict, about metaphors of conflict and about metaphors of resolution that lead to further conflict. Sixteenth-century France, torn by wars of religion which were also social wars, rediscovered its Gaulish ancestors also reft by antagonism and contest, also subjugated and kept in thrall by ruthless, preying foes.

François Hotman, a Protestant convert, spends part of his life as a refugee. His *Franco-Gallia*, written in bitter reaction to the massacre of St Bartholomew, summoned up Gauls and Franks to attack usurping royalty. Étienne Pasquier, a good Catholic, would lose his wife and one of his sons fighting against the Ligue. Writing about the political struggles of his time, Pasquier was to forge an image of Gauls divided and conquered, fated to live in bondage to their conquerors, the Franks. After the conquest, said this version of French history, only Franks were free, only Franks were noble. The people were the Gauls. As a friend of Ronsard put it, a lawyer ennobled by Henri III, 'Entendez toujours pars le mot de François les nobles; car du commencement aucun ne porta ce nom, qu'il ne fut exempt d'impôts.'[1]

But the civil wars passed, the discourse of discord waned and was almost forgotten, to be recalled only in the eighteenth century, and then in increasingly explicit terms. I remind you only of Boulainvilliers, for whom the Gauls had become and remained subjects of the Franks, as much by right of conquest as by the obedience the strong exact from the weak, liberty and liberties being the prerogative of the Franks alone and of their descendants; the only ones to be recognized as nobles, that is, Boulainvilliers insists, as lords and masters.[2]

The Comte de Boulainvilliers was an eccentric. But his argument, however extreme, proved influential because it furnished a basic metaphor for claims and counterclaims, ever more shrill, ever more desperate. It served as premise for the nobiliary reaction – first against the Crown that had nibbled and crunched away their historic rights, but also against the commoners, subjects by definition, because of their Gallic origins.

Those newly identified as Gauls responded. In 1789, Sieyès's famous pamphlet denounced the nobility's *folles prétentions* to rule on grounds of ancient conquest. The Third Estate was indeed descended from the Gauls. That only meant that the time had come to reject the supremacy of Frankish aristocracy and send the aristocrats packing to their German forests.[3]

Even the *fin de siècle* vogue of Ossian's soppy verse was not unconnected with this fashionable debate. Pierre LeTourneur's translation of Macpherson's brilliant forgery was published in 1774, the same year as the French translation of Goethe's *Werther*. It never had the success of *Werther*, but it did very well. And if Ossian, and his father Fingal, found so much success, it was in part because their Caledonians were simply Gauls whom the Romans never conquered. For Tacitus, whom every schoolboy read, Britain had been an extension of Gauldom. For LeTourneur, the Caledonians were colonial Gauls (in the sense that the Carthaginians were colonial Phoenicians) who maintained their liberties not just against Rome, but against their kings.[4] And remember that the best friend of Ossian's father, Fingal, was named Gaul.

Napoleon and Josephine were very keen on Ossian. And when Girodet painted an *hommage* to Napoleon for a salon of Josephine's Malmaison, the homage was really to Ossian, because the picture shows an encounter between the legendary bard surrounded by shades of his characters, and modern French heroes of the recent wars who also died for their fatherland. The interesting thing is that, above the French – indeed, above the whole fierce, bristly mass of figures – a Gallic cock watches over the scene; a rooster who has put to flight what looks like a Roman eagle.

But this is going too far ahead. My point is that the race war soon became a fairly familiar metaphor. There were other arguments in 1789, and other issues; but the metaphor of racial conflict, of historical wounds reopened and decisions up for grabs was handy; and reference to Franks and Gauls made doubly clear that revolution was legitimate, being no more than the justified rebellion (as Boulay de la Meurthe put it, speaking in the Council of Five Hundred) of the Gallic people against the remains of Frankish supremacy. The justification also, as Barère had argued, for wanting to wipe out all historical memories, of subjugation and injustice, for making everything anew.[5]

The revolution did make a lot of things new, but it hardly wiped out historical memories, or images, or fictions, especially of conflict. Rather, it branded them more deeply on the national temper. Struggle had exasperated past visions of struggle. In 1814, the Comte de Montlosier flew at the throat of old enemies: 'race d'affranchis, race d'esclaves arrachés de nos mains, peuple tributaire, peuple nouveau . . . we are not of your community, we are not of your ilk'. For Montlosier, reality had nothing to do with stability restored, let alone with reconciliation. The struggle

Sentiment and ideology

between nobles, descending from free men, and a Third Estate descended from their subjects, was an intrinsic part of French history.[6]

Coming at a particularly sensitive moment, Montlosier's invective was going to drive those he attacked back towards the Gallic nation of commons and of Third Estate – the nation that was also the people: that *peuple* which made first the revolution, then the glories of the empire. More specifically, we know how one of Montlosier's readers reacted. With Montlosier, said Augustin Thierry, 'Internal war was postulated as a necessity of our history'. Montlosier's book established that there could be no reconciliation between past and present. There could be none because one part of the French stood for the past, another for the present, and never the twain would meet except as foes. Whatever happened on the surface of politics, 'il y aurait au fond la même chose: deux peuples ennemis sur le même sol'.[7]

Here was a formula with a future. Bear in mind that Thierry did not claim he had invented it. He attributed it, or at least its gist, to Montlosier, who sketched the picture of a France divided into two hostile camps: the old people and the new, the old masters and those who would displace them. Then, soon after reading Montlosier, in 1817 to be precise, Thierry happened on Hume (in 1817), in whose pages he discovered the parallel between French and English history: 'tout celà date d'une conquête, il y a une conquête là-dessous.'[8] Just like the Saxons in England, the Third Estate in France was descended from the conquered and had to wipe out this conquest, this defeat. Historian of all third estates, of Gallo-Romans conquered by Franks, of Anglo-Saxons conquered by Normans, of the Irish conquered by Anglo-Saxons, Thierry was to hammer away at this theme and, above all, at the racial antipathy that divides the French. The two-nation simile keeps popping up under his pen, from the reviews and newspaper articles of 1817, to the end of his life. And he himself believed that in stressing it as he did, he stoked the fires of conflict, and furnished both parties (since he likes binary models: the party of revolution and that of reaction) with references without which their conflict would not have continued so virulent, and without which the revolution of 1830 itself might not have occurred.[9]

I should add that, if Thierry came to his revelation by reading Hume, he found his inspiration by reading Walter Scott, and notably *Ivanhoe*, which is about the struggle of 'two hostile races', Normans and Saxons, but also about their reconciliation.[10] I mention this partly to show that the two-race simile was part of the idiom of the day, and that by 1845 (when Disraeli published *Sybil*) the famous passage about two nations could not have sounded either strange or novel. But, also, because you will notice the difference between the British and the French: in Scott, conflict precedes reconciliation; in Thierry, reconciliation is refused – the struggle continues.

Of course, Thierry was not alone; he was merely more explicit and more persistent than many. Early nineteenth-century historical writing is full of references to the debate, with people such as Sismondi, and even Pigault-Lebrun, attacking what looks like the dominant thesis (what Thierry describes as 'des propositions qui sont aujourd'hui des axiomes historiques'). But Thierry is in good company; Guizot expresses the same point of view, and literary evidence suggests that they stand on the winning side.[11] The best witness for this is probably Balzac, whose *Cabinet des antiques* (1837) is precisely about the struggle between the proud and pretentious Franks and their inferiors of lesser blood. A dominant figure in Balzac's story, the Marquis d'Esgrignons, dies in 1830, after Charles X has been expelled. His last words are: 'Les Gaulois triomphent!' They do indeed, since it was after the *Trois glorieuses* of 1830 that the fleur-de-lys would be replaced by the *gallus gallicus* – Girodet's Gaulish rooster. From the brass buttons of the July Monarchy, to the Great Seal of the Second Republic, through the more enduring figure of Rude's *Marseillaise*, the vigilant fowl would symbolize those profound origins in which national unity plunged its roots. A generation after Balzac's d'Esgrignons, Flaubert's *Bouvard and Pécuchet* were to plunge into Celtic archaeology, in order to learn about 'les anciens Gaulois, nos aïeux'. And when they seek 'the best history of France', they will be sent Thierry's *Lettres sur l'histoire de France* where, Flaubert explains (no doubt tongue in cheek), 1789 represents a turning back towards the constitution of our forebears.[12]

But the greatest monument to mid-nineteenth century Gallomania – or, at least, Gallophily – must be Eugène Sue's monumental *Mystères du peuple*, which began publication in 1849, and was still marching on when Sue died in 1857. Subtitled 'History of a proletarian family through the ages', the *Mystères* begins in 1848, but quickly switches back to the first century before Christ, to tell the story of the Lebrenn family, once prosperous and free in the democratic civilization of the Gauls (our fatherland, long ago, was 'a republic as glorious, as powerful, but happier and twice as big as the France of the Empire'), but enslaved first by Romans, then by Franks, and having to reconquer their freedom bit by bit. A maxim heading every instalment read:

> There is no social, political or religious reform that our fathers were not forced to conquer from century to century, at the cost of their blood, by Insurrection.

And copious notes urged the reader back to the works of Boulainvilliers, Sieyès, Guizot, but especially the Thierry brothers.[13]

Sue, of course, was a socialist. He had been one since 1841, and he looked upon social conflicts as wars of national liberation. The authorities of Annecy, where his story was printed during the 1850s, found the

Sentiment and ideology

work quite infamous, because 'it tends to raise the people against the existing social order'. Fortunately, it was read only 'by persons of the working class'.

Thierry himself, meanwhile, had tempered his argument after 1848, and started to push back the era of racial distinction and race war to feudal times.[14] But these qualifications never caught fire, or the public ear, as his more violent views had done. We have on this the testimony of the Marquis de Marcère, an eminent though unsuccessful politician, who wrote at the very end of the Second Empire to deplore the incalculable influence of Thierry's formula and its persistence beyond Thierry's own change of heart. But we also have more convincing evidence. When this same Marcère writes his memoirs in 1914 he never stops arguing against Thierry, and he repeats his point as often as three times on one page; no, the Franks did not enslave the Gauls. Gauls, Romans, Franks, a dash of Christianity (crucial), shake well, and that is what makes the French nation.[15]

More impressive, perhaps, at least to a historian, is the fact that in 1877 when Fustel de Coulanges begins to publish his magnum opus, *Les Institutions politiques de l'ancienne France,* no less than four chapters of the first volume are dedicated to exploding the legend of Frankish enslavement of the conquered Gauls. You would think that by 1877 the legend has weakened; but Fustel evidently does not think so. He presents it as still very strong. Its hold on the masses, but also on what he describes as numerous historians, obviously presents a serious problem.[16]

The problem is the more serious because, as Fustel perceives, the race war theory conceals a theory (and magnifies a reality) of social war. 'It is,' says Fustel, 'born of class antagonism and it grows with that antagonism.[17] A dangerous opinion, therefore, and one that weighs upon our present society (remember, this is in the wake of the Commune), that spreads false notions about how society works and changes, but that also spreads 'des sentiments mauvais de rancoeur et de vengeance'. Hatred conceived it, says Fustel, and it perpetuates hatred. That is why an interpretation of history is of more than merely academic importance. Witness the democratic agitator in the *Mystères du peuple,* for whom the real people are not 'French', but 'of poor Gaulish stock' like himself and his audience.[18] Witness also the name of a newspaper founded in 1867 to represent the liberal opposition to the empire: *Le Gaulois.*

Hence, what had been presented as a conflict of races is perceived (or admitted) to be a conflict of classes. The old metaphor is to be superseded by a new one. And the transition is not very mysterious when we remember that (conscious or not) the old formula had been designed to represent, perhaps to conceal, the reality which the new formula expressed. Marx and Engels did not miss the point; the first chapter of their *Communist Manifesto* testifies to a careful reading of Thierry, and to the determination to stand him on his head. In the *Manifesto*, historical determinism, hitherto incarnated in racial conflict, is reincarnated in class conflict.

But the root of the shift lay further back, in the aspirations of the revolution, and those of the Comte de Saint-Simon. A man of the eighteenth century, Saint-Simon too had taken for granted the 'racial' division between the 'heirs of feudal families' and the 'class descended from serfs'.[19] But his vision of history, involving the opposition of the productive and the unproductive, implied ideas of class conflict that required time before they became explicit. In the meantime, Saint-Simon acquired as secretary Augustin Thierry, who would help complete one of the count's major projects, by writing a whole volume – on the political aspects of what Saint-Simon called *Industry*. Thierry's name appears on the title-page identified as 'fils adoptif de Henri Saint-Simon'. The Frankish oppression which kept the Gauls away from the levers of power is here revealed as crucial, because it deprived the French, the immense majority of the French, of political experience. It would be their 'complete, absolute... political ignorance', that prevented the French from making a successful revolution and setting up a social order comparable to that of the United States.[20]

All this was in the logic of Saint-Simon's own thinking and consonant with it, though a good deal more readable than the master's prose. But the logic of theories that favoured producers was driving Saint-Simon towards socialism (or proto-socialism); and socialism was something Thierry could not abide. He knew that history was the tale of struggle between subjects and masters, the replacement of the powerful by those whom they oppress, but he wanted to avoid the issue. So he left Saint-Simon, and went the way of race conflict. When he wrote about the misery and wretchedness of the people, he wrote about Jacques Bonhomme, 'symbol of the conquered Gauls of the Middle Ages'. Also, incidentally, the name under which the *citoyen* Simon had been imprisoned at Ste Pélagie under the Terror.

Then, when socialism became too threatening or, at least, too active, Thierry modified even that. Written between 1846 and 1853, his last (and weakest) work, but not necessarily the least influential, his *Essai* on the formation of the Third Estate was 'a brief on the historical unity of the classes of the Third Estate, a treatise on the embourgeoisement or levelling of all classes', but could also be read as a tale of revolutionary process that displaces now one dominant group, then the next – a process in which the dispossessed await or grasp their turn to possess themselves of power. It was so read by the left-wing press in Germany and France. The *Essai* was translated into German by a socialist (1847). And there is an 1854 letter from Marx to Engels, praising Augustin Thierry for his discovery of 'the conspiratorial and revolutionary character of the 12th century municipal movement'.[21]

So the threat of class conflict discouraged the advocates of racial conflict, and revealed the connection between the two formulae. Soon, reactions to the same threat were going to revive the image of race conflict in a new guise. In one respect, though, the old theme persisted to the end of the nineteenth century in a battle of books and speeches over just who France's founding hero might be: Vercingétorix or Clovis. In a charming book for young readers that he published in 1881, Jean Macé attacks those history books that make French history begin with Clovis. They could not be more wrong: 'c'est de la vieille Gaule que nous sommes les enfants.'[22] Priority for Vercingétorix over Clovis meant not just the priority of Gauls over Franks and the whiff of populism that this implied, but also (and very topical in the early years of the Third Republic) demotion of a royal lineage of Germanic origin. So Vercingétorix continued the special hero of republicans until the early 1890s when, in the wake of the Boulanger episode, admirers of the *brav'general* began to praise *le brave* Vercingétorix.[23]

We know Macé best as the founder of the Ligue de l'Enseignement, in which he worked closely with men such as the editor Jules Hetzel and the historian Henri Martin, who happens to have been Augustin Thierry's testamentary executor and who besides a copious list of French histories also perpetrated a five-act tragedy in verse entitled *Vercingétorix* (1865). The works of Henri Martin, now justly forgotten but very influential in their time as true republican history, and the textbooks and magazines of the Hetzel connection, were to spread the notions of Gaulish or Celtic populism and, after 1871 especially, of a patriotism closely related to the warlike virtues of Gaulish ancestors. Because the Ligue de l'Enseignement, patriotic and populist in the republican tradition, had also shared the generous internationalism of romantic nationalism – an internationalism extending in some cases, like that of Jean Macé, to pacifism. After 1870, after 1871, this was to change. Internationalism and pacifism gave way to resentment and revanchism bolstered by images of divided Gauls conquered by disciplined Romans, but above all of decadent Gallo-Romans conquered by barbarians from across the Rhine. The *barbares* so often cited, not least in 1848, as analogous to oppressors of the *peuple*, were transmuted into enemies of the *people*, of the nation, because they could be identified with German invaders and with a German menace, once again as real in the nineteenth century as it had been in the fifth.

It was in this context that popular education now had to include physical and military preparation. And Macé, though he opposed a proposal to change his league's name to Ligue des Patriotes, collaborated closely with his friend Déroulède who, said Macé, was left to inherit the name he had not wanted. Under the leadership of men such as Macé and Henri Martin (who later actually joined the Ligue des Patriotes), the Ligue de l'Enseignement supported proposals for military instruction in schools, for gymnastics and for musketry training.[24] It was in this context that history was once again recognized as what a revolutionary had called the great lever of public instruction;[25] and that historical formulae, issues, images that once fuelled relatively restricted intellectual and political debate were translated into *programmes scolaires* that set the benchmark for a flood of elementary textbooks. And it was in this context that Jean Macé published his book on *France before the Franks*.

But the formula 'nos ancêtres les gaulois', which is the gist of his argument, does not appear in the book. Nor does it appear in the majority of the 130 textbooks I worked through, deep in the bowels of the Institut Pédagogique. There were variants of the formula, such as 'les Gaulois, nos ayeux', or 'nos pères les Gaulois', but, even so, of the 130 textbooks I looked at, most of them elementary texts, 115 use neither the locution nor any close variant of it; and Lavisse never uses it at all.

My research was far from systematic; others may well do better. However, the first verbatim appearance I found of 'nos ancêtres les Gaulois' was in an article of 1855 by Edgar Quinet;[26] the second, in a history of France edited by Mame at Tours in 1896, for and by the Frères des écoles chrétiennes; with an earlier variant, 'Les Gaulois, nos ancêtres', in 1882.[27] What appears more often is a qualified statement, such as 'les Gaulois nos premiers ancêtres', or 'les Gaulois nos vrais ancêtres';[28] and this for the good reason that, by the 1880s, what most children were taught was not conflict, but reconciliation. There may have been conquest, though that is not always clear; but there was, above all, assimilation and integration. The fatherland was forged, the nation was fused, not by one race against another, but by the amalgamation of several peoples who, together, created modern France. Romans civilize rude Gauls, Franks rejuvenate decadent Gallo-Romans. So, the conservation of Gaulish claims that Thierry and Sue had called for, the fulfilment of the efforts which the revolutionaries of 1848 had demanded, was achieved at least in textbooks. Gaulish swords were sheathed, Frankish axes buried. Just as the Third Republic claimed to have accomplished the revolution, so the *grands ancêtres* come together in textbooks – though Clovis and his Franks are disparaged for their Germanic origins and Gauls are recognized as 'nos *vrais* ancêtres'.

Hence we know that the black hussars of the republic carried more than the regulation marshal's baton in their knapsacks; they carried a message of national unity and integration. Diversity: many peoples, many conquests had forged France, civilized it, made it great, endowed it with its peculiar mission to civilize the world. And reference to French civilization as the fruit of conquest had peculiar advantages.

The example of original ancestors, brave, inspiring, but primitive, uncouth, civilized by Rome and much better off as a result despite the discomforts of conquest, explained and rationalized the contemporary civilization of rural France by urban France, the very educational process being inflicted on the children who used the textbooks. It further justified the colonization of foreign peoples, and especially of Algeria, also expected to benefit from French conquest as France had benefited from Roman colonization, painful but salutary and, in the spirit of the nineteenth century and the republic, inevitably progressive. Eugène Sue had already drawn the parallel between Roman Gaul and French Algeria, and Gustave Hervé was to follow his lead, comparing the careers of Vercingétorix and Abd-el-Kader, both freedom fighters, but concluding to the disadvantage of Rome.[29]

It is important to realize that Hervé and a few other left-minded teachers were following in the footsteps not just of Eugène Sue, but also of respectable republican leaders such as Paul Bert, Jules Ferry's right-hand man, and of equally republican colonial administrators who endorsed schoolbooks of Algerian history which also exploited the analogy between Gauls and north Africans, between Vercingétorix and Abd-el-Kader – not to mention Jugurtha.[30] Which leads me to express strong doubts about the allegation that many young natives, in Algeria or elsewhere, were taught that their ancestors had been the Gauls. Some of the textbooks used in the colonies probably included some variant of the formula;[31] but only about one in ten French textbooks featured it at all. So, when, a few years ago, an angry anti-colonialist published a book entitled *Leurs Ancêtres, les Gaulois*,[32] which refers to the formula only in the title, he was repeating a notorious absurdity, but probably an exceptional one.

While textbooks encouraged an integration easier to operate on paper than in life, other forces took up the race war metaphor not to integrate but to exclude. Among its most pungent users would be the groups associated with that acute version of patriotism that we describe as nationalism.

The 1880s see the rise of republican radicals, in the wake of Clemenceau; and the rise of chauvinist and social urban radicalism, especially in Paris, where the likes of Clemenceau have to run hard to stay ahead of their more radical rivals, and lose that race with Boulanger.

After Boulanger, after 1889, radicalism alters cases. Radical sentiment expresses itself in agitated urban creeds that have much to do with conflict and with protest: collectivism, anarchism, anti-Semitism, nationalism. The radical politics and politicians of an earlier generation discover the virtues of reconciliation. Increasingly empirical and drawing closer to the opportunists, they take refuge in the countryside and in smaller towns, and leave excess and dogmatism to their rivals.

The radical left, now, had its own metaphor of conflict: class war. The new radical right reached for something more familiar: race. Rejecting those *forains* on whom traditional conflict always focused, race was comprehensible, accessible, ideal for demagogic appeals, but also highly appropriate to a time of confusion.

My story started in an age of religious conflict; it reached a turning point in another age of religious conflict – that of the revolution and its aftermath; it culminated in a prolongation or revival of the same. Marcère, the transigent Orleanist whom I quoted earlier, speaks of a 'retour aux luttes de classes et recrudescence de la guerre religieuse'.[33] While the latter was fairly active in a literal sense, I use the term figuratively. For here, in the 1880s, as in the previous *fin de siècle*, indeed as in the sixteenth century, French identity could no longer be taken for granted. It had to be defined and redefined. France and the French had to be identified by what was authentically, historically, French. But what *was* French? Obviously, people differed about that, and sought a resolution.

The revolution had invented nationalism and inculcated it beyond France. But, in France especially, it also sharpened awareness of divisions which threatened its unifying idea. The symbolism of common Gaulish descent, like that of subsequent integrations, provided powerful images to counter or assuage divisive experience. It also suggested the persistence of what were presented as national traits, providing a sense of continuity where there had been fracture, pride where there had been humiliation, and reassuring reminders of military valour certified by the martial record of the founding races, which schoolbooks duly emphasized. The Gaulish, Gallo-Roman, Gallo-Roman-Frankish saga had something for all who wanted all to feel like one; also something for everybody who wanted to pick and choose. And one can see how the latter worked under the Third Republic.

Dispersed and at odds with itself, the country needed a bond to tie it together and hold it firm; a *religio*. Emile Durkheim, who lived through those years, wrote about religion in terms of common practices and obligatory beliefs. In that perspective,

> the flags, the fatherland ... are indistinguishable from religious beliefs, properly so-called. The fatherland, the French Revolution, Jeanne d'Arc [another *illustre Gauloise*, like the fairy Mélusine, especially when her name was spelled Darc] are for us *sacred things* which we allow no one to touch (original italics).[34]

Well, that was one version. Inclusion of the French Revolution in the realm of the sacred would make Durkheim's list unacceptable to a vocal minority – especially in 1899, when these lines were published. Perhaps in 1989 as well. So, one *religio* clashed with another, which is why I refer to religious war; a religious war which, as in the sixteenth century, or the eighteenth, must by its nature proceed by placing opponents outside the pale, seeking to achieve unity not by integration but by elimination, not by the synthesis of contending parties but by the triumph of one over the others.

Given the similarity of circumstances, the unusual search for mass support, the populist efforts on all sides (and, of course, the rejection of political parties as factors and symbol of division), it is not surprising that new political formations called themselves 'leagues', as their sixteenth-century predecessors had done. Augustin Thierry, writing for Saint-Simon, had already equated a nation and a *ligue*: both 'united in the pursuit of the same object and by the will to pursue it'.[35] That, of course, was *a petitio principi*, but it gives us another hint of origins. If the founders of the Action Française read Fustel, whom they made one of their patron saints, is it not likely that they read Thierry? And if they respected Auguste Comte, would they not look into Saint-Simon? As for those who did not read either, the memory of race warfare was in the air as a synonym for social war. Only now, the old formula had to be adjusted, for national unity was at stake, and social war was not to be emphasized to be plastered over.

This is where new-model references to race take the place of traditional ones. We all know how loosely the latter had been used to denote trade, or family origin, or psychological type. Nor am I sure how many of those who used the metaphor I have dwelt on really believed it as historical fact. Now, as a general rule, this changes: the foreign race, and especially the Jewish race, is treated as objective fact, like the phylloxera. But the impetus for this surely dates back to the height of the Gaulo-populist craze, when in 1845 the Fouriérist, Alphonse Toussenel, published *Les Juifs rois de l'époque, histoire de la féodalité financière*. Because, when he identified Jews and feudalism, that is Jews and Franks, Toussenel opened the way to replacing one alien race denounced as exploitative and oppressive by another that could be denounced in similar terms.

We have seen how, in paradoxical and typical fashion, *religio*s with universal pretensions proceed by elimination; excluding unbelievers, and those defined as in- or ill-digestible on a variety of grounds. In the 1880s and 1890s, the exclusions that are the price of unity would be kept to a minimum, at least in theory. Xenophobia and anti-Semitism permit this, again, in theory; for many may be tarred by association. In 1892, for example, one of Drumont's associates published a book that proclaimed 'le Méridional, voila l'ennemi', and called for *La Gaule aux Gaulois*.[36] But, in theory at least, organic unity of the national body is advance when excommunication is prescribed largely for foreigners.

National vagaries meanwhile – disunity, divisions – would be explained, rationalized away, by reference to Gallic stereotypes: brave, but argumentative, undisciplined, hotheaded. And Gallic experience in itself is rewritten by the schools to include civilization by Roman conquest (painful but profitable in the long run); Christianization by way of Rome, but also of the Franks; and integration of hitherto clashing traditions (Gaulish, Roman, Frankish, Christian) under the beneficent rule of Charlemagne.

By pushing conflict far into the past, the schools help to minimize it in the present, and help facilitate its resolution. By 1900, the integrated nation, synthesis of its primitive components, has turned conflict outward – at least, in principle.

So there's no more excuse for division on that score. The Gauls, conceived to represent the mass of people, continue ahead in the popularity stakes. Launched in 1910, *Gauloises* are still going strong, but no one ever tried to market *Franques* (and the *Francisque*, as we know, did not have much of a run). Yet the revolutionary tradition Gauls once represented is forgotten today. The French are no longer the sons of Brennus, as Proudhon hoped they would become, but of Astérix. And at Clermont-Ferrand, Vercingétorix and Joan of Arc, symbols of republican and Catholic patriotism respectively, shake hands below the banner of the fatherland whose deliverance both represent.

Even the Franks (who, one theory has it, may have been migrant Celts in the first place, heading back home), even the Franks in the new canonical version succumb to the Roman and Catholic tradition that takes its captors captive and goes off in turn ('étrange destinée', muses Fustel)[37] to Christianize and civilize the Germanic peoples as Rome had civilized the Gauls. French unity, first forged by Rome, reforged by kings guided by the Church of Rome said some, by the necessary operation of progressive historical forces said others, was part of one long civilized tradition. As Louis Dimier triumphantly concluded at the highly political celebration of Fustel that the Action Française organized in 1905: 'Ainsi point de révolution aux origines de notre histoire. Point de vainqueurs et de vaincus. Une fusion rapide des races.... La paix... entre nos morts.'[38]

It was not to be so easy. Peace, in France, is reserved largely for the dead; but the living pursue their quarrels and contentions. French history continues, as in the days of Thierry and of Fustel, to reflect and affirm political divisions. The war between Franks and Gauls has died out, it is true; but it has been replaced by war between Gauls and Gauls. Curiously, as late as 1985, a Fête Gauloise to benefit Le Pen's National Front featured the slogan 'La Gaule aux Gaulois'.[39] *Nos ancêtres* may be fading away. But in France the dead live longer than in other places.

NOTES

1. Léon Feugère (ed.), *Oeuvres choisies d'Étienne Pasquier* Vol. I, (Paris: Delalain, 1849), pp. 2, 18; Claude Fauchet, quoted by Sir George Carew in Thomas Birch, *An Historical View of the Negotiations between the Courts of England, France and Brussels* (London: n.p., 1749), p. 418.
2. Comte Henri de Boulainvilliers, *Histoire de l'ancien gouvernement de la France* (Amsterdam: n.p., 1727), pp. 33–6.

3 E.-J. Sieyès, *Qu'est-ce que le Tiers État?* (Paris: n.p., 1820 edn), p. 70; also François Furet, *L'Atelier de l'histoire* (Paris: Flammarion, 1982), pp. 172–3.
4 Ossian, fils de Fingal, *Poésies galliques*, trans. M. LeTourneur Vol. I, (Paris: Musier, 1777), pp. iii, viii, xxiii–xxiv.
5 Henri Duranton, 'Nos ancêtres les Gaulois', *Cahiers d'histoire*, XIV, 1969, pp. 362–3. See also Michel Winock, 'Dix Juin 1789', *Le Monde*, 28 July 1988.
6 Comte F. D. de Montlosier, *De la Monarchie française depuis son établissement jusqu'à nos jours* (Paris: Nicolle, 1814), Vol. I, pp. 136, 149, 155, 163, 176; Vol. II, p. 146.
7 Augustin Thierry, *Considérations sur l'histoire de la France* preceding *Récits des temps mérovingiens* (Paris: Tessier, 1840), pp. 172–3; also his article 'Sur l'antipathie de race qui divise la nation française', *Le Censeur européen*, 2 April 1820, reprinted in *Dix Ans d'études historiques* (Paris: Tessier, 1835), p. 292 ff.
8 Thierry, *Considérations*, Preface, p. iii.
9 Rulon N. Smithson, *Augustin Thierry* (Geneva: Droz, 1972), p. 209; and Thierry's review of Benjamin Franklin's correspondence in *Le Censeur européen*, p. iv, August 1817.
10 Scott's facetious dedicatory epistle to the Rev. Dr Dryasdust in *Ivanhoe* (Paris: Richard, 1821, Vol. I, p. vii), refers to 'our Saxon forefathers'.

> For generations had not sufficed to blend the hostile blood of the Normans and Anglo-Saxons, or to mute, by a common language and mutual interests, two hostile races, one of which still felt the elation of triumph, while the other groaned under all the consequences of defeat (ibid., p. 3).

In the end though (Vol. II, p. 350), Wilfrid of Ivanhoe, the Norman, weds Rowena, the noble Saxon, and nobles and lower orders join to celebrate 'this pledge of future peace and harmony between the races which, since that period, have been so completely mingled, that the distinction has become invisible'. Scott's first description, applying to twelfth-century England, could well have been taken to apply to early nineteenth-century France. The second passage would hardly have applied before the latter part of the nineteenth century.

11 Thierry, *Récits des temps mérovingiens*, p. 64; François Guizot, *Du Gouvernement de la France depuis la restauration* (Paris: Ladvocat, 1820), pp. 2, 3.
12 Balzac in *Oeuvres complètes* (Paris: Furne, 1844), Vol. III, pp. 121–2, 139, 243; Flaubert in *Oeuvres complètes* (Paris: n.p., 1972), Vol. V, pp. 119, 125; ibid., Vol. VI, p. 435; Flaubert's *sottisier* included references to Casimir Jules Leflocq, *Etudes de mythologie celtique* (Orleans: H. Herluison, 1869, p. 47), who found in the French Revolution the maturation and emancipation of Gauldom, and to one of Flaubert's favourite absurd historians, the Marquis de Villeneuve, an ex-Napoleonic dignitary heavily involved in controversies concerning Gauls and Franks. Flaubert's letters of the 1860s indicate that he had carefully read both Auguste and Amédée Thierry and meant to refute the former 'à propos de la race', Vol. VI, p. 665.
13 There is an excellent edition of Sue, *Les Mystères du peuple*, 2 vols (Paris: Regine Deforges, 1977–8).
14 Thierry, *Considérations*, chap. 4 and *Essai sur l'histoire de la formation et des progrès du Tiers Etat* (Paris: Garnier, 1867), p. 12. Also A. Augustin-Thierry, *Augustin Thierry*, (Paris: Plon, 1922), pp. 254–64.
15 Emile-Louis de Marcère, *La politique d'un provincial* (Paris: Douniol, 1869), p. 15; *Souvenirs d'un témoin* (Paris: Plon-Nourrit, 1914), pp. iii, 91, 118.
16 Fustel de Coulanges, *Histoire des institutions politiques de l'ancienne France*, Vol I, book III (Paris: Hachette, 1877), chaps 11–14.
17 ibid., Vol. I, p. 452.
18 Sue, *Les Mystères*, Vol. II, p. 583.
19 *Oeuvres de Claude-Henri Comte de Saint-Simon*, Vol. II (Paris: Anthropos, 1966), *L'Organisateur* (Paris: Corréard, 1819), p. 41.
20 *Oeuvres de Claude-Henri*, Vol. I, *L'Industrie*, Vol. I, Part II: A. Thierry, fils adoptif de Henri Saint-Simon, *Politique* (Paris: n.p., Mai 1817), pp. 7, 153, 158.

They proclaimed the rights of man, because they had no idea what the rights of a citizen might be. Ignorant of politics, they appealed to nature. Unable to conceive concrete political needs, they fell for vague, indefinite formulae and talked about abstract benefits rather than concrete projects.

21 Augustin-Thierry, *Augustin Thierry*, p. 222; Smithson, *Augustin Thierry*, pp. 27, 54, 72, 270–1.
22 Jean Macé, *La France avant les Francs* (Paris: Hetzel, 1881), p. 7.
23 Christian Amalvi in Paul Viallaneix and Jean Erhard (eds), *Nos ancêtres les Gaulois* (Clermont-Ferrand: C. Ferrand, 1982), p. 352.
24 Edouard Petit, *Jean Macé* (Paris: Picart & Kaan, n.d.), pp. 442–3.
25 Joseph Lavallée, *Voyage dans les départements de la France*, Vol. VI: *Indre* (Paris: Brion, 1795), p. 5: 'L'histoire! Voilà le grand levier de l'instruction publique.'
26 *Revue des Deux Mondes*, 1 March 1855, p. 933.
27 André Grégoire, *Nouvelle histoire de France* (Paris: Garnier, 1882).
28 For example, as in Pierre Foncin, *Textes et récits d'histoire de France* (Paris: Colin, 1873), p. 5. I owe this reference to Christian Amalvi.
29 Sue, *Les Mystères*, Vol. I, pp. 19–21; Gustave Hervé, *Nouvelle histoire de France* (Paris: Fayard, 1930), p. 19.
30 G. Hervé and G. Clémendot, *Histoire de France* (Paris: Bibliothèque d'éducation, 1904) and *Nouvelle histoire de France* par un groupe de professeurs et d'instituteurs de la Fédération; but also Jules-Edouard Renard, *Histoire de l'Algérie racontée aux petits enfants* (Alger: A. Jourdan, 1884), with an introduction by Paul Bert.
31 Though the one Paul Bert held up to ridicule in his *Lettres de Kabylie* (Paris: A. Lemerre, 1885), p. 63, preferred Merovingians. It is well to remember that the leaders of republican education, who were also advocates of republican colonialism, opposed school programmes inappropriate to the cultural needs of native children.
32 Maurice Lemoine, *Leurs ancêtres, les Gaulois* (Paris: Harmattan, 1979, 1982).
33 Marcère, *Souvenirs*, p. 47.
34 Emile Durkheim, 'De la définitions des phénomènes religieux', *Année sociologique*, Vol. II (1899), p. 20.
35 A. Thierry, *Politique*, p. 21.
36 Gaston Méry, *Jean Révolte* (Paris, 1892).
37 *Revue des Deux Mondes*, 1 September 1872, p. 249.
38 *Le 75e Anniversaire de Fustel de Coulanges, Célébré le 18 Mars 1905 sous la présidence de M. Auguste Longnon* (Paris: Action Française, 1905), p. 58.
39 Article and photograph in *Libération*, 21 October 1985, p. 11. Another reference for which I have to thank Christian Amalvi.

2

The political culture of nationalism

Zeev Sternhell

The aim of this chapter is to demonstrate the continuous existence in France of two very different political traditions. On the one hand, France – and on this point everyone seems to agree – is the country dominated by a universalistic and individualistic tradition rooted in the French Revolution, rationalistic, democratic, and liberal or Jacobin in complexion. From the foundation of the Third Republic until the summer of 1940, this was the prevailing tradition.

And yet, at the same time – and here we are on far more slippery ground – France has also produced a second political tradition: one which is particularistic and organistic, and which is often dominated by a local variant of cultural, and sometimes biological and racial nationalism, very close to the *völkisch* tradition in Germany. This other tradition launched a general attack on the dominant political culture of the turn of the century, its philosophical foundation, its principles and their application. It was not only the theory of the rights of man and the primacy of the individual that were called into question, but also the institutional structures of liberal democracy.

This second tradition, notwithstanding a certain preconception engendering perhaps comfort for national susceptibilities, has been far more than a marginal ideology in twentieth-century France. On the contrary, its influence on the evolution of ways of thinking has been considerable, and it has impregnated society to a far greater degree than is generally admitted. This is so despite the fact that it is indisputably a minority tradition, or, as one would say in the Latin Quarter, a 'dominated culture', for the minority also wields influence: it poses questions, it raises problems and can contribute, no less than the majority, to the intellectual climate of a period. The losers also have something to say, especially when they include some of the greatest minds of the age.

These two traditions have fought each other from the end of the nineteenth century; but they have also coexisted, sometimes in the same work, sometimes in the same system of thought, and independently of the famous dichotomy of left and right. A presentation in terms of the

Political culture

traditional conflict of left and right can give only a very partial idea of the realities of the period and, very often, no idea at all.

Nationalism was the basis of this alternative political tradition which sprang up and developed in the course of the 30 or 40 years preceding the First World War. Let us be quite clear about it: it was not the shock of the defeat of 1870 that produced this anti-democratic and anti-liberal reaction at the end of the nineteenth century. The rejection of the principles of 1789, of rationalism, individualism, utilitarianism and bourgeois values, of democracy and majority rule, of the idea that society is never anything other than an aggregate of individuals and that its ultimate aim is to serve individual interests – the rejection, in short, of the primacy of the individual with regard to society – was not the outcome of particular events, and it came into being independently of them. Essentially, this second political tradition appeared first of all as a cultural problem, in the broadest sense of the term. To be sure, it was not only a cultural problem, but it was a cultural problem first and foremost.

This is the manner in which nationalist politics should be understood: as one facet of a much broader cultural reality. This explains why the nationalist movement as a political force could experience crushing defeats without its intellectual importance being affected or its influence on society diminished. It was precisely when the nationalist intellectuals and militants, former Boulangists and anti-Dreyfusards, considered themselves to have been conclusively defeated, that the nationalist influence really began to grow. It was precisely from the moment when political nationalism grew feeble that cultural nationalism began to play an increasing role in the life of French society.

We know 1902 as the year that marked the end of the old Parti Nationaliste. The legislative elections of April–May ended with the defeat of the Boulangist veterans and the anti-Dreyfusard militants. Zola's funeral was to take place on 5 October. On the 4th, some thirty deputies and city councillors gathered together with Barrès, Rochefort, Coppée and Syveton in order to organize a nationalist counter-manifestation. The plan to take to the streets was abandoned: the nationalist leaders no longer felt capable of mobilizing the Parisian lower classes who had given Boulangism and anti-Dreyfusism their successes. For Barrès, this new proof of incapacity, coinciding with the grandiose funeral of Zola, signified the 'funeral of nationalism'.[1]

Yet, for all that, barely a decade later, the socialist leader Francis de Pressensé observed in *Le Mouvement socialiste* of April 1911 that 'we are witnessing a revival of nationalism. It is up to the brim and running over'.[2] Even more remarkable than this, however, was the conversion to nationalism – at first sight, quite extraordinary – of Gustave Hervé. On the eve of the war, pacifism, anti-militarism and an extreme internationalism constituted the last barriers against the wave of nationalism.

Sentiment and ideology

In the summer of 1912 it was already apparent how frail these barriers were.

The glory that surrounded Hervé in those days seems to us incomprehensible. In the collective memory of the French, he seems only to have been the winner of a famous 'competition' organized in the middle of the war by *Le Canard enchaîné*. He was then called the number one 'bourreur de crânes' in France, Barrès being number two. The unbridled fanaticism he displayed from the time of the battle of the Marne until the armistice, his clumsy attempt at leading a small group of fascists in the 1920s, and his famous call for a saviour ('It's Pétain we need!') in 1936 – all this has obscured the main point, which is that in the early years of the century Hervé was a major figure of the European left.

In the eyes of the average militant socialist, Hervé was one of those nineteenth-century revolutionaries who shrank from no sacrifice for the sake of a cause. An apostle of anti-militarism and internationalism, he went to prison several times for violation of the press laws. Although behind this idealized image there lurked a dangerous megalomania, it was this semblance of an activist capable of boundless self-sacrifice which helped to make 'Hervéism' the symbol of a fight to the finish for socialism and against the bourgeois state. The respectable Section française de l'Internationale ouvrière (SFIO) headed by Jean Jaurès, had to reckon with this leftist agitator whose popularity with militants continued to grow, despite the dislike and distrust of quite a number of leaders of the party. In 1912, Marcel Sembat offered him his seat as a deputy in order to enable him to get out of prison, but true to the principles of extra-parliamentary struggle, Hervé categorically rejected this compromise, which he considered unworthy of a true revolutionary. Together with all the others guilty of press offences, he was freed on 14 July. On leaving prison, Hervé provided a headline displayed over the whole front page of *La Guerre sociale*: 'Et je vous dis merde!'[3]

Such was the man who, in the summer of 1912, was supposed to take his usual place at the head of the anti-militarist and anti-patriotic campaign. One can readily understand the consternation of his followers when, after 26 months in prison, he described in an important article three major points on which his thinking had changed. First, he advocated solidarity with the Socialist Party; henceforth, he believed, it was necessary to avoid the polemics that could diminish the confidence of each individual in the power of French socialism. Second, he claimed that the party was as useful a tool for the preparation of the social republic as the Conféderation Génerale du Travail (CGT) itself, asking, as a result, for a 'disarmament of hatreds' between the syndicalist movement and the party. In other words, the intransigent revolutionary, the sworn enemy of parliamentarianism, bourgeois democracy and 'Marianne III', had rallied unconditionally to social democracy. Then came the final revelation, that of 'revolutionary militarism': Hervé urged the socialists to conquer the army from within in order that, when the time came, it should become the instrument of the revolution.[4] In plain language, he called upon his friends to renounce anti-patriotism and anti-militarism and to accept integration into the national collectivity. All in all, Hervé aligned himself with the most conventional positions of the SFIO.

At the end of September, faced with the revolt of some of his followers, the editor of *La Guerre sociale* defined his thinking. Hervé organized a huge meeting in the salle Wagram. There, in front of a crowd crying treason – some shots were exchanged – he reaffirmed his new positions: he attacked anarchists, recommended a profound reconciliation with the Socialist Party and ended by making a redefinition of anti-patriotism: 'Anti-patriotic: a confusing word, an equivocal word, a word that kills!' He explained that his anti-patriotism had never been anything other than a hatred of bourgeois society, and that his campaign had been directed solely against the exploiters of patriotism.[5] The year was 1912.

One is, therefore, not really surprised to find that, two years later, when war broke out, Hervé embraced a chauvinism that would put Déroulède to shame and was filled with a hatred of Marxism then comparable only to that of a Léon Daudet. It was not the impact of the war which made Hervé transform *La Guerre sociale* into *La Victoire*; he had simply reached the end of a process that had been gestating for several years. With an equal logic, in July 1919 he founded the Parti Socialiste National (National Socialist Party).[6] He was soon joined by Alexandre Zévaès, a former Guesdist deputy and lawyer from Isère who had undertaken the defence of Villain, Jaurès's assassin. At that time, Zévaès headed a small faction, the Action Républicaine Socialiste, which had emerged from the regrouping of the dissident activists opposed to the so-called Marxist character of the SFIO in 1910.

Hervé's most significant achievement, however, was gaining the adherence of Jean Allemane. On 2 August 1919, *La Victoire* published a letter in which the former *communard* agreed to 'enter into the phalanx of the national socialists' in order to 'enlighten the working class concerning its true interests' and to 'show it that they are identical with those of the nation'.[7] Allemane, who had been the founder of the Parti Ouvrier Socialiste Revolutionnaire in 1890, was an advocate of the general strike and a famous anti-militarist. This anti-Boulangist, this earliest of Dreyfusards, this witness to heroic times, was, at the moment when he left the life of political militancy on the eve of the war, one of the most respected figures of French socialism. His decision to join Hervé was one more example of the growing influence of nationalism.

But what happened between 1902 and 1912? Nothing very spectacular. Politically speaking, the old Parti Nationaliste – a party in name only, and so described only to employ the terminology of the period – had practically disappeared. The generation of Rochefort, Drumont and Déroulède was on the way out (although Déroulède's funeral was one of the most magnificent that France had known since that of Victor Hugo), and the generation of Barrès, Lemaître and Coppée was slipping into conservatism or coming under the domination of Maurras. The Parti Nationaliste appeared to be dead, but nationalism had never been so much alive.

Barrès was wrong when he saw the cause of all these troubles ('The smoke of all these lost battles darkens the horizon') in the doctrinal poverty of the movement and its leaders. The Parti Nationaliste had not been lacking in ideas – far from it – but it had not managed to bind them together into a simple and coherent whole; it had a philosophy but had been unable to translate it into a few principles capable of guiding action. Nationalist thought did not lack richness, but it contained a number of contradictions and for that reason was unable to transform itself into an effective weapon of political combat. The Parti Nationaliste had not succeeded in defining clear and unambiguous objectives and was not able to provide a credible alternative solution.

The most striking of the many paradoxes of French nationalism is the fact that between 1885 and 1914 the more modern aspects of nationalist politics are to be found at the beginning of the period and not at its end. The nationalists of the late 1880s and 1890s seem to have been better adapted to mass politics than Action Française. Boulangism and anti-Dreyfusism constituted the beginning of modern politics in France. Boulangism was the first political movement to make use of all the possibilities offered by liberal democracy to destroy that same liberal democracy. Boulangism was an interaction of parliamentary politics and street demonstrations backed by a powerful mass-media campaign. In Paris, it could also avail itself of a strong and quite sophisticated organization. The Ligue des Patriotes and the Blanquist committees provided thousands of dedicated and well-led campaign workers.

With Boulangism the era of mass politics really began. The modernization of the European continent, the technological revolution and the democratization of political life created a new social and ideological reality. These new conditions and the intellectual revolution of the turn of the century produced a new political force supported by an organic nationalism, a tribal nationalism, the nationalism of blood and soil, of the land and the dead. The revolutionary right represented a response to the problems of modern society: it was not only a revolt against parliamentary democracy but also against the individualist and rationalist bourgeois society. Boulangism and anti-Dreyfusism favoured not only a strong political authority freed from the trammels of democracy, but sought also to restore the nation as a harmonious, morally united organic collectivity.[8]

This was Boulangism and anti-Dreyfusism's originality and their contribution to French history and politics. Otherwise, Boulangism would not have amounted to much and the Dreyfus Affair would have been little more than an interesting legal case. Moreover, Boulangism was not another edition of the Bonapartist saga. Bonapartism belonged to the pre-industrial era and it reflected the concerns of pre-industrial society; at the turn of the century it was no more than a memory.

Ideologically, the nationalism of the last 15 years of the nineteenth century combined social Darwinism, racism and anti-positivism, and reflected the intellectual changes of the turn of the century. Whereas Bonapartism was merely interested in a strong political authority and thought in terms of a *coup d'état* supported by the great mass of peasants eager for stability, for whom dictatorship was above all a means of assuring public order and the protection of private property, the new right wished to create a new morality, a new man, a new type of society and new rules of political behaviour. The cultural integration of the lower classes, universal suffrage, the general rise in literacy and the dissemination of daily newspapers politicized society to a degree hitherto unknown. A struggle for public opinion began, a struggle for or against the accepted order.

Boulangism also brought into being within the right two opposing blocs that confronted each other until the defeat of France in 1940: on the one hand, the conservatives and the first social democrats, the Possibilistes, who took their place next to the liberals and accepted the value system of liberal democracy and, on the other, the revolutionaries, who wanted to destroy the political structures of liberal democracy and sweep away its intellectual values. This new revolutionary right had little in common with Bonapartism, which, despite its populist and authoritarian character, belonged to a society where the participation of the people in the political process was extremely limited. Furthermore, Bonapartism lacked two essential modern ingredients of the revolutionary right: anti-Marxist radicalism and organic nationalism. As a result, it did not have an ideology of its own, elaborated – like that of the revolutionaries – by some of the leading intellectuals of the period. Bonapartism, in other words, was pure authoritarianism. It was not interested in providing the country with a new vision of man and society and consequently it lacked the intellectual force that, throughout the half century preceding the defeat of 1940, assured the revolutionary right of its influence.[9]

These were nationalism's strong points. Its main weakness stemmed from the fact that in 1889 or 1899, it was difficult to see exactly what the nationalists wished to put in place of liberal democracy. What was in question was not only institutional structures, but also the French Revolution. Did they want to destroy the whole revolutionary heritage or, on the contrary, to go beyond liberal democracy toward a more radical political and social system? Was constitutional reform to go in the direction proposed in 1885 by Naquet, supported by Michelin, Laguerre, Laisant and most left-wing *Radicaux*, or would one see the rise of a king-dictator?

Sentiment and ideology

It is clear that Boulangism and anti-Dreyfusism had a chance of success only as long as they remained true to their leftist and popular origins. In this respect, the appearance of Action Française added a further element of weakness. Monarchism, intended to serve as a means of breaking with the established order by breaking with the revolution, was the very opposite of what nationalism really needed. How many Frenchmen were ready around 1900 to fight for the king? The Maurrassians created yet another division, and they never succeeded in acquiring the degree of credibility necessary to uproot the existing system.

Faced with the problem of its attitude to the French Revolution, political nationalism fell apart, and the fact that in the first years of the century it identified itself with Maurras and Action Française constituted a weakness which was overcome only 40 years later as a result of the defeat of 1940. Maurras's system was too sophisticated, the movement was too elitist in character and possessed too narrow a social base to win a mass following. In this respect, Action Française was not a credible phenomenon. On the one hand, one could point to the fact that it never passed beyond the stage of a great laboratory of ideas: it was always present in the Latin Quarter, it was influential in the Académie Française, and its journal and reviews were always splendidly produced. It is clear that in the 40 years of its existence Action Francaise never took anything to the streets except printed paper. But, on the one hand, it transpires that in so doing it gained a considerable authority over a good part of the educated public. Action Française became a classic example of an intellectual power. As such, in the interwar period it was to become one of the focal points of French politics.

However, there is one means of mobilization which all nationalisms quickly learned to make use of, and that was anti-Semitism. The left-wing Boulangists were the first to discover its usefulness. Around the year 1890, it was a real revelation for them: it seemed that the one common denominator which all factions of the opposition to liberal democracy so badly needed had been found. And yet, hardly ten years after the first successes of anti-Semitism as a unifying factor, anti-Dreyfusism was defeated.[10]

The eclecticism of nationalism and its internal problems do not explain everything – far from it. Other factors also played a part. Nationalism sported famous figures who spoke on its behalf, but no popular leaders. Boulanger himself was a notorious failure.

And yet all these weaknesses appear secondary when considered in relation to the main point, which is that the conditions in which the nationalist movement developed were unfavourable to a revolt. The problems involved in the adaptation of liberalism to a mass society had undoubtedly created very great tensions, and Boulangism is largely explained by these difficulties of expanding liberalism towards democracy.

Political culture

These tensions, however, were not sufficient to cause a real national crisis.

Indeed, this period of peace, stability, economic growth and unprecedented social progress was unable to create a groundswell capable of undermining the foundations of a regime. The Parti Nationaliste was not the only victim of prosperity; the socialist movement was another. It must be said that, all things considered, modernization, which worked in favour of national integration against revolutionary socialism, also worked in favour of the established order. The extension of literacy to new social classes had the effect of making the worker a good Frenchman and a good soldier rather than a good revolutionary. And it also had the effect of making him a good citizen.

This was of course something totally unexpected. Instead of having the disruptive effects that the Marxists on the one hand and the nationalists on the other had predicted, modernization had produced not only democracy and political equality, but also tremendous improvements on the standard of living of the working people. Around 1900 peasants and workers were no longer what they had been 50 years earlier: mainly draught animals. Even workers now had something to lose; they began to develop a political behaviour not very different from that of peasants and the middle classes. The spread of culture, the rising standard of living, social reforms and political democracy could not fail to have a stabilizing effect.

Finally, one should remember that the nationalist movement had to deal with a state machine determined to resist it, with the elites who had a vested interest in the existing system and who were able to defend themselves. Both the Boulangists and the anti-Dreyfusards confronted social and political forces committed to the conservation of the established order. In this sense, at the turn of the century, French socialism had also become a major force of conservation. The vast majority of organized workers, let alone those who refused to join the CGT, saw themselves as represented by democratic socialism – the kind , that is, which regarded itself as the heir to liberalism and the principles of 1789.

All this leads to the conclusion that a genuine revolutionary situation existed neither in 1889 nor in 1899. Most of the nationalists seem to have understood this instinctively; they knew that the time for armed revolts had passed. Bonapartism was dead and buried. Boulangism, indeed, was a mass movement which made use both of agitation in the streets and universal suffrage, and many of its militants already knew how to exploit in an admirable way the great mobilizing issues of the twentieth century, including anti-Semitism and social resentment. Boulangism had been able to mobilize urban masses, although only for a very short period. Bonapartism, for its part, had never required anything except a passive acquiescence which would allow for a *coup d'état*, and its real power base was in the countryside. The very element which Boulangism had always lacked was precisely Bonapartism's strong point: the support of the army and a leader with singleness of purpose.

Despite all these setbacks the cultural hegemony of nationalism continually increased, for, in the decade that preceded 1914, nationalism not only reaped the benefits of the intense intellectual activity of the generation of 1890, but also those of the tremendous labours of the preceding generation: that of Renan, Taine and Michelet. The distance between these great names of the French nineteenth century and the 'generation of Agathon' was far less than is generally believed, and their importance in shaping the intellectual climate of that period was far greater than is generally assumed. In fact, a close reading of Michelet, Taine and Renan constitutes a *conditio sine qua non* for the understanding of French nationalism. Moreover, their work provides the best possible evidence for the continuous existence within the same system of thought of two antagonistic traditions.

Indeed, the conception of the nation as an aggregate of citizens only really existed in the early years of the French Revolution, that is, for as long as the nation was regarded as the true source of power and legitimacy as opposed to the royal power. The European wars and the necessity of confronting German romantic nationalism, nourished by Herder and Burke, were not without effect on the nature of French nationalism.

The nations were in opposition to each other: once the problem of the source of sovereignty within the country had been settled, the new problem arose of sovereignty in relation to the other national collectivities. Consequently, the nature of French nationalism differs far less than is generally thought from that of German nationalism. It was not only that with Drumont, Barrès and Maurras, French nationalism became very similar to the nationalism of Wilhelm Marr, Treitschke and Stöcker, but, if one looks closely, Michelet's nationalism was not as far removed as is generally thought from that of the liberals of the Parliament of Frankfurt. For Michelet too, the ultimate values were national and not universal, and *Le Peuple* pilloried all adversaries of the nation and condemned values such as cosmopolitanism and humanitarianism which were regarded as opposed to patriotism. It is important to stress this point. Michelet attacked the humanitarians, who in his opinion overlooked the social dimension of man. He associated humanism with individualism, and he deplored the 'sterility' of individualism which led to an exclusive concern for self-enrichment. He consequently condemned 'cosmopolitan utopias of material enjoyments'.[11] For Michelet, man was a social being; individualism was not only immoral, it was against nature and was the source of the supreme evil – materialism.

That, however, was not the whole story. Michelet solved the problem of the potential conflict between patriotism and humanitarianism by making France equivalent to the universe. France, he believed, was not only

Political culture

destined to be 'the pilot of humanity's vessel', but was also the incarnation of humanity. Consequently, if one defended France against some other country, one was not only defending France, one was defending humanity. Michelet was convinced that in defending France, whose vocation was 'to deliver the world' and 'bring liberty to birth in every nation', he was defending, not his country, but the principles of goodness and truth.[12]

How, one may ask, did France achieve this unequalled, unparalleled historical position? Here Michelet made a long digression. In a spirit close to that of the eighteenth century, he conceived of the evolution of humanity as being, on the one hand, a growth of liberty at the expense of all biological or geographical determinism and, on the other hand, a victory of the social and artificial over a presumed natural simplicity. The further away a country is from its state of origin and the more the determinism of physical factors has been neutralized, the more civilized it is. Progress depends on a mixture of races and a liberation from racial determinism. If the French are a sort of chosen people, it is precisely because they are an extraordinary mixture of races, because they assert the superiority of the spirit over matter and the victory of freedom over determinism. Such are the broad outlines of Michelet's thought as expressed in his *Introduction à l'histoire universelle* and in the first volume of *L'Histoire de France*.[13]

The picture is quite different, however, when one comes to *Le Peuple*. Here one begins to feel the full weight of a geographical determinism which now explains the difference among nations. The ideals of the civilized, the artificial and the intellectual, which formerly represented progress, the highest stages of human evolution, now give way to a cult of the instinctive, spontaneous and unreflecting people. Cross-breedings, interactions and borrowings are condemned. Like all European nationalists of his and succeeding generations, Michelet was now convinced that the nation should remain as nature had made it:

> One takes from a neighbouring people something which for it is alive; one appropriates it after a fashion, despite the repugnance of an organism which was not made for it, but it is a foreign body which you are putting in your flesh; it is something inert and dead; it is death which you are adopting.[14]

To be sure, for Michelet the nation is never identical to the race; 'France,' he said, 'is not a race like Germany; it is a nation',[15] but this nation is so unique that being part of this singular product of history in itself constitutes a kind of determinism. France, he said, is unique in everything, superior in its intellectual power and its overall achievements to all other nations.[16] The same applies to the history of the country: 'No people has one like it.... Every other history is mutilated; ours alone is complete.'[17]

Sentiment and ideology

But what is finally even more important is that the French superiority is due to the fact that 'this people, more than any other is, with all the excellence and force implied in the term, a *true* society'. This people possesses the very element which all others lack, and which constitutes the secret of its power and greatness, namely, 'organic unity'. This glorification of the nation Michelet underscores by a whole series of xenophobic clichés concerning foreigners. The Russians and Germans are savages and barbarians and, with regard to German intellectual production, it is obvious that one cannot expect much from the 'vaporous thoughts which fill a northern brain between a stove, tobacco and beer'.[18] In the final analysis, it is their national group which determines the behaviour of individuals, and Michelet's nationalism is much closer to that of Barrès than is often thought.

The same applies to Renan and Taine. Both expounded a cultural determinism strongly influenced by racial determinism. Political nationalism constituted an elaboration of the premises of this cultural determinism. It drew practical consequences from the idea of inequality: 'We reject indeed as a fundamental error of fact the equality of human individuals and the equality of races. The higher parts of humanity must determine the lower parts.'[19] And again: 'an irremediable decadence of mankind is possible, the absence of healthy ideas about the inequality of races can lead to a total degradation.'[20] In 1890, when he wrote his preface to *L'Avenir de la science*, Renan again asserted that 'the inequality of races is an established fact'.[21] The only fault which the Renan of 1890 could find with his text of 1848 was that he had not sufficiently insisted on the hierarchy formed by human societies.

Following this, Renan proceeded to a classification of human races. At the top of the hierarchy one finds the white race, but within the white race itself he quickly asserted the superiority of the Aryan race, destined to become master of the world.[22] However, it is interesting to note that side by side with a thinking on racialism that was really quite banal and very similar to Gobineau's, with which Renan was well acquainted, there was also a definition of race which was subtler and closer to reality. The word 'race' in Renan has two meanings, which explains how he, like the nationalist ideologists of the turn of the century, could make assertions which at first sight appear contradictory.

At the turn of the century, the most striking example of this phenomenon is to be found in Barrès. 'Let us say it once and for all,' he wrote, 'it is inaccurate to speak in the strict sense of the term of a French race. We are not a race but a nation.'[23] Very quickly, however, Barrès adopted the theory of the irreconcilable opposition between the Aryan and the Semitic races and the inferiority of the latter, and finally presumed that physiological factors explained the treachery of Dreyfus:

Political culture

We expect this child of Shem to exhibit the fine characteristics of the Indo-European race. He is not accessible to all the feelings of excitation which our land, our ancestors, our flag, the word 'honour' arouse in us. There are optical aphasias in which one is unable to see graphic symbols or one can no longer understand them. Here the aphasia is congenital and comes from the race.[24]

The Semite and the Aryan, he believed, are unable to react in the same way; there are constants in human behaviour which 'no circumstance or act of will can alter in the case of a Semite any more than of an Aryan'.[25]

There is no real contradiction between these two positions. It was Renan who modified Michelet's distinction between race and nation. In Renan as well as in the following generation, the word 'race' had two senses: one was physical, ethnic and almost biological; and the other was cultural and historical. Renan recognized anthropological races and linguistic races, races in the original sense and races that were cultural. A nation was a 'cultural' race; here, Taine was in agreement with Renan, and both propounded a rigid determinism – a determinism that was not without biological elements. This emerges very clearly in Taine.

According to Taine, an individual is the product of his civilization, which is itself the outcome of 'three basic forces': 'the race, the milieu and the moment'.[26] 'What is called race,' said Taine, 'is the innate and hereditary dispositions which man brings with him to the light, and which are generally joined to marked differences in temperament and in the structure of the body. These vary according to peoples.'[27] Stating ideas that were soon to become the classic theories of racism, Taine said that 'at the source, and at the greatest depth in the area of causes, race appears',[28] and that the element which binds men together is above all 'the community of blood and spirit'.[29] Taine concluded as follows:

> There are naturally varieties of men, just as there are varieties of bulls and horses – some brave and intelligent and others timid and limited; some capable of superior conceptions and creations, and others restricted to rudimentary ideas and inventions; some more particularly disposed to certain works and more richly endowed with certain instincts, as one sees races of dogs – some more suited to running, others to fighting, others to hunting, and others, again, to guarding houses or flocks.[30]

Consequently, there are superior and inferior races:

> With the Aryan races, the language becomes a sort of variegated and coloured epic in which each word is a personage, poetry and religion take on a magnificent and inexhaustible amplitude, metaphysics are

developed with breadth and subtlety, without concern for positive applications; the entire spirit, despite the deviations and lapses which are inevitably part of its effort, is enamoured of the beautiful and the sublime and conceives of a ideal model capable, through its nobility and harmony, of gathering around itself the loves and enthusiasm of the human race.

But as against this:

> With the Semitic races, metaphysics are lacking, religion can only conceive of a God-king who is all-consuming and solitary, science cannot come into being, the spirit is too rigid and complete to reproduce the delicate ordering of nature, poetry can give birth only to a series of vehement and grandiose exclamations, language cannot express the interweaving of reasoning and eloquence, and man is reduced to lyrical enthusiasm, to unbridled passion, to fanatical and limited action.[31]

Thus nationalism, once more, found its justification in science, for cultural and spiritual determinism were essential elements of scientific thought. Racism, whether cultural or biological, was a constituent of nationalism. Le Bon and Vacher de Lapouge simply continued the work of Renan and Taine. When they measured skulls, they were doing research, and when they drew moral conclusions from the exercise, they remained true to the heritage of the two giants who dominated the end of the nineteenth century in France. Similarly, Barrès and Maurras simply adapted to their own needs and in accordance with their own specialities the same premises and the same conclusions. As Renan said:

> Man, messieurs, is not the result of an improvisation. The nation, like the individual, is the end-product of a long past of efforts, sacrifices and immolations. The cult of ancestors is of all cults the most legitimate; our ancestors have made us what we are. A heroic past, great men, glory (I mean the genuine article) – this is the social capital on which a national ideal is based.[32]

And when he described himself, Renan could not refrain from thinking of the ancestors who spoke through him: 'For thirteen hundred years they lived an obscure life, saving up thoughts and sensations – an accumulated capital which has accrued to me. I sense that I am thinking for them and that they live in me.'[33]

Drumont, Le Bon, Barrès, Maurras, Lemaître, Bourget and legions of other nationalist intellectuals said the same thing. With Renan also, as with the men of the succeeding generation, this conception of the nation was not without political implications and, once again, it was not a reaction to circumstances. *La Réforme intellectuelle et morale* is undoubtedly a result of the defeat of 1870. Most of its contents, however, all that is really of importance, are already to be found in a long article published in *La Revue des deux mondes* in November 1869, nearly a year before the battle of Sedan. In this essay, entitled 'Philosophie de l'histoire contemporaine', Renan expressed what came before the 'année terrible' and what was to remain his essential political thinking thereafter. The essay condemned above all

> the idea of the equal rights of all men, the way of conceiving government as a mere public service which one pays for, and to which one owes neither respect nor gratitude, a kind of American impertinence, the claim ... that politics can be reduced to a mere consultation of the will of the majority.[34]

After having poured scorn on the United States, Renan urged Napoleon III to adopt 'the truly conservative programme' which alone could hold back 'the harsh, peevish, pedantic Jacobinism which is stirring up the country', and the 'democratic spirit ... which can be well-described as materialism in politics' and which finally could only give rise to 'a sort of universal mediocrity'. It was 'probable', he concluded, 'that the nineteenth century will be ... regarded in the history of France as the expiation of the Revolution'.[35]

This analysis was repeated, often word for word, in *La Réforme*: 'Enervated by democracy, demoralised by its very prosperity, France has expiated in the most cruel manner its years of aberration', wrote Renan after the defeat at Sedan. And he went on to assert:

> France as formed by universal suffrage has become profoundly materialist, the noble concerns of yesteryear – patriotism, an enthusiasm for beauty, the love of glory – have vanished with the noble classes which represented the soul of France. The judgement and government of things have been transferred to the masses, and the masses are heavy and coarse, dominated by the most superficial idea of interest.

Sedan was thus conceived as the defeat of a political culture which was 'the negation of discipline' and which tended 'to diminish the state to the advantage of individual liberty'.[36] 'While we were going carelessly down the slope of an unintelligent materialism or an over-generous philosophy,' he said, 'nearly losing all memory of a national spirit' [it was] Prussia, which had remained a country of the *ancien régime* and was thus preserved from 'industrial, economic, socialist and revolutionary materialism, which vanquished the virility of all the other peoples'.[37] France was now paying the penalty for the 'philosophical egalitarian conception of society', together with 'the false politics of Rousseau'.[38] Renan taught his own generation and his innumerable disciples in the next that 'a democratic country cannot be well-governed, well-administered, well-ordered'.[39]

But the real root of all evil was materialism. A key idea if ever there was one, anti-materialism constitutes the backbone and the common denominator of all the tendencies which, from Sedan to Vichy, were in revolt against the heritage of the eighteenth century, against liberal and socialist utilitarianism. 'Materialism' was the summation of what Renan called 'le mal de la France'.[40] Materialism was the cause of French decadence; it was liberal and bourgeois materialism which were defeated at Sedan. This basic idea recurred in an almost identical manner at the time of the defeat of 1940: once again, it was materialism which was accused of having eaten away the body of the nation. The difference was, however, that since the turn of the century, liberal and bourgeois materialism had been supplemented with Marxist and proletarian materialism.

It was no accident that Mussolini spoke of Renan's 'pre-Fascist intuitions';[41] nor was it if Barrès was one of the very first 'national socialists', in the strict sense of the term, in Europe.[42] And it was no accident if Drumont was at the turn of the century the best known and one of the most influential anti-Semites in Europe. Around the year 1900 French nationalism thus became a powerful assertion of the rebellion against the spirit of the Enlightenment. This nationalism of *Blut und Boden* flourished on both sides of the Rhine and on both sides of the Alps. In this respect French nationalism did not differ fundamentally from German nationalism. The nationalist militancy of Renan and Taine was in no way inferior to that of Ranke, Mommsen or Treitschke. Drumont, Wilhelm Marr, Jules Guérin, the Marquis de Mores, Adolf Stöcker, the Austrian Georg von Schönerer, Vacher de Lapouge, Otto Ammon, Paul Déroulède and Ernst Hasse, the head of the Pan-German League, were as alike as peas in a pod.

But it is important to note in this context that contrary to another well accepted idea, the defeat of 1871 not only accelerated the emergence of a new tribal nationalism; it also restrained the full development of the anti-democratic current in France. Even those intellectuals who concluded that it was necessary to reject the old nationalism of 1848 and in some respects the whole revolutionary tradition, knew that the right of peoples to self-determination was the sole argument which could be advanced in condemnation of the Treaty of Frankfurt. They knew that, weaker than Germany, unable and unwilling to risk a new confrontation, France needed a universal principle in order to demand the return of Metz and Strasbourg. This is the main explanation for Renan's famous lecture given at the Sorbonne in 1882, 'Qu'est-ce qu'une nation?' In reading this manifesto of natural rights, this proclamation of the rights of men to self-determination which is in flagrant contradiction of the spirit of *La Reforme intellectuelle et morale*, one wonders what Renan's evolution would have been had he not been obliged to justify the demand for the return of Alsace and Lorraine.

Translated into political terms, that revolt against materialism took the name of nationalism. To be sure, the defeat of 1870 helped to create an atmosphere favourable to the revision of rationalist, utilitarian and democratic values, but defeats only accelerate a movement which already exists; they do not create one. The Third Republic was established in September 1870, and France progressively developed the most advanced system of liberal democracy on the European continent. Simultaneously, however, it also gave rise to its antithesis, and stage by stage produced a second political tradition of which nationalism constituted the core.

For this new nationalism, the nation was an organism comparable to a living creature. This 'total' nationalism professed an ethics, a system of criteria of behaviour dictated by the interests of the whole national body, independently of the will of the individual. By definition, this new nationalism denied the validity of any universal and absolute moral norm: truth, law, justice only existed to serve the needs of the collectivity. A view of society as something enclosed and insulated created a truly tribal concept of the nation. From the turn of the century and until the National Revolution of 1940 the struggle for the implementation of these principles constituted the rationale of nationalist politics.

NOTES

1. M. Barrès, *Mes Cahiers*, Vol. III (Paris: Plon, 1931), p. 51.
2. F. de Pressensé, 'Chronique du mois', *Le Mouvement socialiste*, no. 230 (April 1911), p. 28.
3. *La Guerre sociale*, 1–16 July 1912.
4. G. Hervé, 'En sortant de la Conciergerie', *La Guerre sociale*, 24–30 July 1912.
5. G. Hervé, 'La Conquête de l'armée' and 'Un Drame passionnel', *La Guerre sociale*, 2–8 October 1912.
6. Cf. *La Victoire*, 7–12 July and 13, 16, 17, 20 August 1919.
7. Cf. Allemane's letter published by Hervé in 'Le P.S.N. et l'adhésion d'Allemane', *La Victoire*, 2 August 1919. Cf. also G. Hervé, 'Vive le Parti socialiste national', *La Victoire*, 5 August 1919.
8. Cf. Z. Sternhell, *Maurice Barrès et le Nationalisme français* (Paris: Colin, 1972; new pbk edn, Complexe, 1986) and *La Droite révolutionnaire. Les Origines françaises du fascisme* (Paris: Seuil, 1978; new pbk edn, 1984).
9. My analysis differs fundamentally from that of René Rémond, author of *Les Droites en France* (Paris: Aubier, 1982; first published in 1954), who divides the right, from 1815 to the present, into three streams: traditionalist (or legitimist), liberal (Orleanist) and Bonapartist.
10. Cf. Z. Sternhell, 'The roots of popular antisemitism in the Third Republic', in F. Malino and B. Wasserstein (eds), *The Jews in Modern France* (Hanover and London: University Press of New England, 1985), pp. 103–34.
11. Tzvetan Todorov, *Nous et les autres: la réflexion française sur la diversité humaine* (Paris: Seuil, 1989), pp. 236–7.

12 ibid., pp. 238–9.
13 ibid., pp. 240–3.
14 Jules Michelet, *Le Peuple* (Paris: Didier, 1946), pp. 239–40.
15 Quoted in Todorov, *Nous et les autres*, p. 244.
16 Cf. in *Le Peuple*, Michelet's introductory essay 'A M. Edgar Quinet', pp. 3–29, and chap. 6, 'La France supérieure, comme dogme et comme légende. La France est une religion', pp. 245–9.
17 ibid., p. 246.
18 Cf. Todorov, *Nous et les autres*, p. 245.
19 Ernest Renan, 'Nouvelle lettre à M. Strauss', *Oeuvres complètes*, Vol. I, (Paris: Calmann-Lévy, n.d.), p. 455.
20 Renan, 'Dialogues philosophiques', *Oeuvres complètes*, Vol. I, p. 591.
21 Renan, *L'Avenir de la science*, quoted in Todorov, *Nous et les autres*, p. 133.
22 E. Renan, *Histoire générale et système comparé des langues sémitiques. De l'Origine du langage*, quoted in Todorov, *Nous et les autres*, p. 174.
23 M. Barrès, *Scènes et doctrines du nationalisme*, Vol. I (Paris: Plon, 1925), p. 20.
24 ibid., p. 153. Cf. also Barrès, *Mes Cahiers*, Vol. III, pp. 156–9.
25 ibid., p. 159.
26 H. Taine, *Histoire de la littérature anglaise*, Vol. I (Paris: Hachette, 1863), pp. xxii–xxiii. Cf. pp. xxii–xxv on race: pp. xxv–xxviii on milieu; and pp. xxviii–xxxii on moment.
27 ibid., p. xxiii.
28 ibid., Vol. III, p. 616.
29 ibid., Vol. I, p. xxiii.
30 ibid.
31 ibid., pp. xix–xx.
32 E. Renan, 'Qu'est-ce qu'une nation? Conférence faite en Sorbonne le 11 Mars 1882' in his *Oeuvres complètes*, p. 904.
33 E. Renan, *Souvenirs d'enfance et de jeunesse*, quoted in Todorov, *Nous et les autres*, p. 254.
34 E. Renan, 'Philosophie de l'histoire contemporaine. La Monarchie constitutionnelle en France', *Le Revue des deux mondes*, vol. 84 (1 November 1869), p. 92.
35 ibid., pp. 73, 75, 92, 95–6.
36 E. Renan, *La Réforme intellectuelle et morale de la France* (Paris: Union générale d'éditions, coll. 10/18, nd), pp. 46, 90, 93.
37 ibid., pp. 88, 92.
38 ibid., p. 32.
39 ibid., p. 79.
40 ibid., p. 29.
41 B. Mussolini, *Fascism. Doctrine and Institutions* (New York: Howard Fertig, 1968), p. 22.
42 Z. Sternhell, *Neither Right nor Left. Fascist Ideology in France* (Berkeley and Los Angeles: University of California Press, 1986), p. 8 ff. Cf. also Z. Sternhell (with M. Sznajder and M. Asheri), *Naissance de l'idéologie fasciste* (Paris: Fayard, 1989), pp. 22 ff.

3

Nationalist responses to the revolution

Christian Amalvi

The French Revolution can serve as a starting point from which to analyse the divergence, both historiographic and political, that characterized the various tendencies of French nationalism over a period of some 25 years. Raoul Girardet has long maintained that there was a distinction between those, such as Maurice Barrès, who accepted a major part of the revolutionary inheritance, and those, such as Charles Maurras, who considered the whole of the revolutionary decade to be anathema.[1] This opinion, still valid today, can be used as the basis for new and fertile hypotheses, in which three different and frequently antagonistic attitudes can be identified. First, the nationalist approach rejected any compromise with the revolution, which was seen as a satanic and criminal break in the continuity of national traditions. This attitude was dominated by Action Française and its sympathizers. Second, the 'authoritarian republicans', centred chiefly on Déroulède's Ligue des Patriotes, willingly proclaimed themselves the heirs of the heroic Soldiers of the Year II, and acknowledged the Grande Nation, forged by the Committee of Public Safety and the Convention, as a great *professeur d'énergie*. In the face of extreme-left pacifism and internationalism, which they classed as treason, these nationalists even set themselves up as jealous guardians of revolutionary patriotism. The third approach was that of 'ordinary nationalists', drawn from legitimism, Orleanism and Bonapartism, and who had rallied to the republic, or rather through force of circumstance were resigned to it, but accepted the patriotic memory of the revolution only in as much as it had become entirely the property of the army – in particular the tricolour flag, which was seen as the sacred symbol of a century of military glory. Each of these three tendencies, and particularly the first, can be divided into factions of varying size and hostility, as is described below.

Within the *nationalist* approach, three very different tendencies can be identified, notwithstanding their common aversion to the revolution, reinforced by manifest xenophobic and anti-Semitic attitudes. First, there is the traditionalist tendency, which regarded the revolution as satanic. This was essentially made up of ultramontane and legitimist intellectuals, and formed a counter-revolutionary group which was not content simply to revive the old conspiracy theories (masonic, philosophic, Protestant and Jansenist) that had been developed at the time of the revolution by Abbé Barruel and his followers. In Manichean style, it compared an idealized view of a glorious, Catholic, monarchist France during the *ancien régime* with a fallen France resulting from the 'disastrous' revolution. This idealization of a mythical past took place on anniversaries with symbolic importance for the church in France, notably the fourteenth centenary in 1896 of the baptism of Clovis and France at Reims.[2] The anniversary of 496 was also an opportunity to praise the 'martyrs' of the Vendée and condemn the 'executioners' of the revolution:

> Despite the monsters of the Terror, France kept its altars. How magnificent our France was... with the cockade of the Sacred Heart at its side, saying the rosary and biting open cartridges.... How magnificent... with that peasant from Poitou, threatened by 20 bayonets, replying to the cries of his enemies, 'Give yourself up!', with the sublime cry from the soul, 'Give me back my God!'. Yes, France demands that you give back its God. It wants no part of Robespierre's 'Supreme being', nor M. Renan's 'category of the Ideal'.[3]

The Catholic nationalists rejected not only the 'perverse principles' of 1789, but fought with equal energy against the national symbols that the republic inherited from the revolution, particularly the 'Marseillaise'. In 1912, for example, the Association Saint-Rémy wished to replace the 'judeo-masonic' anthem by Rouget de Lisle, with the *Hymne à l'Étendard de Jeanne d'Arc*:

> The Marseillaise was played as the young clergy of France mounted the steps to the guillotine, guilty of being true to their God and their King.... The *Septembriseurs*, the *Travailleurs de Marat*, while they slaughtered priests in the La Force or Abbaye prisons, roared: 'qu'un sang impur!' It was to the sound of the Marseillaise that Lebon bled Arras, that Fouquier-Tinville purged Paris, that gentle, moderate Carnot purified Lyons with torch and guillotine....[4]

Such writers drew a part of their arguments from a flourishing revisionist historiography, such as the work of Gustave Gautherot, a professor of French revolutionary history at the Institut Catholique in Paris, who constantly proclaimed the bankruptcy of the principles of 1789.[5]

While at the same time fighting to convert the cultivated elite to their cause, the Catholics made efforts to popularize their hostility towards the revolution, and to put forward the Vendée martyrs as models: 'Where could one find better or more heroic examples for young Christians! Why not make more people aware of these sublime and holy figures, capable... of inspiring a young man with all that is great, loyal and pure.'6

The second nationalist tendency, that of Drumont and his followers, promoted a strange interpretation of the revolution: for Gaston Méry, a friend of Drumont, it was the work of southerners, and had the effect of ensuring the domination of Jewish capitalism over the Gallic people:

> Our forebears destroyed the Bastille, which was then the symbol of oppression; we will bring down the Bourse, which symbolises oppression today. They drove out the aristocrats and priests; we will chase away the shady dealers of finance and politics. We will show the people that the Revolution profited only the Midi, where it started; that only the Latins and the Jews gain any benefit from it, and that it must be fought again because it did nothing to give us our freedom, but only replaced our masters. The ousted nobles were succeeded by the Jacobins, the Church by Freemasonry. Who would dare maintain that we have gained by the change?[7]

Added to this lunatic explanation are Drumont's own moral analyses. Commenting, in 1893, in *La Libre Parole* on anarchist assassinations, Drumont coldly asserted that they were the inevitable consequence of crimes committed a century earlier by the revolutionary bourgeoisie:

> The anarchists, without doubt, are wicked; but what example has society given them? The Jacobin bourgeoisie... made no attempt to wash away the stain of the crimes of 1793; on the contrary... it solemnly raised a statue to Danton, the initiator of the September massacres, the horror of which will never be surpassed by anarchist murders.[8]

Pushing his logic to its extreme Drumont claimed that President Carnot, under Caserio's dagger, had finally made atonement for his grandfather's crimes: 'The assassin grew from the seed of revolution, left there by the killers in 1793. The terrorist fathered the anarchist and the anarchist killed him who begot him.'[9]

Although this vision of things was accepted by Action Française, Gaston Méry's denunciation of Roman tyranny over the Gallic people was not acceptable to Charles Maurras, who eulogized Romanism and was vehement in his contempt for Gallic anarchy.

This third tendency, that of Maurras and Action Française, saw the revolution as the triumph of precisely this Gallic anarchy. For Maurras there was 'naturally no France, there are naturally only Frances':[10] Gallic France, Roman France, Germanic France. According to him, 'their unification was a royal work'.[11] Furthermore, 'our moral unity has scarcely existed except between 987 and 1789; even so, whenever the king was absent, ill or

Sentiment and ideology

a minor, Celtic anarchy resurfaced'.[12] The revolution, by overturning the monarchy, ensured the permanent triumph of Gallic anarchy: 'De l'anarchie républicaine à des brenn de hasard, notre race française, en se dissociant de la sorte, retourne au primitif régime gaulois.'[13] Starting from this assumption which was, in their eyes, indisputable, Maurras and his followers constantly mocked the republican myths glorifying the revolution, and denounced those who zealously propagated them, Michelet especially. It was, therefore, no accident that as early as his first major work, *Trois Idées politiques: Chateaubriand – Michelet – Sainte-Beuve* (1898), Maurras took on the great pontiff of the revolution in single combat:

> On 14 July (1898), the government of the Republic... arranged the free distribution, in schools throughout the country, of a brochure containing a selection of Michelet's writings... I note pages on the federation of 1790, the volunteers of 92, the Marseillaise and Valmy that are nothing but a farrago of historical, political and philosophical errors.[14]

Although Action Française attacked the revolution as a whole, it nonetheless paid particular attention to one revolutionary myth, that of the storming of the Bastille. Based on some very active revisionist historiography,[15] they tried to show that the republicans had employed deception in what they said concerning the *ancien régime* and the revolution:

> The legend of the Bastille being taken by the assault of the Parisian people has been abandoned: official teaching has even given up the legend of the Bastille as a place of torture. What is maintained is the poetic and legal value of the legend.[16]

Militants and sympathisers took charge of spreading the word through leaflets, public debate and popular tracts, affirming that the Bastille was not taken, but surrendered virtually without a fight, and that this 'exploit' was not the work of the true people of Paris, but the result of a plot devised abroad. Consequently, Action Française demanded that the annual commemoration of an event that was so shameful for France should be ended.

Father Hilaire de Barenton, a fiery Franciscan, proclaimed in 1914 that the fall of the Bastille was

> a sad symbol. *It is the symbol of two Frances*: on one side, the national France defeated, on the other, the France allied with foreign powers, victorious and triumphant.... These men on 14 July, who pillaged and

massacred in a frenzy, represent France infected with the gangrene of bad doctrines from abroad: Jews, Protestants, philosophers, freemasons, bribed by Germany and England to demoralise the country. Their mission was to destroy the Catholicism that gives France its strength and thus prepare for it to be dismembered.[17]

Revolutionary error was mercilessly pursued even in secular school textbooks: George Valois participated, in 1911, in the campaign by Action Française against 'primaires', that is the authors of school books.[18]

The second attitude regarded the French Revolution as a lesson in vigour – a *professeur d'énergie*. While the royalists, of various allegiances, were condemning the criminal rent in the 'seamless robe' of French history which had created two Frances facing each other as mortal enemies, the friends of Déroulède and Barrès, who came together in particular in the Ligue des Patriotes, managed easily to integrate the revolution into their view of national continuity. They considered the heroic Soldiers of the Year II as worthy successors to the military glory of the *ancien régime*, placing these exceptional *professeurs d'énergie* under the banner of revenge. On his return from exile in 1905, Déroulède exhorted his fellow citizens to face the Prussian threat like 'the French of Valmy or Jemappes'.[19] Criticizing pacifists, whom he described as 'internal émigrés', he drew a parallel between the 'white international of 1792' and the 'red international of 1906'.

The royalists, as explained above, hated the emblems of the revolution, revered by the republic, the tricolour flag and the Marseillaise among others. The Ligue des Patriotes, however, made them the object of a veritable cult. Mentioning the subject of the Schnaebelé incident of 21 April 1887 in *L'Appel au soldat*, Barrès wrote: 'Every Lorrainer accepted a share in the necessary sacrifice; they had all the enthusiasm, the almost holy rage of Rude's *La Marseillaise*.'[20] Déroulède invoked this sculpture in even more lyrical terms, in 1905:

> this all-powerful allegory in which all those who can bear arms are seen, standing ready for battle: a people defending itself. Hovering above, urging them to combat, is just Nemesis. What enlivens her features ... is not the spirit of pride, nor of conquest, but the spirit of revolt and independence. ... What she sings of our national anthem is not the phrase about 'jours de gloire', but the verses for moments of national peril ...: 'Amour sacré de la patrie, Conduis, soutiens nos bras vengeurs.'[21]

Maurice Barrès and Paul Déroulède did not only celebrate the external aspects of the French Revolution. For them, the internal politics, or at least a part of it, was just as much a patriotic example. Certainly, Déroulède

Sentiment and ideology

also drew the classic distinction between the positive beginnings of the revolution, and its eventual slide into disaster. Nonetheless, on several occasions in his major speeches, he justified his political proposals, aimed at strengthening the executive, with explicit reference to the revolution. Throughout his career, he berated republicans in the name of the great revolutionary principles, even accusing them of betraying their mother, the revolution. In 1901, while eulogizing the plebiscitary republic of his dreams, Déroulède, having glorified 'this immortal Declaration of the Rights of Man and the citizen',[22] went on to declare:

> whether we study the declarations of 1791 or consult those of 1793, there cannot be two opinions on this point: 'men are born free and equal in rights; Sovereignty resides in the People.' It is expressed thus in both, and for greater clarity the Declaration of 1793 adds: 'All citizens have an equal right to participate in the formation of the law and in the election of their representatives.' (Shouts of 'Long live the People's Republic!' Prolonged applause.) Marcel Habert and I have never asked for anything more.[23]

Barrès noted, on the subject of Taine: 'So many insults to the Jacobin fall on him who believes in energy and heroism.'[24]

One possibility is that Barrès and Déroulède are exceptions, and their attitude – on the whole positive – towards the revolution – is unrepresentative of the main stream of French nationalism. But this seems to be disproved by reading the works of nationalists who are less known now, but were very important in their time: Albert and Georges Duruy, Commandant Driant, Georges Grosjean, Job, Dick de Lonlay and others. Despite varying political backgrounds,[25] all these writers, artists and politicians shared the same admiration for the military conquests of the revolution and for the imperial epoch (to their way of thinking, the exploits of the Soldiers of the Year II cannot be separated from those of the *grognards* of the Little Corporal), to which all of them devoted one or more works imbued with the spirit of *la revanche*, and often intended for the young. These can be divided into three complementary categories: works of historical popularization; anthologies of historical documents contemporary with the revolution, and selected writings by the great nineteenth-century historians on the revolution; and historical novels set in the revolution. Among the works of popularization can be cited those of Albert Duruy, Montorgueil's superb variations on the theme of revolutionary and imperial legend, illustrated by Job, and the series *Nos Gloires Militaires* by Dick de Lonlay. The anthologies of historical texts give pride of place to the exploits of the Soldiers of the Year II, for example, those collected by Charles Bigot or Maurice Loir. Notable among the historical novels are those by Capitaine Danrit (pseudonym of

Commandant Driant) and Henri de Charlieu. The latter's *La Marseillaise* (Paris: Hachette, Bibliothèque des Écoles et des Familles, 1910) contains a number of themes dear to the Ligue des Patriotes: the glorification of the lost provinces, Alsace in particular, and well regulated denunciation of both extremes of opinion, the émigrés and the sans-culottes, whose political aberrations had threatened national unity.

Some of these works, in particular those of Albert Duruy, were published in a context of official republican orthodoxy, since they resulted from Jules Ferry's educational reforms. But their authors, far from disowning these books in later years, accused the republicans of having betrayed the patriotic and revanchist ideals of the republic's founding fathers: Gambetta, Henri Martin and others. It is interesting to compare the itineraries of Georges Duruy, son of minister Victor Duruy and brother of Albert Duruy, and Georges Grosjean. During the course of the 1880s they published two works indisputably republican in tone: Duruy's *Pour la France: Patriotisme, Ésprit militaire* (Paris: Hachette, 1881), and Grosjean's *La Révolution française d'après les témoignages contemporains et les historiens modernes* (Picard, 1887). During the first decade of the twentieth century, these two historians were in the vanguard of those who condemned pacifist teachers who rejected the chauvinistic literature of the Jules Ferry years. In 1906, Grosjean published *L'École et la Patrie*; in 1907 Duruy published *École et Patrie*. While these works were not about the revolution alone, they did feature it very prominently, as can be seen from this extract from a speech by Grosjean to the Chamber of Deputies on 3 June 1905, entitled 'L'Internationalisme à l'école', and quoted in his book:

> and now, gentlemen, let me inform you of the ultimate wish of the new Credo. I have taken it from the *Bulletin de l'Association Amicale des Instituteurs de la Drôme*: 'We will gain millions [from the budget] once we have educated the multitude in pacifism, and once this multitude ... no longer puts the bloodthirsty words of the ... *Marseillaise* into the mouths of its little children.' ... This is the new song![26]

This denunciation could not fail to win the approval of the third major nationalist tendency, that of the 'ordinary nationalists', all devotees of the French army. In contrast to Déroulède and his friends, who willingly defined themselves as 'authoritarian' republicans, their feelings for the republic were tepid, to say the least. Their views were represented by *L'Echo de Paris* and the emblematic figure of Albert de Mun. Although they were resigned to the inescapable existence of the republic, they certainly did not attach any importance to the historical, and particularly the revolutionary, references that legitimized it. Unlike Maurras's partisans, they revered the tricolour flag, not because it contained the three colours

Sentiment and ideology

handed down by the revolution, but because it was the sacred standard of the army, *arche sainte* on which the safety of the nation depended.[27]

Unlike the Ligue des Patriotes, whose fervour for the 'Marseillaise' was unbounded, these nationalists were quite unmoved by the anthem which, they felt, was too revolutionary. Although they freely recognized the revolution's contribution to the glory of France's military history, they were adamant that those immortal pages were not written by 'Republicans', but by the people of an eternal France, shaped by the Catholic monarchy of the Capetians. One of the most distinguished representatives of this tendency was, without doubt, General Cherfils, military correspondent for *L'Echo de Paris*. He blasted Jaurès's *L'Armée nouvelle* for its unthinking glorification of the revolution coupled with a failure to appreciate the revolutionary armies' real shortcomings of weakness, ignorance and indiscipline. Cherfils berrated Jaurès for his failure to understand that the 'warlike enthusiasm that roused France at the time of the Revolution was less the result of an ideal of freedom ... than the explosion of anger of a people fighting for its existence'. In Cherfils's view, Jaurès was blind to the fact that fourteen centuries of Catholicism had prepared France for its patriotic struggle.[28]

Hence, the major grievance that these nationalists addressed to the republicans was that they attributed the birth of patriotism to the revolution, whereas it was indissociable from the glory garnered by the monarchy. General Cherfils, for example, deplored the fact that old regiments

> only carry on their colours battle honours dating back to the Revolution, as if France, in 1791, could not already count fourteen centuries of history written in its blood. . . . By all means honour the victories of that long day of battle that followed the bloody sunset of the Revolution, and let their names be added on the red of our flags. But on the white silk in their centre let the names of our oldest ancestors' victories also be inscribed.[29]

Although these nationalists recognized the worth of the external politics practised during the revolution, this was not so for its internal activities: 'Behind the curtain of heroic soldiers defending our frontiers ... the Convention presented a sorry spectacle. It justified [the] epithet of "murderers".'[30] Murderers and torturers, epitomized by Marat, whose 'criminal' activity sums up the horrors of the Jacobin Terror and the cosmopolitanism of the revolution in the eyes of the nationalists:

> It is important to explain ... the moral and physical hideousness of the bloodthirsty creature executed by Charlotte Corday's dagger ... Marat was a foreigner who, at the tribune of the Convention and in clubs,

spewed out the hatred and bile he had accumulated in three centres of anti-French feeling: huguenot Switzerland, Prussia and England. . . .[31]

As a counterpoint to this revolutionary cruelty, the nationalists celebrated the very French generosity and the chivalric patriotism of the people of the Vendée: 'there is all the difference between the bright sword of the Béarnais [Henri IV] and the blood-clotted cleaver of Santerre, Couthon and Carrier.'[32]

They saw no contradiction in simultaneously celebrating the heroism of the Vendée leaders and that of the young republican generals: 'Henri de La Rochejaquelein . . . the hero of the Vendée, against Marceau, a hero of the Republican armies of the Rhine. Alas! France had then two opposing flags.'[33]

This 'ecumenical' interpretation of the revolution was not confined to the political press and works of historical popularization; it extended to the ceiling of the north gallery of the Petit-Palais, commissioned in 1906 from Fernand Cormon by the nationalist Paris Municipal Council. It covers 86 square metres and shows the French Revolution with, in the centre, the Tennis Court Oath, the National Assembly and the Convention. At the bottom right-hand corner, the people are training a cannon on the Bastille. On the left are some of the women of the revolution: Mme Roland, Charlotte Corday, Mme de Beauharnais, Mme Tallien, Mme Recamier and Théroigne de Méricourt. The heroes of the Vendée are also shown. At the top, the armies of the republic move towards victory (Bonaparte in Egypt).[34]

Apart from a shared hostility towards the liberal, parliamentary and radical republic and a common xenophobia, there are few historical references between 1889 and 1914 to link those who considered the revolution as a satanic tearing asunder, and those who incorporated it into the national tradition; the gulf that separated them could be summed up by this remark made by Jean Lacouture on the subject of the opposing views of history held by Maurras and de Gaulle:

> their conceptions . . . are antinomic: although, for Maurras, there were two Frances – the judeo-protestant and radical-masonic Republic that he completely rejected, and the other – de Gaulle had a basic feeling of continuity in France through the ages from Clovis to Albert Lebrun, with strong times – Philippe-le-Bel, Louis XIV, Robespierre – and weak times.[35]

Although after the First World War, part of the nationalist right showed no hesitation in reclaiming parts of the revolutionary heritage, particularly the Marseillaise, so as to avert 'that great glow in the east', a handful of schismatic traditionalists have still not lowered their guard against the

Sentiment and ideology

Second Vatican Council – and the revolution: the fundamentalists have never accepted that, in the words of Cardinal Suenens, 'Vatican II was 1789 in the Church'.[36]

NOTES

1. Raoul Girardet, *Le Nationalisme français, 1871–1914* (Paris: A. Colin, 1966).
2. *La Décade de Clovis* (Paris and Lyon: Delhomme & Briguet, 1896).
3. Père Léon de Nantes, *La France soldat de Dieu: discours prononcé à Reims dans la basilique de St Rémy le 9 octobre 1896* (Paris: Mersch, 1896), p. 15.
4. Association Saint-Rémy, *Un Chant national pour la France: la Marseillaise ou l'hymne à l'étendard (de Jeanne d'Arc)?* (Reims: Monge, 1912), pp. 12–13.
5. Gustave Gautherot, *L'Assemblée constituante: le philosophisme révolutionnaire en action* (Paris: Beauchesne, 1911), p. xi.
6. Abbé F. Charpentier, *Cent ans après! souvenirs, épisodes et récits* (Poitiers: Imprimerie des Jeunes Sourds-Muets, 1897), p. 8.
7. Gaston Méry, *Jean Revolte: roman de lutte* (Paris: Dentu, 1892), p. 237.
8. *La Libre Parole*, 11 December 1893, quoted in E. Beau de Loménie (ed.), *Edouard Drumont ou l'anticapitalisme nationale* (Paris: Pauvert, 1968), pp. 445–6.
9. *La Libre Parole*, 22 June 1894, in ibid., pp. 450–1.
10. Charles Maurras, *Devant l'Allemagne éternelle: Germains, Gaulois, Latins* (Paris: L'Etoile, 1937), p. 39. The articles in this collection are generally from before 1914.
11. ibid.
12. Maurras, in *L'Action Française*, 8 September 1908, quoted in Alcide Ébray, *La France qui meurt* (Paris: Société française d'imprimerie et de librairie, 1910), p. 126.
13. Maurras, *Devant l'Allemagne*, p. 12.
14. Maurras, *Oeuvres*, Vol. III (Paris: Nouvelle Librairie Nationale, 1922), p. 254.
15. Esp. Frantz Funck-Brentano, *Légendes et archives de la Bastille, préface de Victorien Sardou* (Paris: Hachette, 1898), and Gustave Bord, *La Conspiration révolutionnaire de 1789* (Paris: Bibliothèque d'Histoire Moderne, 1909).
16. Charles Maurras, *Entre le Louvre et la Bastille* (Paris: Cadran, 1931), p. 64 (collection of articles from July 1907 and July 1911).
17. [Père Hilaire de Barenton], *Le 14 Juillet! La Prise de la Bastille* (Le Tract Populaire Illustrée, no. 209, c. 1914).
18. Georges Valois and François Renie, *Les Manuels scolaires: étude sur la religion des primaires* (Paris: Nouvelle Librairie Nationale, 1911), p. 26.
19. Paul Déroulède, *Qui vive? France! 'quand même': notes et discours (1883–1910)* (Paris: Bloud, 1910), p. 118, 'Le Devoir patriotique', 30 November 1905.
20. Quoted by Girardet, *Le Nationalisme*, p. 134.
21. Déroulède, 'Le Devoir patriotique', *Qui vive?*, p. 119.
22. Déroulède, 'La République plébiscitaire: discours lu au meeting du manège Saint-Paul le 23 mai 1901', ibid., p. 252.
23. ibid., pp. 260–1.
24. Quoted by Girardet, *Le Nationalisme*, p. 217.
25. Albert Duruy (1844–87) was, until the death of the Prince Imperial, one of the Bonapartist party's best writers. Émile Driant (1855–1916), Boulanger's son-in-law, was nationalist deputy for Nancy, 1910–15. Georges Grosjean (1865–1934) was at first close to Jules Ferry before taking part in 1899 in the founding of the Ligue de la Patrie Française, and being nationalist deputy for Doubs, 1902–6. Georges Montorgueil and Jacques Onfrey de Bréville (1858–1931), known as 'Job', were members of the Ligue de la Patrie Française. One of Job's first cartoons, *La Définition* (1876), was already hostile to the revolution: 'Petit Père, pourquoi tu dis "c'est la RF qui a rendu Victor Hugo fou?" Qu'est-ce que ça veut dire, RF? Le Père: Rammollissement [sic] fatal!' See François Robichon, *Job ou l'Histoire illustrée* (Paris: Herscher, 1984), p. 9.
26. Georges Grosjean, *L'École et la patrie: la leçon de l'étranger* (Paris: Perrin, 1906), pp. 140–1.

27 Firmin de Croze, *Le Drapeau tricolore* (Limoges: Barbou, 1899), p. 7.
28 Gen. Cherfils, *Pour l'Armée* (Paris and Nancy: Berger-Levrault, 1913), p. 7.
29 *Vers l'Espérance* (Paris: Chapelot, 1913), pp. 112–13.
30 Charles Ponsonailhe, *L'Année française: un héros par jour* (Tours: Mame, 1903), pp. 188–9.
31 ibid., pp. 211–12.
32 ibid., p. 308.
33 ibid., p. 234.
34 Sophie Bussière, *Petit Palais: dossier no. 3: la grande galerie Nord: histoire et décor* (Paris: Ville de Paris, 1984), p. 12.
35 'De Gaulle, le connétable de France', interview with Jean Lacouture, *L'Histoire,* no. 71, October 1984, p. 91.
36 *Libération*, 10 November 1988, p. 36.

4

Families and fatherlands: the lost provinces and the case of Captain Dreyfus

Michael Burns

> On changerait plutôt le coeur de place
> Que de changer la vieille Alsace.[1]

With ink on the Treaty of Frankfurt barely dry in May 1871, French caricaturists, painters, engravers, lithographers and school book illustrators began to fashion images of the 'Lost Provinces' of Alsace and Lorraine which would endure through the decades of annexation and *revanche*. Marianne, that young republican mother of many provincial children, went into mourning for her two temporary orphans to the east and, like the black-shrouded figure of Strasbourg on the Place de la Concorde, she would not shed her grief until the family was reunited in the wake of another war. While Maurice Barrès, Léon Daudet and scores of lesser literary lights stressed themes of uprootedness and the need to recapture the lost provinces in order to retap the sources of national energy, other chroniclers found simpler ways to convey the story of a wider audience. Jean-Jacques Henner, an artist from the Haut-Rhin whose most celebrated female figures wore little more than wistful expressions, added Alsatian clothes to a patriotic portrait commissioned by a group of 'femmes d'Alsace' and presented to Léon Gambetta. A young girl clad in a sombre dress and dark provincial bonnet stands in the shadows and engages the viewer with a look that is both patient and expectant; adorning her bonnet, a small tricolour cockade provides the primary colour of the piece, and above the figure shafts of golden light reveal the date – 1871 – and the title – *Elle attend*. It is, as Jean-Marie Mayeur suggests, one of the early icons of a peaceful but resolute sentiment of *revanche*.[2]

From Henner's academic portrait, through Bruno's school book *Le Tour de la France par deux enfants* (1877), to the colourful illustrations which accompanied Hansi's no less colourful texts 30 years later, images of lost youngsters, in pictures and words, emerged as the principal leitmotif of the 'Alsace-Lorraine question'. The Treaty of Frankfurt not only ended the war, said one Alsatian observer, but 'kidnapped from France its most loyal children'.[3] Eastern deputies attending the National Assembly debates at Bordeaux in 1871 helped set that scene and, in the language of their protest, helped invent those images. They insisted that their children would 'eternally demand' their 'inviolable rights' as members of the great French nation; and as they stormed out of the Assembly they announced that 'Your brothers from Alsace and Lorraine, separated at this moment from the common family, will keep for France, now absent from their homes, a filial affection until that moment when she returns to take her place'.[4] And a dozen years later, when that gymnastic patriot Paul Déroulède chastised Jules Ferry for focusing more on exotic foreign lands than on France's annexed lands, he used the same motifs: nationalists who aimed to rescue their two lost 'sisters' could not care less about Ferry's 'twenty black servants'.[5]

But Henner's orphan, Bruno's two young Lorrainers and Hansi's Alsatian children standing hand in hand at the summit of the Vosges were more than allegorical figures representing an abstract political concept. They enjoyed enormous popularity across the decades on either side of 1900 because they were the familiar portraits of a community of exiles, mirror images of vast numbers of men and women who had been severed from their families in the aftermath of war. Those stories of divided families – of exodus, abandonment, *mal du pays* and unflagging commitment to the return of the homeland – were immediate and concrete. They captured the plight of easterners forced to stay behind as colonial subjects of a new German *Reichsland*, and those relatives and friends who fled to the French interior.[6]

Estimates vary (families who dodged German functionaries have eluded cliometricians with equal success), but as many as 150,000 residents of the annexed areas of Haut-Rhin, Bas-Rhin and Meurthe-et-Moselle took advantage of the 'option' clause which allowed for French citizenship; and thousands more, many already living in the French interior, eventually followed their lead.[7] 'Children of the frontier', they came in the spirit of Bruno's André and Julien – 'to curl themselves up in the bosom of the Fatherland',[8] and in the spirit of Henner's portrait – 'to wait'. Not all remained in France, but most did, and their baggage of exile contained concerns for family members under German rule and vivid memories of those *petites patries* described by Michelet: the villages and towns in which they were born, the land of their fathers. An epigraph from *Le Tour de la France* said it best: 'The memory of our native land, united with the memory of our parents, will always live in our hearts.' And a comment by the Grand Rabbi of France, Zadoc Kahn, confirmed that it was not all fiction: 'How many of us have left along with our childhood memories,' the rabbi observed at the close of the century, 'a part of our hearts in Alsace.'[9]

Sentiment and ideology

In an epoch marked by massive exodus from country to town this was a diaspora – a word often used for this ecumenical dispersion of Alsatians and Lorrainers[10] – with a difference. For easterners who settled in the French interior the way home was blocked by German occupiers, and particularly so after the late 1880s when special passports to the *Reichsland* were required and, for many, were difficult to obtain. Hansi called it that 'abominable police system of passports which isolated Alsatians from their family and friends in France [and] completely severed them from their children. . . . It was the direct and deliberate cause of our immense sadness.'[11] The mountains and forests of the Vosges were not the only barriers between Alsatian parents and children, and the intense patriotism of exiles from the lost provinces was shaped by more than remembrances of war along the 'shock line' of the eastern frontier. Memories of life in a border territory where one had to be either 'Alsatian and German or Alsatian and French' surely gave an added edge to the allegiance of exiles,[12] but so too did family ties forcibly broken by the invader. Reports of the occupiers' brutal tactics (real or fabricated, it made no difference) heightened anxieties, and absence from home and homeland made hearts grow fonder.

This dilemma also influenced attitudes toward *revanche*. While Gambetta (sympathetic to easterners, but with roots in the Lot) concentrated on strategic reasons for avoiding armed conflict over the Alsace-Lorraine question, exiles, many of them in key military and governmental posts, could not help but worry about the personal implications of their political beliefs. Since their families in Strasbourg, Mulhouse, Colmar, or Metz would surely pay the price of another war, it is no wonder that 'the bulk of exiles preferred the opportunist republic of Gambetta and Ferry' to the 'tub-thumping', bellicose movements led by Boulanger and Déroulède. Having just escaped the bombardment of Strasbourg or the invasion of Mulhouse, most exiles knew the consequences of militarism, and most aimed to save their homeland without sacrificing their kin.[13]

No Alsatian military officer thought about these issues more often or with more intensity than Alfred Dreyfus; as he put it, he never ceased to think 'of Alsace trembling under the foreigner's yoke', of family members 'whose hearts remained French and who suffered such oppression'.[14] While Gambetta admonished citizens to 'never speak' about Alsace-Lorraine, but to 'always think about it',[15] Dreyfus did both. He joined the army in 1878 so that his family would have an officer in its ranks 'for the hour of *revanche*',[16] and 16 years later, when colleagues on the General Staff accused him of transmitting military secrets to a German attaché, he cited his Alsatian background as the strongest proof of his innocence. 'Son of a family of protesters [*protestataires*],' he announced to his interrogators with characteristic pride and defiance, 'I left my position in Alsace in order to come to serve my country with devotion. Today, as yesterday, I am worthy of leading my soldiers into battle.'[17]

The captain's public history, from his arrest in 1894 to his acquittal in 1906, is familiar and unique. 'Everyone knows,' wrote Charles Péguy, that 'Dreyfus has become... the most famous name since the death of Napoleon'. With the emperor, the captain was one of the most celebrated and reviled figures of 'that wonderful century' described by Martin du Gard' which began with the Revolution and ended with the Affair'.[18] But the private story of Dreyfus's Alsatian background and of the role that lost province played in his life before and during his affair is, in its essential features, typical of other exiles who fled to the French interior and waited for their family's reunion. Dreyfus's enemies condemned his divided loyalties, his allegiance, as a Jew, to a nation within the nation. But if they were right about the captain's devotion to two fatherlands, they got the geography wrong. French Alsace, not 'Israel', was the focus of his patriotism, and across the years of his exile, Dreyfus, like so many other easterners forced from their homeland after 1871, dreamed of the reunification of his 'dear and ill-starred *petit pays*'.[19]

Alsatians and Lorrainers from every social class and religious group joined the westward migration after the Franco-Prussian War, but eastern 'elites' – functionaries, doctors, pastors, rabbis, teachers and industrialists – travelled in the greatest numbers; and, proportionately, more Alsatian Jews came to France than did Catholics or Protestants.[20] Dreyfus's family had been part of the 'vast human and spiritual reservoir of Judaism'[21] that had settled along the Rhine over the centuries. His ancestors moved from the market village of Rixheim to the textile town of Mulhouse in the 1830s, and life in that 'ville la plus française de l'Alsace'[22] helped shape their national allegiance through the middle decades of the century: French gradually replaced the Judeo-Alsatian dialect of their village past; a Gallicized family name was chosen over the Germanic 'Dreÿfuss'; and, *pari passu* with cultural assimilation, their ties to textile markets beyond the Vosges hastened their economic integration into France. Alfred's father launched a cotton mill in Mulhouse in the early 1860s, and by the eve of the Franco-Prussian War it had become one of the city's more prosperous enterprises. Like other Mulhouse industrialists, Raphael Dreyfus made certain that his children studied French grammar, French literature and French history in order to cultivate the 'essential and distinctive signs of belonging to a "bonne famille"'. And by 1870 they had learned their lessons well.[23]

As part of the city's 'manufacturing patriciate',[24] the family had abundant reasons to stay put in the wake of the German occupation of Mulhouse. Their cotton mill would continue to operate within the German customs system, the *Zollverein*, and they could work through local organizations to combat the 'Germanization' of their town and province (Mulhouse had quickly emerged as 'one of the most solid bastions' of Alsatian protest against annexation).[25] But, motivated by 'patriotism' more than by 'profit',[26] and by the desire to escape the conscription of young Alsatians into the German army, the family decided to separate on the eve of the 'option' deadline. It was their private 'day of mobilization', and a comment in Jean Richard Bloch's novel, *Et Cie*, an account of another Alsatian Jewish family, captures the meaning of that move: 'In one sense, the war may be over; but in another, it has only begun.'[27] The Dreyfuses' choice to resettle in the French interior was inspired by the same sentiments that historian Freddy Raphael has attributed to other Alsatian Jews: they felt a 'fidelity toward the country which was the first in the world to emancipate them'.[28] Through its revolution, France had given the Dreyfus family the gift of citizenship; as Alsatian 'protesters' working to reunify province and *patrie*, they would return the favour.[29]

Like many others, however, Jews and gentiles, they would do it as a family divided. Too ill to travel, Alfred's mother remained behind in Mulhouse with her oldest son, Jacques, who had served in the French Légion d'Alsace and was therefore exempt from the German draft. Jacques would stay on to manage the family business and, later, to oversee its branch enterprise across the border in the French territory of Belfort. Meanwhile, Raphael Dreyfus declared French citizenship for his other children and, following the lead of other southern Alsatians, first took them across the Swiss border to Basel.[30] They travelled along the same route that Alfred Dreyfus's great-grandparents had taken during the French Revolution when, on at least three occasions, peasants had chased Alsatian Jews into the refuge offered by Switzerland.[31] But Basel had always been a temporary sanctuary, and in the autumn of 1873 the family continued its diaspora; setting off for various regions of the French interior, they divided again.

Four years before the publication of *Le Tour de la France par deux enfants* Alfred and his closest brother Mathieu made their first trip across the Vosges, a journey which had much in common with Bruno's young Lorrainers who marked 'their steps like two young soldiers'. 'Let's walk together hand in hand,' said André and Julien, 'united by the same love for our parents, our Fatherland and our sense of duty.'[32] Better off than their fictional counterparts, the two Dreyfus boys, on their way to boarding school in Paris, did not hike around the hexagon with knapsacks and 5 francs to their name; they travelled amidst the comforts of French trains, and they carried luggage filled with provisions they would need at the prestigious Collège Chaptal and Collège Sainte Barbe. But Alfred and Mathieu, roughly the same age as André and Julien, shared the same sentiments – the sense of loss, separation and adventure. And during the years to come they would remain true, in Bruno's words, 'to the great things they had learned to love at such a young age: Duty, Fatherland, Humanity'.[33] Theirs was a precocious patriotism, again like that of André and Julien, informed more by lessons taught in a home now lost than by sophisticated notions of national allegiance. The connections, the blend of personal memories with the abstractions of French nationalism, would come later – in the schoolrooms of the fatherland and in its many military garrisons.

'Pushed by a sentiment natural to an Alsatian in the aftermath of war,' as one family friend put it, Alfred Dreyfus rejected the career of an industrialist and entered the École Polytechnique as a 19-year-old cadet.[34] Promoted to lieutenant in 1885 and to captain four years later, he moved from garrison to garrison and led the nomadic life of an artillery officer. And through those years his assignments included trips to examine fortresses and transportation networks along the eastern frontier.[35] Cited by superiors for his 'lively intelligence' and 'excellent memory', he worked on military maps and assessed the capability of rail lines to move troops and material toward Chalons-sur-Marne, Verdun and deep into the Argonne forest. After years of academic preparation, he was finally involved in projects which fitted his original reason for joining the army: his desire to be part of the strategy of *revanche*, to devise military plans which would return his homeland to France. And like other officers from the lost provinces, he could not resist the temptation to take advantage of his eastern travels and slip across the border 'en fraude', as he put it,[36] for brief visits with Alsatian family and friends. Having applied for passports through official channels on at least ten occasions, and having been refused every time, Dreyfus entered Alsace through areas inadequately policed by German troops, or he came the back way via Basel. When he returned from those abbreviated family reunions, his thoughts echoed those of other secret visitors. Paul Appell, a Normalien with family in Strasbourg, and with a brother who would be imprisoned for involvement in a pro-French Alsatian party, described his native province as 'developing materially' while becoming 'morally oppressed'; the Germans were 'more and more arrogant and blundering', said Appell, and their oppression was increasingly 'severe'.[37] Dreyfus noted similar changes; he commented on the increased presence of Germans in uniform and on the stories (accurate or exaggerated) of arrogant, drunken and violent occupiers.'Saddened and angered' by the German music he heard celebrating the anniversary of Sedan one September day, he renewed the 'pledge' he had made as a teenager: 'I swear to devote all my strength, all my intelligence, to serving my country against those who have so insulted the grief of fellow Alsatians.'[38] Dreyfus's visits were a tonic for his homesickness and they strengthened his resolve. But late in 1894, when the General Staff probed his past and searched for treasonous activity, the captain's clandestine trips to the German

Sentiment and ideology

Reichsland emerged as circumstantial evidence of his 'betrayal'. He paid for his Alsatian travels with another loss and another separation.

After nine o'clock on the morning of 15 October 1894, the hour of his arrest for the crime of high treason, Dreyfus no longer fitted the typical profile of other Alsatian exiles of his station and background. He began that long Odyssey of a dozen years during which he became a unique symbol for allies and enemies alike: symbol of the persecuted Jew and of the 'destiny of Israel', as Charles Péguy, Daniel Halévy and Bernard Lazare believed; symbol of eternal 'Jewish treason', as Edouard Drumont and Henri Rochefort insisted. Barrès called him 'nothing but a pretext' for the struggle over larger, more important issues.[39] But Alsace remained an essential ingredient in the prisoner's strategy of survival, and the same sentiments he held as an exile in Paris he expressed as an exile on Devil's Island; only now he longed for two reunions – with his Parisian family and with his lost homeland.[40]

Forced to remain silent for four and half years, he expressed his thoughts in diaries, journals and letters to family and to government officials. He could never grasp how the son of Alsatians 'whose sentiments had never been doubted by anyone', could be 'condemned for the most infamous crime that a soldier can commit'. Certain that a clear understanding of his Alsatian background would move high government officials, he wrote to the Minister of War in 1897 to make him realize the spirit of this prisoner who, 'through his nights of hallucination, sees his past, his memories of the 1870 war'. He described his father's 'option' for French citizenship, his family's exile and the 'hatred' they had 'for the foreigner'; and he recounted the anger he felt upon hearing the German celebration of Sedan in Mulhouse, and the pledge he had made to serve his fatherland.[41] That letter, like the many others he sent to the Minister of War and President of the Republic, was ignored. But if individual representatives of the French government let him down, memories of France and Alsace – of all the notions of justice, honour and homeland they represented – continued to shape his resolve. 'Above all human passions, above all human error,' he wrote to his wife, 'there is the Fatherland ... and it will be my supreme judge.'[42]

Though Dreyfus would not learn the details of his *affaire* until his return from Devil's Island, his family struggled with a case in which the 'Lost Provinces' loomed large, and in which many of the leading players, Dreyfusards and anti-Dreyfusards, were of Alsatian origin. Colonel Sandherr, head of the army's Statistical Section and instrumental in the captain's conviction, was a native of Mulhouse, the son of a local anti-Semite; Georges Picquart, the General Staff officer who overcame his own deep-seated anti-Semitism to help an innocent colleague, came from Strasbourg; Lucien Herr, librarian of the École Normale Supérieure and tutor to those socialists who, at the eleventh hour, rallied to Dreyfus, had been born in the southern Alsatian town of Altkirch, close by Mulhouse; Scheurer-Kestner, Vice President of the Senate, self-professed' protector of all Alsatians in France', and the first notable politician to believe in Dreyfus's innocence, also came from a town near Mulhouse, the industrial centre of Thann; and Grand Rabbi Zadoc Kahn – whose request to see the prisoner in 1894 was denied (Dreyfus had asked for the 'comfort' of the Alsatian's 'warm and eloquent words') – had been born in Mommenheim, a small town very much like the market centre in which Dreyfus's ancestors had lived and worked.[43] With their ties to the lost provinces these and other Dreyfusards and anti-Dreyfusards helped keep the Alsace-Lorraine question alive at a time when memories of war were beginning to recede 'into the background of public consciousness'[44] – at least for those with no vested interest and no family members on their minds.

The affair also attracted less celebrated Alsatians and Lorrainers who sent letters of support or condemnation to Dreyfus's allies and enemies, and to those newspapers which lined up for or against the captain. Their reactions to the prisoner's plight captured the contradictions which had marked attitudes toward eastern Jews for generations. As a French Alsatian and a soldier, Dreyfus was, for some observers, the 'innocent and ill-fated ... martyred son of our Alsace', an honourable patriot 'incapable of betraying his country';[45] for others, however, he had descended from that long line of 'African hordes', as one Alsatian deputy had put it during the French Revolution, who had 'infested' the province and, through moneylending and trading, had 'ground down' the 'industrious and honest' population. A century after the revolution, the captain's critics echoed that vocabulary when they insisted that the 'Lost Provinces' had been 'betrayed' by Dreyfusards, and when they questioned, as they had always done, the allegiance of Alsatian Jews. One lawyer, expressing the shock of 'all Alsatians', reminded Scheurer-Kestner that 'experience shows us that Jews are not honourable ... that their devotion and patriotism are limited by self-interest. They have exploited their Alsatian qualities long enough,' went this letter which spoke for others, 'and it is high time that we ... deny them the title of compatriot. For the honour of Alsace and for the welfare of France....' Dreyfus may be 'an Alsatian by birth,' said still another observer, 'but he has no Fatherland, because Jews have no Fatherland'.[46]

When it came to the affair, Alsatians and Lorrainers manifested the same prejudices or ideas of tolerance they had held *en famille* along the eastern frontier. For every Scheurer-Kestner or Lucien Herr who supported Dreyfus, there were those who concluded, with Barrès, that Dreyfus was 'capable of treason' because of his 'race'. 'The Jews do not have a country in the sense that we understand it,' Barrès instructed his readers. 'For us, the fatherland is our soil and our ancestors, the land of our dead. For them, it is the place where they find their greatest self-interest.'[47]

Sentiment and ideology

But that very attachment to 'soil and ancestors' – to memories of his native province and kin left behind – was the essence of Dreyfus's patriotism and that of thousands of other easterners who fled to the French interior after 1871. One of the Affair's many ironies is that its central victim, an Alsatian Jew, best exemplified the definition of 'national energy' devised by one of its most prominent anti-Semites. The land of Dreyfus's family, living and dead, had been the touchstone of his allegiance since that moment when he was forced to leave his home as a 13-year-old exile. Across the years of his schooling and military service, and most especially through his long imprisonment, he never ceased to tap the sources of energy – of honour, duty and steadfast commitment to province and *patrie* – which Barrès had enshrined as the key ingredients in the making of the French soul. Just as they had anticipated the westward travels of Bruno's André and Julien, Alfred and Mathieu Dreyfus were, in more ways than one, Alsatian counterparts to Barrès's young Lorrainers who had set off for Paris sustained by a common bond to their provincial homeland. It is no wonder that Léon Blum, born in Paris of an Alsatian Jewish family, sought out Barrès for the Dreyfusard cause. Blum's generation had been seduced by the powerful blend of Barrès's literary gifts and intense nationalism, and Dreyfus's supporters were convinced that this *engagé* novelist and political essayist would rally not to benighted clerics, but to the enlightened Dreyfusard camp of patriots with a social conscience. When Barrès turned them down (a shocking and 'pathetic' blow for Blum),[48] he exposed the old bigotries which lay behind his new national socialism. Talented champion of the lost provinces, he was, it turned out, a provincial of the worst sort. Dreyfus, who shared Blum's admiration for Barrès, and who read the novelist on Devil's Island without knowing his role in the affair, understood the strengths and weaknesses of that author from Lorraine better than Barrès ever understood the Alsatian Jew he reviled. A 'very original' story by a 'very bizarre' man, Dreyfus said of *Les Deracinés*, an odd mix of 'lofty ideas', 'petty vilifications' and 'narrow social views'.[49]

'What do I have in common with this Dreyfus,' Barrès had questioned at the moment of the prisoner's public degradation in 1895. 'He is not of my race. He was not born to live in society.' And nearly a decade later, when the captain's innocence had been established for all but the most virulent anti-Semites, Barrès repeated that Dreyfus 'is very different than us, [he is] impervious to all the emotions which our land, our ancestors, our flag [and] the word "honour" inspire in us'.[50] But the Lorrainer Barrès and the Alsatian Dreyfus had more in common than either man would ever admit; and their close similarities, as well as their key differences, were demonstrated in their respective readings of Numa-Denis Fustel de Coulanges, the classicist and medievalist whose works would be put to many uses in the middle years of the Third Republic.

Families and fatherlands

Best known for his two major studies, *La Cité antique* and *Histoire des institutions politiques de l'ancienne France*, Fustel held the chair in history at the University of Strasbourg until the eve of the Franco-Prussian War. Though born in Paris, his attachment to Alsace – to French Alsace – was profound; and until his death in 1889 he spoke often and eloquently for the return of the lost provinces. For Barrès, Maurras and other champions of the royalist organization Action Française, founded at the height of the Dreyfus Affair, Fustel served as a standard-bearer of that 'historical patriotism' which refused 'to accept theories relating French institutions to Germanic origins'.[51] Much as they had done with the image of Joan of Arc, nationalists aimed to coopt Fustel's memory, and on the seventy-fifth anniversary of his birth, in 1905, they staged a celebration which, though presented as an intellectual enterprise, was nothing more than a demonstration of partisan politics. According to members of Action Française, the French civilization glorified by Fustel was racially superior, royalist at its core and intensely nationalist; and it is no wonder, as Eugen Weber reminds us, that all those 'tainted by Dreyfusard associations' were carefully excluded from the 1905 commemoration.[52]

In the schoolrooms of his youth, however, and in what he called his 'classroom of one' on Devil's Island, Dreyfus read the great historian differently. During his four and half years in exile, the prisoner filled diaries and notebooks with thoughts on 'justice' and 'impartiality', and cited Fustel de Coulanges to illustrate his points. 'No one sensed this [need for impartiality] better,' Dreyfus wrote, 'when he said that before approaching a work of history one must disengage oneself from all *partis pris* . . . one must study history in the context in which it was wrought. . . . Great objectivity was one of the highest qualities of Fustel de Coulanges,' Dreyfus concluded, and what is 'true for history is true for everything'.[53] Fustel's views on the loss of Alsace-Lorraine, shared by Dreyfus, confirmed that desire for impartiality. After a conference in Strasbourg in which the 'burning questions of the causes and responsibilities for the disastrous war' were debated, Fustel condemned the obsession with partisan politics: 'As for me, I aim to speak only for our dear Alsace,' he wrote, 'and when I am driven back to a discussion of French parties, I always respond: No more parties, no more divisions, no more hatred; accept our government as it is, as it can be, and dream only of pushing the enemy out . . . our sole objective should be Alsace.' Fustel knew the trauma experienced by Alsatians and Lorrainers when their homeland and fatherland were separated by force, when one swift and 'disastrous war' violated family unity and national unity. And he concluded with a plea that Frenchmen of conflicting opinions should work together to return the lost provinces; they should 'pardon each other, one and all'.[54]

A generation later nationalists exploited Fustel's call to push the 'enemy out', but parted company with the historian over the question of enemies within. Fustel, who rejected litmus tests of allegiance based on race, stood for a patriotism that was inclusive and magnanimous, for a sense of national community that Dreyfus would trace to that 'ideal of generosity' rooted in the early promises of the French Revolution and in the Declaration of the Rights of Man and Citizen.[55] When Dreyfus insisted through the years of *revanche* that 'the image of the Rhine should never be effaced from our memories',[56] he conjured up, much as Fustel had done, an image of national solidarity which the revolution had secured through its edicts of emancipation, and which Dreyfus's family had honoured as Alsatian *protestataires*. The captain's enemies, however, manipulating the politics of the lost provinces and treating Alsace-Lorraine as a testing ground for national purity, perpetuated a legacy of the revolution gone bad: the idea of a nation unified through exclusion.

NOTES

1 Hansi (Jean-Jacques Waltz), *L'Histoire de l'Alsace* (Paris: Floury, 1915), p. 100.
2 Jean-Marie Mayeur, 'Une Mémoire-frontière: L'Alsace', in Pierre Nora (ed.), *Les Lieux de mémoire*, Vol. 2 (Paris: Gallimard, 1986), p. 88.
3 Ernest Meininger, *Histoire de Mulhouse* (Mulhouse: n.p., 1923), pp. 113 ff.
4 ibid. See also François-Georges Dreyfus, *Histoire de l'Alsace* (Paris: Hachette, 1979), pp. 249–50; and Mayeur, 'Une Mémoire-frontière', p. 88.
5 See Roger Magraw, *France, 1815–1914: The Bourgeois Century* (New York: Oxford University Press, 1986), p. 261.
6 'La séparation de la France,' wrote Jacques Fleurent in 1907, 'ne pouvait que développer cet amour de province, surtout qu'il s'y ajoutait un nouveau motif: la conscience des malheurs communs et le sentiment de cohésion vis à vis de l'élément étranger, qui venait s'installer dans le pays' (see 'L'Idée de patrie en Alsace', in *Revue politique et parlementaire*, 1907, p. 337). Fleurent focused on French Alsatians who stayed behind, but similar sentiments were felt by those who moved on. For a recent study of Bruno's (Mme Fouillée's) book, see Mona and Jacques Ozouf, 'Le Tour de la France par deux enfants: Le petit livre rouge de la République', in Nora, *Les Lieux de mémoire*, Vol. 1, pp. 291–2.
7 For the numbers and motivations involved, see Dan P. Silverman, *Reluctant Union: Alsace-Lorraine and Imperial Germany, 1871–1918* (University Park, Pa.: Pennsylvania State University Press, 1972), pp. 66–69, 220, nn. 11 and 12; and F.-G. Dreyfus, *Histoire de l'Alsace*, pp. 251–2.
8 Ozouf, 'Le Tour de la France', p. 298.
9 Bruno, *Le Tour de la France par deux enfants* (Paris: Librairie Classique Eugène Belin, reprint 1983), p. 34. The Grand Rabbi is quoted in Julien Weill, *Zadoc Kahn, 1839–1905* (Paris: Alcan, 1912), p. 128.
10 See, for example, F.-G. Dreyfus, *Histoire de l'Alsace*, p. 252.
11 Hansi, *L'Histoire de L'Alsace*, p. 96. On the passport system and travel to Alsace, see Paul Appell, *Souvenirs d'un Alsacien* (Paris: Payot, 1923), pp. 181–2; and Meininger, *Mulhouse*, p. 130.
12 Fleurent, 'L'Idée de patrie', p. 342.
13 Frederic Seager, 'The Alsace-Lorraine Question in France, 1871–1915', in Charles K. Warner (ed.), *From the Ancien Regime to the Popular Front* (New York and London: Columbia University Press, 1969), p. 118 *et passim*.
14 Capitaine Alfred Dreyfus, *Souvenirs et correspondance publiés par son fils* (Paris: Grasset, 1936), p. 42.

15 Quoted in Gordon Wright, *France in Modern Times* (New York: Norton, 1987), p. 296.
16 Dreyfus's sister is quoted in H. Villemar, *Dreyfus intime* (Paris: Stock, 1898), p. 10.
17 Archives Nationales (hereafter cited as AN), BB 19/128, interrogation, p. 434.
18 Roger Martin du Gard, *Jean Barois* (Indianapolis: Bobbs-Merill, 1969), trans. Stuart Gilbert, p. 272. Péguy is quoted in Stephen Wilson, *Ideology and Experience: Antisemitism in France at the Time of the Dreyfus Affair* (Rutherford, NJ: Fairleigh Dickinson University Press, 1982), p. 1. The most thorough histories of the affair are Joseph Reinach's *Histoire de l'Affaire Dreyfus*, 7 vols (Paris: La Revue Blanche, 1901–1911; Fasquelle, 1929); and Jean Denis Bredin, *L'Affaire* (Paris: Julliard, 1983).
19 AN, N.A.F. 14307, journal, 7 November 1895. It is important to note that Dreyfus, though highly assimilated, had not severed all connection to his Jewish faith or to the particular notions of justice embedded in the religion of his ancestors; see Michael Burns, 'Majority Faith: Dreyfus Before the Affair', in Frances Malino and David Sorkin (eds), *From East and West: Jewish Experience in a Changing Europe, 1750–1870* (Oxford: Basil Blackwell, 1991).
20 On elites, see Mayeur, 'Une Mémoire-frontière', p. 89, and F.-G Dreyfus, *Histoire de l'Alsace*, p. 252. On Jewish migration, see the two informative articles by Vicki Caron, 'The failed alliance: Jewish-Catholic relations in Alsace-Lorraine, 1871–1914', *Leo Baeck Institute Yearbook*, vol. 26 (1981), pp. 3–21, and 'Patriotism or profit? The emigration of Alsace-Lorraine Jews to France, 1871–72', *Leo Baeck Institute Yearbook*, vol. 28 (1983), pp. 139–68.
21 Patrick Girard, *Les Juifs de France de 1789 à 1860: De l'émancipation à l'égalité* (Paris: Calmann-Lévy, 1976), p. 110.
22 F. Hoffet, *Psychanalyse de l'Alsace* (Paris: n.p., 1951), pp. 73–4.
23 See Michael Burns, 'The Dreyfus Family', in Norman L. Kellblatt (ed.), *The Dreyfus Affair: Art, Truth and Justice* (Berkeley and Los Angeles: University of California Press, 1987), pp. 140–52. On the French customs of the Mulhouse manufacturing 'patriciate', see Jean Schlumberger (ed.), *La Bourgeoisie Alsacienne: Etudes d'histoire sociale* (Strasbourg: Le Roux, 1954), p. 491 *et passim*; Georges Weill, *L'Alsace française* (Paris: Alcan 1916), pp. 96–7; and F.-G. Dreyfus, *Histoire de l'Alsace*, p. 241.
24 F. L'Huillier (ed.), *L'Alsace en 1870–1871* (Strasbourg: Publications de la faculté des lettres de l'Université de Strasbourg, 1971), p. 111.
25 *Mulhouse et le Sundgau: 1648–1848*, n.a. (Mulhouse: n.p., 1848), p. 6. On the economic situation in Alsace after 1871, see Silverman, *Reluctant Union*, pp. 165–89; and on the cultural conflict, see *Centennaire de la Société Industrielle de Mulhouse*, n.a. (Mulhouse: n.p., 1926), p. 14; Raymond Oberle, *Mulhouse, ou la genèse d'une ville* (Mulhouse: Éditions du Rhin, 1985), p. 278.
26 Caron, 'Patriotism or profit?' pp. 147–8.
27 Jean Richard Bloch, *Et Cie* (Paris: Gallimard, 1947), pp. 74–5.
28 Quoted in Caron, 'Patriotism or profit?', p. 139.
29 Alfred Dreyfus often spoke of France and its 'idéal de générosité' (see Bibliothèque Nationale (hereafter cited as BN), N.A.F. 24909, Dreyfus notebooks, p. 257).
30 Archives departementales de Vaucluse, 6 M 303, declarations for French citizenship. On Jacques Dreyfus's military service, see Dreyfus, *Souvenirs*, p. 41.
31 Burns, 'The Dreyfus Family', pp. 141–2.
32 Bruno, *Le Tour de la France*, pp. 10, 25.
33 ibid., p. 300. On the schooling of the Dreyfus boys, see Villemar, *Dreyfus intime*, pp. 10–11; and Dreyfus, *Souvenirs*, p. 42.
34 Villemar, *Dreyfus intime*, pp. 9–10. Dreyfus's thoughts on his own education are in BN, N.A.F. 24909, notebooks, p. 217. On Alsatians returning temporarily to their province, see, for example, Appell, *Souvenirs d'un Alsacien*, p. 177; and Schlumberger, *Bourgeoisie Alsacienne*, p. 324.
35 On the nomadic life of young officers like Dreyfus, see William Serman, *Les Officiers français dans la nation, 1848–1914* (Paris: Aubier, 1982), p. 204. For Dreyfus's military record, see Ministère de la Guerre, Archives Administratives (hereafter cited as AA), 'Feuillet du personnel', Dreyfus, 1878–1920.
36 AN, BB 19/128, interrogation, pp. 418–20.

Sentiment and ideology

37 Appell, *Souvenirs d'un Alsacien*, pp. 179–80.
38 Dreyfus will recount this visit, which took place in the early 1880s, on a number of occasions; see BN, N.A.F. 16609, letter to Lucie Dreyfus, 6 December 1894.
39 See the quotes in Michael Marrus, *The Politics of Assimilation: The French Jewish Community at the Time of the Dreyfus Affair* (Oxford: Oxford University Press, 1980), p. 188. See also the interview with Barrès in *La Liberté*, 1 December 1903.
40 AN, N.A.F. 14307, journal, 7 November 1895.
41 ibid., and BN, N.A.F. 16464, letter to Ministère de la Guerre, 25 December 1897.
42 BN, N.A.F. 16609, 24 December 1896 and 5 February and 10 August 1897.
43 The best overview is Robert Gauthier, 'Les Alsaciens et l'affaire Dreyfus', *Saisons d'Alsace*, vol. 17 (1966), pp. 56–80, On Dreyfus's appeal to see Grand Rabbi Kahn, see DFPC, Dreyfus letter, 23 December 1894; and AN, BB 19/75 for the rabbi's correspondence with military officials.
44 Seager, 'Alsace-Lorraine Question', p. 119.
45 BN, N.A.F. 23821, 9 January 1898; and BN, N.A.F. 17386, 5 August 1898. See also, BN, N.A.F. 23819, 10 October and 23 November 1897.
46 BN, N.A.F. 23821, 6, 13 and 26 January and 11 February 1898. The Alsatian deputy during the revolution was Jean-François Rewbell, quoted in Arthur Hertzberg, *The French Enlightenment and the Jews* (New York: Columbia University Press, 1968), p. 356.
47 Maurice Barrès, *Scènes et doctrines du nationalisme*, Vol. 1 (Paris: Plon, 1925), p. 67. See also Barrès quoted in Pierre Birnbaum, *Un Mythe politique: La République juive* (Paris: Fayard, 1988), p. 129.
48 Léon Blum, *Souvenirs sur l'Affaire* (Paris: Gallimard, 1981), pp. 84–6.
49 BN, N.A.F. 24909, notebooks, p. 244.
50 Barrès quoted in Bredin, *Affair*, p. 7; see also the interview with Barrès in *La Liberté*, 1 December 1903.
51 Louis Dimier, one of the academic members of Action Française, is quoted in Eugen Weber, *Action Française: Royalism and Reaction in Twentieth-Century France* (Stanford, Calif.: Stanford University Press, 1978), pp. 36–7.
52 ibid., p. 37.
53 BN, N.A.F. 24909, notebooks, p. 58.
54 Fustel de Coulanges quoted in L'Huillier, *L'Alsace en 1870–1871*, pp. 380–1.
55 See above, n. 29.
56 Dreyfus quoted in Reinach, *Histoire de l'Affaire Dreyfus*, Vol. 2, p. 160.

5

Joan of Arc between right and left

Gerd Krumeich

[Joan of Arc] was a discovery of democracy, of the people speaking out.

> Maurice Barrès[1]

The experience of the Revolutions made it possible [for us] fully to understand the beauty of this story.

> Jules Quicherat[2]

When the Englishman made himself king, France started to feel herself to be France.... This protest could not have come from the powerful, from the king or from the towns... it came from the people, the country people, from a woman, a virgin, The Maid.

> Jules Michelet[3]

Johanna nostra est.

> Pope Pius X[4]

These quotations, a few of many, give a clear indication of the state of mind of those who tried to revive Joan of Arc's popularity during the first half of the nineteenth century. Augustin Thierry, Sismondi, Barante, Michelet, Lavallée, Henri Martin and others took as their major act of faith the creation of a history of the French people – and it was in this context, that the episode of Joan of Arc took on an entirely new meaning:

> From where did the help come that drove out the English and raised the throne of Charles VII, when all seemed lost...? Was it not the energy of patriotic fanaticism among the ranks of the poor soldiers and the militia from towns and villages? The religious aspect of this glorious revolution was only a veneer: it was the most powerful symbol of popular inspiration.[5]

Clearly, the romantic idea of 'the people' is far from uniform – on the contrary: Michelet's 'people', for example, represent a broad concept,

Sentiment and ideology

embracing different strata of society in a whole from which the nation will spontaneously arise. This concept is somewhat representative of a centrist view and very different in principle from the view of the left, in which the people live in a permanently antithetical position to the 'great'.[6] But important though this distinction was for the later development of the view of Joan of Arc's personality, it must be stressed that the reevaluation of the heroine by leftist historians and writers was based on a very aggressive spirit of freethinking and republicanism; it was in this spirit that Joan was reclaimed by them as the daughter of a peasant, a daughter of the people who, as the most advanced put it, was betrayed by her king and burned by the church. The first romantic historians (Augustin Thierry and Sismondi) who retraced the saga of Joan of Arc from about the 1820s, portray her as a daughter of the people, whose visions and beliefs are supposed only to have been the light of her own intelligence that she was as yet unable to name. And all the 'left-wing romantics' vigorously supported the claim, made during the 1820s, that it was due to her betrayal by the 'great' that Joan of Arc was prevented from pursuing her aim of national liberation. It was their fault, they asserted, that the Maid was taken prisoner at Compiègne, that she was found guilty and burned, without the ungrateful king paying any heed. This was the preferred theme from which they all derived either an ethic or a martyrology of the 'people': 'a poor peasant girl whom he scarcely thought of as he lay in the arms of a courtesan, and whom he let burn without even a care! The people sacrificed themselves for the ungrateful and disdainful monarchy.'[7]

This conviction increased as, through an enormous collective effort of historical research, sources were discovered which proved that Joan had acted, to a large extent, against the advice of Charles VII and his counsellors, who regarded the Maid's exploits with suspicion and who, content with the coronation, started negotiations with the Burgundians instead of continuing the struggle as Joan wanted, to drive the English 'out of all France'. In reality, this process of collective 'discovery' was a multifaceted phenomenon, which combined the discovery of previously unknown sources, and the rediscovery of sources known in theory since the fifteenth and sixteenth centuries, but which had, until then, been neglected or undervalued. Consider the following typical examples of this double process of discovery. Joan's famous 'Lettre aux Anglais' had been widely known since the trial itself, when it was introduced as a proof of her superstition. It was in this letter that Joan declared unequivocally: 'Je suis cy venue de par Dieu pour vous bouter hors de toute France.'[8] But despite this first-hand source, which had always been available and indeed used, the conviction had arisen and gradually come to seem self-evident, that Joan had believed her mission to be over once the king had been crowned at Reims. It was the new conviction, originating in the nineteenth century, that Joan's mission had been a 'national' one that led to this vital source being 'rediscovered'.[9]

But more important, perhaps, than this epistemological renewal was the discovery, in the nineteenth century, of new contemporary sources. The most important of these was by Jules Quicherat of the chronicle of Perceval de Cagny. Perceval was the squire of the Duc d'Alençon, Joan's faithful companion-in-arms. His chronicle, dating from the first half of the fifteenth century, is an absolutely contemporary testimony, the authenticity of which has not been contested since 1850. Perceval bitterly described the Maid's fate after the coronation, ending with the failure of the assault on Paris and her capture outside Compiègne: 'Elle fist choses incréables à ceulx qui ne l'avoient veu; et peult-on dire que encore eust fait, se le roy at son conseil se fussent bien conduiz et maintenuz vers elle.'[10] Above all, Perceval reproached the king and his advisers with preferring to negotiate a truce with the Duke of Burgundy after the coronation at Rheims, rather than continuing the fight for liberation, as Joan had demanded: 'Le roy ... ayma mieulx à donner ses héritaiges de la couronne et de ses meubles très largment que soy armer et soustenir les fais de la guerre.'[11] Clearly, this source was considered by left-wing historians as a welcome and definitive proof of the modern interpretation of the Joan of Arc saga. The disagreement between Joan and the king concerning the tactics to be adopted was interpreted as a deliberate betrayal of the 'national' effort being made by the Maid and the people, and for many this presented a parallel with the betrayal of the national cause by pre- and anti-revolutionary monarchs.[12]

The historian who did most to develop and instil this 'left-wing' view of Joan of Arc in the minds of the public was certainly Henri Martin.[13] Martin became interested in Joan very early on, and wrote a good deal about her in his *Histoire de France* (1883). He immediately appropriated Quicherat's discoveries, most of which were to be found in specialist reviews such as the *Bibliothèque de l'École des Chartes*, and brought them to public attention by simplifying and restructuring them to suite the taste of the wider republican readership which had avidly read his *Histoire de France Populaire* during the 1860s and 1870s. He published as an indictment the new left-wing view of the history of Joan in an article that appeared in 1856, and returned to the topic a year later in his widely read work *Jeanne Darc*;

> We accuse Charles VII of having conspired against his kingdom ... in 1429, when Providence ... had sent an immense power to his aid ... that brought with it soldiers, people, the young nobility, all the elements of action and victory.... We accuse him of having ... rejected this grace and stopped Joan in the middle of her mission.[14]

Sentiment and ideology

In 1884, the deputy Joseph Fabre proposed a bill to institute a national holiday in honour of Joan of Arc. The proposal originated from this same *gauche-républicaine* political tendency, anti-clerical and 'secular', and it was signed by 252 left-wing deputies, including Clovis Hugues and Charles Marie Ange de Laisant, who would soon turn to Boulangism.[15] The 'advanced' nature of the Fabre proposal was made clear both by Fabre's own arguments,[16] and by the parliamentary report on the bill. This stated unequivocally that Joan should be considered as a precursor of 'democracy rising up to save France', as the inspiration of '*popular* patriotism' opposed by 'les grands' and the clergy. This, briefly, was how Joan was 'discovered' and her cult appropriated by the left. This appropriation continued from about 1820 until 1885; at this historical moment, Joan was definitely the sister of Marianne.

The undeniable fact of Joan of Arc's authentic rediscovery by left-wing romantics in the years following 1820 should not be taken to indicate, as is often said, that the Maid was 'forgotten' until that time. Although her personality and individuality had disappeared long before, her image as a heroine had been well maintained by a centuries-old royalist tradition. Her memory and commemoration were well established in the Catholic, royalist, even statist view. She had been celebrated uninterruptedly at Orleans since the fifteenth century, and the historians of the absolute monarchy cherished and transmitted her memory as one sent by God to aid the king.

This image too developed, and the variations generally kept to the following pattern. For Étienne Pasquier, in the sixteenth century, the Maid's existence was a sign of 'the hand of God' protecting France. Although in this view Joan of Arc is seen to be as much an individual as an historical figure, the memory faded and gave way to an increasingly stereotypical evocation of her deeds, that eventually became almost utilitarian.[17] The historians of the *grand siècle* saw only the royalism in this – the proof of their main assertion, that God occasionally worked miracles for the good of the king and France. This instrumentalization is present everywhere in the various *Histoires de France*, in the *Abrégés* from the time of Mézeray, whose books influenced the attitudes of cultivated people even into the nineteenth century.[18] Mézeray even blames the Maid for having continued the fight after the king's coronation. In common with all the historians and the panegyrists at the celebrations at Orleans, he was convinced that Joan's 'commission' ended with the coronation, and that going on with the struggle to drive away the English was tempting providence. From this ideological starting point they all reached the same conclusion. 'As she exceeded her commission . . . and still bore arms after having had the King crowned, God, who wishes to be obeyed exactly, was no longer obliged to continue his miracles in her favour.'[19] Joan was thus found guilty of bringing about her own burning. This theory seems absurd by today's standards, but was present not only throughout the historical discourse of the *grand siècle* and the absolute monarchy, but also in the *Histoires de France* of monarchist leaning until the 1870s.[20]

Alongside royalist historiography, there is another excellent source for the stereotypical and longstanding official Catholic and royalist vision of Joan. This source is the 'Panégyrique' of Orleans – the sermon given each year during the celebrations of the feast of Joan of Arc at the church of Sainte-Clothilde. The occasion became a major social event, and the great ecclesiastical orators considered it an honour to be asked to preach.[21] a few examples, which attempt to combine the current and temporal with what is held to be the universal and eternal, are sufficient illustration. By the nineteenth century, the panegyric already had a long tradition, and one which profoundly influenced the right-wing, monarchist, Catholic view. One of the main affirmations, since the origins of the panegyric,[22] was that the Maid's mission ended with the coronation, and that her continued struggle for liberation, counter to God's explicit will, led directly to her death at the stake. But although the language of the panegyric changed over time, with the rationalist scepticism of the eighteenth century having an influence, it took a distinct step backwards during the Restoration. The traditional notion of Joan's disobedience to her divine 'commission' was sometimes reinforced by the assertion, as absurd as it was remarkable, that Joan had committed the serious fault of conceiving of the country without the king. This was suggested, for example, in 1830, two months after the July Revolution.[23] Even leaving aside the extremist claims of the Restoration, the fact remains that the traditionalist and Catholic position did not alter at all from the seventeenth century until the 1840s.

In about 1840, the two sides of the edifice were clearly visible: on one side was the age-old, ingrained stereotype of a Joan of Arc whose 'mission' was intrinsically royalist and Catholic, and whose existence was proof of the assertion that 'God looks after our kings' and of the 'gesta Dei per Francos'. On the other side, was the recent and enthusiastic support, fuelled by a whole historiographic trend, for Joan as a daughter of the people, 'betrayed by her king and burned by the Church', and whose aim had been to create France, although this she attributed to God, not daring to claim it herself. The latter image had considerable assets, in the romantic, republican feeling of the period, and the sources discovered at that time by an army of researchers, the standard-bearer of whom, because of his erudition, was Quicherat (although Michelet excelled above all because of his genius for combining the new vision with tradition). At that time, a new and very important development took place in the form of another and permanent restructuring of the cult of Joan.

After a period of some 30 years, during which the Catholic world put up only an indirect defence, the 1850s marked the start of an increased interest in Joan of Arc which seems to have been characterized by a

Sentiment and ideology

reduction in the royalist element. Among Catholics who wanted to open Catholicism up to the modern world, there was a second wave of 'romantic' feeling, although this, originating in Paris, would not filter through to the provinces for about 20 to 30 years. Mgr Dupanloup, Bishop of Orleans, is typical of this new movement. His interest in Joan, which first developed in 1849 when he was made bishop, differed from that of the time-honoured royalist, Catholic tradition in that, for him, what mattered about Joan was not 'legitimacy', the saving or restoration of the monarchy. He was not a republican, but felt that the church could function perfectly well without the monarchy. Dupanloup discovered that the story of Joan, as recounted by people such as Quicherat, Henri Martin, Lavellée and Michelet, could be combined perfectly well with a Catholic nationalism: Joan was certainly a daughter of the people, inspired by God for the good of France. The ungrateful king and the clerics of the time (unlike the official church) might indeed have caused her death; but her 'mission' was not over – she should still be the guide of an eternal France:

> and France, restored to the ranks of independent nations by a young girl, resumed her glorious and incomparable destiny which is still not complete; by remaining the eldest daughter of the Catholic Church while other nations fell by the wayside, she would prepare herself to lead the other European peoples, as queen of the civilised world. That was the reward for the sacrifice![24]

Catholic historians of a new generation discovered for themselves a Joan, daughter of the people, of whom a thorough understanding, already achieved by the left-wing historians of recent decades, would lead to the clear and simple statement that by dint of her actions and her suffering, Joan was a saint. Henri Wallon was the standard-bearer for a serious renewal of a Catholic historiography unafraid to accept the more important findings of the left-wing historians, particularly Jules Quicherat. In terms of erudition and sympathies, Wallon's *Jeanne d'Arc* (1860), was close to Quicherat or Michelet. For Wallon, there was nothing scandalous about using the text of the 1431 trial as well as that of the rehabilitation, which had been, almost exclusively, the source for traditionalist historiography. Wallon felt that Joan's true character as a marvel, beyond all rational explanation, was here absolutely apparent, and that more important than the patriotism of which the left-wing writers spoke so freely were Joan's piety and her divine mission. For him she was a 'model of piety', and her mission to liberate France was God-given, and the 'constant, tacit hostility' of Charles VII and his advisers was thus all the more reprehensible.[25] It was as a result of an initiative of Wallon's that the idea of canonizing Joan first occurred to Dupanloup, whose indefatigable historiographical adviser he was from about 1868.[26]

Joan of Arc

Hence, from about the 1850s, the old royalist and Catholic paradigm of Joan of Arc came into question, and was soon rejected even by Catholics, who were then free to argue the issue with the republicans on an equal footing. Although freed from her royalist associations, Joan remained Christian, Catholic, a pious maiden who died with the name of Jesus on her lips, and who had always affirmed her fidelity to the church. Since Wallon and Dupanloup, Catholics had constantly stated that Joan of Arc in no way contradicted the dogmas of the church, but that these had been interpreted wrongly and in bad faith by her ecclesiastical judges, who were in the pay of the English.

Thus the wheels were set in motion for the battle of Joan of Arc, which continued from the 1880s until 1914. On the left, there were the republicans, led by Joseph Fabre, a deputy then a senator, who lobbied for a republican festival in honour of 'the daughter of the people, betrayed by her king and burned by the church', although this phrase was already sounding rather tired and defensive in the 1880s. This side consisted of a strange mix of republican enthusiasts for Joan, such as Fabre, and anti-clericals for whom the debate was a vehicle for secularist propaganda. The centenary of Voltaire's death, on 30 May 1878, was typical of the way Joan was put to use for the *République au combat*, for 30 May was also the day on which Joan died at the stake, and Catholics had always regarded Voltaire as their enemy, who had insulted Joan of Arc.[27] It follows that the celebrations to commemorate Voltaire's centenary were greeted by Catholics with unanimous protest, and the pilgrimage to Domrémy was to a large extent devised as an anti-Voltaire demonstration. Although, strangely enough, Victor Hugo's lecture on tolerance, which was the main event of this commemoration, made no mention of Joan, other orators of the left and extreme left mentioned her in a deliberately partisan way:

> the people's Joan of Arc was inspired by love of the Fatherland and not some higher power. It was not fanaticism that made Joan of Arc, but patriotism. What did they do to Joan of Arc? They turned her into a pile of ashes and dust. Was it the free-thinkers who killed Joan of Arc? No, it was a Bishop of Beauvais, and priests from Rome and Paris.[28]

On the Catholic side, there was a noticeably similar change: the enthusiasm of men like Wallon or Dupanloup, who saw Joan as a model of piety, went hand in hand with considerations of ecclesiastical politics – Dupanloup wrote as much to the pope in 1869, when he pressed for her canonization:

> I would go as far as to say, most Holy Father, that nothing would be more popular in France, and elsewhere, and at the same time this act

would be very opportune under the present circumstances, very much to the honour of the Holy See and the Church.[29]

There followed a lull, with the two opposing tendencies, both consisting of an unseemly mix of sincere conviction put to political use, which lasted from about the time of the Boulangist episode to the start of the Dreyfus Affair. During this decade, various abortive attempts were made to establish festivals and republican commemoration days in honour of Joan, daughter of the people, and in the same period the Catholic-political ascendancy started to appear. There formed a new core of fundamentalist propaganda, and hysterical, unshakeable zealotry around the project for the Basilica of Domrémy, where the Assumptionist fathers found fertile ground for their Catholic propaganda: sermons gradually gave way to invective, groups such as Femmes de France organized a Joan of Arc cult which united revanchism with a rejection of the so-called satanic republic, against which Joan of Arc was called upon to protect France. The Bishop of Saint-Dié, Mgr Briey, addressed this harangue to a crowd of 10,000 'pilgrims of Joan of Arc', who came to Domrémy in 1878:

> There is, in France, a splendid, divine institution that they want to destroy – the Church of Christ. But isn't destroying the Church the same as destroying France itself?... Gesta Dei per Francos! France, the sublime origins of which start in the baptistery at Rheims!... Joan, the saints still watch over France, don't they? Joan, there is great pity in the land of France!... Joan, pray for France, Amen.

It was at that time, at the start of the 1880s, that a new generation of fundamentalist zealots, such as Father Ayrolles, Abbé Mourot of Domrémy, Canon Debout, Abbé Leman, and Cannon Lemerle, spread the message of a Joan who would drive both the Germans from Alsace and the Jews from France. The total lack of restraint exhibited by these and many otherwise cultivated people is astonishing, and leads one to wonder what were the fears and obsessions driving them. The chapter titles from the supposedly scholarly work by Ayrolles called *La Vraie Jeanne d'Arc*, which appeared in four volumes in 1890, are highly revealing: 'la Paysanne est l'inspirée travestie par la libre-pensée. La Jeanne d'Arc forgée de Michelet, la burlesque fillette rêvée par Quicherat.... Siméon Luces insanités.'

An era of rapid modernization which inspired fear and a search for a saviour in many people, opened up a fantastical world in which Satan, by means of the Jews, was thought to run things. The Taxil Affair was famous because it reunited all the morbid and twisted fantasies of these years. Léo Taxil, whose real name was Gabriel Jogand-Pagès, was a convinced and argumentative freethinker who, in 1880, published a book with the

Librairie Anticléricale, the title of which was entirely indicative of the spirit of the times: *Joan of Arc, victim of the priests. Historical study with revelations and documents (the betrayal, the rape, the trial, the execution)*. The main assertion of this semi-pornographic publication was that Joan had been raped by 'the priests' before her execution. Seven years later, in 1887, the same author published confessions in which he explained how Joan of Arc had worked a miracle by making him convert to Catholicism. The Catholic establishment was beside itself with pride, and Pope Leo XIII granted him a private audience. Having been promoted in this way as a champion against the misdeeds of freethinking, Taxil redoubled his efforts and brought out a monthly review, *Jeanne d'Arc*, followed by a rather poor edition of the *Procès de Jeanne d'Arc*. After that, he published other stories of converted freethinkers, then suddenly in 1897 revealed in a blaze of publicity that all this conversion had been a joke intended to lay bare the abuses and absurdities of Catholicism.[30]

On the threshold of the twentieth century, the antagonism over Joan of Arc went through another significant change. After the period of extreme conflict, when struggle in the name of Joan followed exactly the general trend of struggle between the 'two Frances', a centrist movement started to form, focused on the Catholics of the Ralliement who were close to those 'national', centrist republicans who were defenders of 'order'. One of the representatives of this movement, Mgr Pagis, Bishop of Verdun, expressed its sentiments very clearly during the Joan of Arc celebrations at Orleans in 1898: 'Since France wants the Republic, let's have the Republic! Let us keep the tricolour flag.' And Poincaré, the minister of public instruction of the time, echoed this by calling for a patriotic truce: 'Joan can unite all the French people through all the fundamental values of patriotism, above party considerations, because she represents the passionate desire for the independence and greatness of the nation.'[31] Since the centrist republicans made no objection to the fact that Joan was, first and foremost, Catholic,[32] this truce in official commemoration – which has lasted, *mutatis mutandis*, to the present day – could be concluded.

The republican left started to draw back from the dispute, gradually showing less and less interest. The Thalamas Affair, typical of many other such small incidents,[33] was a lively but chiefly ritualistic expression of their fighting retreat, in which internal politics and the hostility between the two Frances, which continued to break out frequently, found a symbolic resonance in the 'management' of Joan of Arc's memory.

When Joan's beatification took place in 1909, the struggle was over. As the pope said, 'Johanna nostra est', and the only opposition the left could make was an entirely individual refusal to ratify the fact: a complete rejection of the 'official Joan'. Alain expressed this feeling of resignation and impotent sympathy in one of his *Propos*:

There was the faith of Joan of Arc and the faith of those who burned her.... In this splendid story I can clearly see... two inimical religions. I see two Gods locked in a struggle, one God who is matter, and one God who is spirit.... A new prayer; revelation from within; a new God! An insult to order, to plans, interests and intrigues, to captains, kings and priests. They killed the new God first of all. And once he was good and dead, they recognised him and believed that they adored him. This is why it is important that Joan of Arc should divide us.[34]

In conclusion, this overview of developments in the cult of Joan of Arc shows that her so-called illegitimate monopolization, of which all left-wing writers from Sanson to Winock speak,[35] is just a repetition of a republican stereotype ingrained since the 1900s. Both from a structural and a historicist point of view, one must accept that there have been various monopolizations and reappropriations, all of which have been of relative importance for the development of the cult. In the final analysis, the essential fact is that through republican scholarship during the first half of the nineteenth century, Catholicism was able to rediscover and rejuvenate its age-old traditional account of an event that appealed directly to faith, going beyond all attempts to turn it to directly political ends.

NOTES

1 In Marshal Foch, Maurice Barrès *et al.*, *Jeanne d'Arc* (Paris: n.p., 1929).
2 Jules Quicherat, *Aperçus nouveaux sur l'histoire de Jeanne d'Arc* (Paris: Renouard, 1850), p. 165.
3 Jules Michelet, *Histoire de France*, ed. P. Viallaneix, Vol. 3 (Paris: Flammarion, 1973), p. 107.
4 At the beatification of Joan of Arc, 1909.
5 Augustin Thierry, *Lettres sur l'histoire de France* in *Oeuvres Complètes*, Vol. 3 (2nd edn, Paris: Furne, 1851), p. 1.
6 See P. Villaneix, *La Voie royale: essaie sur l'idée du peuple chez Michelet* (Paris: Delagrave, 1959).
7 Theophile Lavallée, *Histoire des Français*, Vol. 2 (Paris: Paulin & Hetzel, 1838), p. 151. See for the development of the historiography of Joan of Arc as a whole, Gerd Krumeich, *Jeanne d'Arc in der Geschichte: Historiographie, Politik, Kultur* (Sigmaringen: Thorbecke, 1989).
8 Jules Quicherat (ed.), *Procès de condamnation et de réhabilitation de Jeanne d'Arc*, Vol. 1, 5 vols; (Paris: Renouard, 1841–9), p. 241.
9 See Gerd Krumeich, 'Der "Auftrag" Jeanne d'Arcs: zum verhältnis von politischer ideologie und historischer forschung' (with English and Italian summary). *Storia della Storiografia*, no. 15 (1989), pp. 54–74.
10 The extracts from the Chronical of Perceval concerning Joan were published by Quicherat. *Procès*, Vol. 5, p. 30.
11 ibid., p. 37.
12 For a discussion of the validity of this assertion, repeated today by the most officially approved historians and questioned only by those on the fringes, Gerd Krumeich, 'Recht und macht: verdammung und rehabilitation von Jeanne d'Arc', in A. Demandt (ed.), *Grosse Prozesse der Weltgeschichte* (Munich: Beck, 1989).

13 Henri Martin was one of the most widely read and now forgotten historians of the nineteenth century. He has no biography, but see Charles Rearick, 'Henri Martin', in Walter Laqueur and George L. Mosse (eds), *Historians in Politics* (London: Sage, 1974).
14 *Revue de Paris*, 15 September 1856.
15 For the history of this proposal, see the seminal article by Rosemonde Sanson, 'La fête de Jeanne d'Arc en 1894: controverse et célébration', *Revue d'Histoire Moderne et Contemporaine*, 20 (1973), pp. 444–63; and for more details and a somewhat different approach, Krumeich, *Jeanne d'Arc*.
16 See Joseph Fabre, *Des Bourreaux de Jeanne d'Arc et de sa Fête nationale* (Paris: Hachette, 1915).
17 Etienne Pasquier already complained of this in his *Recherches de la France* (Paris: Sonnius, 1621).
18 See Alphonse Aulard, 'Émules et prédécesseurs du Père Loriquet: les manuels d'histoire depuis le 16ᵉ siècle', *La Révolution Française*, 77 (1924), pp. 5–44; and Guillaume de Bertier de Sauvigny, 'Les avatars d'un manuel d'histoire', *Information Historique*, 39 (1977), pp. 242–7, and 40 (1978), pp. 44–51.
19 F. E. Mézeray, *Histoire de France* (Paris: Thierry, 1685), p. 617.
20 For details, see Krumeich, *Jeanne d'Arc*.
21 A practically complete collection of the panegyrics is held at the Centre Jeanne d'Arc at Orleans; there are several published anthologies, esp. Canon B. Lemerle, *Soixante-quinze panégyriques de la bienheureuse Jeanne d'Arc* (Orleans: Marron 1909).
22 ibid. (Known from the beginning of the seventeenth century.)
23 ibid. (Le Courtier, 'Panegyrique de 1830'.)
24 F. A. P. Dupanloup, *Panégyrique de Jeanne d'Arc* (Orleans: Gatineau, 1855).
25 Henri Wallon, *Jeanne d'Arc* (Paris: Hachette, 1860), p. 103. It is interesting to note that some of his most unorthodox statements were altered in the famous illustrated edition of 1876.
26 For details and documentary evidence, see Krumeich, *Jeanne d'Arc*.
27 See Jeroom Vercruysse, 'C'est la faute à Voltaire', *Studies on Voltaire and the Eighteenth Century*, Vol. 23 (1963).
28 Speech by Thulié, in *Le Temps*, 1 June 1878.
29 Archives Nationales, Fonds Dupanloup AB/XIX/52, dossier 6.
30 See esp. Eugen Weber, *Satan franc-maçon: la mystification de Léo Taxil* (Paris: Julliard, 1964).
31 Lanery d'Arc, *Le Livre d'Or de Jeanne d'Arc* (Paris: Leclerc & Corniau, 1894), p. 359.
32 Typical in this respect is Gabriel Hanotaux's *Jeanne d'Arc* (Paris: Hachette, 1911), a best seller of the day.
33 See below, p. 146, n. 59, and also Christian Amalvi, 'Les Guerres des manuels autour de l'école primaire en France, 1899–1914', *Revue Historique*, vol. 262, no. 532 (1979), pp. 359–98.
34 Alain, *Les Propos* (Paris, 1978), Vol. 2, p. 55 ('propos' of June 1912).
35 Sanson, 'La Fête de Jeanne d'Arc'; Michel Winock, 'Jeanne d'Arc et les juifs: son mythe sous la Troisième République', *H-Histoire*, no. 3 (1979), pp. 227–37.

6

Words and images of nationhood

Pierre Sorlin

Between the era of Boulangism and the Great War politicians and others were used to referring daily to *nation* or *patrie* which were the core of the political debates during the Dreyfus Affair and were also uttered, in opposite ways, by the internationalists (socialists) and the nationalists in the 1910s. *Nation, patrie* are vocables which do not make much sense if we do not 'fill' them with other words or with feelings. In fact Kant has told us we are unable to 'think' except with 'images', that is to say categories constructed by our society which interpose between us and the outer world and allow us to 'reflect' upon this world. I do not want to linger on the philosophical aspect of the problem. Mine is a much simpler concern: what are the tools (the intellectual tools) which enabled people to expand on *nation* and *patrie*, and what occurred to the listeners or readers when they came across these vocables in a speech or paper? How was it possible to conceive of *patrie* and *nation*?

At first the query seems an elementary one: politicians, opinion formers, and journalists enlarged upon the topic; it is up to us to analyse their words. But what about those who were not well up on politics? I am not interested in scrutinizing the language and programmes of those who knew (or thought they knew) what these notions were but in determining what went on in the minds of ordinary readers or listeners when they encountered them. Many of them were doubtless able to hear the words since they were French but not necessarily to understand their specific connotation. For example, it is no wonder that in the political vocabulary of our period the word *ennemi* was important and frequently uttered. It is easy to trace throughout the period: 'Le monde ne marche que par la haine des frères ennemis' (Renan, *Drames philosophiques*, 1885); 'Luc n'était-il pas l'ennemi public, l'étranger venu d'on ne sait où?' (Zola, *Le Travail*, 1901); 'Qui dit voisins dit ennemis' (A. France, *L'Ile des Pingouins*, 1910); 'Vaincre l'ennemi intérieur pour remplir le premier des devoirs qui est de repousser l'ennemi du dehors' (Maurras, *Kiel et Tanger*, 1914). Antagonism, opposition, adversity were presented as normal, not to say necessary, factors of domestic and international relationships. Now if we look at the statistics we see that *ennemi*, which belonged to the most common vocabulary during the first half of the century and will of course come back during the First World War was not currently used round 1900. There was thus a gap between the attitude of the politicians and intellectuals who argued spontaneously in terms of aggressiveness, and the reaction of 'the others' who lived in an aggressive context but did not express it.

Although words play a prominent part in my research I shall, rather, speak of 'images'. When we deal with practical things, food or clothes, the vocables have a well shaped significance, but there is a fringe of meaning around abstract nouns which is closer to mental images or impressions than to defined concepts. Under the general label of images I shall enclose and scrutinize both words which suggest images and pictures which are concrete images. Images are from the outset totally different items which deserve separate treatment. Even if there are many words in a language their number is limited. There are 70,000 vocables in French but most of them are specialized or outdated. 'Common' vocabulary (abbreviated *cv*) which enables one to express everything amounts to 6,500 and it is possible to make oneself understood with a cluster of 900. Those are the words everybody is familiar with (even if they are understood in different ways by different people). They form 'basic' French (abbreviated *bF*) on which we shall focus.

By contrast, the quantity of pictures is innumerable. It is impossible to deal with 'pictures' as a whole and a choice has to be made. Given our premises I shall not examine politically marked drawings, namely caricatures and engravings printed in newspapers,[1] but rather, pictures previously unknown spread over the last decades of the century. By permitting free posting of bills the 1881 press law led to a profusion of wall posters. During election times, even public monuments were covered with printed manifestos. This was not true only of big cities: the Kahn collection, showing views of small townships, proves that in out-of-the-way villages one could not see the walls for the coloured bills. Later the French discovered postcards. In 1885 in France the annual circulation of these items amounted to one fifth of that in Britain and was limited to advertisements mailed out by the big department stores. The postcard developed with exhibition of 1900 and, all of a sudden, became highly fashionable.[2] On the eve of the First World War 300,000,000 illustrated cards were printed and sold every year (which was still far behind the numbers in Britain and Germany).

Photography is also central to our research. It had existed for a long time but expensive equipment reserved it for the well-off. Photographers were either rich men like Atget, who found pleasure in taking pictures, or professionals who were mostly asked to portray politicians and artists. The collotype process invented in 1890 made it possible to reproduce negatives in massive numbers. The press was slow to take advantage of this but there were many potential customers such as department stores, fashion houses and factories. The first decade of the century created a new journalistic category: illustrated reporting. It cannot be compared with its contemporary counterpart since reporters were not required to come back with sensational shots, but only with pictures illustrating topics (sport, industry, fashion, daily life) that had been ignored previously. The great figure of the time is Jules Seeberger, who has to be contrasted with Atget. Atget's works were ignored in the 1910s because he was not interested in circulating them; today they look charming but are strangely deprived of human content – something with which Atget was not concerned. Seeberger was keen on exhibiting his photographs. Already well known in 1905, he was overwhelmed with orders. He took care to have people in his frames to make his pictures more alive and pleasant. Seeberger's works tell us a great deal about what industrialists or managers wanted to have photographed and about what people saw in art galleries, exhibitions, catalogues and advertisements.

Lastly, our period witnessed the birth of the cinema. By 1914 the French were used to attending regularly at movie theatres in towns, and travelling shows covered the whole country offering one hour programmes of news, documentaries and short stories.

It is not possible to deal with words as we do with pictures. We know who creates the latter whereas we ignore how the former are formed and evolve. Words have a life of their own, they are subject to no law of regular periodicity. We must take into account two different facts: the prevalence of a few vocables over the others during a given period – the dominant vocables – and the progression of other vocables which are much more often used in a period than during the previous epochs but are not dominant. We shall call the latter rising vocables. Sometimes it seems easy to understand the general trend of the vocabulary. If we consider the decade 1871–80 the dominant vocables are *ville, milieu, rue* and the rising vocables *médecin, ingénieur, colon*. But during the following decade the rising vocables are *femme, coup, frisson* and the dominant vocables all refer to purely practical things. The first series illustrates some strong concerns of the postwar era, but what is to be said regarding the second? We must take care not to demand too much from vocabulary.

In 1960 the Centre National de la Recherche Scientifique (CNRS) entrusted one of its laboratories in Nancy with computerizing French vocabulary which led to the indexing of 70,000 vocables with their frequency. This *Trésor de la langue française* is a masterpiece, a wonderful collection of examples (from which I have borrowed most of those quoted in this chapter), but we cannot be content with rough statistics. Fortunately, Etienne Brunet has re-elaborated the whole corpus and classified the words along the different decades of the nineteenth century. For instance, consider a word such as *classe*, whose frequency in the 1900s is three times that of the 1880s; are we allowed to say the vocable was discovered at the beginning of the century? Not until we have compared its frequency in the 1900s with its mean throughout the century and with the difference between the 1880–1900 gap and other gaps in the century. It is this gigantic work that Brunet has completed[3] by counterbalancing the use of a word at a certain time with its total use and variations (reduced deviation).

Things are not so simple with pictures. The difficulty is not that there are too many objects, since in the restricted field I have delimited several good tools are available. Seeberger's photographs have been listed and can be consulted at the Caisse Nationale des Monuments historiques.[4] Succinct though it is, Mitry's catalogue of French films is quite useful.[5] There are thousands of postcards or posters but as they are comparatively rare, valuable and well illustrated items, sometimes exhaustive inventories have been drawn up.[6] The problem is that pictures, unlike language, cannot be analysed into separate, countable elements comparable to words. There will always be some uncertainty regarding the interpretation of pictures.

Nationalisme: the word belongs neither to basic French nor common vocabulary. It is a neologism[7] uniquely intended for a technical (political) use. We cannot decide who was able to grasp its meaning and who did not but those who heard it either understood it immediately (as is the case with unusual terms) or missed it. It was therefore the task of nationalists to explain the term using images akin to it (*nation*), similar (*patrie*), or derived (army, flag). *Nation* formed part of basic French. Extensively used during the first half of the century it declined after 1850. It reached its minimum in about 1885 but, in our period, it was constantly below the average for the century. No image can be scrutinized in isolation and we must relate *nation* to other images. The kindred (*national*) or similar (*patrie, patriotisme*) vocables are to be found in common vocabulary. An important notion in this field is the concept of correlation: do words evolve over the years in the same direction, or do they diverge? A correlation is easily calculated by a comparison between the mean deviations:[8] it is positive when the words vary simultaneously, negative when their trends are opposed, neutral when there is no relationship between them. *National* is perfectly correlated with *nation*. The relationship with *patrie* is also very close during the last decades of the nineteenth century but, unlike *nation, patrie* rises after 1900. *Patriote* sticks to *patrie* just as *national* to *nation*. In other words, the two pairs decline from 1870 through 1900. Thereafter *patrie* outpaces *nation* dragging up another, older neologism, *patriotisme* which is used more frequently than *nationalisme*.

From the beginning we are faced with a political inconsistency: the nationalists gather around a label, *nationalisme*, which is not easily understood, and are therefore bound to have recourse to other, more

Sentiment and ideology

familiar words, such as *patrie*. 'Pour nous la patrie c'est le sol et les ancêtres, c'est la terre de nos morts': it is not by chance that Barrès, aiming to evoke the *Scènes et doctrines du nationalisme* (1902) shifted towards *patrie* which is quickly described thanks to concrete, palpable vocables pertaining to basic French. But the *patrie* vocabulary is common to a great many Frenchmen, even Jaurès and the majority of the socialists did not hesitate to use it.[9] I do not know the nationalists well enough to draw any conclusion from this preliminary exploration but I want to raise a question: was recourse to a common property (*patrie*) in order to illustrate their ideas a drawback for the nationalists? How was it possible to move from accepted but imprecise words (the *patrie* family) to more precise but not current terms (the *nation* family)?

Barrès's text exemplifies what has been assumed above: in politics, abstract nouns are best backed by images. Yet Barrès's images borrowed from the trite vocabulary of basic French are not very effective and can be interpreted in too many opposing ways. Less open images were necessary. The first predicate of *la patrie* should be its name. But if *France* belongs to basic French, it is extremely hard to cope with it. Not only is it used by all the political parties, but is a pretext for ambiguity as well. When Clemenceau wrote 'France autrefois grande de justice' (*Vers la Réparation*, 1899) he mixed up two different vocabularies: on one hand *autrefois*, typical of the 1880s, mostly used by the conservatives, on the other *justice*, a rising vocable of the 1900s, characteristic of the left. In other words, he neutralizes the sentence because it is a compound of inconsistent images. Elusive in writing, *France* is more easily reached in pictures where she is infrequently represented: scarcity delimits a precise field of utterance. It must be recalled that illustrated (e.g. engraved and coloured) posters were expensive and were only produced for industrialists, theatres and holiday resorts. The intervention of business points out a neglected aspect of the French economy: the limited but harsh competition with American firms. American high-quality bicycles, cars, threshing machines and fertilizers were imported and cleverly advertised, which led French industrialists to respond.[10] In many cases posters indirectly emphasized the French origin of goods, and it is this bias (the sellers did not dare to say: 'buy French' but they wanted their clients to understand that it was genuine French equipment) which has something to tell us about representations of *la patrie*. I have found four different variations which are probably not the only possible ones: (a) a map of France is the most obvious; (b) a typical landscape; (c) a lovely, slim woman,[11] especially, but not exclusively where Jules Chéret[12] was the designer (we shall consider these cases later); (d) a tricolour or a group of French soldiers.

Thus pictures delineate two other fields which are to be explored. *Drapeau* does not appear in basic French. It was often mentioned in the 1870s, a decade in which it was still represented on plates and in popular drawings. This was of course a period in which France hesitated between the tricolour and the white flag. From 1880 onwards, *drapeau* is constantly used at the average level of the century; it is one of the words that does not vary because unrelated to emotional questions, merely referring to a concrete object. *Armée* on the other hand is included in basic French. To define its images, I have skimmed off the nouns, adjectives and verbs which may be its derivatives. Given the limitations and lack of sophistication of basic French, I believe there is no risk of error. I have spotted no adjectives, 2 verbs and 14 nouns: 16 items out of a total of 687 (the other vocables of *bF* being adverbs, articles, etc.) do not provide us with an extensive choice. *Resistance, victoire, victorieux* do not belong to the sample, let alone *armes*. One verb, *défendre*, and two nouns, *chef* and *soldat* are perfectly stable and seem as unproblematic as *drapeau*. A sentence such as *Le soldat et son chef défendent (la France)* was probably acceptable to any Frenchman, and was thus politically neutral. All other words but one decline throughout the period. Three of them (*courage, devoir, ennemi*) never stop declining. *Paix/guerre* fall until 1910 and then, for obvious reasons, rise; the interesting thing is that *guerre* seems to be systematically avoided, particularly at the time of Boulangism (25 per cent below the standard usage in the 1880s); it might be interesting to examine whether the French hoped they would avoid war by not mentioning it – but how is it possible to answer such a question? Half of the nouns related to *armée*, although declining, expand temporarily during the first decade of the twentieth century (*gloire, général, honneur*). But the great mystery is *battre*, negatively correlated with the vocables just mentioned, which progresses from 1870 to 1900, falls at the turn of the century and rises again a few years before 1914. The verb is at its peak around 1885. *Battre* whom? Only two nations, *Allemand* and *Anglais* are (together with *Français*) among the 900 basic words. Considerably used around 1840 (a period mentioned earlier with *nation*, when popular engravings and earthwares often exhibited flags, soldiers and a triumphant Gallic cock), both are permanently under average during the Third Republic. *Allemand* recommences with *guerre/paix* round 1910, that is to say late in our period. In the 1880s, while the French avoided designating an enemy who was perfectly known to everybody, *battre* was the dominant verb and this is all the more interesting in that no other verbs or nouns similar to or derived from *armée* and *nation* were currently used in the decade.

We can suggest three easily understandable sentences:

1885: *Le soldat et son chef défendent la France et battent.*
1900: *Le soldat et son chef (gloire, honneur, courage) défendent la France.*
1910: *Le soldat et son chef défendent la France et battent les Allemands.*

Sentiment and ideology

These are of course abstract models which were never uttered as such but delineate the framework of images associated with *armée*. The last sounds coherent, not the others. I cannot account for the first. Still I note that factor analysis,[13] which classifies vocables according to their numerical proximity, gives an interesting constellation for the dominant verbs of the 1880s. It must be recalled that it is the frequency, not the significance which is classified; *battre* is at the centre for the period, the other verbs are statistically close to it but also pertain to an earlier or later decade:

aller

passer   *battre*   *pousser*

remettre   *crier*

rentrer

Subjectively, I read the cluster as a mixture of uncoordinated movements, a violent, erratic shaking and stirring. *Battre* might be an intention, not a direction, an imprecise will rather than a programme. Later, we shall try to account for some aspects of this strange constellation. For the moment I shall be content with noticing that semantically it is not a coherent set of verbs. Yet there are two opposite directions, backwards/forwards and all the verbs (except maybe *crier*) express action or endeavour. *Battre* is at the centre of contrasting tendencies but its presence strengthens the idea of going forward (*aller/pousser*). The problem is of course to decide to what extent it is possible to connect these words with the social–political context of Boulangism.

On the contrary, the rather complicated vocabulary of the 1900s will be easily related to contemporary events. The amazing impact of the Dreyfus Affair accounts for the dominance of *loi, verité* (both *bF*) and the progress of *colonel* (*cv*), *justice* (*bF*), both one third above the standards of the century, *état-major, militaire* and *traître* (all *cv*). The same period also shows a strong concern for social problems, *pauvre* (*bF*) being another dominant vocable, *social* (*bF*), *collectif, solidarité, prolétariat* (all *cv*) also rising. I shall not insist on this topic, which is alien to our problem. I only want to emphasize the close relationship between the most obvious shifts in vocabulary and some struggles of the decade. It is true that more vocables are likely to illustrate the idea of army than previously, but it would be useless (and possibly misleading) to decide whether this was a consequence of the affair or the result of a more profound change in French 'mentalities'. Factor analysis of the dominant nouns in 1900 gives a fascinating, puzzling constellation:

avenir

convention   *instant*

couleur

souvenir   *bataille*   *pensée*

The vocabulary is well structured with clear-cut conflicting pairs (*avenir/instant, avenir/souvenir, souvenir/pensée*). Yet the contrast between the wishful, ill-ordered vocabulary of the 1880s and the well-ordered, motionless vocabulary of the 1890s is puzzling, but this is a subjective opinion. All we can reasonably say is that when we compare the 1880s with the end of the century, it becomes clear that, by 1900, the set of images was much larger and that there were more vocables derived from *armée*.

Pictures confirm many of the conclusions inferred from words and statistics. Few, extremely limited clusters of postcards (and no posters) allude to a possible enemy. During the Boer War a minor printer tried to circulate caricatures of Englishmen by post. Other small workshops sold a limited quantity of drawings dedicated to Alsace. These were exceptions. The best example of apparent lack of concern is given by Joan of Arc. A well-known Catholic publisher, Desclée de Brouwer, launched twelve postcards devoted to the life of the Maid. It is absolutely impossible to infer from these naive engravings whom Joan fought; those surrounding the stake on the twelfth in the series look so grieved that one is led to wonder why she was burnt. Simultaneously, Méliès produced a twelve-episode film which practically eliminates the nationality of the adversary. It will be argued that everybody in France knew who killed Joan. Indeed; yet there were no attempts in the field of new pictures to ridicule, insult, or even designate the English – or the Germans.

Unlike the invisible enemy, the army was present in imagery. Every town was proud to sell illustrated cards of the city. Tastes then were different from ours, there were no panoramic views, old houses, or gothic churches but rather official buildings, prefectures, post offices, stations and the inevitable barracks. Clearly, the army was seen as an intrinsic element of local life, but as a whole a limited number of pictures dealt with it. We are lucky enough to have an exhaustive catalogue of postcards devoted to aircraft:[14] there are no military planes, no military pilots, no allusion whatsoever to a military use of aircraft. Things are not as simple with the navy, but even in images of ports sailors do not occupy the foreground. Scarcity results in a strict division between civilians and servicemen. In the Seeberger collection I have come across two photographs of Sunday in Versailles with officers standing among the crowd, and that is all. The

Sentiment and ideology

countless postcards showing towns or villages seldom include servicemen. Conversely, there are usually several soldiers but no civilians in front of the barracks. The military status is pictured as a specific, rather special one. Relaxing just outside the barracks or lingering under an archway the rare servicemen on postcards do not look over busy. I have not spoken of the army until now since we see, at the most, a small group of individuals, and more often than not, of a stereotypical, clumsy, ill-dressed, unarmed character: *le soldat* or sometimes *le soldat et son chef*. Around 1900, postcards and films (especially Lumière's short comic films) still convey the models elaborated after 1870 in military vaudevilles and popularized by Courteline's plays, thus giving a pitiful representation of the inadequate though occasionally clever French infantryman.

It is true that an evolution may be noted before the First World War. In 1906 Seeberger, entrusted for the first time with reporting on the navy in Toulon, took a good many photographs of different types of boats and life on board, the best of which were sold as postcards. Shortly after, other series were published on infantry, artillery, and so on. Soldiers are still taken in restricted groups (but we must think of the limited surface of a postcard), they do not seem as idle as before but rarely perform warlike occupations. Then the cinema entered the field by making and, from 1912, presenting as documentaries films on the navy or the spring army manoeuvres.

There is a noticeable difference between various kinds of images, which do not evolve at the same pace. Vocabulary can be extremely sensitive to events; a crisis as radical as the Dreyfus Affair resulted in an upheaval among words. Pictures resisted day-to-day politics more because they were produced by people who made long-term investments and did not want to risk them on short-lived commotions: if Méliès made a film on Dreyfus in 1899 this was an exception among hundreds of purely fantasy movies.

A few assumptions can already be inferred from what has been said. We have distinguished four stages which confirm the traditional periodization of the Third Republic: the 1870s, the 1880s, the 1900s and the eve of the First World War:

(a) There are no difficulties with the first decade: *nation* and *patrie* are discretely used, the enemy is not identified, popular pictures emphasize domestic issues while the vocabulary reinforces a pre-existing interest in science and positivism that anticipates the forthcoming debate on secularism. The absence of nationalism coincides with the lack of images likely to illustrate it.

(b) In the 1880s, *nation* and *patrie* were at their lowest; there were no pictures concerning either France or her army; variations in vocabulary were the expression of a disturbing uncertainty, of a

wavering between opposing, though ill-defined, potentialities. And yet there was Boulangism.
(c) When the century closed we pick out a crisis or the beginning of a long-term trend more marked in words than in pictures. A new distribution of the most significant words points to a polarization between overtly incompatible options which confirm, or accompany political divisions. Undoubtedly this was a problematic time. Was there room for nationalism? *Nation* was still avoided, *patrie* went through a modest revival, pictures offered a disarming vision of an ineffective French soldier. Would it be excessive to suggest that the conceptual context was particularly unsuited not to the elaboration of a doctrine but to its circulation?
(d) Finally, it was only shortly before the First World War that sufficient pictures provided *armée*, but not *nation* or *patrie*, with an imaginary background.

Nationalism was not isolated; it can only be appreciated by reference to other political tendencies. It has often been said that the development of socialism and the fear socialists triggered favoured the nationalists. It is always dangerous to risk negative explanations. Still I cannot but emphasize the drastic division of French words at a time (1900) when more vocables expressed a concern for social problems. As has been noted, the most numerous images were on the side of the socialists. It was also during that period that Frenchmen were divided not only by contrasting opinions but also by a conflicting structure of their vocabulary. Supporting the anti-socialists was thus easier, more acceptable than during the preceding, more confused decades. I cannot go further. But still in the field of images I have to examine the context. Was the lack of adequate images specific to nationalism or was it common in politics? And how could the French figure France outside the weak, evanescent concepts of *nation* or *patrie*?

Regarding the first question it must be clear by now that I am not looking for political ideas developed by papers, caricatures, or speeches but for images which might enable the French to make sense of politics. Basic French includes a restricted cluster of vocables likely to express political options. After 1870 all abstract notions and especially the contrasting pair *liberté/ordre* decline. The two leading words are *gauche* and *droite*, which were not extensively used before but progress quickly. Not surprisingly 1900 is the moment when both words make a stop while *classe*, *social* and *revolution* briefly increase. At the background of the most obvious division (*gauche/droite*) a closer study of the vocabulary shows religion to be the most important question. Not the word itself since *religion* follows *liberté*, *ordre* and so on; rather the derivatives of *religion*, *prêtre* during the first decades and then *église*. To cut a long story short, the French use a simplified but efficient image of their political conflicts with two groups fighting over one problem. In this respect the 1900 perturbation becomes even more interesting: something new intrudes and modifies the situation. Hence an outburst of rare terms, the unprecedented conflict of opposing vocables. For a few years the impact of the vocabulary derived from socialism is terrific, but on the eve of the war the traditional *droite/gauche* couplet has been restored. It seems that it was hard for nationalism to promote images outside the already established division. Was it then able to modify even temporarily the landscape as socialism did? Or did it insert itself inside the pre-existing landscape?

The couplet right/left was backed by another trite one, conservatism/change. I am not interested in the content of speeches dedicated to reaction/progress but in basic words relating to these issues. The most important vocable associated with progress is *avenir*, which constantly and regularly declined over our period. On the eve of the war it was 20 per cent below 1871 usage, which was already well below the average for the century. My argument is based mainly on statistics, only somewhat on impressions, but I cannot avoid emphasizing the convergence between numerical data and a widespread conception of the future: 'Je n'ai jamais rêvé sur l'avenir' (Barrès, *Mes Cahiers*, 1899–1901); 'Pour mon compte j'aime bien mieux ne pas penser à l'avenir' (Alain, *Propos*, 1908). *Avenir* is significantly correlated with *espérer/espoir* (down 30 per cent during our half-century). *Bonheur/heureux*, which were subsiding in 1871, remained below the standard for the century. They are scarcely used to express contentment, but rather to suggest short moments of fleeting happiness: 'bonheurs immédiats' (Barrès, *Mes Cahiers*, 1909–10), 'palpitation précaire' (Jacques Rivière, letter to Alain Fournier, 1909). *Bonheur* is negatively correlated with *tristesse*, a characteristic vocable of 1900 and, what is more interesting, with *peur*, a dominant word, not of one of the decades, but of the whole half-century.

The impression conveyed by these images is (only partially) reinforced by the pictures. At a time (before 1910) when papers published no or few photographs postcards provided supplementary information illustrating the news in short-lived series of cards.[15] People were offered disasters, fires, firedamp explosions in abundance. In the cinematic field where competition was fierce the French attempted to give their booming audiences something which could not come from Italy or the United States; in 1908 Pathé launched his newsreels which ran continuously, while Gaumont shot a series on *La Vie telle qu'elle est*. In both cases filmed catastrophes alternated with enacted dramas dealing with dangerous, problematic aspects of contemporary life. We are not allowed to say that the French had a pessimistic vision of their time since we shall never know how they reacted, but we may assume that they were confronted with pessimistic images and made an extensive use of tense, dreary words.

We have surveyed the half-century and I would like to focus on the second decade, the 1880s. *Autrefois*, typical of these years (twice the prevalence as in the 1870s or the 1900s), is well correlated with *colère* and its derivative *rage* and *cri*. *Crier* is also a significant verb of the period. There is a specificity of the second decade which, while using the 'pessimistic' vocabulary common to the whole era, developed another tendency more related to uneasiness and dissatisfaction. I see a contrast which must not be overrated between the 1880s and the 1900s. In short, the French used more 'political' words in the latter, more 'emotional' vocables in the former. I would hardly suggest this 'demonstrates' anything, but it might be fruitful to analyse the political discourse of the two decades with reference to the above mentioned difference.

Pictures compel us to be very careful since together with the dramatic vision they develop a much quieter one. Shortly after the war Jules Chéret inaugurated a new style of advertisements which he later abandoned but which dominated agricultural posters until 1914. Whereas the posters of Deering, Johnson and others concentrated on equipment, Chéret and his followers surrounded machines with a setting which is a corner of rural France with its trees, farm houses, cows and its everlasting stillness. The model has its equivalent in postcards. In 1908 Neurdein, the most important publisher in Paris, indicated that his 120,000 stills were almost exclusively landscapes; and Fildier's catalogue[16] documents the dominant topics of the period: the main street of a village, a cart, a few lingering people, or the countryside with the same peaceful inhabitants, or a small area of a town and its humdrum routine. Seeberger, who was more ambitious, is interesting since he depicted a different townscape, crowded, full of hurrying carriages and pedestrians. By contrasting both visions we realize what is obvious: a photograph is an interpretation. Seeberger anticipated the description which spread after the war and is an exception. From 1906 to 1910 Gaumont attempted to challenge the Americans by promoting what has been called the French comic school: it is a rough draft of what quite soon would be the classical American track-race, but unlike his competitors Gaumont located his scenarios in urban districts (not in studios with all-purpose settings) and involved small groups of typical Frenchmen. A wide range of pictures presents an extraordinarily soothing, almost idyllic image of France.

As for France herself, she is sometimes, not very frequently, named on pictures. But there is an ambiguity which must be noted. Today some academics wonder why it is necessary to picture naked women when advertising cars or food. Fashion was no different during the Third Republic: suggestively half-naked women advertised bicycles or fertilizers. A pretty young lady with a low-cut, transparent dress was to be found everywhere, on posters, in films, on postcards. 'Who's that girl?' There is no precise answer but in a few cases she has a name; she is either

Sentiment and ideology

France, or a province, or a town. Is it possible to ascertain a connection between the dominant figure of the pictures and France? Nothing well defined, rather a suggestion: she is sexy, appealing, surely not an armed wife or an imperious mother. If we combine both images (the village, the woman) France seems to be depicted as beautiful, pleasant and peaceful. But I admit these are mere guesses, the only firm ground being the number of circulating images.

Democracies use at least two political vocabularies. The first, technical, precise, open to neologisms is reserved for specialists (politicians, journalists), but their golden rule is never to go beyond the limits of basic vocabulary, a restricted set of words closed to neologisms, when addressing the majority of the citizens. Does this imply that politicians can only speak trifles? Not in the least since:

(a) Basic language (*bF*), for instance, suffices to express the main concerns of people – employment, peace, taxes, income. When the socialists said: 'Nous voulons la journée de huit heures' their images were simple ones which belonged to the most stable vocabulary and everybody knew what they meant.
(b) *BF* was broad enough to admit metaphors. Words linked to religion were often uttered because the issue was central to the political life of the time but also because the derivative of religion could be used metaphorically. By asserting that they were 'le parti de Dieu' some Catholics misused God but contrived a fine political metaphor.
(c) If the elements of *bF* do not change, their positions shift. Thus the progression or regression of some vocables enables the specialists to say new things with old words.

In late nineteenth-century France the *patriotes* encountered a specific problem. They wanted to *défendre la France* but all Frenchmen, except perhaps a small band of anarchists, were in the same mood. As for words derived from *patrie* they were either stable, therefore neutral and unexpressive or declining. This is a historical situation (historical since located in a precise period) which cannot be 'explained' historically and is merely observable statistically. My first assumption is thus that, *linguistically, there was no room for the patriotes*. Eventually they chose to call themselves *nationalistes* and my second assumption is that the label *was not comprehensible* for their fellow citizens because:

(a) It was a neologism which could not enter *cv*, let alone *bF*;
(b) There was no fringe of meaning associated with the label, no network of related words which could 'image' it;
(c) There were no pictures to support it.

Words and images

Does this entail that the word could not be heard? Absolutely not, provided we accept that there is a distance between understanding and hearing. 1900 France was filled with new sounds in the streets, in the air, in music, poetry, philosophy and many, many people were ready to listen to them. Was there an audience for the *nationalistes*? It is not up to me to decide. I only want to make two final remarks. Twentieth-century historians of European nationalism have often emphasized the 'irrationality' of its discourse. Is irrational the right word? In the French case is it not the difficulty of using common vocabulary (rational because perfectly well known) which results in the use of an apparently 'irrational' discourse? If the answer is positive a 'logical' study of nationalist discourse, a study in terms of 'programme' is less urgent, it is rather the capacity to provoke, to impose hearing which should be taken into account.

NOTES

Are my sources reliable?

Of course they are not. *Le Trésor* is based only on printed words and this is a serious drawback where politics is concerned, but is there another solution for a time when tape-recorders did not exist? Brunet's purpose was to computerize *Le Trésor* but he was obliged to make some choices. The most arguable one is technical. Brunet has opted for *lematisation*, which consists in reducing all words to their simplest form (e.g. the infinitive for a verb). Some lexicographers say it is the only possible solution, others that it is an absurdity but their arguments are more philosophical (unity/diversity) than technical. I confess I feel puzzled. On the one side the technique helps to stress the dominant words: we would ignore how important *défendre* was if the aspects of the verb were not compounded. But in some cases variations of form should be taken into account: *battre* and *être battu* are strictly opposed but *lematisation* does not enable us to distinguish them. Clearly, if the study of vocabulary turned out to be of some interest it would be necessary to begin with *lematisation* and then distinguish various aspects of some words. Another problem arises with pictures. If it is easy to define themes, it is almost impossible to decide what their meaning was. There is no doubt about the numerical importance of the quiet landscape or the pretty lady but thereafter we enter the realm of arbitrary interpretations.

I should like to thank Angella Armstong and Steven Englund for their extremely perceptive and useful comments on this chapter.

1. A good sample of these documents is to be found in Paul Ducatel, *Histoire de la III^{ieme} République vue à travers l'imagerie populaire et la presse politique*, 3 vols, (Paris: Grassin, 1973–6) and Alain Gescon, *Sur les murs de France. Deux siècles d'affiche politique* (Paris: Sorbier, 1979). Donald E. English's *Political Uses of Photography in the Third French Republic, 1871–1914* (Ann Arbor: University of Michigan Press, 1981) is well informed but never attempts to analyse the content of the pictures.
2. Georges Guyonnet, *La Carte postale illustrée, son histoire, sa valeur documentaire* (Paris: Chambre Syndicale de la Carte Postale Illustrée, n.d.); C. Martinet, *La Carte postale témoin de quelques-unes des transformations politiques et sociales de la fin du XIX^{ieme} siècle et du début du XX^{ieme} siècle* (Paris: Musée des Artes et Traditions Populaires, 1978); Aline Ripert and Claude Frère, *La Carte postale, son histoire, sa fonction sociale* (Lyon: Presses Universitaires de Lyon, 1983).

3 *Le Vocabulaire français de 1789 à nos jours d'après les données du Trésor de la langue française*, 3 vols, (Geneva and Paris: Slatkine, 1981). See also Alphonse Julliand, Dorothy Brodin, Catherine Davidovitch, *Frequency Dictionary of French Words* (Paris and The Hague: Mouton, 1970).
4 Hôtel de Sully, 62 rue Saint-Antoine.
5 *Filmographie universelle*, Vol. I (Paris, 1963).
6 For postcards, see J. Neudin and G. Neudin, *Premier Catalogue français des cartes postales de collection* (Paris: Neudin, 1975) and better still André Fildier, *Catalogue, Cartes postales anciennes de collection* (Paris: Fildier, yearly since 1975), which lists themes, regions and evaluates the rarity of the items. For posters, see A. Weill, *Affiches et art publicitaire. 7500 résultats de ventes aux enchères* (Paris: Van Wilder, 1987). See also James Laver, *Nineteenth-Century French Posters* (London: Nicholson & Watson, 1944); Jane Abdy, *The French Posters* (New York and London: Studio Vista, 1969); Hermann Schardt, *Paris 1900* (New York: Putnam, 1970).
7 Rare occurrences at the end of the eighteenth century but the word is not currently used before the second third of the nineteenth century.
8 Difference between the value of a word at a given time and the mean throughout the century.
9 *L'Armée nouvelle* (n.p. 1911) stresses the necessity for the socialists *de servir la patrie* and closely links internationalism and *patrie*.
10 Alain Weill, *Campagnes agricoles. Affiches et réclames agricoles* (Paris: Le Chêne, 1982).
11 Who cannot be Marianne. See the characteristics of Marianne in Maurice Agulhon, *Marianne into Battle: Republican Imagery and Symbolism in France, 1789–1880* (Cambridge: Cambridge University Press, 1981).
12 Lucy Broido, *The Posters of Jules Chéret* (New York: Dover 1980).
13 Given a cluster of data, factor analysis reduces the inventory to dimensions that are distinct and transitory and structures them according to their chronological and quantitative opposition or proximity.
14 A. Simon and J. Lemaire, *Catalogue des cartes postales éditées en France. L'aëronautique d'avant 1914* (Paris: CILD, 1979).
15 Béatrix Forissier, *Vingt-cinq années d'actualité à travers la carte postale, 1889–1914* (Paris: Amateur, 1976).
16 See above, n. 6.

7

The national sentiment of soldiers during the Great War

Stéphane Audoin-Rouzeau

The four years of the Great War were closely linked, as far as *mentalités* are concerned, with the prewar period; and yet they are also distinct from it in that the conflict gave rise to a specific 'wartime culture'. From 1914, therefore, the world became a quite different place. This peculiarity of the subject in hand has its advantages – it allows certain hypotheses concerning the prewar period to be tested, and some of the answers already formulated to be elaborated. War constitutes a test of the truth: it illuminates, sometimes very starkly, various phenomena of opinion that may be difficult to discern in peace time. But one point for which it is particularly helpful to use the prism provided by the war (and more particularly that of soldiers at war) is that of the degree to which French opinion was saturated by the concept of nationalism during the years preceding the conflict.

An important question concerns the distinction between national sentiment and nationalism. The problem of differentiation is all the more complex in that nationalism was clearly a protean notion, and there is not necessarily any clear separation between traditional republican patriotism and nationalism in the strict sense of a system of thought and a political current making the nation an absolute value. In any event, the aim of this chapter is to describe, in a more specific way, the national sentiment of combatants between 1914 and 1918, using this concept in preference to that of patriotism, and interpreting it as a network made up of all sorts of associations, more or less conscious but firmly internalized, that linked soldiers to the national community and forced them to defend it against danger from outside. An attempt will be made to assess the possible *nationalist* influence on this national sentiment, and to measure the real impact of various themes of nationalistic thinking on the soldiers' discourse.

A number of comments are relevant here on the interest of studying the opinions of the combatants. The first is quantitative: France enlisted about 8 million men between 1914 and 1918, drawn from all social classes. The army was, in fact, very varied from a sociological point of view, despite a call-up falling unequally on different social strata, in that

Sentiment and ideology

members of the working class were partially spared to the detriment of the peasantry and middle classes. Apart from this, the army of 1914–18 constituted a microcosm that accurately represented French society, and brought together men of very different social and geographical origins, and from diverse cultural and even linguistic backgrounds. Hence, what is being studied here is the mental universe of a very large cross-section of Frenchmen of the period.

This diversity does not, however, imply an absence of cultural homogeneity among the men who made up the French army. While the front was not able to level all the differences between them, the army functioned during those four years as a veritable melting pot. The enforced integration of the individual into the group compelled the majority of combatants to adopt the most generally accepted values and beliefs. This explains the similarity between trench diaries written by different units and at different times. It also accounts for the impression of homogeneity given by the postal censorship, which indicates that although the army contained different currents of opinion, any points of view that diverged profoundly from the norm concern small minorities. There is great variation in vocabulary between soldiers of different social and cultural backgrounds, but there was no real difference in the nature of their discourse. The soldiers' 'speech' was not uniform, but it was usually homogeneous, being united by many common elements. Therefore, while taking into account these important nuances, it is valid to generalize and discuss the attitudes of 'the soldier' of 1914–18.

To gain a real understanding of the national sentiment of French soldiers, it may help to start with this simple statement: between the start of the war in 1914 and armistice on 11 November 1918, they displayed exceptional tenacity, and this presents a serious problem for historians. Prior to any analysis of their mental universe, it is important to assess their capacity of resistance precisely, for otherwise an understanding of the values that motivated them is impossible.

It should be noted, first, that the combatants endured harder conditions than those of the soldiers from any comparable belligerent country, such as Germany or Great Britain. The rudimentary organization of the French trenches and the deplorable leave arrangements prior to the arrival of Pétain as commander in chief in 1917, which were linked to the refusal of the high command to settle down properly into a war of position, made things very difficult for French combatants, and increased their suffering. The casualty rates are also indicative of the plight of French troops: they suffered the heaviest losses of the major European armies – 16.5 per cent of troops mobilized as opposed to 15.4 per cent for the Germans, in second place. Losses among combatants reached 18 per cent, and among officers, 22 per cent.

The problem of interpreting this evident tenacity is considerably confused by two historiographic traditions, both of which originated during the war itself. The first version fitted in with the image of combatants which wartime 'brain washing' (*bourrage de crâne*) and propaganda had tried to create: an unfailing, often heroic, patriotism from start to finish of the conflict, in the face of an enemy judged to be morally inferior. This image presented an idealized and conventional notion of the combatant, to which nationalist authors, such as Maurice Barrès, made a powerful contribution.

In the face of what seemed a disgraceful imposture, many combatants, often setting themselves up as the exclusive historians of their own war experience, transmitted, through their writings and memoirs, a pacifist version quite at odds with the legend developed from 1914 onwards. They stressed the futility of patriotic ideals after a few months in the trenches, the resigned indifference of the combatants, and their absence of hostility towards the other side. During the 1930s these tendencies were exaggerated and pushed to extremes in certain novels, which concentrated on fear, cowardice and abandonment. But well before Céline or Giono, far less famous combatants had ennobled this pacifist tradition: the soldier, wrote Louis Mairet in 1919, 'fights through honesty, habit and by force. He fights because he cannot do otherwise.'[1] In 1917, a trench journal described the combatants in these words: 'poor men who have been toiling for three years, always hoping for some miraculous change of fortune, but probably ending up with our faces smashed in, that's what we are.'[2] Revolutionary tradition tended to push this portrayal in a more overtly anti-militarist direction.[3]

In reality, the picture of the combatants that can be drawn today is far more complex and offers far more nuances than these simplistic images. During the last few years, the history of soldiers during the Great War has, in effect, been profoundly altered by the availability of new sources, not written after the event with the attendant risks of inaccuracy, but actually contemporary with the war: letters, private notebooks, trench diaries and reports from the postal censors have provided the historian of mentalities with new tools which have thrown new light on the issue, allowing certain aspects of it to be completely reconsidered.[4] There is still, doubtless, a long way to go but, admitting later corrections and alterations, it seems that the picture of the mental universe of French soldiers is far more complex and subtle than either tradition has tended to admit.

The national sentiment of the combatants cannot be understood without reference to the very complex relationships they had with the civilian world and, in a wider context, with the national community. Relationships between active combatants, *l'avant*, and those who stayed behind, *l'arrière*, determined to a large extent their will to 'hold on', and were frequently ambiguous and strained. The soldiers, particularly those with an urban background, had a strong sense of being cut off from the civilian world. They also displayed fierce hostility to those who remained civilians, whom they constantly accused of living a normal or even pleasure-oriented life, of whiling away carefree days in total indifference to the fate of the combatants, who nonetheless had the task of defending and protecting them. It was, above all, a feeling of inequality that gave rise to this hostility towards civilians, further complicated by a sense of incomprehension. This very widespread state of mind in the army was fuelled by the rapid discrediting of the press, of which the soldiers were very aware. The soldiers resented the 'brain washing' and war propaganda, which they perceived as an insult to their own experience, suffering and sacrifices. In this sense, the press made a powerful contribution to widening the gulf between the two worlds. Added to this was the disinterest felt by the combatants, sometimes amounting to disdain, for all that happened anywhere but at the front, or even outside their own sector. The combatants affected to ignore the outside world and interested themselves only in the 'here and now'. It seems that the front was described by many of them as an island completely isolated from the 'continent' made up of the rest of the nation.

But on closer scrutiny, this image of insularity among the soldiers is revealed as superficial, since relationships with the civilian world were far more complex than the combatants were prepared to admit. Behind their apparent disdain for the civilian population, there was a deep fascination for everything that involved them. In the trench press and the soldiers' letters this fascination for civilian life illuminates every page. Beneath the disapproval is concealed a deep desire for recognition: it is not so much the inequality in the face of death and their suffering that these soldiers complain of, as the fact of their sacrifice not being recognized and appreciated by the civilian population. But this reproach in itself shows that the split between the two worlds was more apparent than real. A deep moral link was therefore maintained, and was physically reinforced by leave, parcels and, above all, letters. These letters, sometimes written daily during the calm periods of life at the front, maintain a very strong emotional link, a kind of uninterrupted conversation with the soldiers' families. They also touch on material preoccupations: in the management of their lives at a distance, these professional fighters, as the trench soldiers became, showed that they were really civilians in uniform. Their constant preoccupation with their financial and family affairs linked them with the small communities they had left and, beyond that, with civilian society as a whole and the entire national community. Civilians and soldiers were, therefore, interdependent from the start of the war until the end. The changes in civilian and military morale coincided and interacted; this was certainly the case in 1917, when the morale of the whole country plummeted dangerously, then again in the autumn of the same year, when it recovered.

The ambiguous relationship the soldiers had with the media is an additional proof of this close connection between the civilian and combatant worlds. Although exasperation with newspapers and their contents was very widespread, reading papers remained an ingrained habit for those at the front. Postal censorship also proves that the soldiers had a fairly extensive knowledge of news: in 1916, 17 items of current affairs filtered into their correspondence, 6 of which were judged to be negative and 11 positive.[5] The list of positive events may seem rather disparate in the light of what is known today; but it testifies to a real preoccupation with national and international events, and with the conduct of the war in general. The subtle variations in morale which the postal censorship reveals during 1916 closely follow the sequence of news items received at the front, depending on whether these were judged favourable or not. The stability of morale between January and October is linked to the larger number of news items considered to be 'good'. The downturn in December 1916 was, on the other hand, caused by a reversal of this situation, and the improvement in February 1917 by the break-off of diplomatic relations between Germany and the United States.

Not only were the soldiers sensitive to 'news' coming from the civilian world, but they often expressed themselves in the same terms as the papers they read, although they challenged the style vigorously. The insincere heroism tended to exasperate the combatants, but they often used the same language in their letters and diaries, even adopting the most contrived terms and images of 'brain washing'. When it came to describing a battle, commenting on events or the progress of the war and predicting how long it would last, or when it was a question of evoking and judging the enemy, the soldiers adopted the language they read in the newspapers. This explains the heroic flavour of the trench press and letters. In other contexts, the language used for brain washing exasperated the soldiers, particularly when it was adopted by those protected from the conflict. But they did not feel restrained by the same considerations themselves.

This heroic tone sometimes found in the soldiers' writing could indicate a specific penetration of *nationalist* feeling, but this is not the case. Apart from the fact that it had older roots than nationalism proper, it was essentially copied from the vocabulary and images used by the press as a whole at the time. All the details mentioned above should not detract from the main point: the fact is that there was no real rift between the soldiers and the rest of the national community. The link retained with the civilian world, and the strength of the connection between the two worlds, constitutes the base, the precondition, for this national feeling among the combatants, the constituent elements of which can now be identified.

Sentiment and ideology

Since Jean-Jacques Becker has established the fact with certainty, it has been known that the 'nationalist fever' of the summer of 1914 was a myth and that only a minority of conscripted men felt enthusiastic at the start of the war. Despite demonstrations in certain towns and stations, the conscripted men did not set off with 'flowers in their rifles', but resolved to do their duty, believing that their country was in the right, the victim of German aggression that was as sudden as it was premeditated, and that the best thing was to finish Germany off as quickly as possible. Although national sentiment was, therefore, strongly demonstrated in August 1914, it was not with the enthusiasm that historiography has so long attributed to it.

Subsequently, despite the impact of prolonged conflict and the suffering caused by it, the soldiers' national sentiment did not change significantly. To state things simply, there was never a fundamental change in their state of mind from August 1914 onwards. In what they wrote about events at the time, in their newspapers at the front, their letters, their personal notebooks, the themes linked closely or remotely to national sentiment remain in the background. Quantification shows that the combatants mentioned their private lives more than anything else: domestic, family and affective concerns, and life at the front. The soldiers' daily life constitutes the basis of what they wrote about, whatever the source used. However, national sentiment also appears, albeit discreetly. Depending on the time and the individual, the combination of these elements varies; but simplified somewhat, the national sentiment of soldiers can be said to be based on four main pillars: a sense of defending the land and the community; hostility towards the enemy; the concept of duty; and confidence in victory.

First in importance was the desire to defend loved ones against enemy invasion, from which they had, at any cost, to be spared. This was a fundamental point, the importance of which was not surprising considering the strength of the links between soldiers and the rest of the population. This defence of the personal family circle is closely linked to that of the population as a whole, and that of the entire homeland. This accounts for the clear feelings of guilt when civilians had to be evacuated during the last German offensive in 1918; it also explains the particularly combative nature of soldiers from regions that had been invaded, for whom the war became a personal war of liberation. This is one of the peculiarities of the French soldier: the map of the war on the western front, which showed some ten departments partially or wholly occupied by the enemy, whose harshness was known throughout the country, made the war far more concrete for the French soldiers. For them, the conflict constantly remained a war of defence, protection and liberation. Although soldiers from other countries may have felt an identical sense of defence, as Gerd Krumeich has shown for Germans in the Somme in 1916,[6] it could not have been as strong and permanent as for the French soldiers.

This 'defensist' feeling could conceivably be linked to nationalism in that it occupied a significant position in currents of opinion prior to 1914. But the strongly felt obligation to defend seems not in fact to be related to prewar nationalist thinking. It existed to a significant degree in the period before the Third Republic, as shown by the conflict of 1870.[7] In addition, it was among the peasant classes, where pre-1914 nationalist theories had clearly not spread (since nationalism remained an urban phenomenon), that the gut reaction to defend the country was often most marked. Indeed, trench warfare was particularly suited to the way of thinking of the chiefly peasant infantry.

The theme of death is, however, more difficult. A deep sense of respect for the dead is clear in front newspapers. Burying the dead was a priority, but it was also unthinkable to let their graves be overrun by the enemy. Added to the defence of the land was the defence of fellow soldiers, buried in the land that they had defended and on which they had fallen. This is reminiscent of Barrès's theme of 'the land and the dead', and therefore a direct continuation of prewar nationalist themes can be seen in certain writings in the trench press, as in this extract from a front diary, written in 1915:

> This earth that the soldier digs with his hands, that he defends with his life, this earth is soaked with the blood of his comrades: each piece of ground, torn from the enemy, has cost a man's life. Close by him numerous cemeteries bear witness.[8]

Another front journal, written in 1918, continues the theme: 'To lose the dead who believed that, with their blood, they had won the right to be laid to rest in their mother land, causes deep bitterness.'[9] Here, and here only, a link can be detected with prewar nationalist ideas. The presence of this theme of the land and the dead, which has a particular significance at the front, is present above all in the trench press. This was, however, edited by educated soldiers, mostly members of the middle classes, frequently officers or NCOs, and this was one of the milieux in which the spread of nationalism had been most widespread before the war. It is virtually impossible to state, however, if this constituted a resurgence or an invention. In addition, respect for soldiers fallen in combat had been well established in the army since the middle of the nineteenth century, and the cult of the dead was equally based on this relatively recent tradition. It is, therefore, impossible to be certain that it really reflects a direct extension of pre-1914 nationalism.

Hostility towards the adversary is very difficult to pin down today. It was systematically concealed by veterans, who were anxious to give a more elevated meaning to their experience and to present themselves as the artisans of a victory won without hatred. One of these goes as far as to speak of a 'vague sympathy' between the soldiers of the two sides.[10] This rewriting of the war formed an essential part of the pacifist beliefs taken up by some ex-soldiers between the wars, but the reality of what went on was far more complex. It was quite true that the soldiers did not always feel hatred for the soldiers facing them, and whom they could glimpse briefly or even hear when the front lines were close. With this tangible enemy, a whole range of understandings were possible, even leading to the famous examples of fraternization. These, however, remained more limited in number than certain traditions would indicate, and their significance was often highly ambiguous.[11]

Hostility towards the 'German race' as a whole was a far more generalized feeling with particular resentment of German militarism. The hostility of French combatants towards this adversary is strongly confirmed by both the trench press and the postal censors. In the most 'combative' soldiers, it could lead to an increased feeling of hate, as can be seen from the writings of a peasant from the Puy-de-Dôme in 1915: 'I feel a terrible anger against these barbarous people. I'd be happy to see a bunch of them come out, I guarantee they wouldn't stay standing for long ... I'm proud when I see them fall on the battlefield.'[12] This was by no means an isolated opinion; the most insulting terms are sometimes used about the enemy, all based on the accusation of savagery and barbarous behaviour. After battles and the death of comrades, an increased desire for revenge is noticeable, and a wish to destroy the enemy. Most frequently, hostility towards the Germans remains latent and is expressed discretely. But the term 'boche', for example, used by soldiers from every cultural and social background, always has negative connotations. There was no such term in use in 1870, and not by chance, for it was the historical memory of that previous war which played a decisive role in establishing anti-German feeling. This was chiefly based on a sense of difference, often accompanied by the certainty of representing higher moral values. Here again, there is hardly any trace of true nationalism: the anti-German feeling remained, above all, an extension of the will to defend, described above.

As the war continued, this hostility abated slowly: an analysis of coverage in the trench press between 1915 and 1918 shows a slight reduction in the use of hostile terms, which were far more numerous at the start of the war than at the finish. But they never disappeared completely, and even increased slightly as victory approached, and the French combatants affirmed their feeling of superiority.

The idea of duty is also important, and constantly crops up in the trench press and in letters: 'In a few days from now, we will be launching a major attack. Well, come what may, I'll do my duty', were the significant words of a wine grower from the Loire, written to a member of his family in 1916.[13]

This was where the work of the Third Republic's primary education can be clearly appreciated, since it was on this point that its lessons were most ingrained. Direct sources, however, confirm Jean-Jacques Becker's opinion on the relative insignificance of the theme of the lost provinces or the idea of revenge both before the war and at its outbreak. These themes (which belong not only to the nationalist tradition, but also to republican patriotism in its most classical manifestation, hence the difficulty) are scarcely present between 1914 and 1918, and the war did not seem able to reawaken them. Other major themes in the same vein, typified by their extreme abstraction, such as 'the civilizing role of France in the world', or 'the mission of the republic against the empires' are no more prominent. Even the idea of fatherland is scarcely present, those of nation and flag even less so. This was, therefore an important test, not only for nationalism, but also for the republican education system, and for other vectors of national feeling, such as military service, newspapers and the progress of written culture in general; the penetration of patriotic themes seems to have been quite selective.

Duty, on the other hand, was not open to question, and was certainly never disputed by the soldiers. A deep satisfaction from the accomplishment of daily duty can be detected, and a pride in the fact of 'holding out' for as long as possible in the worst moral and material conditions. The soldiers were encouraged in the fulfilment of their duty through the letters they received from their nearest and dearest, which shared exactly the same moral values. In this sense, Jean Galtier-Boissière was perfectly right to describe the soldiers as excellent 'ouvriers de guerre'.[14] For many peasants, the sense of duty often had a connotation of submitting to authority, and to fate. But this deep sense of resignation should not be interpreted as an entirely passive attitude: it was closely linked to the feeling of having a duty to fulfil.

The belief of the combatants in their eventual victory was the most fragile of the pillars supporting national feeling. This belief was not constant, but was better maintained than might have been expected, given the successive setbacks experienced by the Allies and the discouraging changes in the war map up until the middle of 1918. It can be explained by the self-justification current in public opinion from August 1914, which varied very little from that time onwards. The soldiers were, from the outset, deeply convinced of the justice of the French cause, and went on from this to analyse the military situation in a way they believed to be purely objective: since France was 'in the right', it could not lose the war. The reasons for believing in the final victory were entirely moral, and this explains their relative resilience in the face of military setbacks, disappointments of all types and the prolongation of the war. Problems could delay the victory (which was, however, always envisaged in the near future), but never really brought it into question. This is why the desire

Sentiment and ideology

for peace, which was always very strong, must first of all be seen as an expectation of victory, of peace through victory. It would be difficult to say that the connection between these two terms was never broken, and that discouraged combatants never wished for peace even without victory. But it seems certain that the majority did not envisage peace through defeat. The term 'defeat' was, in fact, a forbidden word among the combatants, and the possibility was denied.

This simplified schema requires some further qualification, however. Until spring 1917, the soldiers' mental universe seems not to have undergone any radical change since the start of the war. Verdun, in which every unit served its turn, had no decisive effects; the sheet-anchors of national sentiment still held. However, the years 1917 and 1918, although less well known in some ways, give a more complex and contrasting picture.

The crisis of insubordination in 1917 is often seen as a breakdown in the soldiers' 'will to hold on'. This is certainly incorrect, as the well-known work of Guy Pedronicini demonstrates.[15] The crisis was a limited one, in several ways: quantitatively, in that only a third of the army was really affected, and the number of mutineers proper did not exceed 40,000; sociologically, in that although the mutineers came from all social groups, among those sentenced there were relatively few rural soldiers, who made up the vast majority of the army and who, it seems, were less liable to indiscipline than the men from towns; finally, qualitatively, for the mutinies did not lead to fraternization, desertion, or refusal to hold the front line. In short, it cannot be taken as demonstrating a crisis of national sentiment.

More serious doubts arise concerning 1918, however. In the trench press, most subjects related to national sentiment show a distinct falling off in spring 1918, during the last German offensive. The impression given is that a breakdown in the will to hold on was possible, and that the army perhaps came closer to this than in 1917. However, the most recent studies using postal censorship show that the will to fight on strengthened spectacularly at the beginning of 1918, as soon as signs of a coming German offensive appeared.[16]

Hence, a very complex picture can be drawn of national sentiment among combatants. Direct sources show that this feeling was strong, but with little or no enthusiasm for war, and not much in the way of 'abstract' patriotic ideas either. The combatants' national sentiment was not expressed in fine words, but its solidity cannot be disputed. The links that connected the soldiers to the national community gave them ample reason to hold on, even if there were other reasons too, such as the solidarity that grew up between men within a section or a company. The soldiers submitted to the war, but this submission, far from indicating a lack of national sentiment, constitutes its central manifestation. Doubtless, this national sentiment was eroded during the course of the war, but the process was gradual, and there seems to have been no decisive breaking point. The soldiers never accepted the idea of defeat for their country, and this denial constituted a solid line of mental resistance. It might possibly have been worn down during the last two years of the war, but the strategic conditions, which were of decisive importance, never came close to making this happen.

The roots of this national sentiment go deep. The contribution of prewar nationalism seems insignificant, but it is tempting to consider the role of the Third Republic too as only relative. On this hypothesis, the regime only completed the 'task' begun many years previously. The foundations of national sentiment between 1914 and 1918 were, to a large extent, already complete in 1870, and must be seen as part of a long-term cultural development.

NOTES

1 Louis Mairet, *Carnets d'un combattant* (Paris: Cres, 1919), p. 172.
2 *L'Argonnaute*, no. 31 (August 1917), p. 2.
3 The best example of this tradition is the best-selling *Carnets de guerre de Louis Barthas, Tonnelier, 1914–1918* (Paris: Maspero, 1979).
4 In addition to the pioneering article by Jean-Noël Jeanneney, 'Les Archives de la commission de contrôle postal aux armées, 1916–1918: une source précieuse pour l'histoire comtemporaine de l'opinion et des mentalités', *Revue d'Histoire Moderne et Contemporaine*, (January–March 1968), pp. 209–33, see the thesis by Annick Cochet, 'L'Opinion et le moral des soldats en 1916 d'après les archives du contrôle postale', doctoral thesis, Université de Paris X-Nanterre, 2 vols, 1986. A summary can be found in 'Les Paysans sur le front en 1916', *Bulletin du Centre d'Histoire de la France Contemporaine*, no. 3 (1982), pp. 37–48. On the subject of trench newspapers see Stéphane Audoin-Rouzeau, *1914–1918: Les combattants des tranchées* (Paris: Colin, 1986), and 'Les Soldats français et la nation d'après les journaux de tranchées (1914–1918)', *Revue d'Histoire Moderne et Contemporaine*, (January–March 1987), pp. 66–86.
5 Events judged to be negative include the Serbian retreat, the Zeppelin raids on Paris, an article in *L'Information* stating that the end of the war was a long way off, the government debate on troop numbers, civilian rationing measures and the Rumanian retreat. Events seen as positive include French resistance at the start of the Battle of Verdun, Russian troops at Marseille, the success of the Brusilov offensive, the Somme offensive, the entry of Rumania into the war, the new regulations concerning leave, the recapture of forts Vaux and Douaumont, the German peace proposals and the allied response, news of German–American relations, and those between the USA and other Central Powers. See Cochet, 'L'Opinion', *passim*.
6 Gerd Krumeich, 'Le Soldat allemand sur la Somme', in J. J. Becker and S. Audoin-Rouzeau (eds), *Les Sociétés européennes et la guerre de 1914–1918* (Paris: Centre d'Histoire de la France Contemporaine, Université de Paris X-Nanterre, 1990), pp. 367–74.
7 See Stéphane Audoin-Rouzeau, *1870, La France dans la guerre* (Paris: Colin, 1989).
8 *Marmita*, 21 February 1916.
9 *L'Argonnaute*, April 1918.
10 Pierre Chaine, *Mémoires d'un rat* (Paris: Paris, 1930), p. 66.

Sentiment and ideology

11 See Alain Barluet, 'Les Fraternisations de Noël', *L'Histoire*, no. 107 (January 1988), pp. 77–9.
12 Bibliothèque de Documentation et d'Information Contemporaine (BDIC) (Université de Paris X-Nanterre) archives, no classification mark.
13 Documents in possession of the author.
14 *Le Crapouillot*, no. 7 (December 1917), p. 4.
15 Guy Pedronicini, *Les Mutineries de 1917* (Paris: Presses Universitaires de France, 1967).
16 Annick Cochet, 'Les Soldats français' (see n. 6).

PART 2
Nationalism and politics

Introduction

Albert Vaiciulenas

Nationalism as a phenomenon of modern French politics emerged during the quarter century prior to the Great War, from the consolidation of the republic in the 1880s to the deepening crises of European diplomacy on the eve of Sarajevo. It was the means by which both the left-wing avant-garde and dynastic conservatives, each for their own reasons profoundly alienated from the parliamentary republic, desperately manoeuvred to find new means of effective action in the arena of mass politics. The chronology is straightforward enough. First came the Boulangist assault on the Opportunist republic; this provided the paradigm for a continuation of the Jacobin protest tradition. A hiatus followed, punctuated by Panama, the *ralliement*, anarchist outrages, alliance with Russia and, after the elections of 1893, the formation of a socialist parliamentary group. Then the Dreyfus Affair convulsed the nation, unleashing popular passions whose intensity and violence threatened the established order. In its aftermath, the *Bloc des gauches* triumphed over both church and army, and, in the dénouement of the drama, 'republicanized' the regime. Finally, came the illusion of a *belle époque*, as France, again a major player on the European stage, enjoyed prosperity and the growing political stability of a conservative republican consensus that faithfully reflected the interests, fears and aspirations of her *nouvelles couches sociales*.

During the 1880s political life seemed increasingly polarized between a broad coalition of republicans committed to the defence of the existing liberal order, and the rising forces of organized socialism with its exclusivist critique of bourgeois society. Fearful of losing their traditional constituencies and, indeed, their *raison d'être*, both revolutionaries and conservatives faced hard political choices. Drawn inexorably together by their common opposition to the parliamentary regime, they used the nationalist amalgam of Boulangism to create a new political force. In the process, expediency melded with an intellectual tradition grounded in an emotional rejection of decadent bourgeois materialism and a profound sense of European civilization in decline. The result was a *glissement* of nationalism from left to right: from the bitter radical-socialist critique of the constitutional settlement of 1875 to the dark ruminations of Charles Maurras; from the Boulangist campaign to establish 'the democratic and social Republic' to an utter rejection of both the republic itself and its spiritual underpinnings; from the inheritors of the Jacobin tradition of protest to the creators of what has been termed problematically the radical right.

Boulangism was the crucible. Out of this remarkable mass movement born of the conjunction of popular patriotic protest and the radical reform impulse, arose the ideas, slogans, men and organizations that would animate the nationalist leagues of the 1890s and beyond. Its popular and left-wing credentials were impeccable: Jules Ferry declared it 'a creation of the Radicals'; Terrail-Mermeix insisted that it was 'a democratic, popular, even socialist movement', solidly based on the people of the great working-class suburbs; and Séverine, in a diatribe addressed to the moderate republican Arthur Ranc, described it as

> disgust, not with the Republic, for God's sake, but with *your* republic; the republic as your friends have made it, that heartless, gutless, mongrel regime, which in seventeen years has done nothing for the poor, nothing for the people, nothing for those to whom it owes everything.[1]

Based mainly in Paris, the Boulangist organization spun a web of electoral committees – a practice hallowed by radical tradition – out of elements as diverse as the Fédération des Groupes Republicains Socialistes de la Seine, Granger's revolutionary Blanquists and Déroulède's Ligue des Patriotes. The felicitous coincidence of the *scrutin de liste* and Boulanger's enormous popularity nationwide enabled the National Republican Committee temporarily to marshal the forces of popular protest behind the general's rallying cry of 'Constituante, Révision, Référendum'. And it was that felicitous coincidence that induced Mackau's beleaguered monarchists to conclude their cynical electoral alliance with Boulanger in 1888.

The Boulangist organization never threatened to become anything more than a temporary alliance of like-minded electoral committees, groups and federations dedicated to constitutional revision. Any notion that the National Republican Committee entertained serious thoughts of a revolutionary outbreak in the streets of Paris should be discarded. Police reports discounted any such possibility. Few of the leaders of the National Republican Party had the stomach for anything more than the occasional political brawl. They remained convinced that the road to power lay through the ballot box: they hoped to capture the republic, not to destroy it.

What, then, was Boulangism's legacy? Not the least important for the future of the political system was the reintroduction of the *scrutin d'arrondissement* to preclude the possibility of another plebiscitary campaign. French political energies henceforward would be concentrated on 'la politique de clocher' – parish pump politics. The paramountcy of the provinces over Paris was confirmed. The crisis roused the government from the torpor of corrupt, ineffectual parliamentarism and demonstrated its readiness to defend the regime with vigour. Failure at the polls in 1889 shattered the fragile Boulangist organization – leaderless since the general's proscription and ignominious flight into exile – and reduced it to a welter of rival groups and leaders. No obvious successor to Boulanger would emerge to head a revisionist movement demoralized by the scandal of the monarchist electoral alliance and racked by the struggle between Déroulède and Laguerre for his mantle. The latter argued for a continuation of electoral tactics, the former demanded more direct action. Déroulède's temperament and his experience in cooperating with Granger's Blanquists, with whom he discovered 'a community of ideas...[and a] community of action',[2] would have a profound influence on the future course of nationalist politics. As the revisionist alliance crumbled, his league's activities degenerated into violent confrontations with anti-revisionists. Defeat at the polls merely induced a certain euphoria in the Ligue des Patriotes's militants, who saw the election results as a vindication of their belief that what was needed was less propaganda and more action. They abandoned the National Republican Committee's electoral stance for one not dissimilar to that of the Blanquists, and began to plot a politics of the street far removed from the democratic vision of radicals such as Naquet and Laguerre. It was to come to a ludicrous end in February 1899, when Déroulède staged a bungled *coup d'état* during Félix Faure's funeral.

Anti-Semitism had not figured prominently in the Boulangist movement, but by 1890, militant revisionists were becoming more and more interested in the political possibilities of Drumont's brand of socialism. The progression from the socialism espoused by a majority of the Boulangist deputies elected in Paris in 1889 to a 'national socialism' that decried internationalism and focused on the Jew as the 'internal enemy' marked a crucial stage in the development of a nationalist ideology. It was neither logical nor inevitable that anti-Semitism should become the main plank of the nationalist platform, but the Dreyfus Affair made it so. Nevertheless, anti-Semitism failed to become a politically potent mass movement on the Boulangist model. The organizational jealousies and personal rivalries that had bedevilled the revisionist party since 1889 only increased with the greater opportunities for political action during the anti-Dreyfusard agitation. In spite of anti-Semitism's usefulness as a mortar with which to bond the disparate elements of nationalism into a compact mass, many leading nationalists refused to surrender entirely to its blandishments. Déroulède, for example, resisted all efforts by Guérin's Anti-Semitic League to penetrate his organization, while maintaining an uneasy working alliance with its militants on the streets.

The Dreyfus Affair marked the apogee of the nationalist movement before the war. Not since Boulangism and Panama had the forces of opposition to the regime been presented with such an opportunity to recover popular support. But this in fact did not happen. Boulangism had been the last gasp of a radical reform impulse that developments were rendering old-fashioned or even irrelevant. During the 1890s, nationalists jettisoned most of the Boulangist revisionist baggage. By 1898, only an opposition temperament that married well with a taste for gutter politics remained. Ironically, the Dreyfus Affair found these militants allied with the most respectable conservative elements in the army, church and professions. They had joined ranks with the pillars of the community to defend the status quo. And if the latter looked askance at the likes of Guérin, Dubuc and their bully boys rampaging through the streets, they quickly realized that in the heat of the anti-Dreyfusard frenzy it would be impolitic to scrutinize their allies too closely.

Rallying to the defence of the beleaguered republic, left-wing and moderate republicans exorcized the lingering ghost of anti-Semitism from within their own ranks, and dealt harshly with the enemies of the regime. The antics of Déroulède and Guérin made them an easy mark. Anti-clericalism unified republicans in a determined campaign against the power of the church and traditional notables. The respectable conservatives in such organizations as the Ligue de la Patrie Française were left to the judgement of the electorate which, except in Paris, roundly rejected them. Even the army did not escape the effects of republicanization.

Politically, nationalism lay dormant after the Dreyfus Affair. But its ideology – the sum total of myths, symbols, rituals, slogans and ideas – permeated the nation's mind. During the decade from Boulanger to Dreyfus, nationalists had bitterly opposed a parliamentary regime which they considered corrupt and ineffectual, and totally unable to rally the nation in its inevitable hour of struggle with the enemy across the blue line of the Vosges. The triumph of the radical republic after the Dreyfus Affair would impel men such as Maurras to follow a line in their explorations of French identity and destiny that led to anti-republicanism and the extra-parliamentary leagues of the interwar period. Another route lay open, however. To the majority of conservative nationalists in organizations such as the Ligue de la Patrie Française, a republic with sound social and fiscal policies could be accommodated. The regime had demonstrated its strength and willingness to shoulder burdens vital to the national interest. Their support for the nationalist revival after 1905 and the policies of Poincaré were a testimony to the potency of a patriotic republican creed that had played no small part in transforming a country of peasants into a nation of Frenchmen.

NOTES

1 Jules Ferry, *Lettres de Jules Ferry 1846–1893, publiées par E. Jules-Ferry, mai 1914* (Paris: Calmann-Lévy, 1917), letter to Reinach, 20 August 1988, pp. 486–8. Mermeix (pseud. Gabriel Terrail), *X... du Figaro. Les Coulisses du Boulangisme* (Paris: Cerf. 1890), p. 56. Séverine (pseud. Caroline Rémy), *Notes d'une frondeuse: de la Boulange au Panama* (Paris: H. Simonis Empis, 1894), p. 19.
2 Archives de la Préfecture de Police, Ba 1337, 'Comité directeur et renseignements'.

8

Royalists and the politics of nationalism

William D. Irvine

In 1900 a French royalist observed: 'I believe that serious and careful historians, free of partiality, passion or hatred, will never include Boulangism among the nationalist events.'[1] This was an understandable sentiment since few royalists recalled the Boulanger Affair with much fondness. But it was also bad history. The Boulanger years were a critical turning point in the history of French nationalism and of French royalism. In the quarter century after 1889 the French right underwent radical modifications – it became a 'new right' – the first of a series. What made the post-1889 right 'new' was the appropriation of doctrines previously identified with the revolutionary left and likewise previously anathema to traditional conservatives. The most important of these new acquisitions was nationalism.

In the years before 1889 the most consistent opponents of popular patriotism were the traditional conservatives personified by the royalists. They were, as they invariably insisted, as patriotic as anyone else but their patriotism was not the 'patriotisme de réclame' so much in vogue in the France of the 1880s – the patriotism of Clemenceau, Rochefort, Déroulède or, worse yet, Boulanger. Viewing, as they always would, nationalism through the optic of domestic politics, royalists in those years found much that was profoundly disquieting.

Nationalism could lead to war and under the republic war was dangerous. A decade of republican rule had isolated France diplomatically and weakened her domestically. While the list of republican crimes was long, not least of them was what the regime had done to the army. The royalist *Avenir militaire*[2] excoriated a succession of republican Ministers of War for their systematic disorganization of the military. Much of '*Avenir*'s indictment did not go beyond the traditional gripes of retired officers: politics not merit determined promotions; beards being grown by the lower ranks undermined hygiene as well as hierarchy; the newfangled repeating rifle meant ammunition squandered and marksmanship discounted. (That these things were all associated with General Boulanger did not render them any more acceptable.) But what really frightened '*Avenir*' was the fact that the French army was becoming increasingly a civilian army in a society that was becoming more democratic:

> While, on the other side of the Vosges, a farseeing and strong government snuffs out the dangerous ideas that go along with obligatory military service and is wise enough to prevent 'the nation in arms' from degenerating into a militia, at home, on the contrary, egalitarianism becomes more and more in vogue every day, the levelling tendency destroys the *esprit de corps* and an army of soldiers is transforming itself into an army of citizens.... In the hands of our radicals, the principle of obligatory service has become the most effective of tools of destruction.[3]

The newspaper was not alone in its assessment. Referring to Boulanger's proposed army reform bill, Emile Keller, former royalist deputy from Belfort and one of the party's military experts, denounced 'the military disorganization bill which is one of the most criminal enterprises by the revolutionary mind against the living forces of the country'.[4] Citizens' armies (or 'Militias' as *L'Avenir* invariably called them) were not just militarily ineffective – they were revolutionary. It was hardly accidental that insane ideas, such as the creation of 'schoolboy battalions', emanated from left-wing radicals such as Paul Déroulède. The effect of 'the invading influence of revolutionary ideas' weakened France against her enemies – both foreign and domestic. Upon learning that a colonel of the republican guard had had to chastise some men under his command for too boisterously celebrating 14 July (and for having cheered a now ex-Minister of War) *L'Avenir* predicted: 'We will see once again the deplorable spectacle of February 1848 – troops fraternizing with the populace.'[5] In fact, *L'Avenir*, which knew its counter-revolutionary catechism well, seemed haunted by parallels with the past. When Henri de Rochefort announced that any attempt to fire Boulanger as Minister of War would have 20,000 Parisians in the street yelling 'down with the traitors', *L'Avenir* observed that this was not patriotism but a call for 'civil war and military rebellion' emanating, significantly, from those 'who in 1871 raised the standard of insurrection while the victorious enemy was still camped on national soil'.[6] France had seen such patriots before, 'always drunk with imagination and ready to cry "War against Prussia"'. When military reality got the better of patriotic romanticism, they would be the first to flee the enemy, the first to cry treason, and the first to 'massacre the pretended traitors just as the famous volunteers of the Revolution did in 1793'.

1871, 1848, 1793 – royalist debates about patriotism in the 1880s kept coming back to these dates, especially the first and the last. Patriotism, at least of the 'false' kind meant both war and revolution as the lessons of the past amply demonstrated. Nor were these merely the paranoid fantasies of

Nationalism and politics

retired generals; *L'Avenir* was in fact relatively restrained in its discussions of the *revanchard* patriotism of the 1880s; most royalist newspapers were more extravagant.

L'Espérance du Peuple, the mainstay of western legitimism, assiduously scoured the left-wing press in search of revolutionary bellicosity. A column in Jules Vallès's socialist *Cri du Peuple* announcing that 'the next international conflagration must be the struggle between Reaction and Revolution – on the one side Bismarck, on the other, France', confirmed the royalists' suspicions. The 'furious fools' of Gambetta's time had given way to the 'criminal charlatans'. 'The socialists,' *L'Espérance* declared, 'provoke universal war in order to seize power in the midst of the general confusion, just as did their ancestors in '92.'[7] Partisans of *revanche* such as Rochefort were moved exclusively by 'the social question' and sought a 'future Commune'.[8] *L'Espérance* went to some pains to insist that the conjuncture of war and revolution was in no way adventitious; to the contrary, the left deliberately sought to provoke war as a means of fostering revolution.

> The return of the Commune is impossible against the French army [a proposition *L'Avenir* might have contested].... These republicans know it and reason as follows: it is essential to get rid of the army by occupying it elsewhere. War with Germany serves this purpose perfectly. Our soldiers will rush to the frontier and Paris will fall prey to the insurgents.[9]

L'Espérance was given to provocative rhetorical outbursts. *Le Messager de Toulouse* was not. But it echoed the same themes. 'When our attention and our material and moral forces are turned towards the foreign enemy ... dare we assume that there will not be some terrible explosion? The new Commune will bear the same relationship to that of 1871 that petrol does to dynamite.'[10] In Marseille, the *Soleil du Midi* grimly warned: 'The domestic revolutionaries that today govern us profited from the war of 1870 to overthrow the government and seize power. Why should we believe that the socialists and the anarchists will not follow that example should war break out?'[11] France, *Le Moniteur du Calvados* insisted, was beset by those elements who were 'disposed to play into the hands of foreigners by making a revolution in the face of the enemy just as in 1870. The socialist party will once again, in the event of war, provide a powerful auxiliary for our enemies'. Germany, therefore, enjoyed 'in the very heart of France, allies ready to set Paris and France on fire as they did in 1870 and let the blood flow the minute that the armed forces no longer protect our social institutions'.[12] All of this led to some remarkably dispassionate assessments of France's hereditary enemy. The war scare of January 1887 was not, *Le Nouvelliste du Nord* insisted, really the fault of

Bismarck. 'The ridiculous blustering of the Ligue des Patriotes, a society whose real aim is purely electoral, has exasperated opinion on the other side of the Rhine.' Bismarck's militant language was but 'a response to the provocations of the republican press and a response to our Minister of War'; royalists did not want war 'to satisfy the fancy of Paul Déroulède or the ambitions of M. Boulanger'.[13]

Some of this was pure sensationalism, a paranoid preoccupation with political forces that were, and would remain, relatively marginal. With the Paris Commune still a recent memory, with most adult Frenchmen having lived through two, if not three, revolutionary upheavals, the war–revolution nexus that dominated conservative discussion in the 1880s can hardly be dismissed as insincere fabrication. After all, their obsession with the determining links between war and revolution was no more intense than that of conservatives of the 1930s who had, if anything, rather less justification.

Moreover, the public fulminations of the royalist press closely echoed the privately expressed anxieties of royalist leaders. Eugène Dufeuille, secretary general of the royalist party, and arguably the most sober, cautious and level-headed royalist in France, could write in the aftermath of the Schnaebelé affair (i.e. after the passions caused by the second war scare of the year had subsided):

> I have it on very reliable authority that the Radical party does not fear war, even if they do not wish it. A number of names were mentioned including that of the President of the Chamber, M. Floquet. Can we attribute such Radical sentiments to the blusterings of Boulanger? Or, on the contrary, do such desperate measures come from a realization that the republic is on its last legs and are they prepared to leap into the dark to rescue themselves from such a serious situation?[14]

Albert de Mun, royalist deputy from the Morbihan and something of a political realist, had, at the beginning of the year, reflected on the then current war scare. The source of the problem was the Minister of War, General Boulanger, whose bellicose nationalism was the pretext for Bismarck's recent bout of sabre-rattling. One solution was to overthrow the ministry although de Mun thought that unlikely because the radicals adored Boulanger, the opportunists feared him and the right, in addition to their usual incoherence, were reluctant to overturn a ministry by refusing military appropriations! Worse, so unstable was the existing French polity that toppling the ministry promised no salvation. During the ministerial crisis, Boulanger would remain at the war ministry and would 'just let the insurrection in support of him happen, without doing anything to encourage it but nothing to repress it either'. 'For that whole crowd,' Boulanger would be acclaimed 'more than ever, the necessary man, the defender of *la patrie*'. 'This would mean immediate war' and 'the declaration of war would be the signal for even more serious developments domestically and first, according to all the evidence, the creation in Paris of a Commune government after the expulsion of the Chamber.'[15]

Similarly, Jules de Michon, a former prefect and a perceptive and usually sober commentator on French affairs reflected on the political situation in the wake of the Schnaebelé Affair. After the overthrow of the Goblet ministry but with no new cabinet in sight and with Boulanger still at the rue Saint-Dominique, de Michon envisaged the following scenario:

> General Boulanger, head of the army, could lock up the troops, could let the rioters, whom he had encouraged, invade the legislative body and we could wake up with a dictatorship, military in flavour, Communard in essence. The army playing into the hands of insurrection. I know, of course, that this orgy won't last long but it will only end in foreign war and the break-up of France. Duty will oblige [the Comte de Paris] to fight under the flag of those who brought these calamities upon us. For once I will consider the exile of the Prince and his family to have been a blessing.[16]

Examples like this could be multiplied endlessly. Everyone who wrote to the Comte de Paris decried the 'national peril' inherent in the bellicose nationalism of the period; everyone recognized the need for the French government to adopt 'pacific language'.

But if they feared the domestic consequences of militant nationalism, the conservative right could hardly allow the left to monopolize the slogan 'patriotic'. Indeed, that particular adjective was evoked with increasing frequency – usually to describe positions which were diametrically opposite to those of the 'false' patriots. However much they scorned the patriotic obsession with *revanche*, the royalist right too claimed to be partisans of *revanche*. But there was *revanche* and *revanche* and that of the right was 'La revanche du bons sens ou plutôt de la Providence'.[17] Comte Othenin d'Haussonville gave some indication of what this 'other' *revanche* might look like. 'The Alsatian question,' he wrote, 'can only be resolved by remaining always open just like the Venetian question since the beginning of the century.'[18] For a man as worried about war as Haussonville this was a somewhat dubious example since, after 1815, the Venetian question was responsible for no fewer than four wars, two of them in some sense revolutionary. What he meant, of course, was that in the end the Venetian question had been resolved by big power diplomacy which, had the Italians been less obtuse, would have rendered the fourth war unnecessary. The point was that sooner or later European governments could find a common ground for the resolution of international problems.

That common ground was, of course, fear of the disruptive forces of revolution. After all, former enemies such as Austria and Germany 'who had every reason to detest one another do not hesitate to unite against the imminent threat of revolutionary contagion'.[19]

Faced with a dangerous Jacobin nationalism French royalists preferred an aristocratic internationalism. Typical of such efforts was the Comte de Paris's meeting in the autumn of 1886 at Portofino with the heir to the German crown, Prince Frederick. Here the two putative future rulers discussed ways to improve relations and diminish the arms race between their respective nations. Such 'bucolic fantasies' and the prospect of French royalists 'appearing to be the accessories of our enemies' prompted much sarcasm among republicans.[20] Royalist Images d'Epinal (propaganda prints), one of them sardonically observed, had traditionally depicted the military exploits of the Comte de Paris. Would they now portray the pretender embracing a Prussian prince?[21] By contrast, the Portofino meeting stimulated a royalist journalist to begin a press campaign in favour of bilateral disarmament.[22]

Early in 1888 Comte Edmond de Martimprey, a confidant of the Comte de Paris, wrote to Baron Armand de Mackau proposing a secret meeting between the pretender and Bismarck to discuss an imminent monarchist restoration. Since it was 'in Germany's interests to have a Christian monarchy as a western neighbour instead of a socialist republic' and since a monarchical France 'having reduced its armies to the size necessary to assure internal security' would no longer appear as a threat, restoration was the key to European peace.[23] Martimprey, of course, lived in something of a dream-world since the whole project hinged on the return of Alsace-Lorraine, something he thought could be arranged by a monetary indemnity and the cession to Germany of Tonkin or Cochin China. Yet Mackau, who was nothing if not a hard-nosed politician, shortly thereafter contemplated a trip to Rome seeking 'an intervention of the Pope with Bismarck in the hope that the latter turn away from the Republic completely and promise the restoration of Lorraine as soon as there has been a peaceful restoration'.[24] Many royalists took these ideas seriously, most notably Comte Paul de Leusse who was forever insisting that as soon as France ceased to be 'a revolutionary foyer in the midst of Europe' and restored the monarchy, the German and French Crowns could join in 'a mutual struggle against democracy, socialism and the materialistic philosophy that produced them'.[25] Nor, Leusse insisted, was exchanging European territory for colonies Utopian. Germany's population, unlike that of France, was growing and she, unlike France, needed colonies.[26] The Marquis de Beauvoir, a former diplomat, thought enough of Leusse's ideas to prevail upon him to enlist the support of a German cousin, aide de camp for the Crown Prince Frederick, in getting articles reflecting French royalist views on foreign affairs inserted in the *Kreuzzeitung*.[27]

Nationalism and politics

It was easy enough to assert that a monarchist restoration was the critical precondition for a lasting Franco–German *rapprochement*; it was another matter to persuade Bismarck to accept the logic. Granted, in many ways his criticism of French foreign policy was the same as that of the royalists. When, during the war scare of January 1887, he complained of the unpredictability of French policy owing to governmental instability and the constant fear that a French government might 'look to war as a diversion from domestic difficulties', he was speaking the language French royalists knew so well. Nor was he unaware of the pacific sentiments of the French right; when the Centre Party leader Windthorst challenged Bismarck's assertions of an eternally warlike France, the chancellor countered that his Catholic opponent could believe that France did not seek revenge only because his French contacts were limited to the clerical milieux.[28] Yet, as royalists were uncomfortably aware, no matter how much he distrusted the revanchist proclivities of the radical republicans, Bismarck persisted in believing that the moderate republic of the opportunists was a better guarantee of peace than a restored monarchy.

From this perspective Boulanger was not entirely without utility to the royalists. Bismarck might believe that those such as Grévy, Goblet and Ferry were an adequate guarantee of peace but the elections of 1885 and the emergence of Boulanger ought to suggest to him that the moderates would not hold power much longer. The Marquis de la Ferronnays, reporting on his conversations with contacts in the German embassy, noted in 1886 that although the view that 'a monarchist restoration would have as a corollary war has not yet been abandoned, the agitations of General Boulanger increasingly force our neighbours to understand that the greatest danger of war can come, not from the restoration of the monarchy but by preserving the republic'. The 'pacific' utterances of the pretender had been well received in Germany and he urged that 'no occasion be neglected to confirm this impression'. 'In the presence of the threat that [Bismarck] believes he sees in the coming to power of Boulanger–Clemenceau, it is not impossible that Monseigneur will cease to have his route to power blocked by the persistent hostility of the chancellor.'[29] If nothing else, Dufeuille noted, Boulanger's behaviour would disabuse France's neighbours of the idea that the republic was 'incapable of being bellicose'.[30]

Within a year, of course, Boulanger ceased to represent the spectre of war and revolution and became, instead, the last great hope of monarchist restoration. By the end of 1887, royalists had confirmation of earlier rumours suggesting that his flirtation with radicalism would be of short duration and that Boulanger saw a more permanent home among the ranks of conservatives.[31] But proving the sincerity of his conversion was something of a challenge and both Dillon and Boulanger went straight to the heart of what they feared would be the principal royalist concern about

Boulanger and attempted to allay their anxieties about his belligerent nationalism. What is striking is how little problem they had.

In their celebrated meeting of 18 April 1888, Dillon informed the Comte de Paris that in exchange for putting the pretender on the throne, Boulanger wished only that the count use his influence among the courts of Europe:

> He asks you to be a guarantor *vis à vis* Europe, to answer for him until he has time to prove his pacific intentions. It is critical that before he comes to power Europe be enlightened as to his intentions lest there be an explosion that would be impossible to stop later on.

Such talk was so transparently ingratiating and manipulative that it ought to have prompted an irritated rejoinder. But, on the count's own retrospective account, it did nothing of the kind. He seems to have appreciated the sentiment and engaged in an extensive discussion as to the best means of spreading Boulanger's new pacific image to Europe. His chief link with the Crown Prince Frederick was through the Prince of Wales, whom he promised to see the next day. He and Dillon discussed at length just how much the prince should be told and the pretender agreed that it was best 'to tell him something and hint at a lot'. Specifically, he agreed to inform the prince that Boulanger could restore the monarchy if foreign difficulties did not intervene and that he would be 'the guarantor of Boulanger's true sentiments and [would] ask Europe for three months' credit to permit him [Boulanger] to prove himself'. Better yet, the pretender actually did what he said he would, spoke to the prince on 23 April, very specifically assured him that the Boulangist phenomenon no longer carried with it the danger of war with Germany and engaged the Prince of Wales so to inform the Germans.[32] On the basis of the glib assurances of a political adventurer and the formal promises of a notoriously unreliable scoundrel, the Comte de Paris radically altered his party's stance on war, peace and General Boulanger.

Selling this conversion to royalists at large was more difficult. In a speech at Marseille designed explicitly to convince doubtful royalists, the Marquis de Breteuil directly addressed the linkage of Boulanger with war. Some, he noted, still feared that Boulanger would lead the nation to dictatorship and war. But a dictatorship was unlikely, especially if conservatives won a majority in the 1889 elections, something Boulanger's help might ensure. Moreover, the notion that Boulanger's ascendancy would inevitably lead to war was belied by recent events:

> Europe does not question our pacific sentiments, which are the monopoly of no one in France; she has better things to do than to concern herself with our internal affairs. Nowhere were the recent

electoral developments [i.e. Boulanger's victories] treated as a sign of bellicosity; instead they were considered to be the most severe blow yet delivered to an unsympathetic government and conservative victories never alarm reigning monarchs.

'Europe has ceased,' he concluded, 'to get excited about our choice of government or the versatility of our ideas.'[33]

He had a point. Whereas Boulanger's 16 months as Minister of War had seriously disquieted the chancelleries of Europe, his year and half of openly bidding for power in France did not. Jules Herbette, French ambassador in Berlin, had spent some uncomfortable moments in 1887 trying to defend the conduct of the French Minister of War to Germans who took his every action as tantamount to a declaration of war. Now he had to listen to Herbert von Bismarck assuring him that 'it is not self evident that the success of [Boulanger's] enterprise would not be to our advantage' since 'the Orleanists, for whom he is no doubt working, would not be worse disposed towards us than the Republic'.[34] Nor did Boulanger's further adventures prompt more than some snide observations by Bismarck about the internal difficulties within the Orleanist family occasioned by their new tactic.[35] Boulanger may have been *le général revanche* but the Boulanger Affair was almost entirely about internal politics.

What can explain the phenomenal ease with which French royalists embraced a man and a movement that had terrorized them a scant few months earlier? Were their cries of alarm in 1886–7, like Bismarck's, mere tactical ploys? Certainly, some royalists had hoped that Boulanger might lead Bismarck to reconsider his views about a monarchist restoration; others saw Boulanger as a wedge to be driven between the opportunists and the radicals. But the fears expressed privately concord so closely with the public alarms that one can only conclude they were very real. Perhaps frivolity and stupidity best explain the royalist role in 1888–9. Some royalists said so during (although more typically, after) the affair. But the architects of the Boulanger alliance, notably Mackau, de Mun, Piou, Bocher, Dufeuille, Beauvoir and Breteuil, were neither frivolous nor stupid. They were in fact remarkably astute politically.

These *fin de siècle* royalists recognized that the very thing that made Boulangism so disturbing to royalists – its popular dynamism – was also potentially very attractive to them. The urban masses clamouring after the latest Boulanger song, 'nouvelles couches boulangistes' one royalist called them,[36] were what stood between the royalists and any hopes of regaining power. By themselves, royalists could never hope to appeal to those segments of the population; allied with Boulangism, they might.[37] Boulangism, in short, could provide royalists with the populist dynamism they so notoriously lacked. Harnessing these popular energies was an inherently difficult project and success hinged, in the end, on the ability of conservatives to channel erstwhile Jacobin patriots in a right-wing direction. But Jacobinism had lost its political bearings by the end of the nineteenth century and the prospect of monarchist support, electoral or, especially, financial, was usually enough to persuade 'republican' Boulangists that they were more at home with royalists, old and especially new, than with Clemenceau, to say nothing of Jaurès.[38]

Even those few Boulangists who remained disturbingly independent adopted a stance that could trouble few conservatives. Gaston Laporte, ex-radical from the Nièvre, outraged royalists by his stubborn refusal to 'remain bought', but he certainly knew what the 'new' nationalism was all about. When asked by an unemployed worker if he were prepared to adopt the eight-hour day in order to create more jobs, Laporte brightly responded that 'the only means of attaining that reform is to send a Boulangist majority to the Chamber in order to tear up the Treaty of Frankfurt which ties us to Germany'.[39] By making the social question hostage to the national one, Laporte was talking the language of the new right. The kind of language that once seemed dangerous because it risked provoking war, international and civil, now served to deflect real social issues into the nebulous, and safe, realm of foreign affairs. Nationalism was no longer an extension of domestic political radicalism. It was a safe substitute for it.

The language of nationalism became a permanent part of the lexicon of the French right.[40] Of course they preferred not to remember the man who introduced it to them – General Boulanger. Now, 'the crime of General Boulanger' was not, as *Le Soleil du Midi* once observed, that he represented war, dictatorship and revolution, but that he was 'guilty of the most shameful failure' in not staging a coup on 27 January 1889.[41]

But if they forgot Boulanger, French royalists certainly did not forget some of his nationalist *compagnons de route*. In the past, hardly an issue of *Le Nouvelliste de Bordeaux* failed to denounce the crimes of Henri de Rochefort. By 1900 his appearance in the city was the occasion of extensive and sympathetic press coverage.[42] *L'Espérance du Peuple* no longer considered the feverish patriotism of Paul Déroulède to be the work of 'dangerous charlatans'. Now they were simply 'the left flank' of that 'great nationalist party' whose programme 'strangely resembles' that of the royalists on the 'right flank'.[43] Now it was the 'generous Déroulède,'[44] 'Déroulède, barde suprême de la patrie',[45] whose 'bold initiative', 'guts' and 'patriotism' earned him 'our sympathies'.[46] As far as royalists were concerned, Déroulède's only flaw, and one he shared with Jules Lemaître's Ligue de la Patrie Française, was his perverse insistence that he belonged in the republican tradition. This annoyed royalist leaders such as Edouard de Lur-Saluces who 'strongly suspect[ed] him to be an unconscious royalist'.[47] 'Your ideas are royalist ones. They are,' pleaded Charles Maurras.[48]

Nationalism and politics

Perhaps the best symbol of the evolution of French royalism was André Cordier, political director of the influential *Nouvelliste de Bordeaux*. From 1886 until near the end of 1888 there was no more articulate opponent of the superheated patriotism of the likes of Déroulède, Rochefort and, above all, Boulanger. Boulanger and his friends represented not 18 Brumaire or 2 December but 1793 and 1871, 'the hideous despotism of the people, the bloody tyranny of the streets . . . war, and worse, civil war'.[49] Conservatives who found the anti-parliamentary language of the radical nationalists to be attractive were bluntly reminded that 'parliamentarianism is not as black as it is often depicted'.[50] By 1889, however, Cordier had been won over to the logic of the 'parallel march', allied with the Boulangists in the general elections and, in effect, assured the election of three of them in Bordeaux. A decade later he insisted on the same alliance with the nationalists. 'Let us not be afraid,' he wrote, 'of being swept away by the nationalists. . . . We must be closely allied with them against the common enemy.'[51] The *revirement* was of course more apparent than real. The basic conservative project and the conservative enemy remained what they had been a decade earlier. Cordier was still evoking 1793, 1848 and 1871 and still predicting that France would 'witness the scenes of murder and pillage that bloodied France during the First Republic . . . and which will return us to the days of June 1848 and the Commune of 1871'. What was different now, however, was that responsibility for this civil war fell no longer on the false patriotism of a demagogic Jacobin left but on 'international sects'.[52] In André Cordier's political career there were two constant preoccupations: he lived under a regime he detested and he adhered to a political party that had no popular base. All that changed in 1889 was that he discovered that a newly domesticated nationalism might solve both these problems.

NOTES

1. Paul Frank in *Le Soleil du Midi*, 5 January 1900.
2. *L'Avenir militaire* pretended, without much success, to be above politics. It was, in fact, entirely dependent on subsidies from the royalist pretender, the Comte de Paris.
3. *L'Avenir militaire*, 16 September 1886.
4. Keller to Comte de Paris, 19 May 1887; Archives Nationales (AN) 300 AP III, 615.
5. ibid., 2 August 1887.
6. *L'Avenir militaire*, 26 January 1887.
7. *L'Espérance du Peuple*, 2 April 1886.
8. 5 February 1887.
9. 25 May 1887.
10. *Le Messager de Toulouse*, 10 February 1887.
11. *Le Soleil du Midi*, 24 April 1887.
12. *Le Moniteur du Calvados*, 2 February 1888.
13. *Le Nouvelliste du Nord*, 13 January 1887.
14. Dufeuille to Comte de Paris, 3 May 1887; 300 AP III 615.
15. De Mun to Comte de Paris, 27 January 1887; 300 AP III 613.
16. Jules de Michon, 21 May 1887; 300 AP III 615.

17 *Le Salut Public*, 13 April 1888. William Francis Ryan has a good discussion of how the right distinguished their *revanche* from that of the radicals. See his, '*La Croix* and the development of rightist nationalism in France, 1883–1889', PhD thesis, University of Connecticut, 1970, pp. 162 ff., 207–8.
18 Haussonville to Comte de Paris, 27 February 1887; 300 AP III, 614.
19 *L'Avenir militaire*, 11 August 1886.
20 Arthur Ranc in *Le Matin*, 24 December 1886; Henri des Houx in *Le Matin*, 24 October 1886.
21 Henri des Houx in *Le Matin*, 24 October 1886.
22 Joseph Cornély in *Le Matin*, 27 December 1886.
23 Martimprey to Mackau, 10 February 1888; AN AP 151 I 102.
24 Beauvoir to Comte de Paris, 18 February 1888; 300 AP III, 624.
25 Paul de Leusse to Comte de Paris, 1 February 1886; 300 AP III, 601.
26 For a further elaboration on these ideas see his *La Paix par l'union douanière franco-allemande* (Strasbourg: J. Busseniers, 1888).
27 Beauvoir to Comte de Paris, 10 December 1886; Leusse to Comte de Paris, 14 December 1886; 300 AP III, 611.
28 From the Reichstag debates documented in the Archives du Ministère des Affaires Etrangères, Correspondence Politique Allemande (1871 à 1896), 74.
29 La Ferronnays to Comte de Paris, 4 July 1886; 300 AP III, 606.
30 Dufeuille to Comte de Paris, 18 October 1886; 300 AP III, 609.
31 On the royalists and Boulanger, see Philippe Levillain, *Boulanger, Fossoyeur de la monarchie* (Paris: Flammarion, 1982) and William D. Irvine, *The Boulanger Affair reconsidered: royalism, Boulangism and the origins of the radical right in France* (New York: Oxford University Press, 1988). The possibility of 'buying' Boulanger occurred to royalists quite early but they thought it unlikely that the general would come to them. 'As long as the Duc d'Aumale [whom Boulanger had expelled from the army] is alive,' Beauvoir noted, 'what kind of future would he have under the monarchy? None.' As soon as he lost his ministerial portfolio, Boulanger seems to have lost little time in disabusing royalists on this score. At the end of June 1887, the royalist Senator Lacave-Laplagne was informed by a source he respected that Boulanger 'has decided to lend himself to a project for restoring the monarchy with or without an intermediate step of a royal president' (30 June 1887; 300 AP III, 616).
32 The source is the pretender's retrospective account of his dealings with the Boulangists, the 'Recit sommaire' (300 AP III, 634).
33 *Gazette du Midi*, 12–13 November 1888.
34 Herbette to Goblet, 5 June 1888, Archives du Ministère des Affaires Etrangères, Correspondance Politique Allemande (1871 à 1896), 82.
35 See Herbette to Foreign Minister, 25 January 1889, in ibid, 86.
36 Beauvoir to Comte de Paris, 16 March 1888; 300 AP III, 625.
37 On the links between Boulangism and the royalist need to adjust to mass politics, see William D. Irvine, 'Royalists, mass politics and the Boulanger Affair', *French History*, Vol. 3, no. 1 (1989), pp. 31–47.
38 Just how aware 'republican' nationalists were of the royalist domination of their movement remains open to debate. I have recently argued that from very nearly the beginning all of them knew perfectly well what was happening. See William D. Irvine, 'French royalists and Boulangism', *French Historical Studies* (Spring, 1984) pp. 395–406.
39 Archives Départementales (AD), Nièvre, 3M 1126/5 (1889), commissaire spécial to prefect, 15 September 1889.
40 Until the 1930s when a 'New Jacobinism', i.e. communism, and a new bellicosity on the part of a French left, some fraction of which wanted to resist Hitler, threw the French right back on positions analogous to those held in the 1880s.
41 *Le Soleil du Midi*, 9 May 1900.
42 *Le Nouvelliste de Bordeaux*, 18 and 19 February 1900.
43 *L'Espérance du Peuple*, 22 April 1900.
44 *Le Soleil du Midi*, 9 January 1900.

Nationalism and politics

45 ibid., 6 January 1900.
46 *La Revue de l'Ouest*, 1 June 1899; 7 March 1899; *Le Nouvelliste de Bordeaux*, 18 July 1899.
47 *La Revue de l'Ouest*, 7 March 1899.
48 *Le Soleil du Midi*, 26 April 1900.
49 *Le Nouvelliste de Bordeaux*, 20 March 1888.
50 ibid., 12 April 1888.
51 ibid., 8 January 1900.
52 ibid., 22 August 1899.

9

The nationalists of Meurthe-et-Moselle, 1888–1912

William Serman

In 1888, the six deputies, the two senators, the majority of the *counseillers généraux* of Meurthe-et-Moselle and a large number of mayors, including the mayor of Nancy, as opportunist members of the Alliance Républicaine, won 52 per cent of the votes at the legislative elections of 1885, against 5 per cent for the radicals and 39 per cent for the conservatives/reactionaries. They represented a current of opinion that was at the same time republican, patriotic and moderate. But their dominant position was shaken by the dissidence of part of their electorate and by the formation of an anti-ministerial coalition, directed first by extreme left-wing revisionists, then by so-called 'nationalist' or 'national' right-wingers.

At Nancy, discontented republican workers formed the vanguard of the Boulangist phalanx and the bulk of the revisionist troops. They wanted social reform and a change of political personnel, and the idea of protecting the national employment market against competition from foreign manpower attracted them. They blamed the government majority and the local leaders of the Alliance Républicaine for allowing a large number of Italian, Swiss and Luxembourg workers into the department's mines and building sites. The barrister Larcher, who was a *conseiller général* and influential member of the opportunist governing party of the town, outraged this group, in a speech delivered in August 1887, by comparing the hard work of the Italian labourers with the idleness of certain French workers.[1] Volland, the senator and mayor of Nancy, increased their irritation with the moderate representatives by coming to the defence of Grévy in parliament over the Wilson scandal.[2] They wanted these men, who spoke in support of Wilson's father-in-law in Paris and the foreigners in Lorraine, to be removed from power. Their adversaries, if not their objectives, were the same as Boulanger's. The general's name was popular, so suddenly and defiantly, they acclaimed him.

On 26 April 1888, about 500 people demonstrated at Nancy with cries of 'Long live Boulanger', and stoned the windows of the Cercle des Étudiants and the offices of the republican newspaper, *Le Progrès de l'Est*, two local centres of anti-Boulangism. On the 28th, a new demonstration was hastily summoned with improvised posters, but was curtailed by the police, who dispersed the initial gathering. During these two days, 43 individuals were arrested and prosecuted. They were mostly young people: a woman of 24, 12 adolescents between 14 and 20 years old, 13 men between 21 and 29 years old, plus 14 people of between 30 and 39 and three of at least 40 years old. Three quarters of them (exactly 32 out 43) were workers. A variety of trades was represented by one or two individuals, occasionally three, but a third of the effective total was made up of 14 cobblers and shoe workers alone. There were a number of shoemaking businesses in Nancy, several of which had been established at Metz before 1871, and their workers were particularly sensitive to the need for social reform, nostalgia for the lost provinces and the patriotic theme of revenge.[3]

The police, of course, were looking for the leaders, and identified three: Aron, Marconnet and Margonnet.[4] Armand Ernest Aron, who wrote and distributed the posters for the demonstration on the 28th, was 27 years old, came from Metz and was the son of a wealthy flannel producer at Nancy. His role was secondary; the anti-Semitic nature of the movement soon disillusioned him. Henri Margonnet, a 35-year-old travelling salesman, with no capital or regular income to his name, was the archetypal activist, always ready to raise his voice or throw a few punches in the street or meeting place. Ferdinand Marconnet was born at Strasbourg in 1866. He gave his official address as Nancy, where his mother, who had a comfortable private income, lived, but he resided in Paris where he studied medicine. The police considered him to be the founder of the 'Boulangist Party' at Nancy, but in fact he acted more as recruiting sergeant, by virtue of his enthusiasm and generosity. His youth and lack of local status stood in the way of his becoming the real leader of the movement. He had none of the trappings necessary for legal political struggle: he had no newspaper, no electoral committee and no network of family or friends in the local community. This is why he was eclipsed by a man who already had a certain influence in Nancy: Alfred Simon Gabriel.

Born at Toul on 14 September 1848, Gabriel[5] was the son of an employee of the Chemin de Fer de l'Est. Having joined up as a volunteer and fought against the Germans in 1870, he mixed with students and bohemians in Nancy, took part in the publication of two small newspapers, *Le Masque* and *La Sentinelle*, became an accountant in about 1877, and became involved in political struggle from about 1879 onwards. He took part in pre-syndical meetings and the preparation of the workers' congress of Le Havre in 1880, and published a draft socialist programme. As the founder of the Comité Radical in Nancy, editor-in-chief of *Le Patriote de l'Est*, then the *Reveil Démocratique de l'Est*, he presented himself as the leading figure of the local extreme left. Although defeated in the elections of 1885, in which he won less than 4,700 votes compared with the 45,000 of the previous opportunist elected, and was far out-performed on the same list by his fellow candidate from Toul, Dr Chapuis (future radical, anti-revisionist deputy), he was not discouraged. After his newspaper closed, he wrote articles in various extreme left-wing publications. In 1888, he wrote several for Séverine's *Le Cri du Peuple*, under the pseudonym Jacques Dest. Despite his slovenly dress, his bushy beard, dishevelled hair and club foot, he exercised a fascination over his audiences because of his vigorous style of oratory and his aggressive verbal attacks on the clergy and bourgeois moderates.

Just before the municipal elections in May 1888, he sided with the malcontents. He invited workers who had supported Boulanger to join the Comité Radical, for which he divised a motto reminiscent of the Blanquists: 'Socialism and Revenge'. He was careful, also, to mention 'revision', a key word certain to unite all sorts of opponents of the regime. *L'Express de l'Est*, established in February by Oswald Leroy, supported Boulangism more through commercial self-interest than political conviction[6] and represented the themes that were developing in public opinion. On 6 May, the radical candidates in the municipal elections at Nancy won almost 1,200 votes more than in 1884, to the detriment of the opportunists who, nonetheless, retained the Mairie.

In the following months, renegades from the opportunist camp came over to the Boulangists. On one hand, ex-members of the dissolved Alliance Républicaine moved closer to Gabriel; typical of these was Nicolas Emile Gouttière-Vernol. An ex-solicitor turned insurance agent and editor of the illustrated newspaper *La Lorraine Artiste*, he was born in Nancy in 1855 and enjoyed the reputation of being comfortably off, bourgeois, honest and a sincere republican. On the other hand, from June 1888, the regional committee of the Ligue des Patriotes broke up into rival groups. The majority declared themselves anti-Boulangist and formed the Union Patriotique de l'Est[7] while the minority approved Déroulède's politics and joined the revisionist forces under the leadership of the local Ligue president, Alphonse Victor Bouttier,[8] a retired and fairly wealthy chandler. Born in Paris in 1834, he had lived in Nancy since 1859, and was a minor local notable, presiding over the very bourgeois club, Sport Nautique. He was a committee man, active and ambitious and always ready to take on a committee chairmanship, although lacking political imagination or a talent for oratory.

Although considerable, these reinforcements were not enough. In about October, *L'Express de l'Est* had only a few readers, and the radical committee in Nancy had only 200 members. No one local was prepared to represent the revisionists at the next cantonal and legislative elections, and the national committee in Paris decided to intervene to revive the movement. On 8 November, one of their number, the radical deputy Vergoin, called a meeting of the Boulangists at Nancy, helped by Gabriel, Marconnet, Bouttier and Henri Edmond Soulard, a 40-year-old radical and patriotic wine merchant, and invited them to form an electoral committee. On 17 December, he returned accompanied by Laisant and found he had succeeded: the radical committee had transformed itself into a revisionist committee.[9] At Nancy a few days later, between 19 December 1888 and 5 January 1889, the Prince de Polignac negotiated and financed the acquisition of a small bankrupt newspaper, *Le Courrier de Meurthe-et-Moselle*, by four revisionists: Barrès, Gouttière-Vernolle, Doctor Raymond and the restaurateur Clérin, who ran the Buffet de la Gare. From 22 January, the title of the periodical was changed to *Le Courrier de l'Est*.[10] The youthful editorial team included two journalists recruited in Nancy: the 22-year-old Marconnet and the 20-year-old Gobert, under the direction of two men from Parisian literary and press circles: the 26-year-old Maurice Barrès, and the 27-year-old Paul Adam.

Although originally from Lorraine, Barrès had been living in Paris, and in January 1889 he had no influence in Meurthe-et-Moselle. Few people knew him in Nancy. For his part, he knew nothing about local political personalities and problems: he arrived with a few general ideas on questions of national interest and a desire for self advancement.

His friend Paul Adam[11] originally came from Arras, and had published articles in *Le Voltaire*, a collection of risqué stories and a few novels, one of which emerged from obscurity because it caused a scandal: *Chair molle*, a study of prostitutes and their world, was judged to be too raw, and Adam was generally considered to be a 'decadent' writer.

Le Courrier de l'Est failed to make its mark as a regional daily. It was short on news and substantial comment concerning local events, often settling for repetition of what appeared in the Parisian press, and endless parroting of national revisionist slogans and arguments. Pamphlets would have been as effective, and certainly cheaper. Indeed, brochures, songs and Boulangist caricatures, distributed by pedlars, had more success than *Le Courrier de l'Est*, which was changed to a weekly from 17 March 1889. Another periodical fulfilled the role of diffusing revisionist propaganda: *L'Express de l'Est*, which had as its new editor Henri Teichmann,[12] a little known writer just 22 years old, who was born in Strasbourg but resident in Paris, and was held to be a polemicist close to Barrès, but more aggressive.

With the support of these two papers, the Comité Révisionniste de la Meurthe-et-Moselle[13] developed rapidly in Nancy and in the neighbouring workers' communes. In February 1889, it had over 1,500 members and by July, more than 2,500: 1,460 in Nancy, 264 in Saint-Nicolas-de-Port, 180 in Pompey, 164 in Jarville, 153 in Malzèville, 129 in Frouard, 96 in Dombasle, and so on. Revisionist meetings[14] held with a view to the cantonal elections in July, and the legislatives in September–October, drew 120–800 people in Nancy and 80–200 elsewhere. Everywhere, workers made up the majority of the public. Margonnet directed the cheerleaders and stewards, who violently expelled trouble makers, particularly at Pont-Saint-Vincent and Neuves-Maisons in July. Gabriel and Barrès were the main speakers, and in addition to them, the Prince de Polignac, presented as an 'honest and sincere republican', took the floor at Nancy on 9 February. Elsewhere, local militants occasionally spoke: Adam, Teichmann, Jean-Baptiste Klein (a Moselle metal worker, 36 years old, employed in the ironworks at Nancy), or the notary's clerk Rosz.[15] From the start, Gabriel adopted a socialist, anti–Semitic and xenophobic tone, while Barrès started on a more anti-ministerial, anti-parliamentary level, but soon changed to being more in tune with his team-mate, who had a better understanding of public feeling. This cultivated scholar transformed himself into a crude demagogue: on 17 August, for example, he denounced Italian workers as spies, sent by Crispi and protected by Larcher.

Although the enemies to be defeated were easily identified, the candidates and a constructive programme to offer electors were more difficult to find. At the cantonal elections in July, the revisionists settled for supporting the symbolic candidacy of Boulanger against Larcher at Nancy-Ouest. Boulanger won, but the Conseil d'État annulled his election and the seat was finally taken by an opportunist, Dr Henrion.

For the legislative elections in September, Gabriel, Adam and Barrès were candidates in the three Nancy constituencies, the first because he was head of the local revisionist committee (known as the 'Gabrielist party'), and the other two out of devotion to duty, since no one else was prepared to take on such a risky task, and also in the hope of an amusing adventure. The National Committee in Paris sent them the social programme that the revisionists were to defend everywhere, featuring the creation of workers' pensions, the development of occupational training and the protection of French workers against foreign competition. Gabriel tried to negotiate with the local conservative right, whose opinions were expressed in the *Journal de la Meurthe*, but met suspicion on the part of the monarchist nobility and upper bourgeoisie for plebeians claiming to be republican and/or socialist. He was not welcomed by liberal Catholics, readers of *L'Espérance*, who disapproved of Boulangism's Caesarist tendencies, and certainly had no prospect of support from the Bishop of Nancy, Mgr Turinaz,[16] who had forbidden all the clergy of the diocese to participate in the electoral battle. Nevertheless, an agreement was reached with the conservatives against the government: a non-aggression pact was concluded for the first round and it was agreed that, in the second round, the anti-ministerial candidate most likely to succeed would stand alone.

In the second constituency of Nancy, Adam was beaten by the opportunist Papelier, but in the first and third, Gabriel and Barrès were elected deputies. They owned their success to the revisionist votes on the extreme left and particularly to the mass rallying of electors, three quarters of whom had previously voted for the government republicans and only a quarter for the monarchist conservatives.[17] Soon, however, the two men revealed themselves unequal to the task of maintaining the stability of such a heterogeneous coalition.

Early in 1890, the revisionists claimed to be republicans and socialists. They formed various committees at communal and departmental level, which recruited most of their members and sympathisers from among workers. In April, the Comité Républicain Révisionniste Socialiste de la Meurthe-et-Moselle[18] included 83 members on police files. Nine of these stood out as forming a steering committee, and among them there were several well-known Boulangist personalities, namely, the chairman, Soulard, and the vice-chairmen, Bouttier and Jean-Baptiste Paris, a furniture worker and manager of *Le Courrier de l'Est*. Information supplied by the police on the 74 other members of the committee reveals the principal characteristics of the revisionist militants in Meurthe-et-Moselle. Some 58 per cent were born in communes of Lorraine that remained French (44 per cent at Nancy, 14 per cent elsewhere); 33 per cent in the annexed territories; and 9 per cent in departments that were neither in Lorraine nor Alsace. A third, therefore, came from the lost provinces and were, as a group, likely to be particularly sensitive to the patriotic theme of revenge. Analysis by age reveals that 10 per cent were under 21, 36 per cent between 21 and 29, 30 per cent between 30 and 39, and 24 per cent 40 or older. The generation brought up in the bitterness of defeat, and emerging on to the job market during an economic crisis accounted for 46 per cent of the total, but it would be unwise to conclude from this that youth is a distinctive characteristic of revisionists, since the majority of them were adults aged at least 30.

Far more remarkable is their socio-professional background: 15 per cent were petit bourgeois, almost all running small artisan or, more commonly, commercial businesses, such as grocery shops or bars. Another 5 per cent were employed in shops or offices, while *petits métiers*, such as newspaper vending, also accounted for 5 per cent. The remaining 75 per cent were manual workers, mostly wage earners in the industrial sector. Out of these, there were 5 file makers, 7 joiners or cabinetmakers, 7 day labourers and, in particular, 17 shoemakers and other workers in the shoe industry who represented almost 23 per cent of the total. Police records indicated that two members of the committee were ex-Communards and that two others had defected from the 'clerical' party.

The workers, who formed a large majority, intended to stress the socialist orientation of the revisionist movement. Soon, the more impatient and 'advanced' among them would start to reproach Gabriel and Barrès for not keeping their promises, and the leaders in the department for being too timid concerning social reform. From the summer of 1890, dissident feeling started to grow. Involved in this were discontented activists, such as Margonnet, and many of the militant shoe workers, whose newsletter, *Le Tire Pied*, edited by the 28-year-old shoe worker, Jules Flageolet, was involved in the formation and propaganda of a new group, L'Essor Socialiste. This was a 'radical society' and 'social studies group', which concentrated on the issues of class struggle and was committed to fighting 'the selfish and ferocious bourgeoisie'.[19]

Between 1891 and 1893, the trend of the workers' movement towards autonomy was illustrated by the appearance of an independent socialist tendency (close to Gérault-Richard and hostile to revisionists, but weak) and by the will of most union militants to affirm their independence from politicians. Although Guichon and his friends could still expect a favourable reception from the carpenters, they came up against opposition from almost all the shoe workers, the majority of skilled cobblers and filemakers, from among whom the vast majority of revisionists had only recently been drawn.[20] Moreover, revisionist propaganda among workers was hampered by the attitude of employers: many threatened their workers with sanctions if they took part in the meeting organized by Barrès, Gabriel and their colleagues. In August or September 1893, employers dismissed three bricklayers from their yards, because they were organizing a 'workers' movement to expel the Italians'.[21]

However much Gabriel and Barrès declared their devotion to socialism or to the democratic and social republic, many workers distanced themselves from them, reproaching them with having betrayed their commitment and neglected their constituencies. In the cantonal elections of 1891 and the municipals of 1892, a large proportion of workers again voted for moderate republicans. The decline of the socialist-revisionists became even more marked, and by the time their committees decided to call themselves simply 'socialist' for the legislatives in 1893, they had lost virtually all their members. Under these conditions, Gabriel and Barrès preferred to stand down: the first disappeared altogether from the political scene, the second was elected in Neuilly. The government republicans retook the first and third constituencies in Nancy.[22]

Soulard, Bouttier and their friends nonetheless tried to keep their committee going, and in order to strengthen it, they attempted, in 1894, to reform the links between revisionism and socialism by means of a small group in their sphere of influence: the Union Socialiste, directed by the accountant, Leloir. In December, the attempt to join up with other socialist groups failed, because the independent socialists supported the struggle on two fronts: against opportunists and against revisionists.[23] The result was that in 1895, the Comité Socialiste Révisionniste, with Bouttier as chairman and Leloir as secretary, had only a dozen members in Nancy.[24] The standing of the ex-Boulangists was at it lowest in Meurthe-et-Moselle.

Between 1895 and 1902, the fortunes of the movement launched by the revisionists underwent a change for the better, but they altered both their direction and their name. The conservative notables took control, with anti-Semitism replacing socialism as the mobilizing theme. The term 'nationalist' gradually came to signify the members of a coalition that was both anti-ministerial and anti-socialist.

Jules Brice[25] set the example. Born in Abancourt (Meurthe-et-Moselle) in 1830, this 'farm owner', who was vice chairman of the Societé d'Agriculture of Meurthe-et-Moselle and *conseiller-général* for Pont-à-Mousson from 1889, was a well-known conservative republican. In 1893, he was elected deputy for the first constituency of Nancy. In the Chamber, he declared himself to be a nationalist republican. The growth of anti-Semitism and the Dreyfus Affair actually won him electoral alliances in the department.

In Nancy, Bouttier (again!) took the initiative in exploiting the political use of a centuries-old anti-Semitism. In September 1895, at his invitation, the Marquis de Morès gave a speech in front of 2,000 people against Ribot 'and his gang', against the English and, above all, against the Jews.[26] After the violent anti-Semitic and anti-Dreyfusard demonstrations in January 1898[27] he organized public meetings with Guérin, Houdaille and Millevoye, then formed a section of the Ligue Antisémite, assuming the chairmanship with the solicitors' clerk, Léal, as his vice chairman. A few months later, the Ligue had 2,800 members in Nancy (where they provoked serious anti-Jewish agitation in November and December) and 500 at Lunéville.[28] In parallel with this, from March 1898, the Union Catholique held increasing numbers of lectures attacking Jews and freemasons in the parishes of Nancy. The organizers, particularly the lawyer Renard and the editor of *La Croix de l'Est*, Dombray-Schmitt, formed an electoral committee which called for 'resistance against the judeo-masonic coalition' by voting for candidates in favour of protectionism, the rights of home distillers, freedom of education and freedom of association.[29]

The Ligue Antisémite decided to support the candidature of Ludovic Gervaize in the third constituency of Nancy. Gervaize[30] was a lawyer, born in Nancy in 1857, with a reputation of being a deceitful schemer. Having been rejected by Barrès in 1889, he positioned himself in Brice's wake in 1893. In the legislative elections of May 1898, he stood as an 'independent republican', and based his whole campaign on the fight against the Jews. The *Ralliés* supported him against the progressist Demenge-Cremel and the 'socialist' Barrès, who was dismissed as a *revenant* supported by outsiders, *déracinés*, revolutionary workers and anti-clericals. Barrès was the candidate for the Comité Socialiste Nationaliste, in which there were two union members, Jolz and Georgel, who were influential among mechanics. In April, *Le Courrier de l'Est*, which had disappeared in 1892, restarted publication, and Habert and Ferrette came from Paris to bring Barrès the support of *La Libre Parole*. Part of the working-class electorate was won over by socialist-nationalist demagogy,[31] but Barrès scared the conservatives by mentioning socialism and disappointed the clericals by refusing to commit himself to defending Catholic interests.

The right had agreed not to be too aggressive towards him during the campaign, but were overtly supporting the other nationalist candidate, the anti-ministerial, anti-Semitic Gervaize, because he was, above all, anti-socialist. With the support of the Ligue Antisémite, *La Croix de Nancy* and many local elected representatives, Gervaize defeated Barrès in the second round, winning 6,015 votes against 5,786. The left-wing republican candidate was crushed with only 3,140 votes, while between them the two nationalist candidates won 11,801.[32]

The fate of the other conservative and anti-Semitic candidates was little better: Brice was re-elected as 'Catholic republican' or 'moderate' at Nancy (first constituency), but otherwise all were beaten. More interesting than their electoral score is their choice of label: two stood as 'Catholic, republican, anti-Semites'. These were Dr Baraban in the second constituency of Nancy and the lawyer, Corrard des Essarts, at Lunéville.[33] Baraban disseminated pseudo-scientific racist theories aimed against Jews at the medical school, where he taught. Corrard des Essarts was a conservative town councillor, supported by his colleague Becker de Scholtz, the leader of Drumont's supporters at Lunéville. At Toul, a suspended priest, the 'abbé démocrate' Hémonet, launched a violently anti-Semitic campaign under the label 'Catholic and French'. He won only a few dozen votes, however, because the readers of *La Croix* and the bishop's faithful flock voted instead for a conservative candidate who styled himself simply 'Catholic', as did the candidate for Briey.[34]

In the following years, the evolution of anti-Semitic nationalism towards conservatism, anti-socialism and clericalism continued. The Ligue de la Patrie Française[35] contributed to this, and its first meetings were held in Nancy and Lunéville in June 1899. In these two towns, it formed committees under the direction of the urban patriciate. In 1900, the committee at Nancy had 1,800 members, the most eminent of whom were: the brother of General Mercier; a former officer, de Pourville; Comte Ferri de Ludre, Mayor of Richardménil; and the dean of the Faculté de Lettres, Krantz. The Lunéville committee was led by a former officer, de Pully, but dominated by a traditionalist notable, Keller, who was co-owner with the Guérin family of a large pottery factory. At Dombasle, where Barrès was to call for 'a union of patriots', the working class was in the majority. In the area of Briey, the Ligue had a belated success by founding a section at Joeuf. But it did not gain a foothold in Toul, although the regional weekly that it published in 1901–2 *La Cause Lorraine*, must have had some readers there.

The Ligue Antisémite[36] for its part was increasing its action and influence. In 1900, it launched a new periodical, *Le Petit Anti-juif de l'Est*, and organized anti-Semitic banquets at Nancy, attended by deputies Brice and Gervaize, conservative *conseillers-généraux* (several of whom came from noble families), town councillors and various notables,[37] including the lawyer Henri Déglin, who fashioned himself after Jacques Piou, and exerted an increasing influence on parish associations or 'fraternités' in Nancy. These were pious associations. In 1901, Mgr Turinaz requested that their entirely religious character should be respected, but this did not prevent their being put to political use for electoral ends by the leaders of the Union Catholique, the Comte de Malval and Dombray-Schmitt (of *La Croix*), who enjoyed the active support of many members from respectable bourgeois backgrounds: doctors, lawyers, civil servants and merchants.[38]

The former monarchists ('reactionaries') were often closely allied with these new movements, but were intent on preserving their traditions and individuality. Prior to the elections in 1902, they formed a Comité Conservateur, the chairman of which was a former artillery officer, Picquemal. The other members were notables, drawn from some of the great aristocratic dynasties (Guerrier de Dumast, Metz-Noblat), from bourgeois owners of medium-sized industries (Meixmoron, of Dombasle, and the miller Bertin), and from the professions.[39]

The Ligue de la Patrie Française, the Ligue Antisémite, the Union Catholique and the Comité Conservateur joined forces against the left-wing government majority. Their propaganda was disseminated through several periodicals: *Le Journal de la Meurthe*, *Le Petit Anti-juif de l'Est*, the versions of *La Croix* for Nancy, Lunéville and Toul, *L'Echo des Fraternités*, which appeared monthly, and *La Frontière de l'Est*, which was published weekly in 1901 and 1902. In addition, the two main republican papers in the region, *L'Impartial de l'Est* and *L'Est républicain*, owned by Léon Goulette, drifted to the right, as the anti-Dreyfusard progressists had done, moving closer to the reactionary conservatives and showing their candidates either open support or benevolent neutrality.

On the political chessboard of 1902, the right-wing, supposedly 'nationalist' candidates were united in whom they recognized as friends and enemies. Their friends were Déroulède, Guérin, Marchand, the Assumptionists, and the anti-Dreyfusard officers; while their enemies comprised Jews, freemasons, socialists (whether international or not), radical or moderate republicans, supporters of secularism, anti-clericals and supporters of Dreyfus, in short, the left and its 'accomplices'. They abstained from attacking the anti-Dreyfusard progressists, such as Papelier at Nancy and A. Lebrun at Briey. Their programme was characterized by demands supporting the Catholic clergy and its rights, in terms of worship, education and association. On a local level, they considered the decision taken in 1900 to open a *lycée* for girls at Nancy as particularly outrageous. The slow evolution of the early 'nationalists' into 'clerical' conservatives escaped no one's attention. On 19 April, the republicans of Saint-Nicolas-de-Port called Gervaize a *calotin*, and interrupted his speech by singing the 'Ave Maria'.[40] A parallel transformation was not, however, evident in the various labels adopted by candidates. At Nancy, in the first and third constituencies, Brice and

Gervaize stood as 'anti-Jewish, anti-ministerial republicans'. At Lunéville, Corrard des Essarts, who was supported by conservatives of the monarchist tradition (including the *conseiller-général* Michaut, all-powerful master of the glassworks and the town of Baccarat), stood as a 'Catholic republican'. At Nancy, in the second constituency, the Comte de Ludre relied chiefly on playing his trump card – being a notable – and affected a variety of adjectives: conservative, Catholic, anti-Semite and/or 'liberal'. All four candidates were elected, but the 'nationalist', Villeneau, at Briey and the 'anti-Jewish nationalist', Gillet, well-known doctor and *conseiller-général* at Toul were both beaten.[41] Without a disguise, it seems that 'nationalism' was doomed to failure, particularly against adversaries whose unshakeable patriotism and social moderation were known (Lebrun at Briey and Chapuis at Toul).

After 1902, the nationalists of Meurthe-et-Moselle rapidly transformed themselves into so-called 'liberal' conservatives. The Ligue de la Patrie Française disappeared without a trace, the Ligue Antisémite survived, but became far quieter, *Le Petit Anti-Juif de l'Est* ceased to appear in 1908, and *L'Action Française* had hardly any audience in the department. Fashion swung away from calls to arms and popular xenophobia to opposition to the parliamentary republic, and priority was given to the legal conquest of central or local power.

In this respect, the major event was the formation, between 1904 and 1906, of a right-wing Catholic coalition, composed of the Action Libérale Populaire (ALP) and secularist republicans of the centre-right: the Antibloc. From 1904, the Antibloc Lorrain comprised the friends of Déglin, linked to the ALP, and those of Goulette, of *L'Est républicain*, and it won the *mairie* at Nancy for a 'nationalist' university lecturer, Ludovic Beauchet.[42]

Brice died in 1905, and Louis Marin,[43] a native of Lorraine living in Paris, canvassed to become his successor. A patriot, conservative, anti-Semite and anti-Dreyfusard, he had connections in many areas of activity and he applied himself to cultivating them. In Paris, he associated with nationalists and members of the Catholic group Sillon, such as Georges Delavanne. In Lorraine, where he had an old friend in Ducrocq (Catholic, anti-Semitic, but Dreyfusard), who had founded the regionalist review *L'Austrasie*, he reached an agreement with Déglin and Goulette, who helped him to obtain the support of many local notables and elected representatives. In order to consolidate this influential network, he claimed in turn to be republican, progressist or liberal, as the need arose – all terms that were sufficiently ambiguous for him to maintain his independence and play the part of unifier of the conservative right. And so he was elected. During the legislative elections of 1906, the Antibloc coalition made its views very clear within the department. Certainly, Goulette and his friends in the centre-right tried to moderate the anti-Semitism and clericism of their allies in the ALP, but they no longer shrank from using the nationalists' xenophobia as a weapon against the enemy within: the left. In the words of *L'Est républicain*[44] it was vital 'to bring all these foreigners to heel', by whom they meant anarchists and internationalists who, they believed, threatened the state and society with subversion, because of the weakness and complacency of the Bloc des Gauches. The Antibloc was committed to fighting them. As in 1849, the defence of property and of the traditional hierarchy acted as the unifying theme for all conservatives, whether they were believers or not, and brought about the alliance with militant Catholics. Against socialism, against state secularism and the state education system, and against the radical republic's anti-clericalism, this new 'party of order' scraped the barrels of nationalism and anti-Semitism in order to excite prejudice and hatred in frightened electors, whom they essentially asked to take a stand against the separation of church and state, and in favour of a 'liberal' law on workers' pensions.

Except in Nancy, where Marin and Ludre were re-elected, the results were disappointing. Gervaize, Corrard des Essarts, F. de Wendel and E. Billiet were all beaten at Nancy (third constituency), Lunéville, Briey and Toul respectively by three left-wing republicans and a radical.[45] In the same year, General Langlois[46] became a senator for Meurthe-et-Moselle. A progressist and moderate republican, he did not participate in the excesses of the right, or the strategic plans of one nationalist officer who, having failed in the legislative elections at Pontoise in 1906, sought a seat in the third constituency of Nancy in 1910: Commandant Emile Driant.[47] The right in Nancy welcomed this newcomer, born at Neufchâtel (Aisne), with open arms, but more because of the nature of his network of friends and relations, the spirit of his adventure and war novels and the nature of his political ideas than his military record. Driant was Boulanger's son-in-law, a member of the Ligue Anti-maçonnique, affiliated to Action Libérale Populaire, a former contributor to the *Petit Anti-juif de l'Est*, and was already known for his Anglo- and Germanophobia, his hostility towards Jews and freemasons, his hatred of socialists and of the members of the CGT. Under the label 'independent' or 'liberal republican', he skilfully mounted his campaign on the theme of patriotic unity around the army, while stressing two subjects close to the hearts of the people of Lorraine: the frontier to be protected or altered, and the fortification of Nancy, requested in the National Assembly before 1875 by the republican Berlet[48] but refused since then by the military authorities. With more success than the ardent left-wing patriots, he won over the faithful flock of Mgr Turinaz, 'the frontier bishop',[49] who praised the virtues of Joan of Arc (a heroine whose popularity was on the increase during this period),[50] took part in the glorification of the army and defined 'real patriotism' in France as being fundamentally Catholic, a view shared by all the so-called nationalist, liberal and independent candidates in the legislative elections of 1910 in Meurthe-et-Moselle. Three of these were elected: Marin, Ludre and Driant. The four others were beaten by republicans marked by strong secular patriotism.

In the senatorial elections of 1911 and 1912, two patriotic radicals, Chapuis and Octave de Langenhagen, won against the conservative candidates, Keller and Castara, who were supported by the 'nationalist' deputies.[51] These results confirm that, in this frontier department, in the eyes of the local elected representatives and citizens, the right had not managed to gain the monopoly on patriotism. In the same way, the right was not alone in displaying a certain interest in the renewal of 'Lotharingism', marked by the establishment of the Pays Lorrain in 1904 and Union Regionaliste Lorraine in 1905.[52] But the novels of Barrès, in celebrating the land and the dead of Lorraine, show the direction that the conservatives and reactionaries felt should be taken in studies and essays on the history and culture of the province: that of traditionalism.

In politics, the influence of Catholic traditionalism on the nationalism of conservatives in Meurthe-et-Moselle was already clear between 1910 and 1912. The right soon shook off the socialist and pagan elements that characterized the nationalism of Gabriel and Barrès. Like Mgr Turinaz, the right took as its point of reference a Catholic idea of the French nation, in order to characterize itself simply as 'national'. This comes close to the position of Action Française. Whether affiliated to the ALP or the Fédération Républicaine, all the members of the new 'party of order' started to describe themselves as 'national', thus presenting themselves as the only 'real Frenchmen'. At the same time, they excluded from the nation all radicals, liberal democrats, socialists, anarchists, freemasons and Jews as being 'bad Frenchmen': in short, anyone they contemptuously labelled *les apaches*. Their religious, racist, xenophobic and political intolerance eventually split France in two: on one side was 'true France' – traditionalist, right-wing France; on the other was a tainted France – left-wing, afflicted with an incurable malady since 1789 and, furthermore, contaminated with a great many foreign bodies.

NOTES

1 *L'Est républicain* (*ER*), 'Les coulisses du boulangism à Nancy', 1 October 1890.
2 Gabriel Richard, 'Le Boulangisme à Nancy (à propos du *Mystère des foules* de P. Adam): l'élection au conseil général de Nancy-ouest: la région nancéienne vers 1888', *Le Pays Lorrain*, 1962, pp. 10–28.
3 Archives Départementales de la Meurthe-et-Moselle (ADMM) 1 M 638; *ER*, 30 September 1890; Richard, 'Le Boulangisme', p. 12.
4 ADMM 1 M 638 and 647.
5 J. Jolly (ed.), *Dictionnaire des parlementaires français*, 4 vols, (Paris: Presses Universitaires de France, 1960–72); *ER*, 30 September 1890; Richard, 'Le Boulangisme', p. 14.
6 *ER* 'Les Coulisses', 1 October 1890.
7 ADMM 1 M 638 (16 June 1888).

8 ibid., 2 April 1890.
9 *ER*, 'Les Coulisses', 1 and 3 October 1890.
10 ADMM 1 M 638 (5 and 24 January 1889); *ER*, 3, 4 and 5 October 1890; Zeev Sternhell, *Maurice Barrès et le nationalisme français* (Paris: Colin, 1972), p. 120.
11 Richard, 'Le Boulangisme', p. 47; *ER*, 4 October 1890.
12 ADMM 1 M 638 (2 April 1890).
13 ibid.; Richard, 'Le Boulangisme', p. 17; *ER*, 12 October 1890.
14 ADMM 1 M 647; Richard, 'Le Boulangisme', pp. 21–5.
15 Alphonse Zéphirin Rosz (or Roz), b. 1850 at Laines (Jura), had been a freemason, secretary of the radical deputy Vergoin, then would-be police informer. Considered to be a very active Boulangist agent at Nancy, he is the presumed author of the articles on 'Les Coulisses du boulangisme à Nancy' published by the *ER* between 30 September and 20 October 1890. On him, see ADMM 1 M 647 (28 January 1890).
16 See Marie Christine Pierre, 'Les Idées politiques de Mgr Turinaz', thèse de 3e cycle, Nancy, 1982, p. 55; *ER*, 12 and 13 October 1890.
17 J. Bourdon, 'L'Evolution politique en Meurthe-et-Moselle de 1885 à 1893', *Annales de l'Est* (1952), p. 156.
18 ADMM 1 M 638 (police files of April 1890, used by Richard, 'Le Boulangisme', p. 17, to describe the committee in 1888).
19 ibid. (25 and 26 April, 6 August and 21 September 1890). There is only a single number of *Le Tire-Pied* at the Nancy municipal library – research continues.
20 ADMM 1 M 647 (9, 11 and 17 May 1891).
21 ibid. (10 September 1893).
22 ADMM 3 M 84; Bourdon, 'L'Evolution', pp. 159–61.
23 ADMM 1 M 638 (December 1894).
24 ADMM 1 M 647.
25 See Jolly, *Dictionnaire*; Jean-François Eck, 'Louis Marin et la Lorraine, 1905–1914: le pouvoir local d'un parlementaire sous la IIIe République', thèse de 3e cycle, Institut d'Etudes Politiques, Paris, 1980, pp. 112–13; *ER*, 21 and 26 April, and 6 May 1898, 7 and 24 April 1902; ADMM 3 M 84 (note of 14 August 1893).
26 ADMM 1 M 647 and 646 (10 September 1895).
27 Zeev Sternhell, *La Droite révolutionnaire, 1885–1914: les origines françaises du fascisme* (Paris: Seuil, 1978), pp. 230–1; Colette Hirtz, *L'Est républicain (1889–1914): naissance et développement d'un grand quotidien régional* (Grenoble: Presses Universitaires de Grenoble, 1973), ch. 2.
28 Sternhell, *La Droite*, p. 222; ADMM 3 M 85 (20 March 1898), and 1 M 646 (1898–1904).
29 *La Croix de Nancy*, 20 and 27 March, 10 April, 1 and 8 May 1898.
30 Jolly, *Dictionnaire*; ADMM 1 M 638 (2 October 1890), and 3 M 85 (1898 elections).
31 Sternhell, *Barrès*, pp. 226–7; Maurice Barrès, *Mes Cahiers*, 14 vols (Paris: Plon, 1929–49), no. 4; ADMM 3 M 85; *ER*, 5 April to 21 May 1898.
32 ADMM 3 M 85; *ER*, 23 May 1898.
33 *La Croix de Nancy*, esp. 8 May 1898; ADMM 3 M 85; and on Corrard des Essarts, Jolly, *Dictionnaire*.
34 On Hémonet, see ADMM 3 M 85 (police report of 13 March 1898); on the 'Catholic' candidates, see *La Croix de Nancy*, 1 May 1898.
35 ADMM 1 M 636; Barrès, *Cahiers* (no. 6); Jean-Pierre Rioux, *Nationalisme et conservatisme: la ligue de la patrie française 1899–1904* (Paris: Beauchesne, 1977), pp. 57 (map) and 60.
36 ADMM 1 M 636 and 646, collection of *Le Petit Anti-juif de l'Est*.
37 On Déglin, see Eck, 'Louis Marin', pp. 89 and 108.
38 ADMM 1 M 636 (notably October 1902), 1 M 646 and 3 M 86; Eck, 'Louis Marin', pp. 107 ff.; Hirtz, *L'Est républicain*, ch. 2; Jean-Claude Liedot, 'Les Elections législatives en Meurthe-et-Moselle de 1902', *Annales de l'Est* (1960), pp. 326–90.
39 ADMM 1 M 636 (notes of 12 June 1899, 25 February and 7 August 1901), and 3 M 86; *La Croix de Nancy*, *Le Journal de la Meurthe* and *ER* from March to May 1902.
40 ADMM 3 M 86.
41 ibid., and on the Comte de Ludre see Jolly, *Dictionnaire*.

42 Eck, 'Louis Marin', pp. 109–10.
43 ADMM 3 M 87, and esp. ibid. pp. 36, 41, 44, 48, 51, 233, 330, 353–4.
44 Issue of 6 May 1906. On the 'antibloc' coalition of 1906, see Eck, 'Louis Marin', pp. 119, 122–6, 129–32; and Hirtz, *L'Est républicain*, ch. 3.
45 ADMM 3 M 87. For the campaign overall, it is essential to consult the press, especially *ER, Le Journal de la Meurthe, Le Petit Anti-juif de l'Est* and, after 1905, *L'Éclair de l'Est*.
46 Françoise Gaucher-Tonnelier, 'Les Sénateurs de la Meurthe-et-Moselle, 1876–1914', *Annales de l'Est* (1963), p. 332; and Jolly, *Dictionnaire*.
47 Daniel David, 'Le Lieutenant-colonel Driant, officier-journaliste-parlementaire-écrivain', *Revue Historique des Armées*, no. 3 (1985), pp. 84–95; Eck, 'Louis Marin', pp. 208 and 337–8; *Journal de la Meurthe*, 16 March, 10, 11 and 22 April 1910; ADMM 3 M 88 and 1 M 636 (note of December 1910).
48 Gaucher-Tonnelier, 'Les Sénateurs', p. 332.
49 Pierre, 'Idées politiques de Turinaz', pp. 50–4, 237–49.
50 Michele Lagny 'Culte et images de Jeanne d'Arc en Lorraine, 1870–1921', doctoral thesis, University of Nancy, 1973, pp. 148–9, 279–306, 360–9, 427–9.
51 Gaucher-Tonnelier, 'Les Sénateurs', pp. 341–4.
52 Eck, 'Louis Marin', pp. 393–4.

10
Nationalists and Bonapartists

Bernard Ménager

In 1952, in a work that has become a classic, *La Droite en France*, Professor René Rémond established an ideological filiation between Bonapartism and nationalism, both of which formed part of a single political current (later prolonged by Gaullism), and which he labelled the authoritarian right. This analysis suggests questions concerning the relations between the two political forces, one in the ascendant, the other in decline, during the period of their coexistence. Was there any convergence of ideology and, if so, did it lead to unity of action? Did proximity generate tension between rival militants, or did it lead to a strategy of 'entryism'?

The field of observation is complex. The multiplicity of nationalist leagues and groups reveals significant doctrinal oppositions. Déroulède's plebiscitary movement should not be confused with the nationalism of certain radicals, or that of republican moderates who were affiliated to the Ligue de la Patrie Française. The group Action Française, which was in permanent conflict with the Bonapartist party, is not, therefore, included in this study. The Bonapartist party itself was very divided, between an imperialist tendency represented by Paul de Cassagnac, and the heirs of the Jeromists, who supported a consular-type republic. The plebiscitary label adopted by Prince Victor did not resolve the difference and it was not until 1911 that he abandoned the idea of an empire and made a republican act of faith. His temporizing policy did not meet with the approval of the party leadership in Paris, who were anxious to get to grips with the parliamentary republic, and these divergences had their effect on relations between Bonapartists and nationalists.

These relations developed over a period of time, as a function of the changing balance of power and political preoccupations. Bonapartism was in total decline at the time of the Dreyfus Affair, whereas the nationalist Ligues exerted a real attraction. In the years just before the war, however, they were all in the doldrums (with the exception of Action Française), while the Bonapartist party was increasing in popularity. At the same time, external political preoccupations became more important than internal political quarrels and the problem of the form of government, which had dominated the news at the turn of the century. This study, therefore, has as its background an eventful period. It considers the legacy of Boulangism, the first occasion of cooperation between Bonapartists and nationalists.

The Dreyfus crisis merits a thorough analysis because of what it reveals of the convergences and divergences, while the struggles of the beginning of the century suggest an examination of political and electoral tactics in a classic confrontation between government and opposition. Finally, the renewal of national feeling after 1905 must be considered in terms of its consequences for the relationship between Bonapartists and nationalists, associated in joint demonstrations, which bore witness to their similar political culture.

The Boulangist episode cemented an initial alliance between Bonapartists and nationalists, and was the logical step for the Jeromists rallied to the republic. Prince Napoleon, who received Boulanger at his Prangins residence on 2 January 1888, considered him as a stepping stone in the acquisition of power. The coalition was more artificial for those supporters of Prince Victor who had remained imperialists, but like the royalists involved in the same coalition, they envisaged that Boulangist success could lead to a plebiscite that would call the republic into question. The result of the undertaking was a bitter disappointment for the Bonapartists, who were reduced to a meagre cohort of 35 deputies after the elections of 1889, despite the vogue for plebiscitary ideas. The loss of activists was even more worrying. Many adherents rallied to the Boulangist cause after having, on occasion, obtained unwisely awarded electoral endorsement. The image of the 'brave general' supplanted that of the heir to the Napoleonic dynasty in the hearts of the people. Finally, the alliance, extended to the royalists, was rejected by the electorate.[1]

Prince Victor, who reunited the party after the death of his father in 1891, learned his lesson from these events, and rejected definitively the strategy of the Conservative Union, imposed on him by its supporters in the 1880s. The rejection of any collusion with the monarchists during the Dreyfus Affair can be explained in part by the memory of the Boulangist disappointment. It was also important for Bonapartism to reorient itself and to reaffirm its links with the revolutionary tradition. The centenary celebrations of the republic in 1892 provided the occasion: Prince Victor asked his supporters to remain attentive to the worries of the poor. The 'plebiscitary' label, adopted in 1891 without resolving the problem of the future form of government, allowed all legitimist-type imperialism to be rejected.[2]

These new tactics did not, however, prevent another electoral defeat in 1893, when the party was reduced to 13 seats. The *Appel au Peuple* was suspended and many provincial newspapers disappeared. This increased the strength of the party leadership in Paris, since the committees in the capital were the only ones to remain relatively active. Their lack of electoral strength made them susceptible to the temptation of a coup. They would have preferred more resolute action against the parliamentary republic, by making use of the Panama scandal and the anarchist outrages. The Parisian Bonapartists then developed a new strategy, based on the presidential election. A plot was even said to have been hatched in 1894, but the assassination of Sadi Carnot led to its being abandoned.[3]

Anxious to discipline the party, Prince Victor named Baron Legoux, who had been president of the plebiscitary committees of the Seine since 1889, as his delegate-general to the committees, and made *Le Petit Caporal* the official party paper. He entrusted the running of it to Cunéo d'Ornano, deputy for the Charentes and proponent of a Napoleonic republic. Prince Victor's leadership was still contested, however, and in 1895 some Parisian committees rallied to Cassagnac, an intransigent imperialist and inventor of *solutionnisme*, which meant supporting any leader who could overthrow the republic.[4]

The last years of the nineteenth century saw the first joint demonstrations by Bonapartists and nationalists: protests against the performance of *Lohengrin* at the Paris Opera in 1891, and against sending a French squadron to Kiel for the inauguration of the canal in 1895. Contacts were established with Drumont and the anti-Semites. *Le Petit Caporal* applauded Drumont's article against the Senate after its refusal to vote funds for the funeral of Marshal Canrobert.[5] The Bonapartist Lasies undertook an anti-Semitic campaign and his influence increased following his election to the Chamber in 1898.

When the Dreyfus Affair broke, *Le Petit Caporal* boasted of the agreement between nationalists and Bonapartists. During the legislative elections in May 1898, it supported both the Bonapartists and the revisionists on the subject of the constitution (19 May 1898). Rejoicing over the election of Déroulède, Millevoy and Drumont (9 May), it welcomed the formation of the new nationalist party (25 May). After the official reconstitution of the Ligue des Patriotes in September 1898, it approved Déroulède's programme and contrasted it with the sterility of royalist action (24 October). This convergence was founded on a militant anti-Dreyfusism, nourished by a cult of the army, which was outraged by Dreyfusard attacks. Zola's 'J'accuse' was described as a 'jumble of filth and insults against our beloved Army' (15 January 1898). This sentiment was shared by Prince Victor, who sent General Villot to represent him at the Napoleonic ceremony on 15 August 1898 in order to register his disapproval of the attacks against the army (17 August). According to certain sources, Prince Victor considered that a retrial of Dreyfus would be 'a crime against the Fatherland'.[6]

Anti-Semitism was a second point of convergence. Certainly, *Le Petit Caporal* did not make it part of its programme for government, and admitted that it was contrary to the principle of civil equality, but it laid the responsibility for it at the feet of the Jewish community, because of their alleged infiltration into the state and hidden role – thus restating the traditional themes of anti-Semitic propaganda (6 August 1899).

The Ligue des Patriotes, which was not afraid of the Bonapartists having too great an influence, was in favour of joint action. On 7 December 1898, the chairmen of the plebiscitary committees were invited to take part in street demonstrations. The reception accorded to this proposition was, however, lukewarm since the Bonapartists were afraid of dividing the population.[7] The dossiers of the Ligue des Patriotes show the importance of Bonapartist penetration. At the constitutive general assembly, members of the *Appel au Peuple* committee were present alongside Blanquists, revisionists, members of the Jeunesse Antisémite and Jules Guérin's league. Two well known Bonapartists, Le Provost de Launay and de Cuverville, sat on the steering committee.[8] In Marseille, at the only important provincial section, there were two Bonapartists among the ten officers: the editor of the newspaper *L'Aigle* and the chairman of the Redingote Grise club.[9] Paul Pugliesi Conti, the son of a Ajaccio town councillor, and member of a Bonapartist family of long-standing, worked for *Le Drapeau* from 1892. In 1900, he was elected as a nationalist deputy for Paris, without the Bonapartist label.

The question was whether the understanding between Bonapartists and the nationalists of the Ligue des Patriotes could be extended to the preparation and execution of a coup against the parliamentary republic. Activism among Parisian Bonapartists was a long-standing phenomenon, and the Dreyfus Affair gave an opportunity to demonstrate it openly. In May 1898, after another electoral defeat, the chairmen of the Parisian committees put pressure on Prince Victor by threatening to resign unless he took a bolder stance.[10]

From the start of the revision procedure of the Dreyfus case, *Le Petit Caporal* (15 September 1898) openly called for a *coup d'état*. It urged General Zurlinden to arrest the Dreyfusard leaders. Cunéo d'Ornano (18 October 1898) justified the Napoleonic *coup d'état*, on the basis of the will of the nation, in contrast with the Orleanist coup which confiscated national sovereignty. On 19 November, he returned to the subject, defending the violation of the law in the higher interest of the nation. These journalistic liberties fuelled rumours in the Dreyfusard press of a plot, which the police took quite seriously, because of seemingly suspicious movements by Prince Victor,[11] but it seems likely that the whole manoeuvre was merely intended to pressurize the prince into taking a more definite stand.[12]

Those in charge in Paris judged the situation to be revolutionary. They also became involved in the nationalist plot that ended in Déroulède's abortive coup on 23 February 1899 during Félix Faure's funeral. The hurried activity in Brussels in the preceding days indicates that Déroulède's intentions were known.[13] The president of the Jeunesses Plebiscitaires, Moro Gaffieri, who went to join Prince Victor, stated later that the Bonapartists were ready for action.[14] A retrospective police report explained the attitude of General Roget, who refused to march on the Elysée, by his belief that Déroulède was only a stalking-horse for the Bonapartists.[15]

Nationalism and politics

The Bonapartists hoped that after a successful coup, they would be able to steer events towards an imperialist restoration. To this end, *Le Petit Caporal* had submitted to Prince Victor, in January 1899, a plan for Bonapartist propaganda, which included posting portraits of the prince and a massive distribution campaign for the paper. The cost of the operation was estimated at fr.1,000 a day. Brussels agreed, then reduced the offer to fr.200.[16] The Bonapartists certainly overestimated their forces compared with Déroulède's numerous and disciplined troops. This adventurist strategy was not, moreover, universally accepted in the party, and its leader, Prince Victor, refused to adopt it.

The imperialists of Paul Cassagnac's tendency were hostile to the republican programme supported by Déroulède and the Ligue des Patriotes. After the fiasco of 23 February, *L'Autorité* (27 February 1899) condemned all military pronunciamentos and stated that only action by the people could legitimately overturn the government. In June 1899, Cassagnac and *L'Autorité* attacked united action by Bonapartists and nationalists, while *Le Petit Caporal* continued to defend it, on the occasion of a profession of republican faith by Déroulède. Dugué de la Fauconnerie worried about the risk of Bonapartists being excluded in Déroulède's new republic,[17] to which Cunéo d'Ornano retorted that the restoration of rights to the people was a sufficient guarantee.[18] Déroulède had the merit of bringing a new prestige to plebiscitary ideas.[19]

Prince Victor was in favour of an agreement with the Ligue des Patriotes, and had authorized members of the Bonapartist committees to belong to it individually.[20] But, to the despair of his impatient supporters, he never abandoned his prudent line throughout the whole of the Dreyfus Affair, while preparing himself for all eventualities. In October 1898, he asked the committees to avoid public meetings for or against Dreyfus;[21] in February 1899, he was sceptical of the chances of a coup succeeding and reined in Bonapartist propaganda;[22] and during the last months of the crisis, he maintained his reservations at the risk of accentuating discord in the party.[23] The reasons for his attitude were explained by the publication of his manifesto-letter to the mayor of Ajaccio, on the occasion of the celebrations for the centenary of the consulate. The prince justified his refusal to involve himself in the Dreyfus quarrel when the Waldeck-Rousseau cabinet was trying to restore calm in the country by quoting the success of Napoleon's national reconciliation policy: 'I did not wish to trouble my country with fruitless arguments or pointless gestures.'[24]

Concern about national unity explains the rejection of anti-Semitism. From the start of 1898, he had worried about the excesses of *Le Petit Caporal* and instructed Baron Legoux, president of the plebiscitary committees, to be cautious, hoping that the party would define its position on the question of anti-Semitism and that approved candidates would conform to this during the legislative elections in May.[25] In October, he renewed his instructions, and recommended that participation in anti-Semitic demonstrations be avoided.[26] In March 1899, he asked *Le Petit Caporal* to stop its attacks on the Jews.[27] In January 1900, anxious to reaffirm his authority, he demanded a retraction from Lasies, after a particularly violently anti-Semitic article, which was judged to be damaging to national reconciliation. Lasies resigned after claiming that Jewish influence was being brought to bear on the editorial content of the paper, which continued nonetheless to defend a 'respectable anti-Semitism', which was not a programme of government and was limited to denouncing excessive Jewish influence in the state.[28]

This incident revived the old polemic over the reasons for Bonapartist moderation during the Dreyfus Affair. From the start of 1899, Drumont and *La Libre Parole* had accused Prince Victor of being subject to Jewish influence, claiming that he was in the pay of Jewish banks.[29] The police took notice of these accusations, referring to a loan of fr.20,000, offered to Princes Victor and Louis, and to the takeover of several newspapers by Jewish investors, to the profit of the Bonapartist cause.[30] Prince Victor's private correspondence provides some enlightenment: in a letter addressed to the Duc de Morny, he stressed the need to avoid anti-Semitism, since the help of Jewish financiers was important. The prince, sceptical of the efficacy of partisan newspapers, which 'serve only to increase the zeal of the converted', felt that the purchase of republican papers was more effective.[31] It is clear too that his desire to assume the revolutionary inheritance and achieve national unity prevented Prince Victor from falling into the anti-Semitic way of thinking, unlike his Parisian followers, who were subject to the intellectual turmoil of the capital.[32]

The reserve and caution imposed from Brussels were not entirely innocent of Machiavellian calculation, according to observers. The balance of power was distinctly to the disadvantage of the Bonapartists in their alliance with the Ligue des Patriotes, so it was in their interest to turn to good use the disarray that followed the arrest and exile of its leaders and win over its wavering activists.[33] In the short term, it seemed they had miscalculated, since the Ligue was able to reorganize in 1901 and kept close contact with Déroulède, in exile at San Sebastian. In the longer term, it seems likely that a certain increase in vitality may have been due to the new blood brought to Bonapartism by former Ligueurs. The role of Gauthier de Clagny, vice president of the Ligue des Patriotes in 1898, was significant. In 1902, Prince Victor congratulated him following his success in the legislative elections and praised the firmness of his plebiscitary beliefs. In 1911 and 1912, his regular correspondence with the prince showed that he was closely associated with the reorganization of the Bonapartist party.[34]

The Dreyfus crisis revealed two opposing views of France. For Déroulède, in common with the Bonapartist leaders, the lead came from Paris, and

Nationalism and politics

the provinces followed the capital. For Victor, this was not self-evident following the failure of the Commune and Boulangism, and he saw a change of regime as implying the support of the provinces.[35] But this disagreement did not have to be resolved until 1902.

The relationship between nationalists and Bonapartists existed in an electoral context after 1900. The latter had organic links with the secret national council of the Ligues, formed following the Dreyfus Affair with a view to coordinating propaganda and political action.[36] Agreement was total during the municipal elections of 1900 and the legislative elections of 1902, but the relationship maintained with the Ligue des Patriotes and the Ligue de la Patrie Française was not so clear cut. It seems that the friendly relationship that existed during the Dreyfus Affair, between the Ligue des Patriotes and the Bonapartists, at least as concerned the strictly plebiscitary wing, deteriorated somewhat later on. The Bonapartists were irritated at Déroulède's taking over the plebiscitary issue,[37] while Déroulède, without actually breaking with the Bonapartists, distanced himself from the many monarchists and, from his exile in San Sebastian, affirmed his republicism.[38] The Ligue des Patriotes, constituted according to the law of 1901, included in its title the phrase 'plebiscitary republican'. Its vice president, Galli, who led it in Déroulède's absence, was a republican of the left, who had entered politics by way of Boulangism, and had worked for *L'Intransigeant* before taking over *Le Drapeau*, where he redoubled his attacks against the monarchists, including the imperialists who followed Cassagnac.[39] The Bonapartists, who had remained strictly plebiscitary, were treated with greater respect until 1903, since their competition was not considered to pose a threat, but the reorganization of the party in 1903, marked by the formation of an *Appel au Peuple* central committee (led by the Marquis de Dion, as a parallel body to the national plebiscitary committee, led by Arthur Legrand, responsible for electoral questions), was a source of anxiety for the Ligue des Patriotes. The Ligue expressed its irritation after the new Bonapartist manifesto appeared, and Galli complained that plebiscitary themes could be discredited by the action of their allies.[40] He went to San Sebastian to ask Déroulède to order the removal of the word 'plebiscitary' from the Ligue's programme, so as to avoid any confusion, and obtained satisfaction.[41] Galli was hostile to any agreement with the Parisian Bonapartists during the municipal elections in May 1904,[42] and continued, throughout the year, to condemn Lasies's plebiscitary demonstrations, in Paris and the provinces, referring to 'disloyal and plagiaristic competition'.[43] It seems that the alliance formed at the time of the Dreyfus Affair dissipated slowly because of its many ambiguities: the Bonapartists had not made a definite choice of republican institutions, and propaganda for a third empire, drawn up during the first years of the twentieth century, only served to reawaken the touchy republicanism of members of the Ligue des Patriotes.

Another potential ally was presented to the Bonapartists in the Ligue de la Patrie Française, formed during the Dreyfus Affair. The ideological similarities were less striking than those with the Ligue des Patriotes. The vagueness of its programme, and the sentimental aspiration to unity displayed in its first manifesto drew ridicule from Paul de Cassagnac in *L'Autorité* (5 January 1899), who mocked the 'Ligue that wants to have its cake and eat it ... in Academicians's language, refusing to speak loud and clear'. *Le Petit Caporal* (16 February), with practical politics its main priority, refrained from passing comment until 26 January 1899, when it launched an appeal for forces hostile to the regime to unite, so as to defeat parliamentarianism; and it approved the fund-raising activities of the new organization. In fact, the Ligue de la Patrie Française was a very disparate organization. It included a tendency not far from that of moderate republicanism (which included the president, the Academician Jules Lemaître, and the future president of the Paris municipal council, Dausset) anxious above all to refrain from attacking the republic's institutions, and an anti-parliamentary tendency similar to that of Déroulède, represented by its treasurer, Syveton. The poet and Academician, François Coppée, another figurehead of the new movement, was known for his Bonapartist leanings.[44] Like Cunéo d'Ornano, he hoped for a coup against the Elysée, but the directing committee dissociated itself from the agitation in which, it seemed, a number of militants had been involved and Coppée, who had been alongside Déroulède on 23 February, soon found himself marginalized.[45] Under these circumstances, it was still Déroulède who interested the Bonapartist leaders most during 1899. However, his disappearance from the political scene, following the trial before the Haute Cour, and the approach of the electoral period, for which the Ligue de la Patrie Française was preparing, led quite naturally to the Bonapartists moving closer to the Ligue, and all the more so since the new editorial policy of *Le Petit Caporal*, which had altered in March 1900 after the collapse of the company that had run the paper previously, was less attached to an accord with Déroulède.[46]

The difference between respective political programmes remained the main obstacle to a closer link. Soon after the municipal elections in 1900, the Bonapartists attempted to influence the political leaning of La Patrie Française,[47] but they did not achieve any results until the electoral defeat of 1902, when they profited from the Ligue's 'identity crisis'.[48] Lemaître made a public statement supporting the plebiscitary doctrine,[49] but his initiative drew criticism from his own organization.[50] Contact continued nevertheless during 1903. *La Patrie*, which was in favour of a large plebiscitary party being formed, published an interview with the municipal councillor, Jousselin, who was optimistic as to its chances of realization.[51] In this context, the success of the Bonapartist, Flayelle, in the by-election at Remiremont is significant.[52] The defeat in the municipal elections of

1904, however, dispelled all illusions and precipitated the decline of the Ligue de la Patrie Française. Despite continued contact,[53] with a view to preparing joint action for the presidential election of 1906, the Bonapartists acted autonomously from then on, making their priority the reorganization of their party, which they continued during 1904 and 1905, and seeking new, more effective allies in the form of the Action Libérale Populaire[54] and Biétry's *syndicat jaune*.[55]

Overall, the alliance between the Bonapartists and nationalists was not repaid, at least for the former, by substantial electoral gains. Among the newly elected right-wingers in the Paris municipal council only one was a Bonapartist,[56] although several elected as nationalists, in 1900 and 1902, were in fact Bonapartists, for example Pugliesi Conti and Lasies. But the Bonapartists' hopes that the two movements would join forces[57] because of their complementarity, remained vain.[58] Their association did, however, mean that the exclusive relationship with the royalists, which had been the rule up to the start of the 1890s, could be ended.

After 1905, external problems tended to overshadow internal politics and the dispute over the form of regime. While continuing to reorganize, and undergoing a major political evolution in 1911 by formally recognizing the republic, the Bonapartist party took part in joint action with the various nationalist movements. This was particularly the case for the Étudiants Plébiscitaires, who joined with various nationalist groups (Fédération des Jeunesses Républicaines Patriotes, Républicains Nationalistes, Jeunesses Républicaines, and even Action Française, despite violent antagonism between the two organizations), for the classic patriotic demonstration – such as marches in front of the statue of Strasbourg, and the celebration of the feast of Joan of Arc – which intensified between 1910 and 1913. The Bonapartist students joined the nationalists too in disturbances in the Latin Quarter, during the Thalamas Affair, and for the protests against Andler and Bernstein.[59] The Bonapartists also combined their protests with those of the nationalists against the Franco-German agreement of 1911.[60] In 1913, the three elected representatives from Calvados broke the rule of confidentiality after the presidential election, by declaring that they had voted for Poincaré.[61] Their preference for a regular army caused them to have reservations during the campaign for the three-year law, in 1913. Thus, Bonapartism started its process of reintegration into the national community, just as its eventual acceptance of the republic dispelled the suspicions of the republican nationalists.

The relationship between nationalists and Bonapartists, therefore, was a complex one, which varied over time, with agreements being made only with certain organizations and for particular types of action. In terms of ideological similarity, the affirmation of the plebiscitary principle, the desire to strengthen the executive power and augment national greatness certainly brought the Bonapartists and nationalists closer, despite petty rivalries. The appearance of a nationalist movement changed the Bonapartist party: influenced by the *ligues*, it became more urban and, just prior to the First World War, it undertook the democratization of its structures, which made it easier for its members to join the organizations of the twentieth century, such as the Jeunesses Patriotes. But the Dreyfus Affair exposed a basic difference between the nationalists, who were already denouncing the 'Anti-France', and stirring up public anger against certain categories of citizen, and the Bonapartists, who remained faithful to the Napoleonic tradition of reconciliation and national unity, and who, therefore, were ineluctably opposed to Action Française and the totalitarian nationalist movements of the twentieth century.

NOTES

1 Bernard Ménager, *Le Napoléon du peuple* (Paris: Aubier, 1988), pp. 337–47.
2 ibid., p. 348.
3 Note of 10 July 1894, Archives de la Préfecture de Police, APP Ba 70.
4 ibid., note of 24 April 1895.
5 Archives Nationales (AN), F7 12.419.
6 Note of 24 October 1898, AN F7 12.717.
7 Note of 7 December 1898, AN F7 12.451.
8 Note of 29 December 1898, AN F7 12.449.
9 ibid.
10 Note of 26 June 1898, APP Ba 70.
11 The rumour that Prince Victor was in Paris in mid-October arose because for a time he was unaccounted for during a trip from Brussels to Monza, where he met Generals Pellieux and Zurlinden. Note of 17 October, AN F7 12.717.
12 The Duc de Flêtre was said to have originated the rumour. Note of 15 October, APP Ba 70.
13 The 20 chairmen of the plebiscitary committees were said to have insisted that the prince should act, and offered him financial assistance. Annoyed by this pressure, the prince was said to have thought of going to Paris the day after the day of action planned for the occasion of Félix Faure's funeral, while reserving the right to alter his plans according to events. Note of 22 February 1899, APP Ba 70.
14 Report on meeting of plebiscitary students, 1 March 1900, AN F7 12.868.
15 Note of 26 May 1904, AN F7 12.867. A *gendarmerie* report (18 October 1899), closer to the events, refers to telegrams compromising the Bonapartists, which by collusion were excluded from the inquiry. APP Ba 70.
16 Correspondence of Prince Victor and Cunéo d'Ornano: letters of 8, 10 and 17 February 1899. AN 400 AP 183.
17 *L'Autorité*, 2 July 1899.
18 *Le Petit Caporal*, 4 July 1899.
19 ibid.
20 Note of 9 October 1898, APP Ba 70.
21 ibid.
22 see n.16 above.
23 Note of 16 October 1899, APP Ba 70. Baron Legoux was alarmed by numerous defections among the keenest activists.
24 *Le Petit Caporal*, 24 December 1899.
25 Note of 26 January 1898, APP Ba 70.
26 ibid.; note of 9 October 1898.
27 ibid.; note of 28 March 1899.
28 *Le Petit Caporal*, 10 and 11 January 1900.

29 *La Libre Parole*, 4 January and 9 February 1899.
30 Reports of 13 June 1900 and 22 January 1901, AN F7 12.867.
31 Letter of 23 March 1900, AN 400 AP 203.
32 Victor's brother, Louis Napoleon, was said by the police to be more anti-Semitic. Report of 20 April 1900, AN F7 12.719.
33 Notes of 29 November 1899 and 4 January 1900, APP Ba 70; report of 15 December 1899, AN F7 12.867.
34 AN 400 AP 190.
35 Correspondence of Victor Napoleon and Cunéo d'Ornano, AN 400 AP 183.
36 Zeev Sternhell, *La Droite révolutionnaire 1885–1914: Les origines françaises du fascisme* (Paris: Seuil, 1978), pp. 140–1. Report of 31 March 1905, AN F7 12.717.
37 Note of 28 July 1900, AN F7 12.867.
38 Note of 5 June 1900, AN F7 12.719; note of 18 December 1901, AN F7 12.451.
39 *Le Drapeau* attacked Cassagnac vigourously in September 1901.
40 Note of 5 September 1903, AN F7 12.867.
41 Notes of 2 February and 16 March 1900, AN F7 12.451.
42 ibid.; note of 6 February 1900.
43 ibid.; note of 29 July 1900.
44 A laudatory article on the Napoleonic achievement in *Le Petit Caporal* (11 January 1894) had earned a letter of thanks from Prince Victor; AN 400 AP 183.
45 Sternhell, *La Droite*, p. 133.
46 While the editorial of 3 March 1900, signed 'Alceste', denied the assertion made by *L'Aurore* that the alliance between the Bonapartists and Déroulède had been broken off, and said that the two movements would continue to work on the common plebiscitary ground, it doubted that their ultimate aims were the same and expressed reservations concerning Déroulède's programme. *Le Petit Caporal* was to give priority to the Napoleons.
47 Note of 11 August 1900, AN F7 12.719.
48 J.-P. Rioux, *Nationalisme et conservatisme: la ligue de la patrie française* (Paris: Beauchesne, 1977).
49 Note of 15 October 1902, AN F7 12.719.
50 ibid.; notes of 21 November and 2 December 1902.
51 Note of 7 December 1903, AN F7 12.867.
52 Note of 26 January 1904, AN F7 12.719.
53 Note of 20 August 1905, AN F7 12.867. The Comte de Beauregard, an influential Bonapartist agent, was in correspondence with the leaders of the Ligue de la Patrie Française.
54 Several Bonapartists sat on the steering committee of the ALP: Baron Reille, Comte de Cuverville (member of the Ligue des Patriotes in 1898), Dansette, Dussauchoy (see AN F7 12.719). A police note (6 November 1905) refers to the ALP recruiting among the lower-level Bonapartist committees.
55 Sternhell, *La Droite*, pp. 262 and 267; these were principally Cassagnac's imperialist committees.
56 D. Watson, 'The nationalist movement in Paris, 1900–1906', in David Shapiro (ed.), *The Right in France, 1890–1919* (London: Chatto, 1962), p. 73.
57 The Bonapartist deputy Arthur Legrand wrote to Prince Victor about 'la poussée habile' of Lemaître and Coppée: 'I believe that the two causes are complementary.' Letter of 9 May 1902, AN 400 AP 196.
58 The Ligue de la Patrie Française was strongest in the eastern half of the country, while the remaining strongholds of the Bonapartists were rather in the western half.
59 The Bonapartist students were even disavowed over the Thalamas Affair (Latin Quarter agitation during 1908–9 against a lecturer accused of having 'insulted' Joan of Arc by questioning her divine mission) and this caused a split (report of 21 February 1909, AN F7 12.868). The socialist Charles Andler received similar treatment in 1908 after being accused of taking his students to Germany during the Easter vacation. In March 1911 there were demonstrations against the 'Jewish' play, *Après Mai*, by Bernstein.
60 Report of 15 February 1912, AN F7 12.868.
61 ibid.; note of 20 January 1913.

11

The Jeunesse Antisémite et Nationaliste, 1894–1904

Bertrand Joly

Of all the *ligues* that went to make up the anti-Dreyfusard forces, the Jeunesse Antisémite et Nationaliste (JAN) remains one of the least known. The obscurity of this tiny group is quite understandable if its action, the mediocrity of its leaders and the role it was able to play are considered. In addition, the JAN suffered because of the, perhaps excessive, importance attached to Jules Guérin's Ligue Antisémitique.

The first appearance of a Jeunesse Antisémitique was at Lyons in 1893 where, on 21 February, it gave a banquet in honour of Morès and Guérin,[1] but there is no further record of this doubtlessly short-lived movement. The group of anti-Semitic students who were first to adopt the name JAN was formed soon afterwards, in April 1894,[2] under the patronage of Drumont or Morès,[3] and led by Camille Jarre, future nationalist lawyer, and stammerer. The group's quiet beginnings amounted only to a few meetings and brawls,[4] and unsuccessful attempts at expansion in the provinces.[5] In the context of these relatively anodine activities, the meeting that took place on 21 June 1895 is of interest, in that the speeches and the response of the crowd of 250 (of which 200 were students) exactly prefigured the rallies of 1898, both in form and content: racial hatred, the Algerian problem, slight hints of socialism, Anglophobia, and condemnation of the 'cosmopolitans who govern us'. The parallel was complete, even to the cries of 'Down with Dreyfus!'.[6]

Until 1896, the group was scarcely active. A few provincial committees were formed, in Bordeaux, Dijon, Lyon and Marseille,[7] the size of which, although undoubtedly small, cannot be estimated. This inaction was so severely criticized that Jarre resigned in the autumn of 1896, and was replaced by a young, ambitious and aggressive engineer, Edouard Dubuc.[8] Under his leadership, the JAN appeared to shake off its torpor, to some extent at least: Dubuc and his lieutenant, Jacques Cailly, made an appearance at meetings in the Latin Quarter and at other patriotic meetings, sometimes in the company of Jules Guérin. They were seen at Buzenval, Viroflay, and above all, on 21 November, at the Pascaud gymnasium where the JAN organized the first anti-Dreyfus meeting.[9] Under the chairmanship of Dubuc, d'Hugues, Millevoye, Jarre, Guérin and others could be heard to rage against 'the gorilla Reinach' and 'the senile fool, Scheurer-Kestner'. The JAN had really taken off by this stage, and appeared at all the anti-Dreyfus demonstrations.

Despite its student beginnings, the JAN was notable for its strong dislike of theoretical discussions. Anti-Semitism was the sum total of its beliefs, but of a knee-jerk variety, stripped of any doctrinal pretensions. The same was true of its nationalism, which was simply a crude chauvinism accepted as self-evident, the basis of which did not even have to be discussed. The socialism displayed by Dubuc before the Haute-Cour,[10] and which he claimed to base on Proudhon and Blanqui,[11] is scarcely worthy of mention, and was often nothing but a fairly crude anti-Marxist device. These limitations became clear whenever discussion turned to social questions: on 22 April 1901, in a meeting of the Étoile group, the man named Troili made a statement of belief in collectivism and declared himself at war against capitalists; he was also ready to fight in support of the principle: 'what one must be above all, no matter the political party one belongs to, is anti-Jewish.'[12] The same went for political allegiance; although officially republican, the JAN did not hesitate to vote, if necessary, for a monarchist or dubious republican. Thus the group's official programme was reduced to an unimaginative list of half-hearted demands. Apart from the customary anti-Jewish measures, the JAN wanted 'freedom of education'; the extension of local liberties and the creation of regional authorities; an end to *parlementarisme* (parliamentary intrigue) and interest-group politics; profit-sharing, pensions and insurance for workers, and so on; such was the JAN's programme as expressed by Cailly in 1901.[13] The social content gradually dwindled to almost nothing, and it is symptomatic of this that Cailly made the following juxtaposition, with a meaningful parenthesis: 'the abolition of certain monopolies, the prevention of profiteering, the fight against collectivism (state monopoly)', making this kind of socialism sound very similar to social Catholicism.

To match this spineless programme, the JAN had an extremely loose structure, manifested in its repeated changes of name: it became La Jeunesse Antisémitique de France towards the end of 1897, then La Jeunesse Antisémite (et) Nationaliste in the spring of 1899, then finally Le Parti National Antijuif, which title was officially adopted at the congress of May 1901. Moreover, Dubuc's colleagues referred to it, between themselves, by the mysterious name 'La Tethaire', from the Greek letter theta.[14] The statutes were marked by an extreme wish for decentralization, with each member group enjoying a level of autonomy that verged on independence;[15] in the local groups, about which very little is known, power was concentrated entirely in the hands of a committee elected by the general assembly, and within the committee, the president had great authority.[16] In reality, Dubuc (as president) and Cailly (as general secretary) decided the general policy of the movement on their own, although a certain influence was exercised by Drumont and the regional strongholds, such as that established by Brenier in Normandy. The other characters involved – Jarre, Delpech Cantaloup, Jacques de Biez, Jean Baffier, Favre, d'Hugues, Thiébaud, d'Élissagaray and the rest – were reduced simply to playing more-or-less effective walk-on roles after 1898.[17] A badge helped to rally the members,[18] as did the composition of a number of songs, the titles of which give a clear indication of their gist: 'La Carmagnole Antijuive' 'La Marseillaise Antijuive' of which there are several versions, including 'Les Juifs à la Frontiere'.[19]

As is the case with all the *ligues*, it is almost impossible to estimate how many members the JAN had.[20] With the meagre data available, any results must be treated with utmost caution. In addition, the partial figures provided by the leaders were almost invariably wrong, and the number of people listed as members included many totally inactive sympathisers. With these reservations, it is clear that the group began in a very modest, almost clandestine way.

In a letter to Déroulède, Jarre claimed 20 founding members and 350 in 1897, with 25 provincial groups.[21] For 1901, a report[22] set out the state of groups in the Paris region. According to this document, the JAN had slightly more than 1,200 members in Paris and about 150–200 in the suburbs, but these figures are not convincing and are contradicted in another report, written three months earlier.[23] The figures for the following years are very similar: in October 1902, Dubuc's troops, on the verge of collapse, were estimated at about 100 men, and in January 1904, Dubuc sent 100 telegrams to call his supporters to a demonstration, but without success.[24] It seems plausible, therefore, that in spring 1901 the JAN had between 200 and 300 active members, at the most, in the Paris area. But this period probably saw the movement's peak, when it was making the most effort to establish itself prior to the legislative elections of 1902. At the start of 1900, the JAN had only three groups in Paris: Étoile (16th and 17th *arrondissements*), Bastille (3rd, 4th, 11th and 12th) and Louvre (1st and 2nd), all still in the process of formation.[25] At the congress of May 1901, Paris was represented only by the central group (rue de Cluny), the two recently formed groups in the 6th *arrondissement*, and those from Bastille, Étoile and Belleville.[26] The triumphal proclamations in *Le Précurseur*, the JAN's official organ, must also be treated with suspicion. It is revealing that more than a third of all *arrondissements* (7 out of 20) were not represented by a delegate at the congress held in Paris on 4 August 1901. Thus, apart from a few exceptions (notably Étoile and Bastille), the committees set up were dwindling away, and often lasted only as long as their electoral ambitions or the commitment of a single organiser. This impression is further supported by records of attendance at meetings, even for the most stable groups. For the year 1901, figures for those present swing between 10 and 40, with the average about 15. On 10

Nationalism and politics

June, the police informant who was observing the Étoile group noted: 'Very few people. About 15 comrades from different groups, the same as usual.'[27] As a further indication of decreased militancy, the collection taken up that evening amounted to only 35 centimes.

In the provinces, the situation is even more difficult to evaluate, since *Le Précurseur* would refer to a single member as the committee. Two equally unsatisfactory methods can be applied: the first is to scrutinize the column 'Vie des Groupes' in *Le Précurseur* (and although this does not supply any real figures, it can provide a map of where in France the groups were established), and the number of mentions can be taken as a crude but valid indication of a group's size and vitality. Between 1898 and 1902, *Le Précurseur* mentioned 69 towns with committees of the Jeunesse Antisémite, but 36 of them were mentioned only briefly; 26 were named only once, and 10 only twice. Taking an arbitrary lower limit of five mentions, there are 22 towns whose JAN appear to have been genuinely active. Yet, this method of assessment is of limited value. For example, the Caen group, which was the largest in 1899, was not mentioned, having been disbanded in the repression of August 1899. In addition, the federal structure is not accurately represented in this town-by-town calculation. Nonetheless, the activity of the JAN was clearly divided into two main categories: there was a mass presence in a few large towns, such as Lyon, Marseille, Lille, Rouen, Saint-Étienne and Nîmes, and a more diffuse membership in the subprefectures of rural France, such as Meaux, Issoudun, Elbeuf and Langres.

The second method is based on scrutiny of police files. Prior to 1900, the JAN had no real foothold in the provinces, except for the groups in Caen and Marseille. The first of these was established in February 1897, as described in Brunet's letters and diary between 23 February and 30 May 1897. Under the leadership of two adventurers, Maurice Lefèvre and Edouard Brunet, the group started to prepare for a Normandy version of the *coup d'état* planned for the summer of 1899, but this childish plot against the prefecture cannot be taken seriously. The group was wiped out by a police roundup on 12 August, and compromising papers were found, providing the prosecution with ammunition for the trial. Although all the accused were acquitted, a sobered Lefèvre was unwilling to reestablish the group.[28]

At Marseille, the JAN was mentioned in 1899, but the group had certainly been formed between 1896 and 1897. Closely connected to the lodge of the Amis de Morès, an anti-Semitic group loosely affiliated to Guérin, the JAN owed the slight measure of dynamism that animated it to two men J. Balansard, an active member of Catholic organizations, and Ravoux, connected to the Amis de Morès. The JAN in Marseille was content to organize fruitless meetings and argue with the other local nationalist groups. When it invited Dubuc to a banquet, only about 30 were present

– proof of its limited influence. A disagreement weakened it still further, towards the end of 1900, and the special commissariat considered it to be inactive from May 1901. Further efforts to revive it failed, and records state that in 1903, all anti-Semitic and nationalist groups had disappeared from Marseille.[29]

It seems that from 1900, Dubuc had started to restructure his movement in the provinces[30] by reassembling the local committees into regional federations. A comparison between the chart drawn up by the police in September 1901 and the list of groups represented at the congress in May of the same year[31] provides a relatively satisfactory picture of the state of affairs.

The Normandy federation seems to have been the most solid, despite the break-up of the Caen group. About 20 towns had a committee, at least in theory, the best being those in Elbeuf, Fécamp, Flers, Laval and, above all, Le Havre. This success appears to have been the work of just one man, Flavien Brenier, leader of the Le Havre group and of the federation, who used his position for his own ends in playing the various *ligues* off against each other.[32] The federation in the Midi, the first to be formed, no longer existed in any significant way. In the Marseille area, there were nine groups, but sometimes in conflict with each other. La Ciotat,[33] Nice, Toulon and Le Cheylard were the only ones to show any activity. The Lyon federation, the largest after Normandy, had shrunk until it consisted only of Lyon and Saint-Étienne,[34] and at Lyon, various associated and rival groups were in competition to win favour with the Ligue des Patriotes.[35]

To complete the picture, it is worth mentioning the federations of central France (Bourges and Issoudun), of Algeria (Algiers, Mustapha and Oran),[36] of Burgundy-Champagne (Dijon, Langres, Troyes), of Brie (Meaux, with the very active municipal councillor, Caldine), the north of France (Lille), the Ardennes (Charleville), and the south-west (Toulouse-Montpellier). The Parisian federation was limited, in the suburbs, to a handful of groups: Rosny-sous-Bois, Bois-Colombes, Saint-Mandé, Saint-Germain-en-Laye and Gentilly.

Two conclusions can be drawn from this long list. The first is that whole regions are missing, for example Brittany and the entire Atlantic coast, Dauphiné-Savoie, Lorraine, Picardy and the Auvergne. The second is that the movement's growth took place between summer 1899 and spring 1901, which suggests that the JAN was able to gain some of the ground yielded by the retreat of the other nationalist movements, particularly Guérin's Jeunesse Royaliste and, to a lesser degree, the Ligue des Patriotes.

In about 1898, the make-up of the JAN changed, with the student element yielding to young, aggressive white-collar workers and shopkeepers. In Jarre's letter to Déroulède, mentioned above, he regretted this phenomenon and hinted that the Association Nationaliste de la Jeunesse was formed for those who rejected the 'genre vadrouille'.

Nationalism and politics

In this less interesting group, Dubuc was the only one to stand out even slightly. From a Normandy family, he was born in Paris in 1872, and had been an engineering student at the École Centrale at the time when, in 1896, he became politically active. The support for socialism that he expressed before the Haute Cour he later reiterated in the columns of *Le Précurseur*, but although he certainly had strong left-wing sympathies[37] he was not doctrinaire. He had a taste for action, and was always ready to appear wearing his hard hat, accompanied by two 'minders' whenever there was a chance of a fight.[38] This physical courage and his ostentatious admiration for Déroulède won him an honourable rank in the nationalist army.

Jacques Cailly, on the other hand, was 'difficult to take seriously', according to the investigative commission of the Haute Cour.[39] His real name was Louis Ferdinand Émile Davout, and he was born at Segrée-Fontaine (Orne) in 1877, but adopted as his pseudonym the name of a forgotten seventeeth-century poet. A childish and inconsistent man, his position was due solely to Dubuc's friendship, and the same could be said of Brunet, whose mental stability was questionable even to his close friends.[40] This limited world held sway through the columns of *Le Précurseur*, an irregular and remarkably feeble publication which disappeared altogether between 1902 and 1906.

Various satellite groups revolved around the JAN, and the lack of information available seems an accurate reflection of their insignificance. The Fédération Antisémite des Lycées, founded in July 1900 (or earlier), was intended for the pupils of Parisian *lycées* and constituted the JAN's junior wing. With no newspaper and no premises, it had to function through propaganda meetings and by joining in the JAN's street demonstrations. The role of its representative, Masson, was derisory and the movement appears to have faded out after autumn 1901.[41] The Jeunesse Républicaine Nationaliste appeared in about 1901, but was active only in the 17th *arrondissement*. In 1902, Lepelletier gained control and removed the group, which at that time consisted of only about 30 members, from Dubuc's influence.[42]

With Guérin's Ligue Antisémitique de France (LAF), the conflict of personalities was immediate. From its earliest days, the LAF had proposed amalgamation with the JAN, really intending to absorb it entirely, a proposal Dubuc could not but refuse. Guérin and Dubuc did not like each other, and Guérin, hoping to disrupt Drumont's guardianship, tried to separate the JAN from *la Libre Parole*. Before forming his group, he had associated with anti-Semitic students, particularly at the memorial service for Morès in 1896,[43] but the relationship started to deteriorate in early 1898: Guérin supported Gervaize against Barrès at Nancy, then turned his attention to tempting away the few JAN local committees.[44] Despite an attempt by Drumont at reconciliation,[45] the following months were marked by a tiresome succession of skirmishes between the two anti-Semitic movements: *Le Précurseur* never mentioned the LAF, and Guérin accused Dubuc of being an informer.[46]

The JAN received a warmer welcome from the Ligue des Patriotes, who appreciated this auxiliary 'security force'. In 1896, Jarre was pleased with the favour shown him by Déroulède, and took advantage of it to solicit an authoritative 'patriotic and truly anti-Semitic' song from the poet's pen for the use of the JAN.[47] Dubuc continued this good relationship, and virtually worshipped Déroulède, particularly since the Ligue des Patriotes was providing him with a financial subsidy, albeit rather small.[49] Brunet and Cailly followed suit, with Cailly even obtaining a position at *Le Drapeau* after being dismissed from *L'Intransigeant*.[49] The situation deteriorated somewhat during Déroulède's exile, partly because the JAN tried to infiltrate a number of patriotic committees, at Lille for example, and partly because the Jeunesse Républicaine Plebiscitaire was fishing the same waters as the JAN, and was extremely suspicious of Dubuc.[50] This touches on some of the main reasons why the JAN stayed so small: the rivalry with Guérin was manifest, it was semi-dependent on Déroulède, it had very little in the way of funds and few committed members, thus making it unattractive, and was not able to establish a position in the nationalist ranks.

Dubuc won his spurs at the Tivoli Vaux-Hall on 17 January 1898, during a meeting organized by and for Guérin, when he suffered some rough treatment while defending the speaker. He had his revenge on the 23rd at Mille-Colonnes, by roughing up Janvion and his anarchists.[51] Throughout the unsettled period of the Dreyfus Affair, the JAN also fought against the Dreyfusards, sometimes very violently, as on 27 January 1899 at the Palais de Justice, then at the salle Moncey,[52] with the rest of its activity taking place at reasonably calm meetings in the provinces. It warmly applauded Déroulède's attempted coup on 23 February 1899, but was subjected to various police searches in the following days, and exercised more discretion at Auteuil and Longchamp in June.[53] On 12 August, Cailly, Brunet and Lefèvre were arrested, as was Dubuc in September. The investigation and trial before the Haute Cour revealed the childish and inconsistent nature of the defendants, despite their noisy impertinence. The verdict was indicative of the court's view of the threat they posed: they were freed.

Dubuc and Cailly became travelling salesmen of anti-Semitism and nationalism, and criss-crossed France and Algeria purveying exactly the same boring and violent ideas. In May 1900, Dubuc was elected municipal councillor for the Arts-et-Métiers district of Paris thanks to a tide of nationalism that swept the capital, but he did not fulfil his role well.

The effort of organization and recruitment culminated in the anti-Semitic congress of 4 and 5 May 1901.[54] Dubuc hoped to federate the movement's efforts more with a view to transforming the JAN into a viable party in time for the elections of 1902. Before an audience of some 200 delegates, the JAN became the Parti National Antijuif, elected Dubuc as its leader and got bogged down in pointless discussions. This congress marked the movement's high-point and, at the same time, the start of its decline. Dubuc later recognized that the party scarcely survived its foundation.[55] There were a number of reasons for this decline, but the principal one was the open hostility of *La Libre Parole* to the new party, which was independent of Drumont and the direct rival to the group he intended to form.[56] From 1 August 1901, the police informer 'Drôme', who seems to have been very close to Dubuc, stated that members were leaving.[57] At the end of August, however, things were not yet irreparable: the congress of the Paris federation declared, on 4 August, that it had decided on a reconciliation with Drumont.[58] At the same time, Dubuc rejected the mediation of Dr Lorenzi, who wanted to help reconcile him with Guérin and, on 30 August, stated that he thought everything would turn out well.[59]

It seems that the JAN imploded at the beginning of autumn 1901. Reports in *Le Précurseur* on the activities of provincial groups reduced dramatically both in number and size, and meetings of the Paris groups were few and far between. In October, Dubuc publicly broke off relations with Max Régis[60] then in November, obviously desperate, he took the plunge and moved closer to Guérin's Grand Occident de France. He travelled to Brussels on about 10 November and negotiated an alliance at Drumont's expense, in exchange for the exclusion of d'Élissagaray, which Guérin had demanded.[61] A violent incident was soon to occur. On 27 November, Dubuc and some 20 supporters invaded a meeting of the Comité National Antijuif, the party formed by Drumont, but violence was narrowly averted.[62] Three days later, the Bernay Affair took place. It started as an ordinary propaganda meeting organized by Drumont's group. Dubuc, who claimed to have been invited, also went to Bernay with a group of thugs recruited from the staff of *L'Antijuif*, Guérin's paper. Short but violent scuffles broke out on the way into and out of the meeting, and continued in the streets outside.[63]

It seems that this upset in the anti-Semitic groups was essentially caused by financial problems. Because of his reputation and his newspaper, Drumont attracted most of the electoral funds, and the subscriptions to *La Libre Parole* brought in a tidy sum, despite various deductions. He therefore considered, and with some justice, that he was head of the whole anti-Semitic movement. Neither Guérin, who had large personal financial needs, nor Dubuc and Cailly, who had claimed to be martyrs to the cause since the Haute Cour and were bitter at not deriving any advantage therefrom, were prepared to accept this and were not satisfied with the small subsidies on offer. For their part, Drumont and the disturbing Devos needed, in order to stand up against the electoral imperialism of the Ligue de la Patrie Française, to present themselves as undisputed heads of a united anti-Semitic movement, and felt it essential to eliminate the less presentable (Guérin) and more turbulent (Dubuc) elements among the anti-Semites. As they could not accept a direct rival to their own Comité National Antijuif, they closed the purse-strings, which impoverished the JAN and led to the violent reactions mentioned above. Insincere reconciliation between Dubuc and Devos led to an armistice on 6 December, but Dubuc remained the loser, ostentatiously disavowed at Bernay by Flavien Brenier and his powerful Normandy federation. Devos patronizingly consented to release a little more money.[64]

Until the legislative elections of 1902, the JAN remained inactive, due to insufficient funds. The poll marked the rout of the anti-Semites, as Dubuc was well aware.[65] When the Boers were received in Paris on 13 October 1902, only the Téthaire demonstrated against the British,[66] in what was to be their last street protest. The JAN was not mentioned again until the municipal elections of 1904, when Dubuc had a seat to defend. He did so in deplorable conditions, attacked by *La Libre Parole*, betrayed in an underhand manner by what was left of the Ligue de la Patrie Française and his own committee,[67] and let down by the poor record he presented to the electors. His defeat in the first round was predicted by everyone, but he reacted furiously.[68] Cailly, who had found a new dupe to subsidize him,[69] was fought by Drumont and abandoned by Rochefort, and suffered the same fate. Despite a final attempt at reconstruction in December, the JAN, alias the Parti National Antijuif, ceased to exist in the summer of 1904, and the Ligue des Patriotes took the survivors on board.[70]

The return of Déroulède at the end of 1905 put Dubuc back in the saddle.[71] In 1906, he campaigned for Déroulède in Charente, and in 1907 was heading the security for the Ligue at Champigny. In the same year, he published a boring catalogue of nationalist clichés entitled *Socialisme et Liberté*, with a preface written by Barrès. He then returned to private life once and for all,[72] becoming involved in mine prospecting and going to war as an artillery sergeant. He was a passive sympathizer for Action Française, in which his two sons were active, and he retained his ardent admiration for Déroulède. He died in November 1945 at Villiers-sur-Marne. In common with most of the professional anti-Semites,[73] Cailly and Brunet also joined Action Française. Between the wars, the former worked for the royalist daily without attracting much attention. Flavien Brenier was to be found at Coty's *Ami du Peuple* in 1930 and at the Institut Antimarxiste in Paris.

It is difficult to assess whether, in this turbulent episode in French anti-Semitism, Dubuc and his followers merit close scrutiny, or to establish what they represent in the history of nationalism. The movement was certainly of only minor importance in terms of its size and activity: a few hundred members, a handful of loudmouths and thugs as in any *service d'ordre*, an inconsistent programme and mediocre leaders. The JAN carried so little weight that the nationalists could do without it in preparing for the elections of 1902. From the summer of 1901, the team at *La Libre Parole* stifled it with an ease that speaks volumes for the group's vitality. But nevertheless, the Téthaire cannot be ignored for two reasons. First, the JAN constituted a failed but remarkably similar prefiguration of the Camelots du Roi. Despite its republican, socialist and revolutionary protestations, these had no real substance, and the later transformation to royalism was achieved almost naturally, and certainly without any insurmountable problems of conscience. Second, if it is accepted that Guérin's Ligue was a huge swindle, and that its influence has been generally overestimated by historians, the JAN was the only anti-Dreyfusard movement that belongs incontestably to a kind of pre-fascism. Originating from the Blanquist and anti-Semitic left already corrupted by post-Boulangist aberrations, Dubuc and his supporters ended up with Action Française, more out of necessity than conviction, as victims and symbols of the transition of left-wing nationalism towards the extreme right. From 1898 onwards, they were split between their populist, racist and violent nationalism and the respect they owed to the conservative hand that fed them. If pre-fascism existed in France about 1900, there it was, already with all its contradictions.

NOTES

1. *La Libre Parole*, 22 February 1893.
2. *Le Précurseur* (*LP*), 15 March 1900. Founded on 20 October 1898 by Richon, alias Claude Actan, alias A. de Rochetal, and run by Dubuc from April 1899.
3. Pamphlets by Dubuc, Archives Nationales (AN), F7 12720 (n.d.); F7 12461 dossier Seine-et-Oise, 27 March 1898; interrogation of Dubuc, in *Haute Cour de justice: affaire Buffet, Déroulède, Guérin et autres inculpés du complot*, Vol. I, (Paris, 1899), pp. 75–6.
4. Archives de la Préfecture de Police (APP) Ba 103 (11 May 1894, 12 October, 13, 23, and 30 December 1894); Ba 105 (8 and 11 February 1896).
5. See n. 3 above.
6. AN F7 12459, 4 December 1896, and *LP*, 19 April 1899.
7. *La Libre Parole*, 26 June 1896.
8. AN F7 12459, 4 December 1896, and *LP*, 19 April 1899.
9. AN F7 12461, two reports of 22 November 1897; APP Ba 1104, same date.
10. Hearing of 21 November 1899 (in *L'Éclair*, 23 November): 'Je suis socialiste, parce que c'est le long espoir de ce siècle.... Je suis socialiste, parce que je considère que j'appartiens au prolétariat.... Je suis avec les révolutionnaires, citoyens.'
11. AN F7 12458, 6 November 1901. JAN members called each other 'camarade' (ibid., pamphlet of April 1901). See also J. Cailly, 'Au prolétariat', in *LP*, 5 November 1898. Cailly contributed a feeble column on 'the social question' to this review, the group's official organ.
12. AN F7 12461, 23 April 1901. Same reaction when Cailly identified himself with the red flag at a meeting of the Barillier committee, F7 12458, 9 October 1901.
13. AN F7 12461, 17 June 1901.

14 AN F7 12459, 30 March 1900, contains much information on the coded language used by the JAN.
15 Statutes in *LP*, 27 October 1901.
16 Judging by the statutes of the Nice group (copy in AN F7 12720, 4 July 1901).
17 Two lists of leading members exist in AN F7 12459, the first undated, the second of September 1901. Also seen at meetings were Le Menuet, Poccaton, Poirier de Narçay, Barrillier *et al.* (see *LP*, 5 February 1899).
18 A copy in AN F7 12720, dossier JAN, 21 January 1909.
19 *LP*, 19 April 1899 and 5 November 1898; and AN F7 12453 (chorus: 'Chassons tous les Youpins / A grands coups de gourdins' etc.); Bibliothèque Nationale, 4⁰ Y² 896.
20 Very little is known of the financing of the JAN, especially in its early days. On 19 April 1896, Abbé Dabry passed fr.500 to Jarre, and it seems that Drumont and certain Catholic circles were the group's usual patrons. AN F7 12459, 20 April 1896.
21 AN 401 AP 10, letter of 22 January 1900.
22 AN F7 12459, September 1901.
23 AN F7 12461, 17 June 1901.
24 AN F7 12458, 9 October 1902, and F7 12451, 15 January 1904.
25 *LP*, 15 March 1900.
26 AN F7 12461, 17 May 1901, and *LP*, 25 May 1901.
27 AN F7 12458, 11 June 1901; F7 12720, 23 February 1901; F7 12459, 7 December 1901.
28 AN F7 12453, 28 January 1898; F7 12449, telegrams of 29–30 August 1899; F7 12462, 27 and 30 August 1899. See also the documents discussed before the Haute Cour during the questioning of Brunet (22 November), in *L'Éclair*, 24 November 1899, and AN F7 12460, dossier Calvados, 6 March 1901.
29 AN F7 12460 dossier Bouches du Rhône, 24 June, 8 July, 8 September 1899; 28 June, 4 and 12 December 1900; 2 and 31 May, 12 and 15 June, 10 September 1901; and F7 12455, 8 May 1900.
30 AN F7 12460, 19 March 1900.
31 AN F7 12459, September 1901, and *LP*, 25 May 1901.
32 The beginning of the Le Havre committee was difficult, however. In July it had only seven or eight members, whom Brenier assembled at the office of his newspaper *Le Tocsin Normand* (AN F7 12463, 17 July 1899); later the committee grew, lost its anti-Semitic focus, and then collapsed (F7 12457, dossier Seine-Inférieure, 17 December 1901).
33 This group, founded in June 1900, had about 100 members on paper. AN F7 12455, 7 June 1900.
34 The Saint-Étienne group was founded early in October 1899, with some dozen members of whom some had come from the moribund Jeunesse Royaliste. An anti-Semitic committee close to Guérin already existed. AN F7 12460, dossier Loire, 6 October 1899.
35 According to *LP*, 23 March 1902, 15 committees, half of which were based in Lyon, took part in the congress of the Lyon federation, 15–16 March 1902.
36 Max Régis was for a time the organizer of the Algiers group, which was still in existence in 1904, though in an enfeebled condition. AN F7 12461, dossier Seine, 24 September 1904.
37 *LP*, 15 April and 14 October 1900, and 24 January 1901.
38 AN F7 12453, 29 April 1899.
39 *Haute Cour*, Vol. VIII, p. 112.
40 AN F7 12462, 25 September 1899.
41 AN F7 12459, 16 January 1899, 14 June and September 1901.
42 AN F7 12458, 6 November 1901 and 12461, 26 May 1902.
43 APP Ba 1104, 14 January, 12 and 18 July 1896; 25 February and 9 June 1898.
44 On the occasion of a party given in honour of Dubuc, injured in a brawl, *La Libre Parole* lauded his bravery and wrote sarcastically of the 'parlotes' of 'phraseurs' greedy for 'gloriole'; Guérin had a furious scene with Drumont, who sacked Cravoisier, author of the sacrilegious article, despite the intervention of Gaston Méry and Jean Drault. See *La Libre Parole*, 23 January 1898, and APP Ba 1104,

same date; also the bitter letter of 27 July 1898 from Dubuc to Greslay, published in *Haute Cour*, Vol. IV.
45 APP Ba 1104, 28 June and 12 July 1898; AN F7 12459, 25 and 28 June, 1 July 1898.
46 AN F7 12451, 15 October 1898; 12459, 9 January 1900; Charles Spiard, *Les Coulisses du Fort-Chabrol* (Paris, published by author, 1902), p. 23.
47 Letter to Déroulède, 13 June 1896. AN 401 AP 10.
48 AN 401 AP 7, letter of Dubuc, 16 March 1900.
49 ibid. Cailly joined, left and rejoined the Ligue des Patriotes (see AN F7 12451, 18 September 1902, and 12870, 21 June and 18 September 1902). He contributed to *Le Drapeau* under the pseudonym Pierre Legrand, and had only fr.150 he earned there to live on (ibid., 22 November 1901 and 8 December 1902).
50 AN F7 12456, dossier Nord, 4 February 1900; 12720, dossier of Jeunesse Républicaine Plébiscitaire, 23 June 1900.
51 Spiard, *Les Coulisses*, pp. 21–3.
52 AN F7 12454, 3 February 1899.
53 E. Dubuc, 'Déroulède', in *LP*, 5 March 1899; AN F7 12459, search of Dubuc's residence, 26 February 1899; F7 12457, 16 June 1899.
54 On this congress, see *LP*, 27 April and 25 May 1901; *L'Intransigeant*, 6 and 7 May 1901; AN F7 12459, 2 and 6 May 1901; and F7 12720, 5 May 1901.
55 E. Dubuc, *Socialisme et liberté* (Paris: Sevin, 1907), p. 1.
56 All informers were agreed on this: see e.g. AN F7 12458, 8 May 1901; 12459, 8 and 29 May; 12461, 9 May and 6 August.
57 AN F7 12459, 1 August 1901.
58 ibid., 6 August.
59 ibid., 31 August; APP Ba 1105, 7 August.
60 AN F7 12459, 12 October 1901; *LP*, 27 October.
61 AN F7 12459, 13 November 1901; APP Ba 1105, 19 November.
62 AN F7 12461, 27 November 1901.
63 *La Libre Parole* and *L'Antijuif*, 2 and 7 December 1901. APP Ba 1105, 1–5 December; AN F7 12455, dossier Eure; 12459, 4–11 December; 12882, 30 November and days following.
64 AN F7 12459, 8 January 1902.
65 *LP*, 18 May 1902.
66 AN F7 12458, 14 October 1902.
67 APP Ba 1337, 7 April 1904; AN F7 12870, 16 April 1904.
68 APP Ba 1337, 3 May 1904.
69 AN F7 12458, 22 March 1904.
70 AN F7 12459, 5 December 1904; APP Ba 1340, 13 June 1904.
71 AN F7 12451, 23 January 1906; 12870, 18 December 1905.
72 APP Ba 1340, 30 December 1907. The following details were given by M. Dubuc (son of E. Dubuc) at the interview he kindly gave me on 19 November 1987.
73 Eugen Weber, *Action Française: Royalism and Reaction in Twentieth-Century France* (Stanford, Calif.: Stanford University Press, 1962), p. 200.

12

Parisian white-collar employees and nationalism in the belle époque

Lenard R. Berlanstein

This chapter attempts to identify the electoral clientele of the Parisian nationalists in the era of the Dreyfus Affair. Such an endeavour quickly leads to a reexamination of the politics of the petite bourgeoisie. Behind the likes of Déroulède and Drumont was the army of the lower middle class. Its *prise de conscience* at the end of the nineteenth century heralded, in no uncertain terms, the arrival of mass society. What historians actually know about the lower middle class is a great deal less than is often assumed or acknowledged.[1] Two models guide research and writing, but their mutual inconsistencies are not generally examined. The first – classically Marxian – posits a petite bourgeoisie doomed to polarization in a two-class society as a result of proletarianization. As commercial bureaucracies grew, employees supposedly lost their prospects for independence and control over their work. Jobs were downgraded through subdivision and routinization. Employees began to define themselves as victims of capitalism and to identify with the rhetoric of the organized working class. Small property-owners, on the other hand, reacted forcefully against the emergence of collectivism and aligned with big capital and finance.

Arno Mayer has articulated most clearly the alternate model of lower middle-class development.[2] In his view, it was a class with a permanent existence, destined to remain a buffer between capital and labour. The constituent elements – artisans, shopkeepers, labour aristocrats, clerks, and civil servants – had a fragile coherence much of the time. Yet, Mayer finds two sources of unity emerging at moments of social instability: first, a 'sense of negative commonality', being neither bourgeois nor proletarian; and, second, a cohesive belief system, encompassing respect for property, resentment of elites and contempt for cultural innovation. Mayer casts the petite bourgeoisie in a crucial role for preserving social stability. On one hand, its political choices betrayed an 'inner core of conservatism'; on the other hand, by favouring neither *laissez-faire* nor class conflict, it facilitated gradual adjustments to social change.

To the limited extent French historians have examined the lower middle class, it would appear that Mayer could not possibly be correct. The constituent groups seem to have gone their separate ways, as the

Nationalism and politics

Marxian model would predict. Philip Nord has brilliantly illuminated the rightward drift of shopkeepers.[3] Once paladins of radicalism, merchants found their xenophobia, anti-Semitism and anti-modernism drawing them to anti-Dreyfusard nationalism and, then, to Poincarist conservatism. No other group has been studied in such detail, but what we know about them defies Mayer's thesis. Commercial employees and civil servants seem to have drifted leftward. The socialist connections of the largest union of sales clerks, the Chambre Syndicale des Employés de Commerce, were well known. The rallying of school teachers to the CGT, the strikes by postal clerks and the repressive measures used against civil servants under the Radical Republic challenge the reality of an inner core of conservatism.[4] Indeed, a 'proletariat of the pen' seems to have emerged by the dawn of the twentieth century.

But let us look more closely. Much room for further research exists and in this study we intend to test the two models as far as office employees at the end of the nineteenth century were concerned. The approach will be a case study, using the corporate records of the Parisian Gas Company (the Compagnie Parisienne de l'Éclairage et du Chauffage par le Gaz, hereafter referred to as the PGC).[5] This was one of the very largest enterprises in France of the nineteenth century. Founded in 1855 to supply coal-gas for heating and lighting, the firm was probably the biggest private employer of office clerks in the capital. Starting with about 450 book-keepers, the PGC had nearly 1,600 employees by 1880 and 3,200 by the turn of the century.[6] We seek to determine whether proletarianization created a new sort of office workforce that came to define itself as a leftist victim of capitalism or whether a core of conservatism emerged among employees in the era of Boulanger and Dreyfus.

A generation of the new labour history has revealed the central role of the work experience as a determinant of industrial relations.[7] The model of proletarianization proposes that the downgrading of clerical work radicalized employees. It would be easy, however, to overestimate the intensification and routinization of office tasks within the PGC. Labour in most of its offices was not far more downgraded than in that legendary bureaucracy, the French state, which hardly stood as a paragon of efficiency. A parliamentary commission of 1871 concluded that ministerial employees accomplished no more than 3 or 4 hours of effective work per day. The civil servant's relaxed work culture entailed numerous informal breaks each day, and the inappropriate design of offices in the ministries made close supervision impossible. The pace with which office machinery simplified and specialized tasks was glacial. Underlying these conditions was the principle of unitary recruitment of personnel: entry-level jobs (copying documents) went to people with the background to move up to the post of office head. The practice ensured that civil servants would have careers and pass through a hierarchy of tasks. Only around the turn of the century, with the entry of women as typists, did specialization and dead-end jobs begin to appear.[8]

The PGC probably had higher work standards than the civil service, and tasks were rather routinized in some offices, but continuities outweighed differences. The offices of the gas firm were not particularly regimented. Keeping clerks from congregating in the halls, taking a break to smoke, or leaving to retrieve hats purposely left behind at the café were beyond the power of supervisors. Very early in the life of the firm, the executive committee rejected the fining of book-keepers as 'unworkable' and retained fines only for uniformed, active agents (bill collectors, meter readers and lighting inspectors) who worked on the outside. The records of the active agents show that sanctions failed to disrupt a lackadaisical work culture. The PGC built a new headquarters during the 1860s which allowed for oversight of the clerks but quickly outgrew the space during the next decade, so supervision suffered. Even with its failures at disciplining employees, the PGC was actually slower than the ministries in fashioning a pliant personnel through structural change. Unitary recruitment persisted. In 1891, the firm possessed only one typewriter and no key-board adding machines. Females never entered the bureaux of the PGC.[9]

Managers were complacent about clerical work because office expenses were marginal, about 1 per cent of total costs. Clamping down on shirkers would not have mattered much. Moreover, management placed its faith in spurring zeal rather than regimentation. Pensions were not a right but a favour that the company could (but rarely did) withhold. It insisted on promoting clerks up the salary scale (at fr. 300 per step) entirely on the basis of individual performance, not seniority. The problem was that the centralized decision making was ill suited to rewarding merit, and employees thought advancements were arbitrary. The policy produced more contention than zeal.

The case of the PGC thus suggests that large private bureaucracies failed to transform office work in a fundamental manner. Nonetheless, employees did develop a lively sense of grievance, and when the opportunity appeared, were prepared to act collectively. Underlying the discontent was the perceived inadequacy of compensations. Clerks were paid better than workers, and they had more fringe benefits and far more security; but employees also had high expectations and material standards. Even a socialist, class-conscious clerk argued that 'by reason of his education, the demands of his condition require the clerk to have proper and costly attire. His wife and children spend more [than those of workers]. To be an employee is to live in poverty but appear above it.'[10] In 1892, the director of the PGC spoke of fr. 2,700 a year as a 'living salary' for office clerks, but 70 per cent of his clerks were below the figure. Such limited rewards necessitated a household economy of makeshifts. Clerks' wives worked at manual labour. Employees frequently moonlighted (several collected

Nationalism and politics

tickets at the dance halls of Montmartre). Widespread indebtedness was a sign that these expedients failed to stretch budgets far enough. The offices of the PGC were havens for loansharking. Try as it might, management could not eliminate or even reduce the activity significantly.[11]

Exiguous circumstances made employees sensitive to managerial decisions about raises and bonuses. 'Promotion fever' gripped the personnel each 1 January, the day the decisions were announced. One anti-union office chief, a self-styled 'friend of order', warned the director that the perceived unfairness of the decisions brought new members to the union each year. Clerks charged that advancements were arbitrary, mercurial and nepotistic. Moving from salaries of fr. 1,800 to 2,100 took some clerks three years, and others seven or eight; reasons for the differences were not evident. Regular, orderly promotions by seniority were the ideal. Increasingly, the attraction of regular promotions transcended economic considerations; employees defined freedom from the discretionary authority of the boss as a matter of dignity.[12]

There were other discontents as well. Clerks wanted to receive free coke, as workers did. Active agents claimed the company should pay for their uniforms. Some employees resented the refusal of their bosses to consider requests for minor changes in work schedules and routines. Anxieties about retirement rights were especially troublesome. The PGC, holding its gas concession until 1905, had shrewdly (perhaps callously) decided not to fund clerks who would retire after that date, despite its enormous profits. Presumably, younger clerks would be left without pensions, or the company would take care of them if and when the concession was renewed. These clerks were unsettled by such callous treatment.

Thus, office clerks had a distinct sense that their interests and those of the firm were in conflict even though their work had not been proletarianized. Their grievances concerned compensations more than 'shop-floor' issues. They led to a feeling of victimization, and clerks organized to defend their interests. However, as we shall see, very few were willing to proclaim themselves 'proletarians of the office'.

A fateful coincidence governed the collective protest of the clerks, which occurred in 1891. Negotiations between Paris and the PGC over the new gas concession began at the same time that the radical-dominated municipal council came to seek a new relation between the state and emerging industrial society. Radical councillors enraged by workers' support of General Boulanger and contesting the loss of its constituency to socialism, were now willing to countenance moderate intervention into private enterprise to secure social peace. The notion of republicanizing the workplace – removing the personnel from the arbitrary power of employers – guided their programme.[13] If the PGC wished to survive the end of its charter in 1905, it would have to become a model employer.

The left majority of the council encouraged unionization of manual and white-collar workers in the PGC. It supported union demands. The most devastating critique of the promotion policies at the PGC came from the radical councillor Alexandre Patenne. Reviewing the centralized, superficial process of awarding advancement, Patenne concluded that clerks were 'absolutely subjected to arbitrary will and favouritism'. He spoke for the majority when he proclaimed it 'perfectly reasonable' to insist that the PGC declare 'a precise and inviolable regulation that any agent who does his work conscientiously can expect a salary of 3,000 francs at the end of fifteen years and 3,600 francs at the end of twenty-four years'.[14] Management was not in a position to intimidate its personnel, so the union and these sorts of demands persisted.

Information gathered by corporate spies on the 200 or so clerks (out of 2,200) who joined the union in its early years permits further analysis of the origins of employee militancy.[15] The members were concentrated in the most proletarianized divisions, customer accounts and the lighting sections. Most who rallied to the union had not been with the firm very long and had an average of five years of seniority. These two features coincided with lower than average pay. These young clerks were the ones who had to worry about their retirement benefits. This profile emphasizes the quest for security and better compensation as the mobilizing forces. The older employees, who might have been more sensitive to a long-term deterioration in the work routine, remained unorganized.

There are a few signs – by no means conclusive – that the limited minority of clerks who entered the early union identified with the working-class left. Certainly, the man they chose as their leader, Maurice Claverie, intended to run his union as an organization of the left. Though flexible, Claverie was an antagonist of capitalism and an enemy of the bourgeoisie. The former gas clerk founded the union in the hope that workers and employees would organize together. Indeed, he revived the effort at unity from time to time, always without success. Claverie became prominent in the circle of reformist syndicalists. While he expressed suspicion of 'politics', he supported socialists in elections, and opponents accused him of using union funds to underwrite their campaigns. What characterized the employees' leader above all else was an absolute faith in gradualism. 'Any reform that takes even a bit of capital or authority from the boss, and gives it to workers,' he wrote, 'is a revolutionary act.'[16]

Despite Claverie's leftist orientation, we must resist jumping to two conclusions: (a) that the unionized minority represented the political views of the majority; and (b) that employees who were troubled by arbitrary authority at work necessarily expressed discontents through leftist politics. Neither assumption appears justified. A sign that the leftist orientation of the union offended many gas clerks came in 1899. As the nationalist movement gathered strength in the capital, Claverie

Nationalism and politics

abandoned his support for the socialist goal of municipalizing the gas company. Instead, he proposed giving 'the gas works to the gas workers', a syndicalist solution with some obvious corporatist elements.[17] Among the gas 'workers' he included 'the directors, department heads, and factory managers'. His organic vision of administration – with managers as 'the brains' and workers as 'the muscle' – must certainly have raised eyebrows among socialists. Claverie seemed to be preparing the union for a shift to the right as a mass, anti-Dreyfusard movement grew in the capital.

Claverie's responsiveness to the nationalist movement was fully appropriate, much as Mayer would have predicted. In the Parisian election of 1900, gas employees joined the municipal revolution which turned city hall over to the right. The socialist deputy Gustave Rouanet specifically cited gas clerks as a group that voted for the nationalists.[18] Changes in the union after 1900 also document the rightist stance of a great number of clerks. The union grew prodigiously owing to the encouragement and approval nationalist municipal councillors gave to it. By 1902, it had 1,200 members, 55 per cent of the office personnel. The influx forced Claverie to abandon all pretence to a leftist orientation. Deferring to the 'diverse opinions' in his enlarged organization, Claverie vowed to discontinue politics entirely and to focus exclusively on practical gains for clerks. His narrow mission succeeded in bringing 2 out of 3 employees into the union by 1905.[19]

Even neutrality was not sufficient for some enthusiastic nationalists. They challenged Claverie's leadership in 1903. Though the rightist movement was already on the wane in Paris, they nearly won. The nationalist slate scored a victory in the lighting section, where pay was the lowest and work most routinized.[20] Even here there were few 'proletarians of the pen'.

It does seem, then, that office clerks accompanied shopkeepers into the nationalist camp during the Dreyfus crisis – the closing of ranks which Mayer expected. And no more than shopkeepers were gas employees defenders of the status quo, pure and simple. In fact, nationalist clerks had the same work grievances as the early, presumably leftist, union members. In 1899, anti-union employees formed a 'Corporate Association of Gas Employees' and condemned colleagues 'who act like workers'. At the same time, the association made the same demands upon the PGC as the union. It called for 'an elevation of salaries by regular advancement and an absolute right to early and regular retirement'. Petitioners from the customer accounts service proclaimed that their 'dignity, love of their work, and respect for bosses' prevented them from joining the 'red' union. Yet, their 'respectful wishes' mirrored union demands for promotions by seniority, secure retirement rights and higher pay. The questioning of management's discretionary authority transcended preferences for the left or right.[21]

Gas clerks could vote for nationalist councillors in 1900 without fear that their interest in reducing arbitrary authority at the workplace would be jeopardized. Anti-Dreyfusard councillors had shown themselves quite sympathetic to the goals of the union, proclaiming the need for the gas monopoly to treat its personnel more generously. For a time they endorsed Claverie's syndicalist–corporatist proposal. As political realities forced them to create a new, private gas company to replace the PGC, rightist councillors made the union programme a condition for awarding the concession. Despite their frequent fulminations against *functionnaires*, nationalists sponsored the solution which employees finally settled upon, 'assimilation' into the personnel of the municipality.[22]

The good will which nationalist politicians showered on gas clerks is not surprising. The new majority comprised an eclectic group, including former radicals, socialists and plebeian street rebels. Their campaign platforms had contained attacks on monopolies and calls for returning the republic to the people. Among their number was none other than Patenne, elected as a 'patriotic socialist'.[23] Although the majority of nationalists ultimately betrayed their anti-capitalist rhetoric, gas clerks were well positioned to win preferential treatment. The Parisian public despised the PGC because of its notoriously high gas prices, its monopolistic profits and its indifference to the public interest. Nationalists realized that their well publicized effort to compel the hated firm to treat its agents more generously was a harmless way to bash *les gros* and champion *les petits*. Unionized employees were only too glad to exploit the image requirements of the nationalists. The clerks were in the privileged position of being able to vote as their conscience dictated – against Dreyfus, the Waldeck-Rousseau government and the corrupt republic – while enjoying favourable labour ordinances.

The rightist stance of most gas employees may not have been a foregone conclusion, but it was encouraged by their social background, material circumstances and political culture. The large majority of clerks were sons of property-owners, often shopkeepers. For all the employees' complaints about work, their alienation from their jobs was far from complete. Indeed, they expressed a commitment to their posts by spending their careers at the PGC. Most recruits had already passed through several jobs before arriving at the gas company, but once they entered the firm, they stayed. The rate of quitting was negligible.[24] The corporate director had once told union officials bluntly that 'if clerks could find more favourable positions, they would'. The statement was tactless, but it contained a large element of truth. The pay and personnel policies of the PGC were not notably worse than those of other large firms. The employees could expect secure jobs, pensions (management eventually made concessions on that matter), and the hope of ending their careers as assistant office heads. They did not have to endure a frenzied work

Nationalism and politics

pace nor iron discipline. And if a clerk had a son or nephew who needed a job, the company gave the applicant priority.

Mayer's notion of 'negative commonality' does apply to the gas clerks. The rank and file never sympathized with Claverie's desire to amalgamate with manual workers. Clerks insisted on the separate and superior needs of employees. Sharing a dining hall with wage-earners was a threat to their dignity. The clerks may even have developed a resentment of the workers' union as a result of competition with it for the favour of the company and the municipal council.

Gustave Rouanet's analysis of the 1900 election focused on the political culture of Parisians such as the gas clerks. He argued that economic interests were not the determining factor. Far more crucial was the skilful manipulation by the press of xenophobia, the cult of the army, anti-Semitism and the failures of the republic. Philip Nord's more recent and sophisticated appraisal shows how anti-Dreyfusard publicists refashioned the idioms of radical republicanism to make them useful to their cause.[25] Shopkeepers and office clerks had different economic grievances, but they defined their wider political concerns through a similar set of symbols and slogans.

This case study of office employees demonstrates that Mayer was correct, after all, about the inner core of conservatism of the lower middle class at the end of the nineteenth century. Capitalistic development had not driven a wedge between small property-owners and salaried clerks as a result of proletarianization. Though the unity was not visible in normal times, the crisis at the end of the century drew them together in Paris in defence of patriotic symbols and against collectivism. Theirs was not, however, a defence of a world made safe for a liberal elite. Shopkeepers and clerks shared a sense of victimization as 'little people' in a republic supposedly controlled by foreigners, Jews and faceless bureaucrats. The employees denied financial elites the right to exercise authority over working people in an arbitrary manner. The nationalist right spoke to their concerns. In the case of gas clerks, nationalist councillors even redeemed their promises.

Arno Mayer's affirmation of the durability of the lower middle class over the long run is beyond the scope of this study. It may be that the First World War, the huge influx of women workers into offices, and the world depression initiated such disorder as to rend the component groups asunder. That had not happened in the age of Dreyfus, however. The leftist stance of a few leaders, the expression of grievances about work and signs of alienation from authority relations on the job do not provide sufficient evidence of the polarization of the lower middle class. Parisian nationalists of 1900 never doubted their appeal to white-collar clerks, and they were correct to count on that constituency.

NOTES

1. Heinz-Gerhard Haupt and Geoffrey Crossick (eds), *Shopkeepers and Master Artisans in Nineteenth-Century Europe* (London: Methuen, 1984) is an excellent guide to the current state of the literature.
2. 'The lower middle class as historical problem', *Journal of Modern History*, 47 (1975), pp. 409–36. For commentary on this article, see Jonathan Wiener, 'Marxism and the lower middle class: a response to Arno Mayer', *Journal of Modern History*, 48 (1976), pp. 666–71.
3. *Paris Shopkeepers and the Politics of Resentment* (Princeton, NJ: Princeton University Press, 1986).
4. Archives de la Préfecture de Police (hereafter, APP), Ba 1523; A.-J.-M. Artaud, *La Question de l'employé en France* (Paris, 1909); Judith Wishnia, 'French *fonctionnaires*: the development of class consciousness and unionization, 1884–1926', unpublished PhD thesis, State University of New York at Stony Brook, 1977.
5. The 1,600 cartons of corporate papers are conserved in the Archives de Paris in series V 8 0^1.
6. Technically speaking, not all employees at the PGC were book-keepers. 'Employee' status entailed a special relation to the company rather than a specific sort of job. Among them were manual labourers with supervisory roles and uniformed agents who worked primarily outside the office.
7. Joan Scott, *The Glassworkers of Carmaux* (Cambridge, Mass.: Harvard University Press, 1974); Steven Kaplan and Cynthia Koepp (eds), *Work in France* (Ithaca, NY: Cornell University Press, 1986).
8. Guy Thuillier, *Bureaucratie et bureaucrates en France au XIXe siècle* (Geneva: Droz, 1980); Guy Thuillier, *La Vie quotidienne dans les ministères au XIXe siècle* (Paris: Hachette, 1976); Jean Tulard and Guy Thuillier, *Histoire de l'administration française* (Paris: Presses Universitaires de France, 1984).
9. The most useful documents on the regime of the *employés* are in Archives de Paris, V 8 0^1, nos 150–3, 156, 1081.
10. *L'Echo du gaz. Organe de l'Union syndicale des employés de la Compagnie parisienne du gaz*, no. 18 (16 December 1897), p. 1.
11. Archives de Paris, V 8 0^1, no. 153 (various reports).
12. ibid., no. 151 (various reports).
13. For an introduction to the general spirit of industrial reform, see Judith Stone, *The Search for Social Peace* (Albany, NY: State University of New York Press, 1985).
14. Archives de Paris, V 8 0^1, no. 154, 'Mesures prises par le Conseil municipal...'; *Procès-verbaux du Conseil municipal de Paris*, 30 December 1895.
15. Archives de Paris, V 8 0^1, no. 151, 'Syndicat des employés'.
16. Pierre Carcangues, *Le Mouvement syndicaliste réformiste en France* (Paris: Schleicher, 1912), pp. 24–48, 60–3.
17. Maurice Claverie, 'Une Expérience intéressante. Le Gaz aux gaziers', *La Revue socialiste*, 31 (1900), pp. 63–7.
18. 'Les Elections de Paris et le parti socialiste', *La Revue socialiste*, 31 (1900), p. 722.
19. *Echo du gaz* (1900–5).
20. ibid., no. 134 (15 October 1902); no. 155 (September 1903).
21. Archives de Paris, V 8 0^1, no. 150, 'Union corporative des employés du gaz'; no. 153, 'Les Employés non-syndiqués du bureau des recettes'.
22. *Echo du gaz* (1900–1); *Procès-verbaux du Conseil municipal de Paris*, 1900; APP, Ba 695, dossier: 'Elections de 1900'.
23. APP, Ba 1214, dossier: 'Patenne'.
24. Archives de Paris, V 8 0^1, nos 164–73 (personnel records).
25. Rouanet, 'Elections de Paris', pp. 716–32; Nord, *Paris Shopkeepers*, p. 386.

13

La république et la patrie: *the radicals' nationalism under attack*

Judith F. Stone

All nineteenth-century radicals identified militant republicanism as an essential element of French national identity. For politicians nurtured on Michelet and Hugo, the republic and the fatherland were indissolubly joined. No one better personified this union than the radical leader Camille Pelletan. In an 1899 campaign speech Pelletan passionately defended the genuine – in other words republican – patriotism of radicals and socialists against the false nationalism of the republic's latest critics. He was proud of his old beliefs which promoted the traditions of 1792. His 'blood boiled' to hear those who were the political heirs of the aristocratic *emigrés* criticize the loyalty of true patriots, sons of the revolution. Not unlike Barrès he paid homage to 'a material fatherland of native soil which has given us our life . . . and to which we owe the last drop of our blood'. But the fatherland was not only a physical reality; in addition there was a *patrie* of ideals in which all humanity shared. 'France is also . . . that glorious country which has given the world its men of genius . . . great literary figures . . . those who struggled against theocracy . . . It is the country of the eighteenth century . . . It is the country which revealed itself . . . with the sublime explosion of the French Revolution . . . and our sublime motto: *Liberté, Egalité, Fraternité*.'[1] This union of *la république et la patrie* found itself attacked in the first years of the twentieth century.

Since the late 1880s radicals, led most notably by Georges Clemenceau and Pelletan, had identified their nationalism with republican defence, even defence of the less than perfect Third Republic. By 1902 the radicals had become the largest group in the Chamber.[2] The shift from left-wing opposition to arbiters of parliamentary power created enormous strains among radical deputies, party militants and the growing radical electorate. It also generated new tensions between the radicals and their competitors to the right and to the left. Central in this transformation was a debate over what constituted genuine devotion to the nation. This issue was linked to concerns about state power and about the extent to which radical politicians would use their new parliamentary force to fulfil their reformist programmes. The nationalists asserted that the parliamentary regime and its most committed supporters, the radicals, were incapable of governing and defending the nation. Conservatives feared the consequences of the radicals' egalitarian ideals. How could a party so dependent on its electoral alliance with the socialists be trusted with real power, especially power over the military services? Similar questions of national defence and military preparedness surfaced among republicans and radicals themselves. An influential group of republican moderates and radical dissidents began to feel that the party would have to abandon some of the old slogans. A reevaluation of the relation between *la république et la patrie* must occur. This tension among radical parliamentarians contributed to an important redefinition of both nationalism and radicalism.

Uncertainty about the reliability and the programme of a radical government was at its height during the ministry of Emile Combes (1902–5). One of the most effective criticisms launched against this government was its alleged incapacity to defend the nation and to maintain France's military strength. The governing radicals were portrayed as dismantling the armed forces both materially and spiritually. It was claimed that discipline – the essence of all military organization – was being undermined by the government, the very authority which must uphold it. To understand these charges and their impact we must consider what the radicals were in 1902, and perhaps more importantly what they were perceived to be.

The election of 1902 was experienced as a critical confrontation between broad coalitions of right and left. The left associated itself with republican defence and the right with the protection of the church and the army. For weeks violent, confrontational rhetoric characterized the campaign.[3] The large number of seats won on the first round suggests that the electorate had recognized the ideological polarization despite the fact that few candidates presented clear programmes. The victory went to the left, but only by a small margin. Within the left, the recently formed radical republican and radical socialist party made the largest gains. A wave of popular enthusiasm greeted the left victory in May. Toasts, parades, demonstrations and occasional brawls with supporters of the defeated right all accompanied the announcement of radical success.[4]

The election resulted in a radical-dominated Chamber which supported the Combes government. Few governments of the Third Republic have been so closely tied to their parliamentary majority – one of socialists, radicals and a small group of moderate republicans – or so aware of the electoral coalition which stood behind these deputies. In an effort to satisfy moderate forces and allay the concerns of President Loubet, Combes asked Théophile Delcassé to continue in foreign affairs and appointed Maurice Rouvier, opponent of the graduated income tax, Minister of Finance. In order to balance these concessions to moderates and financial interests, Combes called on Camille Pelletan to become Minister of the Navy.

Pelletan spoke for the left of the party, had excellent relations with the socialists and was a popular, nationally recognized journalist. His appointment was intended to satisfy party militants and the electorate. He also had had considerable experience with naval affairs as the naval expert of the Chamber's budget commission. Almost immediately he became the most controversial member of the government.[5] In the summer of 1902 enthusiasm ran high for the new government and for Pelletan in particular.[6] Not surprisingly the socialist Francis de Pressensé cheered the Minister of the Navy, seeing his presence as a guarantee that the reform programme – separation of church and state, the progressive income tax, two-year military service and workers' pensions – would be enacted. Pressensé hoped that now there would finally be an authentically republican and radical ministry.[7]

Pelletan certainly intended to fulfil these hopes. He had an ambitious programme to upgrade and democratize the French fleet. He was anxious finally to implement policies which would introduce democratic values into the military services, thus fully incorporating them into the republican state. The navy would become a model republican service. The new minister was certain that such harmony among the state, the military and popular beliefs could only strengthen national defence and enhance France's military stature. He was equally convinced that the admiralty had failed miserably in its responsibilities, giving greater priority to privilege and rank than to national interest. Since the 1880s Pelletan had been an advocate of Admiral Aube and the Jeune École who argued for small ships capable of a mobile defence of the French coast.[8] Now at the rue Royale Pelletan planned to increase the number of submarines and torpedo boats, restrict the influence of the admiralty's *conseils supérieurs*, and reduce, if not eliminate, his predecessor's 1900 building programme, which had emphasized larger cruisers. By shifting authority from the military to civilians, greater power would be given to a representative of popular suffrage. The smaller crews of the new submarines and torpedo boats would lead to closer bonds between sailors and officers. The officers' impregnable authority and privilege would be further reduced by permitting sailors to appeal against officers' decisions to the civilian minister, by recruiting officers from the ranks, by eliminating all clerical personnel and religious ceremonies and by relaxing military discipline for arsenal workers.

All these policies raised an enormous furore; especially controversial were those applied to the arsenal workers. A ministerial circular introduced an eight-hour working day in the naval arsenals. Pelletan accepted the arsenal workers' union and met with its representatives, members of the CGT. There was considerable support for Pelletan among the workers. Unionized workers in Brest greeted the Minister of the Navy with 'Vive Pelletan', red flags and the 'International'.[9] His opponents were appalled; the naval establishment was convinced that anarchists were in control and that Pelletan was consorting with subversives. By November

1902 outraged contributors to the *Courrier maritime de France* were demanding Pelletan's resignation.[10] High-ranking naval officers would encourage their friends among moderate republicans and within the radical party itself to mount a campaign against Pelletan. But, before this powerful centrist opposition was fully mobilized, the nationalist right initiated its own strident attack against the minister whom they called a 'joke and a liar'.[11] While there was no coordination between these two distinct political groups, their criticisms amplified one another.

The nationalist and right-wing campaign lay primarily outside the Chamber of Deputies and polite political circles. The right-wing press reiterated their central theme: the French political system was decadent and all politicians were corrupt or corruptible. The parliamentary system, especially as defined in the constitutional laws of 1875, could never authentically represent the 'will of the people'. The dangerous new *féodalité financière* could easily buy deputies who then served the bankers' interests rather than those of the nation. This portrait of a prostituted republic contained a powerful combination of insurrectionary rhetoric, anti-capitalist slogans, shades of anti-Semitism and populist suspicion toward *les gros*. It was hurled at Camille Pelletan between 1902 and 1904 with particular vehemence. Pelletan was a preferred target since his republican nationalism during the 1870s and early 1880s had been shaped by the very rhetoric and criticisms which the nationalists now sought to monopolize.

As Minister of the Navy Pelletan found himself accused of behaviour ranging from espionage to venality, to fraud, to drunkenness.[12] None of these attacks was ever formally proven, but they circulated in the press, in the corridors of the Chamber and drifted into some of the capital's political salons. They convinced the already convinced that Pelletan was a menace to national security. They suggested to the uncertain that the Minister of the Navy was possibly a hypocrite, often a fool and perhaps even a drunken buffoon. Throughout 1903 Pelletan was forced to devote considerable time to defending his past and his character. The most damning and damaging scandal raged from the spring of 1903 to the spring of 1904. It connected Pelletan with one of the most spectacular fraud cases of modern France.[13] For at least a year the right had been waiting for the Humbert scandal to ripen into another Panama affair. The Humberts, awaiting trial for fraud since 1902, had had an exceedingly long list of connections with the republican political world: Thérèse Humbert had organized an important political salon; Frédéric had been a radical deputy; his father, Gustave, was considered one of the founders of the republic, having served as Freycinet's Minister of Justice.[14] Nonetheless in the summer and autumn of 1902 the criminal case, in which the Humberts were charged with borrowing tens of thousands of francs against the collateral of an entirely fictitious American inheritance, was not leading to a major political exposé. Then in the spring of 1903 came the allegation that Frédéric Humbert had suborned Camille Pelletan.[15] Finally the right could link corruption, fraud and hypocrisy to the controversial Minister of the Navy.[16] Furthermore, this information had been leaked by a functionary in the naval ministry, demonstrating opposition to Pelletan in his own service.

Responding to the accusation, Pelletan addressed a tumultuous Chamber on 28 May with an impassioned speech denouncing the 'monstrous calumnies' against him. He insisted that he had never received one centime for his support of Frédéric Humbert. He concluded with his own character defence, reminding the republican majority of his ardent convictions, his modest personal resources and the irreproachable legacy of his republican father.[17] The speech was effective. One journal reported that Pelletan left the podium 'surrounded, acclaimed and congratulated by all'; he received the Chamber's vote of confidence.[18]

Nonetheless, by November 1903 the unrelenting newspaper campaign created enough clamour for the Chamber to support the proposal of the Parisian nationalist deputy, Georges Berry, to create an extra-parliamentary commission of inquiry. The commission was charged 'to throw light on the involvement of politicians in the Humbert affair'.[19] Despite the presence of powerful spokesmen,[20] the right did not control the commission.[21] The investigation proceeded fitfully until February 1904 when the commission's majority concluded that no evidence pointed to the collusion of politicians in the Humbert fraud.[22] Strictly speaking this seems to have been the case although there were, as one deputy admitted, many 'private' connections.[23] Most of this information, including the details of Camille Pelletan's contacts with the Humberts,[24] was not made public or even widely disseminated among the political elite. There can be little question that the republican majority succeeded in squelching the general investigation of the Humberts' political ties, including those with the naval minister. A very large circle of republicans, well beyond the radicals, had had financial and/or social dealings with the Humberts.[25] Except for the extreme right, parliamentarians agreed to end the search for corrupt politicians connected with the Humberts.[26]

In the midst of the parliamentary inquiry into the Humbert Affair, during December 1903, right-wing circles and their press promoted yet another, even juicier Pelletan scandal, replete with sexual innuendos. A music-hall satire, *La Revue à poivre*, written by a young protégé of Edouard Drumont,[27] presented the antics of a ludicrous couple just returning from their wedding. Both were very drunk; the dishevelled, elderly groom stumbled about while the young bride danced the 'cake-walk'.[28] Everyone immediately recognized the Minister of the Navy and his new wife. Not only was Pelletan exposed as a 'degenerate', but even more damning in the bright lights of the boulevards he was revealed as laughably old and old-fashioned. This risqué farce sparked brawls between republican and anti-republican students. The censor suppressed the scene. The right delighted in its defence of free speech and artistic expression.[29] The radicals denounced the dissolute world of 'reactionaries, music halls and Montmartre cabaret filth'.[30] Republicans claimed to defend good taste, womanhood and French traditions.[31]

Initially, Pelletan and the radicals seemed to have emerged from these scandals relatively unscathed. Despite the variety of the nationalists' accusations, the supporters of the Bloc des Gauches had little difficulty in presenting themselves and believing themselves to be the defenders of the republic, the revolution and *la patrie* against their enemies. In May 1903 a key spokesman for the Bloc, Francis de Pressensé, predicted that the aspersions surrounding Pelletan would not unseat either the naval minister or the government. He characterized Pelletan's accusers as 'the party of order, the church, the army, property, and public morality caught in the act of dirty tricks, up to their elbows in the muck, agreeing with crooks, blackmailers and swindlers!'[32] Nonetheless, the extreme right's campaign of character assassination had not been entirely fruitless. Pelletan's political position and image had been tarnished.[33] In the press he had been portrayed as a hypocrite whose denunciations of *la féodalité financière* were mere posturings. The right had associated him with the flashy world of the nouveaux riches and Parisian salons, an awkward place for a man of the people. His ability to command the loyalty of subordinates at the Ministry of the Navy was in doubt. Most importantly this assault on Pelletan's character and integrity prepared the way for more powerful opponents who would take up *La Libre Parole*'s accusation that Pelletan was 'disorganizing and dishonouring the navy'. These republicans and moderate radicals would refrain, however, from calling him a 'stingy Huguenot'.[34]

The nationalist right had sought to reveal Pelletan as morally unfit to be associated with, let alone direct, a military service. In their view, his character, the product of radicalism and parliamentary experience, made him incapable of shouldering the serious and 'manly' responsibilities of the navy. Nationalists hoped to demonstrate the thorough incompatibility of the republic and the fatherland. On the other hand, moderate republicans, former radicals and moderates within the radical party aimed to update the relation between *la république et la patrie*. They focused on more tangible complaints about Pelletan's inefficiencies as an administrator and his pursuit of policies which weakened national defence. These politicians, wielding their significant power within parliamentary commissions, centrist political groups and the government majority, hoped to protect their associates in the naval hierarchy and industry from the minister's reforms. In some cases they feared for themselves and the radical party which they regarded as having become more vulnerable to the criticisms of the nationalists. More generally they experienced a deep uneasiness about the security of the republic and the nation should Pelletan's radicalism succeed.

Paul Doumer, Antoine de Lanessan and Edouard Lockroy led this group which opposed both Pelletan and the Bloc des Gauches. When they began this campaign all three were at least nominally radicals. Paul Doumer had been a minister in Léon Bourgeois's brief radical cabinet of 1895–6. He had then accepted Méline's offer of the governor generalship of Indo-China, quickly becoming an ardent advocate of colonialism. From 1900 on he held the position of vice president of the Union des Industries Minières et Métallurgiques, the steel and iron lobby. Long-time deputy from the northern department of Aisne, Doumer replaced Pelletan in 1902 as the president of the powerful parliamentary budget commission. Antoine de Lanessan had preceded Doumer as governor general of Indo-China in 1891 and had been one of the few radicals to serve in Waldeck-Rousseau's government as Minister of the Navy. He had secured a 1900 naval construction budget which mandated the expansion of the French fleet.[35] The most expensive items were eleven armoured and unarmoured cruisers which had been bitterly opposed by the then president of the budget commission, Camille Pelletan.[36] Edouard Lockroy had been Pelletan's colleague on the editorial board of the radical daily *Le Rappel*, but they had drifted apart by the 1880s. Despite radical losses in the capital Lockroy easily maintained his Parisian electoral support. He was welcomed by a variety of republican governments as a highly 'ministerial' radical first serving as Freycinet's Minister of Commerce (1886–7). In the governments of Bourgeois, Brisson (1898) and Dupuy (1898–9) he was Minister of the Navy and became a staunch advocate of the admiralty. As early as June 1902, police reports indicate that these politicians were actively encouraging journalists' attacks on the new Minister of the Navy and building opposition to his programmes within the Chamber.[37]

From their point of view Pelletan's ministry posed a set of serious dangers to closer associates, national interests and the republican state's ability to govern. Most immediately, Pelletan's efforts to block or reduce the naval building programme of 1900 clearly placed certain contracts in jeopardy[38] and upset established relations between the ministry and major suppliers.[39] Still more disturbing to parliamentary friends of the navy, Pelletan completely circumvented the admirals' power to control, or even influence decisions on naval construction and strategy. He simply refused to meet any of the naval *conseils supérieurs*, which he considered to be staffed with clerical and royalist enemies of the republic and therefore the nation.

For committed colonialists such as Doumer and de Lanessan, as well as the head of the colonial lobby, Eugène Étienne, there was no question that Pelletan endangered the existence of France's colonies, particularly Indo-China. Pelletan, unlike the radicals who now criticized him, had never renounced his anti-colonialism. In addition, his support for the Jeune École naval strategy with its emphasis on the mobile defence of the French coasts relegated the protection of distant Asian territories to a very low priority. The colonialists' fears were further exacerbated by the deterioration of international relations. The most concerted parliamentary attack against Pelletan took place immediately following the outbreak of the Russo-Japanese War, which revealed the naval weakness of France's major ally.[40] In early February 1904 moderate republicans met the president of the republic to point out the danger 'which Pelletan's presence posed in case of an international conflagration'.[41]

While these specific questions of international relations and vested industrial and colonial interests were pressing to Pelletan's republican critics, no issue was more important than that of the maintenance of authority and discipline within the navy. Police reports of late 1903 and early 1904 again and again identify 'disorganization and negligence' within the naval administration as the principal cause of anti-government sentiment among former members of the republican majority.[42] In the winter of 1903–4 the traditional radical critique of the military hierarchy as undemocratic seemed increasingly inappropriate to many moderate republicans and even some radicals. In their view, the radicals as a governing party could ill afford to question the loyalty of the French officer corps in a world of rapidly escalating international tension and domestic class conflict. A radical minister who called for a more democratic navy was viewed as a dangerous liability to the party, the state and the nation.

The major republican attack on Camille Pelletan came early in 1904 in the Chamber and especially in its commissions. Lockroy and de Lanessan, important members of the naval commissions, called for an inquiry into the state of the navy in the critical months of February and March. Questions of the Far East, the defence of Indo-China, the 1900 building programme, conditions in the arsenals and the state of reserve forces were all pursued. Although Lockroy in particular had an opportunity to express his criticisms, the final report of the naval commission was sympathetic to Pelletan.[43] It implied that he was the victim of an orchestrated rumour campaign in the press and the corridors of the Chamber. Nonetheless, uneasy about the crisis of the Russo-Japanese War, members of the Délégation des Gauches agreed that a special parliamentary commission should continue the investigation of the naval ministry.

This special commission developed the most serious and damaging condemnations of Pelletan's ministry and his conception of republican national interest. His most important opponents served on the commission. Paul Doumer, president of the budget committee, headed the inquiry; Lockroy and de Lanessan dominated the meetings. The most important testimony was taken in March 1904 while the special investigation of political complicity in the Humbert Affair was just winding down. In contrast to the nationalist right's sarcasm and search for moral outrage, the republicans' tone was one of gravity. Their concerns were the essentials of state power – cruisers, port construction, coal, naval supplies, boilers and colonies. Using testimony from French colonists and admirals, Lockroy accused Pelletan of not spending enough on ships and development (a rare complaint during the Third Republic).[44] In addition, evidence was given of insufficient reserves of troops and coal to support a French naval presence internationally, and particularly in the South China Sea. The expertise and experience of the admiralty were being ignored.[45] In one stormy session when Pelletan attempted to defend his policies on reserves, Lockroy sternly rebuked him, reminding him that he was faced with men experienced in naval matters. 'Truly one hears things here that are extraordinary.... Whom do you take us for? Do you think that we don't understand what reserves are? What you have done has never been done. The entire navy protests and I protest as well.... And please don't tell us any stories.'[46] Hardly the usual tone in which deputies addressed ministers during commission hearings.

Throughout his interrogation Pelletan maintained that, while disagreements about policy might exist, his procedures differed little from those of his predecessors and he was as committed as they had been to building a strong navy and national defence.[47] The real issue was his efforts to introduce greater democracy.[48] Pelletan declared, 'I have upset certain officers of the old school, but I have not encouraged insubordination. On the contrary, I have done everything to maintain the most strict discipline by giving the humble the right to air their grievances.'[49] *République et patrie* were indissolubly linked for Pelletan. A navy more responsive to the needs of sailors and arsenal workers would be a more effective military force. Only a genuinely republican navy could defend the republican state and nation.

For Pelletan the moment had not yet arrived to make peace with members of the military hierarchy. *He* was not the one undermining principles of discipline and devotion to the nation; rather his opponents were threatening a vital institution of the republic and undermining the authority of one of the highest representatives of the state. Pelletan described the circumstances:

> You see my situation. There has been a permanent inquest... into the activities of a man who, right or wrong, is nevertheless at the head of one of the most important military services of the nation.... It has been conducted, let me not say by outright treason or revolt, but rather by the removal of documents, indiscretions, the leaking of all sorts of information, by a campaign of semi-insurrection which has unfortunately found men to foment, encourage and exploit it.... Letters of military chiefs, perhaps disappointed in their ambitions... have been

revealed. This is certainly a novel way to develop the habits of good order and discipline.'[50]

Pelletan insisted that he must protect ministerial authority and prerogatives. He refused to turn over documents which dealt with the internal administration of the Naval Ministry, claiming that to relinquish them would place him under the surveillance of his subordinates and compromise the authority of his position.[51] That authority could not be violated; it was the authority of the state.

The most vocal members of the commission adamantly rejected Pelletan's assertions. In a concluding statement Edouard Lockroy claimed that the minister's refusal to turn over all documents irrefutably demonstrated the 'disorder and anarchy of his ministry'. In Lockroy's opinion Pelletan's testimony proved without doubt 'the lack of preparation for war [and] the failure to meet with the experts [i.e. the *conseils supérieurs*]'. Lockroy stressed the precarious situation of France's national interests and defence:

> We do not know what the European repercussions may be because of the events in the Far East.... We have a great colony there.... It is more vital than ever to prepare a battle plan, to place ourselves in a state of defence.... I do not want to say anything unfavourable about the honourable man who has appeared before us, *but* we do not have a chief of staff here whose authority and influence... could lead either colleagues or superiors.[52]

This damning evaluation by a former Minister of the Navy and fellow radical injured Pelletan's standing with the Chamber and his ability to carry out his responsibilities. Lockroy's conclusions were shared by at least Antoine de Lanessan, another former naval minister, Eugène Étienne, leader of the colonial lobby, and Paul Doumer. Nonetheless this powerful republican coalition failed to oust either Pelletan or the Combes government. The government survived the Chamber debate on the naval budget of 29–30 March 1904; Lockroy had been dissuaded from interpellating Pelletan. Police reports, which in mid-March had predicted the imminent collapse of the government on the Pelletan issue, concluded by late March that the Combes ministry and Pelletan had weathered a difficult period and the political waters were now calm.[53]

Genuine popular support for Combes and Pelletan existed outside the Chamber in the spring of 1904. It was this sentiment among republican and radical voters which probably accounted for Lockroy's decision not to interpellate Pelletan and explained other radicals' unwillingness to vote against the government. The elections of municipal councillors in May 1904 reconfirmed the radicals' success of 1902. Throughout the entire spring, at the time when the campaign against Pelletan reached its crescendo, the Combes ministry and especially Pelletan were inundated with messages of support from mayors, municipal councils, a broad range of political and fraternal organizations, trade unions and masonic lodges.[54] Those republicans and radicals who were leading the anti-Combes/anti-Pelletan campaign were often condemned. The *félicitations* of the Bouches-du-Rhône, Pelletan's department, addressed Combes and Pelletan as *citoyens ministres*; most closed with 'Vive la république sociale, démocratique et laïque'.[55] In late March, following the failure of the effort to unseat Pelletan, the Association Patriotique des Alsaciens-Lorrains de Provence congratulated the naval minister on his victory of which 'all true patriots could be proud'.[56] Pelletan's republican nationalism still had devoted followers.

Nonetheless, despite this support, the Combes ministry did eventually fall in January 1905, the result of a bitter controversy concerning the traditional avenues of military authority and discipline. The distinct campaigns of the nationalist right and the republican moderates against Pelletan and his reforms had well prepared the ground for the furore over army staffing which exploded in the autumn of 1904. In order to identify and promote republican officers, the Minister of the Army, General André, had relied on information supplied by masonic lodges. This revelation elicited an extraordinarily powerful protest. André resigned in November and Combes himself two months later.

The radicals of Pelletan's circle regarded the end of the Bloc des Gauches government as only a temporary setback, a view which the 1906 radical electoral victory seemed to confirm. However, the former Minister of the Navy and his supporters entirely underestimated the deep transformation which had begun within the new political elite. Although the three leading dissident radicals were expelled from the party by 1906, they had nonetheless expressed sentiments shared by segments of the radical electorate, by certain party stalwarts and by a growing number of radical deputies. Now that they were a governing party radicals had to redefine their principles. State power and authority, often viewed as synonymous with national interests, must be defended. In order to serve *la patrie*, some egalitarian and democratic principles might have to be reexamined. This emerging reconceptualization of *la république et la patrie* was in part the result of new parliamentary and electoral strength. But it was also a response to the mounting pressure from nationalists who despised the ties between republican parliamentarianism and the nation. With increasing stridency they insisted that the Third Republic itself was a threat to the integrity of the fatherland. These issues came into sharp relief during the controversy which surrounded Camille Pelletan's tenure as Minister of the Navy. Following his fall and that of the Bloc des Gauches government a significant and growing group of radical deputies and republican politicians found it easier to call for the reordering of political and ideological priorities within the non-socialist left in France. They emphasized national interests, the protection of state authority and social defence. The century-old ties between *république et patrie* had been loosened.

NOTES

Research for this chapter was made possible by awards from Western Michigan University. The American Council of Learned Societies supported travel to the April 1989 Cambridge conference on nationalism where an earlier version of this chapter was presented.

1. *Le Progrès du Loiret. Organe démocrate et républicain*, 18 June 1899.
2. Jean-Marie Mayeur, *La Vie politique sous la Troisième République, 1870–1940* (Paris: Seuil, 1984), pp. 185–6.
3. Madeleine Rebérioux, *La République radicale? 1898–1914* (Paris: Seuil, 1975), p. 56 and Mayeur *La Vie politique*, p. 185.
4. Police reports of May 1902, AN, F7 12541.
5. During the first weeks of the new government Pelletan criticized both his colleague, Rouvier, for his opposition to the income tax reform and the president of the republic for his plea of caution in implementing the campaign's reform commitments. Police report of Pelletan speech, Versailles, 30 June 1902, AN, MI 25359.
6. Police report, 10 August 1902, AN, MI 25359.
7. *L'Aurore*, 1 July 1902.
8. Paul Baquiast, 'La Jeune-École de la Marine Française, La Presse et l'opinion publique', unpublished paper, Universitè de Paris IV, 1987, pp. 107–9.
9. Police report, 7 July 1904, AN, F7 13638. This enthusiasm, however, did not prevent the first arsenal workers' strike in November 1904. The strike over wages was settled fairly quickly, but Pelletan had threatened to fire the strikers.
10. *Le Courier maritime de France*, 11 November 1902.
11. Paul de Cassagnac, 'L'Anarchie', *L'Autorité*, 1 July 1902 and Henri Rochefort, 'La Révolte au sérail', *L'Intransigeant*, 1 July 1902.
12. In one instance Pelletan had employed a Swiss engineer to advise on the development of a new submarine. Not only was he Swiss, but he had also been a Dreyfusard, which was clear evidence for the right that Pelletan had introduced a German spy into the Ministry of the Navy (*La Libre Parole*, 5 January 1903). Another paper uncovered a story which dated back to the 1890s when Pelletan's long-time companion pawned some jewellery and misrepresented herself as Mme Pelletan. *L'Intransigeant*, 29 October 1902 and 16 January 1903.
13. Benjamin F. Martin in *The Hypocrisy of Justice in the Belle Epoque* (Baton Rouge: Louisiana State University Press, 1984) devotes a long chapter to this fascinating case.
14. ibid., pp. 82–6.
15. The assertion first appeared in the moderate republican journal, *Le Figaro*. The paper and its influential editor had been important supporters of Waldeck-Rousseau's government which preceded Combes'. After 1902, however, *Le Figaro* endorsed republican opposition to the Bloc des Gauches. Because of the close ties between the paper and Waldeck, rumours circulated that it was Waldeck-Rousseau himself who had encouraged the attack on Pelletan. Pierre Sorlin, *Waldeck-Rousseau* (Paris: Colin, 1966), pp. 459–60 and police report, no. 148, AN, C3717.
16. *Le Soleil*, 29 May 1903.
17. *Journal officiel*, Chambre des Députés, Débats, 28 May 1903.
18. *Gil Blas*, 29 May 1903.
19. Report of the special parliamentary commission on the Humbert Affair, 20 November 1903, AN, C7313.

Nationalism and politics

20   In addition to Berry, Gabriel Syveton of the Ligue de la Patrie Française was a member of the commission.
21   Special commission meeting, 8 November 1904, AN, C7313.
22   Report of the special commission, 23 December 1903, AN, C7314.
23   Rouanet, special commission meeting, 8 November 1903, AN, C7316.
24   Between November 1899 and January 1902 Frédéric Humbert regularly paid Pelletan sums which totalled fr. 16,900. Humbert *agenda* and *série de caisse*, special commission, AN, C7315.
25   All republicans of all varieties had been invited to Thérèse Humbert's salon. The Humberts also associated with the aristocratic staff of the Russian embassy and donated to Catholic charities. Paul Deschanel, a leading moderate republican, seriously courted the Humberts' daughter, Eve. Humbert correspondence, special commission, AN, C2317.
26   The Humberts themselves were convicted of fraud and each served a five-year sentence at hard labour. After their release there is no record of their activities. Martin, *Hypocrisy*, pp. 142–3.
27   *La Libre Parole*, 20 December 1903. The playwright, Paul Lafargue had some connections with the political elite; his father had been Casimir-Perier's secretary-general.
28   *La Libre Parole*, 20 December 1903; *Le Figaro*, 20 December 1903; *Le Gaulois*, 20 December 1903; *La République française*, 20 December 1903; *L'Aurore*, 20 December 1903; *La Lanterne*, 21 December 1903. Some accounts had the 'bride' doing the cancan.
29   *Le Gaulois*, 20 December 1903.
30   *L'Aurore*, 20 December 1903.
31   *La Lanterne*, 21 December 1903.
32   *L'Aurore*, 31 May 1903.
33   The damage from the Humbert Affair, however, did not end Pelletan's career as Martin concludes, *Hypocrisy*, p. 147. In 1906 Pelletan was reelected to the Chamber by his largest plurality and then elected president of the radical party.
34   Jean Diault, *La Libre Parole*, 20 December 1903.
35   Baquiast, 'La Jeune École', p. 96.
36   Police reports frequently commented on the long feud between de Lanessan and Pelletan. It was rumoured that Pelletan encouraged candidates to run against de Lanessan in Lyon during the 1902 election. 21 October 1901, AN, MI 25359. In the 1906 election de Lanessan was defeated and his leadership of the anti-Pelletan campaign was an important issue.
37   19 June 1902, 16 December 1902, 28 December 1902, AN, MI 25359.
38   Deputies from the maritime departments of the Gironde were especially concerned about the impact of such cutbacks in their districts. ibid., and Baquiast, 'La Jeune École', p. 87.
39   Police report, 22 November 1902, AN, MI 25359.
40   Pelletan had never been an enthusiastic supporter of the Franco-Russian alliance of 1893. One German paper reported that the press campaign against the naval minister was funded by the Russian foreign office. *Frankfurt Gazette*, 22 March 1904.
41   Police report, 11 February 1904, AN, MI 25359.
42   Police reports, 1 October 1903, 23 February 1904, AN, F7 12553.
43   Naval commission, 16 April 1904, AN, C7258.
44   A slowdown of construction in the Tunisian port of Bizerte was an especially contested issue. Report on Bizerte given to the special commission on the navy, 16 March 1904, p. 3, AN, C7283; report on Bizerte, 18 March 1904, p. 17, AN, C7283.
45   Special commission on the navy, 16 March 1904, AN, C7283.
46   ibid., pp. 66/149.
47   ibid., 15 March 1904, p. 43.
48   ibid., p. 51.
49   ibid., p. 154.
50   ibid., pp. 65–6.
51   ibid., pp. 69–70.

52 ibid., 24 March 1904, p. 5 (italics added).
53 Police reports 1, 18 and 29 March 1904, AN, F7 12553.
54 Gérald Baal, 'Combes et la république des comités', *Revue d'histoire moderne et contemporaine* (April–June 1977), pp. 260–85.
55 Groupe Républicain Radical et Radical Socialiste de Salon, 20 January 1904, AN, AP 73/3.
56 This was the second of five letters sent by this fervently patriotic organization based in Marseille between 15 March and 31 December 1904. 1 April 1904, AN, AP 73/3.

14

Dividing and uniting: sports societies and nationalism, 1870–1914

Pierre Arnaud

The history of sporting nationalism is linked as much to the development of the sporting movement (as it became increasingly autonomous and international) as to changes in French society. In opposition to the myth of sport as an eternally unifying factor, and an instrument of peace and brotherly feeling between peoples, is its image as a warlike activity, quick to glorify the national identity. Sporting nationalism, seen as chauvinist but basically well-meaning, has a darker aspect in its extreme form – aggressive, xenophobic and even racist – and this contrast accounts for the disparity in the forms of sporting nationalism.

There were two distinct cycles in the history of sporting nationalism: the first was that of national-patriotic mobilization, in the golden age of military training clubs (1870–89); the second, from 1905, glorified patriotic union based on fierce ideological rivalry (a sort of unity through division). But the appearance of athletic sports from about 1880, and their gradual federalization and internationalization, introduced a break in nationalist discourse, for reasons most probably concerned with the opposition between sporting and military training ideology. Under these conditions, sport seemed to divide more than unite, while still contributing to the mobilization of the masses. The history of sporting nationalism, for this short period, was part of social and political history, the main events of which are described below.

The defeat of Sedan was followed by the republicans gaining power, leading to a desire for revenge clearly shown by Gambetta's speech: 'gymnasts and military men must be placed alongside teachers everywhere, so that our children, our soldiers, our fellow citizens are all able to carry a sword, handle a rifle ... bravely withstand all trials for the Fatherland.'[1] Ten years later Jules Ferry, at the federal festival of the Union des Sociétés de Gymnastique de France (USGF) held in Reims, praised the educational and patriotic role of the gymnastics, shooting and military instruction clubs:

> gymnastics is inseparable from military training, the latter being the end, the former the means ... we believe that military training will

not become a full part of scholastic practices until the teacher himself has become a teacher of military exercises.[2]

For the first time in the history of France, there was a political desire to organize and control the physical, military, civil and moral training of the young. This integral educational project became a reality when the republicans came to power in 1879. Applied in the context of a complete reorganization of teaching programmes, it achieved its greatest success through private initiative. Men such as Paul Bert, Jules Ferry and Ferdinand Buisson held it to be the only way of restoring France's image in the world. Had not the Prussian schoolteacher won the war of 1870?[3] In this period of national identity crisis, the idea was to mould each Frenchman into a future soldier, to regenerate the race and make it more virile, particularly in the aftermath of the Commune, when internal peace had to be maintained, the French people reconciled to one another and the safety of the frontiers guaranteed.[4]

It is difficult nowadays to appreciate the fervour and mobilization this type of message could produce unless three elements are considered: patriotism and nationalism were to become 'unique factors unifying a whole people',[5] and would bring about 'the nationalization of the masses', which was vital to the strengthening of republican institutions. For Zeev Sternhell, the republican ideal was based on patriotic feeling, civic virtues, bracing vigour and military training.[6] But it is difficult to comprehend this enthusiasm without taking into account the fact that the military training clubs had benefited greatly from the financial support of the leaders of the Third Republic – the highest-ranking politicians, ministers, deputies, senators, municipal representatives, and so on. The 'sporting movement' was largely concerned with military training between 1870 and 1914. In 1911 the sporting clubs had attracted about 2 or 3 per cent of the population, representing some 900,000 members, more than half of whom were from military training clubs.[7] Another important phenomenon was that, while athletic sports (associated with the Union des Sociétés Françaises de Sports Athlétiques (USFSA)) were growing in popularity chiefly in urban and industrial areas, the military training clubs were being set up all over the country, including rural areas, even though some departments were uninvolved. The figures available for some of the towns and departments show that, between 1870 and 1914, their growth was very rapid: for example, from 4 to 142 military training clubs in Meurthe-et-Moselle, from 4 to 190 in Rhône, from 4 to 76 in Doubs.[8] This growth was not uniform or continuous and sometimes met with cultural resistance or republican political opposition, but it is still accurate to say that 'nationalist fervour' largely corresponded to 'military training fervour'.

This first cycle was characterized by a series of political decisions that largely fuelled, then supported national patriotic mobilization. The first of these was the integration of gymnastics and military training into teaching programmes by the law of 27 January 1880, followed by the establishment of the school battalions in the decree of 6 July 1882. These two decisions illustrated the political desire to regenerate the race and prepare from childhood for eventual military service. But the failure of the school battalions, which disappeared gradually from 1889, and the criticisms levelled at them during 1884 and 1885, led to their transformation into gymnastics, shooting and military training clubs. From that time onwards, such clubs became the link between schools and the army, and formed a teaching network, the role of which in the acculturation of the masses has been clearly shown.[9]

Republican and patriotic propaganda were strongly supported by important political figures. Although the club members were of modest means and relatively young – military training clubs had large schoolboy sections – they were, in fact, placed under the direction of leaders elected from among the older and more prominent members of society: politicians, high-ranking military men, professionals, and so on. The orthodoxy of the republican opinion held by both members and leaders was guaranteed by police inquiry.[10] Despite the officially apolitical character of these clubs, the leaders were exponents of republican ideology. There is no shortage of evidence of the close collaboration between the republican government and military training clubs: between 1875 and 1892, for example, all competition festivals held by the USGF were presided over by the most eminent politicians of the republic, including ministers and even the president of the republic in person. This close link between politics and the military training clubs suffered during crises in French political life.

The Boulanger Affair rang the death knell for Jacobin patriotism and nationalism inherited from Déroulède. The politicization of the USGF, resulting from its brief alliance with the Ligue des Patriotes (between 1882 and 1887) led to breakaway movements being formed. From 1887, in the Ain and then the Rhône, as well as other departments, the military training clubs underwent a transformation within the Unions Patriotiques, initiated by local worthies. From then on, the leaders of the regional federations, whether or not they were affiliated to the USGF, felt obliged to maintain a show of apoliticism confining themselves to patriotic militancy and, in Raoul Girardet's phrase, 'defensive nationalism'.

This national patriotism based on military training can be characterized by two trends. One was typically warlike, xenophobic, chauvinist and hot-blooded and fuelled by propaganda from the militants of the Ligue des Patriotes. The USGF was briefly involved in this tendency, in the name of revenge and the recapture of the lost provinces. Nationalist and patriotic themes were mixed so as to raise national consciousness, firmly rooted in the cult of memory. This type of mystical nationalism, represented by the charismatic figure of Déroulède, became so extreme as to endanger the republic. The USGF could certainly have provided the Ligue with stormtroops, but had the foresight to dissociate itself from an undertaking that would certainly have compromised it irrevocably; J. Sansboeuf, president of the Ligue des Patriotes until December 1887 became president of the USGF the following year. The other trend was more moderate, and took its inspiration from the French Revolution. The year 1889 provided an opportunity for military training clubs all over France to embrace republican ideals. These were less nationalist than patriotic, and true republicans could not but be patriots. They were citizen-soldiers, whose image overlapped with that of the revolutionary armies of 1792. This phenomenon was all the more apparent because 1889 saw the three-year military service law voted in for all Frenchmen. The gymnast thus became the living symbol of resistance to the oppressor, of freedom won and regained through struggle, and was the ideal presented as an example to a population still in need of inspiration.

This form of nationalism was defensive, but the question of whether, in 1889 and the years following, it was truly warlike and xenophobic is not so easy to answer. Indeed, such a view seems doubtful, if the remarks of leaders of military training clubs and the triumphal reception for the Czech Sokol gymnasts in Paris and Lyon in 1894 are considered. Inspired by the revolutionary philosophy of 1789, military training patriotism after 1889 was closer to pacifism than belligerence and even to socialist and revolutionary ideology: N. Cuperus, founder of the Fédération Européene de Gymnastique in 1881, established close links with the leaders of the USGF. According to R. Barrul, he was politically 'advanced', and participated in the First Workers International in London in 1864.[11] The military training clubs were certainly patriotic if their mottoes and aims were anything to go by. But they were just as attached to such ideals as work, peace, comradeship and brotherhood as they were to military ceremonial, national emblems and symbols: music, flags and uniforms. Important to the understanding of this complex amalgam is the fact that the gymnasts' patriotism was one of action: 'There are better things to do for a virile nation than exploit sensitivity and patriotism with pictures of women in tears, representing our lost provinces.'[12] Gymnastics was intended to glorify virile strength, and the imminent regeneration of the race.

The Boulanger Affair and the commemoration of the centenary of the French Revolution did not facilitate the development of an anti-republican, right-wing military training nationalism. Between 1870 and 1903, the year the Fédération Gymnastique et Sportive des Patronages de France (FGSPF) was formed, the opponents of the republican regime, particularly those involved with the church, still had no sporting clubs of their own. In Lyon, for example, the Catholics formed only one gymnastics club in 1887, and that was about the only one up to the turn of the century. The year 1889

Nationalism and politics

marked a break in the history of sporting associations in France: in addition to the gradual disappearance of the school battalions, the passing of the law on universal male military service and the creation of the USFSA signalled the arrival of a relatively stable form of moderate patriotism, until 1905. This could indicate the growth of socialism in these clubs, so largely frequented by manual and white-collar workers, but various signs show that feelings of patriotism and Germanophobia were on the decline.[13]

The unity called for by Gambetta, which was reflected in the military training clubs' embrace of republican values, soon yielded to the divisions caused by France's internal and external politics.

Attract in order to convert, for the good of the fatherland – this could have been the motto of the clericals as well as the republicans. The stakes were high: to win over the young, through education, and gather them under the partisan banner. Games, gymnastics, military instruction and sport were the preferred weapons of a war which would contribute to patriotic mobilization 'once school was out'. The creation of the FGSPF in 1903 corresponded, according to M. Lagrée, to the appearance of a new form of nationalism in which love of the church led to a new type of mystical patriotism which would support and enliven national patriotism.[14] From 1898, a muscular Catholicism grew up and was encouraged by the leaders and prominent members of the ecclesiastical hierarchy.

The development of Catholic sport was definitely related to anti-clericalism. The FGSPF consisted of about 1,500 clubs in 1914, assembled into 27 regional unions, with a membership of 150,000 (thus, in metropolitan France, a number equivalent to that of the USGF). It was the keystone of a whole network of institutions opposed to the post-scholastic organizations of the secular republic. The big gymnastics festivals thus added a new type of Catholic gathering to the pilgrimages and eucharistic congresses.[15] The growth of the FGSPF after 1905 is impressive: 234 clubs in 1907, 480 in 1908, more than 1,000 in 1911, and 1,250 at the beginning of 1912.[16]

The second cycle of the national-patriotic drive took place between 1905 and 1914 and was given an unintentional boost by the republican government in the form of the law on liberty of association (1 July 1901) and, after 1907, by the creation of school and post-school shooting clubs, instigated by the Ministry of Public Instruction. The FGSPF set about increasing the number of these clubs, competing with its rivals on the same grounds: ideological defence and the glorification of patriotism – without ever making it clear which had priority.[17] This competition to win over the young resulted in fierce opposition between secularists and Catholics, with the formation of a 'clerical' club resulting in a 'republican' club being set up, and vice versa. The aim, on both sides, was to remove the young from the insidious influence of the other side. *Le Progrès* of

Lyons (45 October 1913), stated that 'The church wants everything, soul and body... to attract the young, the church knows how to create an attractive, modern image. Its motto is, make them play to pray.' This is clearly a comment on the introduction of games and sport within Catholic parish groups, which constituted a powerful weapon against the secular movement. The republicans had to defend themselves against the offensive dynamism of the Catholic organizations and sporting and gymnastic clubs. This is shown by the reports submitted by E. Petit each year to the Minister of Public Instruction.[18] The influence of the FGSPF was certainly not uniform throughout the country, nor was its popularity inevitably linked to the intensity of religious practice or, conversely, to that of anti-religious feeling. In the Rhône department, for example, less than one-third of sports clubs belonged to the Catholic Fédération du Rhône.

How could a movement so much smaller nationally than the secular and republican federations have had such an important influence? The FGSPF derived its dynamism from its defence of religion: it concentrated on developing a recruitment network for young people between school and their military service. Although its ideology was rather shaky, it was on safer ground socially and patriotically: 'to be a christian certainly, but also to be a citizen.'[19] From this point of view, the social themes of Catholic mobilization were hardly different from those of the republican and secular military training clubs, hence the success of the values of solidarity, mutualism and thrift.

Nonetheless, sport, gymnastics and military training remained the preferred instruments of mobilization in the name of God and country (the FGSPF motto). Religion was easy to associate with nationalism and patriotism, while glorifying a youth that demonstrated its religious enthusiasm at a time when the new century was marked by the crisis of Catholicism. The ostentatious celebration of the feast of Joan of Arc was the ideal occasion, providing a symbol of both faith and patriotism. This was the point made by E. Aynard to the Chamber, when submitting a report suggesting that the second Sunday in May should be adopted as the national festival.[20] The moment was a good one: the international situation was tense and Poincaré's government was reviving a bill drawn up 18 years previously, to establish the anniversary of the deliverance of Orleans as a national holiday ('patriotism day'), and for many French people, Joan of Arc was the symbol of national unity. Patriotism was easily nourished with themes of racial regeneration, physical and moral development, and all in the name of France, while Dr Michaux, President of the FGSPF, judged to have been weakened: 'whatever party they adhere to, all who still love their fatherland and worry about the defence of the nation agree on the sad reality – France is weakened, its birth rate is dropping, its mortality rate rising.'[21] Germans, Swedes and Czechs served as examples for the FGSPF:

'Most of our strength is being drawn from this association of physical, moral, religious and patriotic education.'[22] These themes were taken up by the Catholic press and developed in a sometimes rather curious way during the gymnastic and sporting demonstrations by the FGSPF:

> All great ideas, and all the loftiest sentiments need to be expressed with a symbol. The flag is the symbol of the fatherland and carries with it all the aspirations and traditions of the French soul. White for the memory of past glories, the colour of Joan of Arc and St Louis; blue for the city of Paris and its motto . . .; Red, colour of the future and of Lyons.[23]

The gymnastics competitions were propaganda for the defenders of a muscular and conquering faith, supported by political and religious networks. In the special atmosphere of the years 1905 to 1914, it was no surprise that the rivalry between republican and Catholic gymnasts was an occasion for real pitched battles, which were sometimes bloody if not deadly. The liveliness of nationalist and patriotic feeling was not solely the province of the USGF, therefore. Although such feeling expressed a consensus of sorts, the deep divisions that existed between competing ideologies should not be forgotten. Although Catholic gymnasts were 'affirming their Christian feelings, as energetic Catholics', they did so in the name of 'Christ and our beloved country', while the republicans celebrated or commemorated the values they had inherited from the French Revolution. The latter did not have a monopoly on patriotism, however, which was a powerful mobilizing force in the early 1910s, when the threat of German invasion was growing stronger. Related sporting clubs found that their competitions provided an opportunity to try out their mobilization exercises and build up patriotic feeling through the unified effort. From this point of view, the combination of 'sabre and holy-water sprinkler' was equalled only by that of 'sword and schoolbook'. Marches, processions and flags were the visible symbols of support for the fatherland (which constituted a worthy and legitimate theme for union, and one which was socially and politically acceptable), but also for God, the republic or secularism (which were the dividing, contentious themes that were at stake in these gatherings, and the cause of confrontations). This cult of patriotism contained connotations of both religion and militarism that accentuated the ceremonial aspect of the demonstrations, and apparently smoothed over the most irreconcilable differences. Patriotism and nationalism were never so well expressed as in the popular gatherings for gymnastic contests – before they were faced with their ordeal by fire.

Military training clubs, associated with the USGF, the UST, or the two national federations of military training clubs, to which must be added the 'confessional' federations, the FGSPF and the secularist groups of the

LFE, did not represent all sporting associations. There were also the clubs devoted to traditional games – bowls, skittles, *boule*, blowpipe, and so on, and occupational/recreational societies – life-saving, swimming – the members of which were for the most part manual and white-collar workers. All these clubs shared most of the values of the military training clubs, accurately reflecting the fact that, at the turn of the century, the workers were attached to the practice of mutual help, solidarity, fraternity and patriotism.[24] Physical exercise during leisure time was still influenced by the values applied to work, with corporate or socio-professional links being developed. The aim was almost always to improve the race, and develop physical attributes so as to make good soldiers and citizens, and to bring these objectives closer by organizing festivals, the edifying nature of which could not be missed. Even swimming was brought into the military training context, as with the creation of the Société Lyonnaise de Natation in 1833 (motto: Hygiene, Fatherland, Humanity), which was intended to teach young people to swim in order 'when the time comes, to swim across the Rhine'.[25]

Such ambitions were not common in the middle-class and aristocratic clubs, although there must have been exceptions, in particular the Club Alpin Français, whose motto 'Pour la Patrie, par la montagne', was very similar to that of the Ligue de l'Enseignement's 'Pour la Patrie, par le livre et par l'epée'.[26] These middle-class clubs became gradually more exclusive as the practice of sport was popularized and democratized; cycling is a good example.[27] The clubs for 'academic arts', such as fencing and archery, and 'mechanised sports', such as regatta sailing, were still popular with the wealthy and the intellectual elite. But the heads of these clubs and of their guardian federation soon became anxious to instil into their activities a competitive logic, in which the values of individualism and human, technical and technological development could be combined with innovation and economic competitiveness. The aims of patriotism and solidarity never featured in the statutes of these clubs, and were not mentioned by their leaders, although this did not prevent them from taking part in 14 July celebrations, such as the regatta on the Saône at Lyon. The challenge, the game, and the competition were the driving force for the progress of man and machine.

Athletic sports, also known as 'English' or 'outdoor' sports, are of particular importance. Although they appeared late (between 1870 and 1882 in Paris, in about 1888 in Lyon, and after 1890 in most provincial towns), their popularity grew dramatically and contributed to the increasingly sporting element in traditional games and military training practice from 1900 to 1905.[28] The founding of the USFSA and the dissemination of the first rules for athletic sports (31 January 1889) introduced a new relationship between sport and nationalism. This federation, formed during the hygienists' campaign (1887–90) engaged in the promotion,

Nationalism and politics

inspired by P. de Coubertin and G. de Saint Clair, of so-called sporting practices, which were actually anti-gymnastic in many respects. Games, competition, risk, the desire to surpass oneself and others, progress and willing discipline based on the respect of rules formed the basis of an entirely new image of hygiene, the pursuit of human perfection and the physiology of exercise, based particularly on the work of F. Lagrange and E. J. Marey. For de Coubertin, sport remained 'the pleasure of the strong', and was to contribute to racial regeneration. Influenced by Le Play, he wanted the youth of France to become 'bronzed again' and to make sport 'a leaven of international peace'. It is easy to imagine that this bard of the Olympic spirit was not impressed by the Déroulède-style *patriotards*.[29] But whether it follows that the sportsmen of the USFSA were neither patriots nor nationalists is quite another question, and one that requires careful and nuanced answers.

A thorough scrutiny of *Lyon-Sport* (newsletter of the USFSA regional committee, which was published regularly between 1898 and 1939) reveals no patriotic or nationalist leaning. The governing bodies of the USFSA seem to have restricted themselves to propaganda for athletic sports, and hence mark themselves off from the patriotic clubs. But as Spivak points out, athletic sports clubs were never supported by the republican government,[30] which only backed the military training clubs. Thus the USFSA had to depend solely on private backing in its development. Moreover, de Coubertin's ambitions were made clear from the outset: sport should become an instrument of peace and understanding between peoples. It was to this end that, from 1886 onwards, international competitions were organized, and the Olympic Games were revived. At a time when international tension was mounting, to preach international peace on the playing fields certainly required tremendous optimism, or possibly a huge lack of understanding. De Coubertin was an idealist: 'sport is intended to strengthen, not to militarize'[31] was an absurd belief at a time when the Ministry of War controlled sporting policy.

Although most international sporting events met with total indifference,[32] the period between 1910 and 1914 saw the development of a new type of sporting nationalism that, to some extent, paved the way for what emerged between the two world wars, both in Italy and Germany. A number of observations should be made on this subject. First, this burgeoning of sporting nationalism took place as both politicians and public became painfully aware of the imminence of war. Franco-German tension over Morocco and the Franco-Russian-British entente contributed to an increase in belligerent nationalism. Second, these circumstances no doubt explain the appearance of a number of studies into French youth. Benneton suggests that this was intended to offer a reassuring picture, for adults at least, of youth (soon to constitute the French army) symbolizing the rebirth of French pride.[33] Third, the organization of the Olympic

Games in Stockholm in 1912, at which the French performance was very disappointing, may explain in part the birth of a sporting nationalism fuelled by the desire for revenge.

In reality, it was propagandists and not sportsmen who saw the Olympic results as damaging the nation's prestige. The victory of Georges Carpentier over Bombardier Billy Wells in 1913, widely covered by the press, gave reason to hope, and victory in the stadium was seen to augur well for victory soon to be achieved on other fields of battle. From there it was only a small step to establishing links between sporting ideology and that of Action Française, or relating the spirit of competition to a kind of social Darwinism, and even finding justification for applying the theories of Vacher de Lapouge and Gustave Le Bon to sporting achievement. A number of intellectuals took this step.[34]

The reaction of nationalists to the relative failure of the French at Stockholm is one of ill disguised disappointment, particularly at the defeat of J. Bouin. Reference by journalists to a sporting Waterloo, and calls for revenge – France came sixth with 17 medals, just behind Germany – are indicative of the general feeling. Some journalists called for radical measures to ensure better physical and moral training for French athletes; the next Olympic Games were to take place in Berlin in 1916: 'will we display our weakness before the very eyes of our hereditary enemy?'[35] Taking a more reasoned line, many commentators attributed the poor results to the lack of preparation of the French athletes; for years the Americans had shown what was needed to win medals. The formation of the College d'Athlètes at Reims, on 1 April 1913, answered this patriotic and eugenic need to train a sporting elite in a kind of human training stable.[36] Thus, for the first time, a kind of 'medal race' was undertaken, justified by nationalism in the interest of restoring French prestige.

But this nationalism had very little in common with patriotism, nor was it an official expression of the state: sport had not yet become the emblem or shop-window of a political regime. It was more an emotional sporting nationalism, based on simple assumptions concerning the pre-eminence of the race, its power and the moral qualities of the victorious nations – in this case Sweden and the USA. This was an intellectuals' nationalism, with the sportsmen who actually performed sharing very little of this specious reasoning.

Just before the war broke out, most people still regarded sport as an instrument of peace. Although the USFSA represented only about a fifth of the membership of all the sporting clubs – about 200,000 members for some 30 regional committees and about 1,200 associations, the audience it reached through newspapers and reviews such as *La Vie au Grand Air* and *L'Auto*, and through large national and international competitions, was far greater than any stadium could hold. None of the international competitions ever resulted in nationalist disturbances, even during diplomatic crises.[37] For example, *La Vie au Grand Air* (25 June 1910) published an article on sporting relations between France and Germany. André Glarner, the winner of the 400 metres at the 'Olympic' meeting at Frankfurt, stated that 'The Germans were worthy of their reputation. The courtesy with which they received us and applauded our victories was very noticeable, and gave us hope that a match between France and Germany will soon be scheduled in our athletic calendar.' But the political calendar contained other fixtures!

That indefatigable promoter of sporting internationalism, de Coubertin, found other unexpected allies. He called on the FSGSPF, and in particular Charles Simon, to spread the Olympic ideal in the secularist circles he thought were most resistant.[38] The progressive democratization of athletic sports eventually won over politicians, even persuading a timid socialist party to form a Fédération Sportive Athlétique Socialiste (FSAS) in 1908.[39] From then on the pacifist and anti-militarist theories of the socialist party and the trade unions found a new area of application. Internationalism and pacifism found in sport a means of mutual strength since the Olympic Games organized in London in 1908 during the international exhibition had an ever increasing audience, even in the midst of Franco-German tension. *L'Illustration* (8 July 1908) was not afraid to proclaim that it was a scene of 'peaceful struggles'.

Eventually, just before the outbreak of war, sport seemed torn between contradictory tendencies. On one hand, it was seen as a pawn of extreme nationalism, though this was certainly the work of journalists and intellectuals who stoked up the fires of a 'sporting war' within the Olympic Games. On the other hand, it could be seen as an instrument of peace between nations: this view was upheld by sports ideologists and the Socialist International, who came together from widely different starting points. But the facts were far from simple: *L'Humanité* on 15 November 1913 called for a 'revenge for Stockholm' while calling for the means to 'specialize to the hilt'.

A single example shows up this ambiguity: all the major international meetings, and particularly the Olympic Games, were full of ceremonial. National anthems, processions and flags could be the symbols of aggressive nationalism and xenophobia as well as of ecumenical internationalist feeling. Sport could help forge a national identity, but this could be a means of affirming its pride and individuality or alternatively a channel for narcissism, chauvinism and hatred. But for all that, there is no automatic parallel between the political forms of nationalism and their sporting manifestations, even though international politics can, from time to time, provide a pretext for intellectuals eager to whip up passions. Sport had still not become a diplomatic instrument, nor was it closely involved with state policy.[40] Its practice, however, would always be a focus for nationalist discourse, since nationalists tended to see it as a means for racial regeneration, and the struggle between races and peoples was a substitute for the class struggle.

The discourse of journalists and intellectuals seems to have been more influential than that of sportsmen themselves, doubtless a sign of the effectiveness of the Third Republic's effort at acculturation and nationalization of the masses. This, in any case, is the interpretation suggested by Louis Pergaud:[41] war becomes a game, its rituals, language and values thoroughly absorbed by children, even if patriotism is the winner in this fight.

To conclude, if nationalism was 'a major phenomenon of European history in the nineteenth and first half of the twentieth centuries, a decisive factor in the general development of societies',[42] sporting clubs in France were sometimes modest but effective helpers. Sporting nationalism, however, could not truly be expressed until after the First World War, under the joint effect of the internationalization and professionalization of sport, and the rise of authoritarian regimes.

NOTES

1. Speech at Bordeaux, 25 June 1871.
2. In *Bulletin Administratif de l'Instruction Publique*, no. 495 (2 June 1882), pp. 424–5.
3. A. Dupuy, *Sedan et l'enseignement de la revanche* (Paris: INRP, 1975).
4. Marcel Spivak, 'Éducation physique, sport et nationalisme en France du Second Empire au Front Populaire: un aspect original de la défense nationale', doctoral thesis, Université de Paris I, 4 vols (1985), p. 162. The author emphasizes the military aspects of sports policy. Part of the thesis is to be published by Presses Universitaires de Lyon.
5. P. Contamine, 'Mourir pour la patrie', in Pierre Nora (ed.), *Les Lieux de mémoire* (Paris: Gallimard, 1987).
6. Zeev Sternhell, *La Droite révolutionnaire, 1885–1914: les origines françaises du fascisme* (Paris: Seuil, 1978).
7. For quantitive data see Pierre Arnaud, 'Les Athlètes de la République: gymnastique, sport et idéologie républicaine', doctoral thesis, Université de Lyon II, 3 vols (1986), the first part of which has been published as *Le Sportman, l'écolier, le gymnaste* (Lyon: Presses Universitaires de Lyon, 1989). These figures are confirmed by B. Dumons, G. Pollet and M. Berjat, *Naissance du sport moderne* (Lyon: La Manufacture, 1987).
8. See also Arnaud, 'Les athlètes'; Spivak, 'Éducation'; and A. Bourzac, 'Les bataillons scolaires', thèse de 3e cycle, Université de Lyon II, 2 vols (1982).
9. See also Arnaud, *Le Sportman*; P. Chambat, 'Les fêtes de la discipline: gymnastique et politique en France', in P. Arnaud and J. Camy (eds), *La Naissance du mouvement sportif* (Lyon: Presses Universitaires de Lyon, 1986).
10. Freedom of association was still governed by article 291 of the Penal Code of 1810, but with different levels of tolerance over time. The law of 30 June 1881 conceded greater freedom of assembly (distinct, however, from freedom of association, which would only be acquired under the law of 1 July 1901).
11. R. Barrul, *Les Étapes du gymnastique au sol et aux agrès en France et dans le monde* (Paris: Féderation Française de Gymnastique, 1984).
12. D. Mamoz, *De la gymnastique en France* (Angoulême, published by author, 1891).
13. See, e.g., E. Bocquillon, *La Crise du patriotisme à l'école* (Paris: Vuibert, 1905).
14. M. Lagrée, 'Les origines de la F.G.S.F.P., du catholicisme social au mouvement de jeunesse', master's dissertation, Nanterre, 1969.

15 Yves Lequin, *Histoire des Français*, Vol. III (Paris: Colin, 1984), p. 182.
16 Lagrée, 'Les Origines', pp. 51–2.
17 Spivak, *Éducation*, p. 490.
18 E. Petit, 'Rapport sur l'éducation populaire', in *Bulletin administratif de l'instruction publique* (yearly from 1896).
19 E. Turmann, *L'Éducation populaire: les oeuvres complémentaires de l'école* (Paris: Lecoffre, 1907), p. vii.
20 The Catholics tried in vain to oppose the cult of Joan of Arc with that of Marianne, demanding in 1912, for example, that the former's feast day should replace the 14 July as a truly national day. See C. Ponson, *Les Catholiques lyonnais et la chronique social* (Lyon: Presses Universitaires de Lyon, 1979), p. 98, and also Gerd Krumeich, above p. 70.
21 Report on 'The race and the gymnastic societies' presented by Dr P. Michaux at the annual meeting of the Société d'Économie Sociale, in *La Réforme sociale*, 1 December 1911.
22 ibid.
23 Sermon of Mgr Petit, in *La Semaine religieuse*, 15 May 1908.
24 See Arnaud, 'Les Athlètes'.
25 A. Poullaillon, *La Natation, étude d'éducation physique* (Orleans: Gou, 1911), p. 14; see also ADR 4 M 603.
26 D. Lejeune, *Les Alpinistes en France 1875–1919* (Paris: Comité des Travaux Historiques et Scientifiques, 1988), p. 166.
27 See esp. P. Gaboriau, 'Le Vélo, lenteur des riches, vitesse des pauvres' in *Actes du colloque sport et société* (juin 1981), CIEREC St Étienne (travaux XXXII), and also Eugen Weber's remarkable papers 'La Petite Reine' in Arnaud and Camy, *La Naissance*, and in Eugen Weber, *France Fin de Siècle* (Cambridge, Mass.: Belknap Press, 1986).
28 See Arnaud, *Le Sportman*; Arnaud, 'Les Athlètes'; and Dumons *et al.*, *Naissance*.
29 M. T. Eyquem, *L'Épopée olympique* (Paris: Calmann-Lévy, 1966), p. 117.
30 Spivak, 'L'Éducation'.
31 Eyquem, *L'Épopée*, p. 61.
32 On these aspects see Spivak, 'L'Éducation'.
33 E. Rey, *La Renaissance de l'orgueil français* (Paris: Grasset, 1912). P. Benneton, 'La Génération de 1912–1914: image, mythe et réalité', in *Revue Française de Science Politique*, no. 5 (1971), pp. 981–1009.
34 H. Massis and A. de Tarde wrote under the pseudonym Agathon *Les Jeunes Gens d'aujourd'hui* (Paris: Plon, 1913). On their inquiry see Benneton, 'La Génération', and Arnaud, 'Les Athlètes', pp. 277ff.
35 Quoted in J. Thibault, *Sports et éducation physique 1870–1970* (Paris: Vrin, 1972), p. 148.
36 This question was widely commented on in the specialist press. The college was a private venture in which the state took no part. See Spivak, 'L'Éducation', pp. 767ff.
37 An examination of the national press (*L'Illustration*, *La Vie au Grand Air*, *Le Figaro*) and the local (*Le Progrès de Lyon*, *Lyon-Républicain*, *Lyon-Sport*) provides no evidence of such disturbances. Spivak, 'L'Éducation', makes the same observation.
38 Quoted in R. Hervet, *La Fédération sportive de France, 1898–1948* (Paris: n.p., 1948), p. 44.
39 The two best studies of socialist sport are T. Davet, 'Du Sport rouge au sport populaire en France de 1919 à 1939', master's dissertation, Université de Paris (directed by M. Rebérioux), and W. J. Murray, 'The French workers' sport movement and the victory of the popular front in 1936', *International Journal of the History of Sport*, vol. 4, no. 2 (September 1987), p. 31.
40 See R. Girardet, 'Pour une Introduction à l'histoire du nationalisme français', *Revue Française de Science Politique*, vol. 8, no. 3 (September 1958), pp. 505–28; J. M. Brohm, *Sociologie politique du sport* (Paris: Delarge, 1976); P. Milza, 'Sport et relations internationales', *Relations Internationales*, no. 38 (Summer 1984), pp. 155–74.
41 L. Pergaud, *La Guerre des boutons* (Paris: Mercure de France, 1912).
42 Girardet, 'Pour une Introduction', p. 505.

15

Exploring the sexual politics of republican nationalism

Karen Offen

Most historical analysis of French nationalism to date have had one feature in common – they have been male-centred stories. For decades historians simply took for granted that nationalist discourse was *ipso facto* a form of male discourse, by virtue of its foreign and military policy perspective on national power. What is hidden by this approach is that although the designers, practitioners and critics of foreign and military policy have been exclusively male, the components of national power have not. Domestic policy and the conflicts that it entails constitute an essential (though often unexamined) element; moreover, the contributions to national power of women – as half the population (as childbearers, as participants in the labour force, as supporters and sustainers of men as well as independent actors) – have far too often been silently assumed. Yet women are not – and have not always been willing to be – men's cyphers; they may have distinct interests and points of view. This essential fact has become increasingly apparent in the late twentieth century as historians of women have retrieved and investigated nineteenth-century women's writing, activities and organizations, including that of the French feminist movement, and have introduced a feminist critique of earlier historiography, embracing that of French nationalism.[1]

Not only are women's contributions and concerns vital to national power, but the rhetoric of nationalism is itself heavily freighted with gender issues: an analysis of the language and practices of both the anti- and pro-republican nationalists in early Third Republic France reveals them to be highly sexualized, and often profoundly anti-feminist, if not altogether misogynous. Their claims and counterclaims depend significantly on assertions about sexual hierarchy, domination and submission, manliness and womanliness, and on notions about the elaboration of the roles and respective contributions of French women and men, which women actively contest or qualify. The tracts of the authoritarian high priests of French anti-republican nationalism, Maurice Barrès, Paul Déroulède and Charles Maurras, not to mention those of their acolytes, are replete with arguments about virility, about masculine energy, which sporadically reveal resentment of women who resist staying in their assigned places as men's muses or the objects of their desires. They exude alarm about the 'femininity' or 'effeminacy' of intellectual culture, and castigate men who do not command and women who do not obey.[2] Thus, to raise the issue of gender, of sexual politics, with respect to French nationalism is not to make a claim for *silences* but for *heretofore unacknowledged presences*. In these discourses, the cultural construction of French masculinity itself often seems to be at stake.[3]

This chapter, however, is less concerned with authoritarian nationalist constructions and reconstructions of masculinity than it is with the closely related and more complex sexual politics of depopulation, nationalism and feminism as manifested among the more progressive republican nationalists during what Eugen Weber has called the 'nationalist revival' of the early twentieth century. In what follows I will extend to the period between 1905 and 1914 my earlier analysis[4] of these intricately entwined factors, in which I posited the importance of gender issues to a fuller understanding of nationalistic thinking in French political life during the *fin de siècle* and, conversely, examined the impact of nationalistic thinking on the development of French feminist theory and practice.

During the Third Republic most women presented their claims for equality of the sexes by arguing that women's differences from men, in particular their incipient motherhood, gave them an irrefutable claim on citizenship in the French nation, including full civil and political rights. Feminist claims increasingly were made not on the basis of generic individual rights but on the rights of women *as individuals of the female sex*, by virtue of their differences from men and their acknowledged importance to the French state as citizen-mothers.[5] Since the French Revolution, this had been the dominant French feminist approach to renegotiating what political theorist Carole Pateman has called (for the British case) 'the sexual contract' that preceded the 'social contract'.[6] In the population-conscious political atmosphere of the early Third Republic, such a 'relational feminist' argument had the advantage of appealing far more to contemporary male sensibilities than did arguments based on individual rights. In conclusion, I argued that 'the emphasis on motherhood by French republican feminists...was a realistic, even astute, response to difficult political circumstances'.[7] In the game of Bridge that was nineteenth-century sexual politics, this card was, in fact, their trump.

NATIONALIZING FRENCH FEMINISM; FEMINIZING FRENCH NATIONALISM

Two interlocking developments, which we may call 'nationalizing feminism' and 'feminizing nationalism', set the stage for developments from

1905 to 1914. By the mid-1890s, the words *féminisme* and *féministe* were spreading from France throughout the civilized world.[8] By 1897 even Charles Maurras was contemplating *féminisme*, and before 1900 other anti-republican nationalists had attempted to brand feminists (along with Protestants, Jews, and freemasons) as cosmopolitan, internationalist, un-French.[9]

French feminists quickly and successfully countered such misinformation. Already in 1896, for example, Eugénie Pontonie-Pierre and Marya Cheliga both attempted to ensure widespread recognition of the intrinsic 'Frenchness' of feminism itself, by insisting on its historical links to the founding principles of the revolution – liberty and equality – and, more specifically, the rights of (generic) man, the slogan of progressive French republicanism, which was increasingly emphasized following the Dreyfus Affair and the reactivation of the Ligue des Droits de l'Homme. Here the French feminists were on solid ground. Indeed, the case of indigenous origins was bolstered by the research of subsequent male historians of the French Revolution. These historians argued against the notion of Anglo-Saxon origins for feminism, even as they insisted on its tight links to the revolutionary tradition. Such support was essential in neutralizing the objections of the anti-feminist authoritarian nationalists.[10]

Indeed, from 1900 on, the leaders of the French republican women's movement seemed to be making a concerted effort to identify feminism with the national community; *les Françaises* repeatedly asserted their claims to equal standing with *les Français*. Witness, for example, the founding in 1901 of the Conseil National des Femmes *Françaises* (which by 1909 boasted of 75,000 members), the naming of the feminist newspaper *La Française* in 1906, and of the Union *Française* pour le Suffrage des Femmes in 1909. In 1909, one group convoked a *national* congress on women's rights and suffrage; the organizers appealed to French women's solidarity above and beyond differences of religion, politics and socio-economic class.[11]

Such efforts to reformulate and reclaim French women's intrinsic connection with the national community may seem exaggerated in retrospect. But they should not surprise us. Such shifts in vocabulary are extremely meaningful; they deserve analytical attention, not least because they suggest the sheer force of nationalist sentiment on both sexes in early twentieth-century France. Few men, including those of the dominant radical parties, dared to stand apart. And some women from all points of the political religious spectrum – Catholics, Protestants, Jews – had begun to insist that they be fully included. They had, after all, been educated since 1880 to become *citoyennes* of the democratic French republic.[12] For many of them, the unanswered questions became not 'would they be admitted' but when, and under what conditions? What, in a political climate marked by increasing international tension, armaments races and escalating chauvinism, might be the price of women's full citizenship?

The counterpoint to the nationalization of French feminism was the feminization of French nationalism, and the key to understanding this aspect was the population question. To comprehend its importance, we must briefly review its development during the nationalist revival between 1905 and 1914, since even the most recent scholarship in French demographic history continues to ignore both the centrality of women's participation in reproductive decisions and the political connections of depopulation, nationalism and feminism.[13]

Following the separation of church and state, the advocates of population growth regrouped to implore the French state to take immediate action on the population issue. In 1907 the French statistical office released a new set of census figures; deaths in France again exceeded the number of births. Why was the birth rate down? Some nationalists on the right insisted that it was a male problem: that Frenchmen were experiencing a crisis of virility, or at least a disinclination to marry and father legitimate children, due (they claimed) to erosion of the legal and economic authority vested in husbands and fathers. Others blamed the women's rights movement and women's increasing access to other options in life besides childbearing. But the explanation that men found most convincing, and that indeed bore on the situation of the vast majority of women, was poverty and women's employment, which was thought (not completely without reason) to restrict their ability to bear and raise legitimate children. The overwhelming response of French men – from patriarchal social Catholics inspired by *Rerum Novarum* (1891) to secularists who variously invoked Rousseau, Comte, or Le Play – was to attempt to return employed women to the household and to childbearing, dependent on a male (or 'family') wage. French working women had been resisting this solution throughout the nineteenth century, arguing repeatedly, as had Paule Mink in 1868 against the First International, that 'by denying woman the right to work, you degrade her; you put her under man's yoke and deliver her over to man's good pleasure.... It is work alone that makes independence possible and without which there is no dignity.'[14]

The first extensive French legislation to restrict women's work (apart from underground work in mines) had been enacted in 1892, following years of wrangling over the wisdom of intervening in the choice of adults of either sex. Protective legislation of other sorts, both for women workers and for mothers, remained controversial; debates raged but little was done. In the face of continuing debate, in 1907 the radical and radical-socialist party had adopted a tepid statement on women's rights, proclaiming its partisanship for 'the gradual extension of rights to woman', but adding that a woman 'must be protected by law in every circumstance of her life'.[15] This was the same year that the International Socialist Women's Conference, meeting at Stuttgart concurrently with the Second International, endorsed the still-radical principle of unrestricted suffrage for all adult women, whether married or single.[16]

Meanwhile, the perceived population crisis only seemed to get worse and birth control had meanwhile become a controversial political issue in France. And in a climate of increasing German hostility, populationist propagandists insisted on linking the issues of national population, the state's readiness for war and motherhood. 'La maternité est la pépinière de la nation', exhorted Henri Vedette in a 1906 book, *L'Art de vaincre les Allemands*.[17] In 1907 Jean de Valdor, author of *Le Vrai Féminisme*, argued that women who demanded independence would only be 'crushed by men's force'. 'Demand, insist on maternity; it is your right and your duty. God will aid you!'[18]

God's aid not being immediately forthcoming, French republicans were forced squarely to confront the significance of the woman question for the future of the French nation. In this sense, republican nationalism itself had been 'feminized'. Would republican men henceforth be able to address the population issue in a way that might serve both the interests of women and the requirements of a male-dominated and increasingly militaristic French political establishment?

MEN AND WOMEN DEBATE MATERNITY AND THE FRENCH NATIONAL INTEREST, 1908–13

In 1909 a series of carefully orchestrated pronatalist articles by former Depopulation Commission members began to appear in the *Revue Hebdomadaire*. Writers ranging from the bishop of Versailles to one of Professor Pinard's physician-disciples, espoused the most conservative slogans, voicing strong opposition to the increasingly vociferous birth-control advocates and urging the government squarely to confront the seriousness of the population issue.[19] Such male writers were absolutist in their insistence on women's maternity; clearly, men could not repopulate the nation by themselves. 'Woman is essentially designed to give birth; she cannot arrive at her complete realization unless she realizes her destiny by becoming a mother,' asserted Dr Burlureaux in the issue of 22 May.

There was, however, a broader range of male opinions as to what ought to be done to improve the situation of women, especially of mothers and infants, than those expressed in the *Revue*. Although many men still considered women as instrumental, the means to an end – walking wombs to provide population growth and more regiments – others articulated more sophisticated positions. Progressive republican members of the medical establishment, citing the turn-of-the-century studies by Dr Pinard and his students, insisted less on breeding than on improving the conditions for maternity in France, especially for the great number of employed women. But their primary goal was to reduce infant mortality, and only then to assist women as individuals with a particular set of sex-specific needs.[20]

Among the most radical proposals put forth by any male writer prior to 1914 was that of Dr Just Sicard de Plauzeoles, a professor at the Collège Libre des Sciences Sociales, and author of a book entitled *Maternity and National Defence against Depopulation* (1909). Echoing suggestions that originated with a cluster of socialist women in the late nineteenth century, Sicard de Plauzeoles proposed that the national state be substituted for the family by underwriting motherhood as a paid service to the nation. Countries such as Germany, Austria and Switzerland, he pointed out, had set an example by insisting on a period of rest from work by wage-earning women before and after confinement and by compensating them through national health insurance.

> France should do still better; it should outlaw work for women who are pregnant or just delivered; mercenary nursing and artificial feeding should be outlawed; maternal nursing should be made compulsory; mothers should be indemnified, put on salary, subsidized; a [state] budget for maternity must be created.

Sicard called for the establishment of a national budget to support these services, to which the state would contribute an amount equal to one-third of the defence budget, complemented by contributions from the departments and the communes.[21]

Not all men envisioned such intrusive statist measures. Some, such as the lawyer A. Vallin (who had made a comparative study of medical literature and pertinent foreign legislation), did not think it possible to eliminate arbitrarily the employment of working-class women. But he also advocated compensating women for obligatory maternity leaves (on the German model) in order to reduce infant mortality, which still ran to roughly 14 per cent of births.[22] The solutions envisaged by the men of the Alliance Nationale pour l'Accroissement de la Population Française continued to run along a line that culminated in Fernand Boverat's *Patriotisme et paternité* (1913). Although Boverat emphasized men's primary responsibility ('Le devoir de paternité doit être assimilé au devoir militaire', read one chapter heading), he did accord limited agency to women: in fact, he lectured women that the only way to establish a lasting peace was through French population growth. All healthy women, he insisted, should give their country *at least* four children. Women who did not fulfil this foremost duty were 'no better than deserters!'[23]

The solutions preferred by French feminist activists, however, were articulated at the governmental level by Paul Strauss, the solidarist republican senator who worked closely with the republican women's movement on a comprehensive body of legislation to benefit women as mothers and workers, and by the deputy Fernand Engerand in the Chamber of Deputies. I will not rehearse the slow development of this legislation, which has been perceptively analysed by Mary Lynn Stewart.[24] Suffice to say that before the First World War, only two modest laws and one programme resulted from their efforts. The law of 27 November 1909 provided job guarantees to women who took (voluntary) maternity leave. A private programme of mutual maternity insurance, partially subsidized by the government, was established. Lastly, the law of 17 June 1913 established obligatory paid maternity leaves, both pre- and postpartum, for all waged women workers.[25] Male rhetoric about national need as they defined it far outweighed appeals to the principles of women's rights.

French republican feminists also argued the case for the improvement of the sociopolitical conditions surrounding motherhood, and for government intervention on women's behalf, even as they sought the vote and major changes in family law. In 1907, only Hubertine Auclert openly dissented from the Radical Party's protectionist position on the woman question, and it was left to Dr Madeleine Pelletier to challenge the notion that motherhood defined a woman's social role.[26] Most early twentieth-century feminists tried to work closely with progressive republican men such as Strauss and Viviani to compel state action on behalf of mothers.

Republican feminists rejected the pronatalist nationalist men's notion that birth rate was the primary issue. Some, such as Maria Martin, argued for 'quality not quantity', which would later become a favourite argument of the eugenics and family-planning movements.[27] More frequently they insisted on the dramatic problem of infant mortality, and some, such as Ida R. Sée, judged others of their own sex harshly on the question of maternal care for infants.[28]

For example, Dr Blanche Edwards-Pilliet, whose principal work was in the area of gynaecology and obstetrics (and who presided over the Ligue Française des Mères de Famille as well as working in the Conseil National des Femmes Françaises (CNFF)), called for the establishment of shelters for pregnant women, for a two-week rest-leave from employment for women workers and for a four-week paid maternity leave following birth.[29] Such constructive ideas did not go unheeded either by other women or by the radical republican ministries.

Women affiliated to the CNFF pressed forward with a broad-based programme of woman-centred social action to enhance women's status in (and contributions to) French society, and especially to address the problems of poor women. Their projects included the establishment of homes for unwed mothers, refuges for released female convicts and prisoners, crêches and other childcare facilities, and concerted efforts to combat the ravages of alcoholism, tuberculosis and inadequate housing. In the meantime Edwards-Pilliet called for full governmental support for mothers, on the grounds that both soldiers and mothers were social servants.[30]

A series of political manoeuvres on the maternity issue can be detected in the wake of the renewed woman suffrage campaign, following the founding in 1909 of the Union Française pour le Suffrage des Femmes (UFSF).[31] In August 1909 the CNFF section on legislation, headed by Mme Abbadie d'Arrast, reported what appeared to be a political compromise with the government, focusing on 'the protection of the unborn infant'. Significantly, it included a restatement of the long-standing feminist demand for the abolition of the much criticized Article 340 of the Civil Code, which since 1804 had prohibited paternity suits.[32] More surprisingly, perhaps, the CNFF also supported a government proposal for the decriminalization of abortion (which would effectively remove abortion trials from lenient juries and place defendants in the hands of sterner judges), and urged that an educational effort be launched to inform women how dangerous abortion was for their health. The CNFF report further called on the state and welfare agencies to give adequate assistance to women with children. Marguerite Pichon-Landry assured members that this endorsement of decriminalization was contingent on radical support for the abolition of Article 340.[33]

In 1910 the women of the CNFF, with misgivings, endorsed Rivet's far more restrictive proposal on *recherche de paternité*.[34] In the end, however, the law passed in 1912 satisfied no one very much; among other things, it exempted married men from possible prosecution! In an unpublished letter, Cécile Brunschwicg remarked sourly that it was a 'law made for women – without women'.[35] Still, the principle of *recherche de paternité* had been restored to French law. Its apparent counterweight, the decriminalization of abortion, would not be not enacted until after the war, and then only by ministerial decree.[36]

In view of the intensity of the population issue and nationalist sentiment, the question that historians of women must ask of these early twentieth-century feminists concerns their stand on women's reproductive rights. This question cannot be adequately answered with the evidence available to date: both abortion and birth control were controversial and relatively hush-hush topics in France during the first decade of the twentieth century. Only a few French women staunchly defended (at great personal cost) women's reproductive rights against the intrusion of the militaristic state; these women included the eloquent Nelly Roussel, Gabrielle Petit, and Madeleine Pelletier. Of particular ideological and propagandist significance was Petit's paper, *La Femme affranchie* (established 1904), which Francis Ronsin has described as 'revolutionary feminist, violently antimilitaristic, and neo-Malthusian'.[37]

Sexual politics

Such uncompromising assertions of women's reproductive rights were apparently unpalatable to the women of the Third Republic elites. Yet even in this quarter an earlier prudery gave way to discrete discussion. One response to the French neo-Malthusians and pronatalists was forthcoming from CNFF activist Jeanne Leroy-Allais. She was a staunch opponent of neo-Malthusianism and abortion, which she condemned as criminal. Yet she was no blind pronatalist; she advocated responsible sex, and even published a sex education tract for girls, built around a tasteful dialogue between mother and daughter.[38] By 1913, such progressive republican women were openly advocating sex education at the Paris international congress of women.

Despite their reluctance to insist forthrightly on women's right to control their own bodies, republican feminists nevertheless obliquely criticized the efforts of the Third Republic's all-male commission on population. In a short note published in the CNFF's *L'Action féminine* (December 1912), the anonymous writer huffed:

> How ridiculous is this chaotic and interminable list of members of the 'depopulation commission'. It would have been far more useful to ask women from different social strata. Then one would learn a lot more about why people don't want children and whose fault it is.[39]

There would be no solution to this or other major national problems, French feminists maintained, without consulting French women.

NATIONAL HONOUR, NATIONAL SHAME, WOMEN'S RIGHTS, 1913–14

By the time of the June 1913 international congress on women's rights in Paris, there was virtually no overt mention of depopulation in the women's press; indeed, there hardly needed to be. National laws establishing paid maternity leave and assistance to large families were on the verge of enactment by the Senate and Chamber of Deputies.[40] *Les Françaises* had consciously rejected British suffragette tactics in favour of exemplary citizenship behaviour: good wives and good mothers (and accompanying entitlements) were much celebrated. Senator Paul Strauss himself attested:

> The tumultuous suffragettes on the other side of the Channel are not the only representatives of international feminism, and the women's congress, now meeting in Paris, suffices to prove it, in case public opinion should be misled on the importance and universality of the feminist movement.[41]

Nationalism and politics

Evan as Strauss wrote, his colleague Fernand Engerand insisted in the Chamber of Deputies that

> By protecting maternity, the nation protects itself, assures its power and its very being.... For France, this is a question of national dignity and national security.... By protecting maternity and early infancy, we assure the primordial element of our national defence.[42]

The congress, and the concurrent debate on the maternity leave law, testified to the love-feast between feminists and the progressive nationalist leaders of the Third Republic. Convened in the grand amphitheatre of the Sorbonne, delegates from many countries listened to Barthou's Minister of the Interior, Louis-Lucien Klotz, wax lyrical on women's social role and women's duty to ameliorate social wrongs. Fêted at the Senate, at the quai d'Orsay and at the Elysée Palace by the leaders of their country, French feminists demonstrated proudly to their guests from abroad that in 1913 everything seemed to be going as they wished.[43]

Engerand and his colleague Strauss were not alone in linking women's situation to the national cause; they dusted off and refurbished a time-honoured republican argument that linked the status of women with regeneration of the nation. In fact, both women and men relentlessly used honour/shame arguments to underscore the point that France was lagging behind other nations (notably England, Germany and, occasionally, the United States) as a means of inducing the French government to enact and finance the desired programmes for mothers. In 1913–14, however, inflated rhetoric invoking national pride on behalf of solutions to the woman question and to the population problem may have reached an all-time high. In 1913, Engerand argued in the Chamber: 'It is difficult to have to attest that France is ... with Turkey, the only country in the world that has not enacted protective legislation for maternity.' Such legislation was a 'national duty', he proclaimed. He capped his speech by reminding the deputies of Kaiser Wilhelm's insistence that money did not count when it came to insuring proper rest for working mothers after their delivery.[44]

WHAT PRICE CITIZENSHIP? AN AFTERWORD

The convergence of depopulation, nationalism and feminism in the early Third Republic assured that as women sought to secure major reforms through governmental action, certain political choices would have to be made. There was, of necessity, a price to be paid for engaging the rhetoric of sexual difference, particularly in the forms of citizen-motherhood and women's social role in the name of the nation–state. However, this price only became apparent well after the outbreak of the war in August 1914.

On 12 August, the president of the UFSF, Marguerite de Witt-Schlumberger, convoked the 'sisters of the Union' to do their duty, not only to offer their services to the Red Cross or other good works, but to keep the country running in the absence of the men. It was not the time, she said, 'to launch a feminist manifestation against the war, as some have asked me to do: no French woman has that right.... We must demonstrate... that we are worthy of assisting in running our country because we are capable of serving it.'[45]

And on the 25th, the officers of the CNFF, Julie Siegfried and Ghenia Avril de Sainte-Croix, dispatched a similar communiqué: 'As women of our soil and our race, we will consent with absolute courage and faith in the final victory to the sacrifices that are demanded of us.'[46] In early 1915, the leaders of both organizations would issue a joint manifesto, explaining why they could not attend the international women's peace conference at the Hague. Wrapping themselves not in the blanket of chauvinism but in the principles of human rights and national self-determination that France had bequeathed to the world, they refused to talk of peace until there was some guarantee that such rights would be respected.[47]

By 1917, however, France's tremendous war losses had reinvigorated pronatalist claims, even among progressive republican women.[48] UFSF's Witt-Schlumberger was arguing in the pages of *La Française* that women had a 'particular duty'. 'We consider that mothers have an obligation to the nation just as soldiers do at the frontier... the country is their child.' And she argued that all young couples in good health should give France a new baby in the year following the end of the war. If they did not, she insisted (echoing Fernand Boverat) public opinion should treat them as deserters.[49] The following month, Viviani, then *garde des sceaux*, assured the women that the government would support the municipal suffrage bill.[50]

Was this only coincidence, or was there a deliberate political trade-off underway? The evidence raises more questions than it answers. Some contemporary critics would argue that French nationalistic thinking had totally ensnared French republican feminists; that they were unable – because of their lack of political power and the demands of war – to maintain a critical distance, to remain alert to women's reproductive interests, to oppose male dominance and male constructs of war and the state. The price of women's admission to the French nation, they would say, would be their sacrifice of reproductive independence.

Yet a careful chronological analysis of subsequent events qualifies such a harsh retrospective judgement. Even a cursory reading of *La Française* for 1917 clearly suggests a resurgence of women's activism on women-centred concerns: calls for women superintendents of women workers in war production plants, special facilities for infant and childcare in armaments factories, etc. These measures were implemented by the War Ministry. In May 1918, the CNFF called for substantive aid to mothers as a precondition to any legal repression of abortion; in 1919 the group met in Strasbourg, in symbolic celebration of the reunification of Alsace-Lorraine with the French nation. In 1919 French women believed that they had nearly won the vote; the Chamber had passed the necessary legislation by a great majority. It was only in 1920, while the Senate dragged its heels on woman suffrage, that a new and far more pronatalist ministry enacted by decree strict controls on abortion, banned all contraceptive propaganda and instituted medals for motherhood. It appears that there was little overt opposition by women's rights advocates to these measures; were the republican feminists afraid of jeopardizing the Senate vote on suffrage (which, though it seemed imminent, was not achieved until 1944–5), or is there another explanation? What is clear is that for the next 20 years women of most political persuasions from Catholic to communist unceasingly advocated measures to support and empower mothers; few came out openly against reproductive repression. When the Third Republic ground to a halt in 1939, women still lacked the vote, but in the meantime they had made signal gains in reform of marriage law, family allowances, access to the *baccalauréat*, and had managed to defend their right to work.[51] Only during the Vichy regime did matters really take a turn for the worse.

Could one argue, then, that reproductive servitude was the ultimate price of women's admission to French citizenship? Could it be said that French republican feminists – or women generally – capitulate unconditionally to the pronatalist demands of the male-dominated national government? Or should such questions be rephrased?

What we do know is that in spite of the stringent legislation, the relentless prescriptive rhetoric, the maternity leaves and the beribboned medals, the broader mass of French women were not responding to the populationist campaign. During the 1920s and 1930s the birth rate continued to drop. The relationship between prescription and behaviour in this instance seems less than simple.

What seems clear is that the feminist groups most closely associated with the republican leadership deployed the rhetoric of republican motherhood for all it was worth, but they also tried to place conditions on any governmental manipulation of women's reproductive rights. They continued to invoke the very ideals and rights that France had claimed for the world, but had not yet extended to women. Did their commitment to the national need, to republican rhetoric, ensnare them? Perhaps, in the short term. But the historian must also ask what other options were open to them, given their goal of incorporation in the national community. Most French feminists sought equality and justice for women within the French republic. They sought to realize fully the meaning of being *françaises* and – it must be said – to break the all-male hold over the power of the state and to harness it, in cooperation with sympathetic males, for their own purposes. In the climate of intense nationalistic sentiment in which they struggled, and without the vote, this entailed some difficult political manoeuvring.

French feminists did succeed to a remarkable degree in 'nationalizing' feminism, in 'feminizing' French nationalism, and in the short term in influencing the development of a broad range of beneficial policies for women as wives and mothers. In the years before 1914, this seems no small achievement. Women's stakes in the sexual politics of French nationalism were of the highest order – the future of the national community itself, and their inclusion therein.

NOTES

1. Karen Offen, 'Depopulation, nationalism, and feminism in fin-de-siècle France', *American Historical Review*, vol. 89, no. 3 (June 1984), pp. 648–76. Space in this collection does not permit full development of either the historical evidence or pertinent historiography on which this chapter is based; an expanded treatment of these issues will appear in my forthcoming book, *The Woman Question in Modern France*. The author wishes to thank various colleagues for their counsel during the truncation of this essay, especially Rachel Fuchs, Steven Hause, Judith Stone and Steven Englund.
2. Paul Déroulède, chief of the Ligue des Patriotes, was a declared foe of female suffrage. For Maurras's neo-Comtean ideas about virility and women, see Eugen Weber, *Action Française* (Stanford, Calif.: Stanford University Press, 1962), pp. 6–7 and 12; for his condemnation of literary romanticism as both feminine (because emotional) and un-French, see *L'Avenir de l'intelligence* (3rd edn, Paris: Flammarion, 1905). The case of Barrès is more complex; his deep ambivalence about nature, reproduction, and death exhibits itself clearly in his ruminations about women, as in *Un Homme libre* (1889) and *Je Jardin de Bérénice* (1891).
3. See, for a beginning, Peter N. Stearns, *Be A Man! Males in Modern Society* (New York: Holmes & Meier, 1979); Annelise Maugue, *L'Identité masculine en crise au tournant du siècle* (Marseille: Rivages, 1987).
4. See above, n. 1.
5. Offen, 'Depopulation', pp. 674–5. See also Offen, 'Defining feminism: A Comparative Historical Analysis', *Signs: Journal of Women in Culture and Society*, vol. 14, no. 1 (autumn 1988), pp. 119–57.
6. Carole Pateman, *The Sexual Contract* (Stanford, Calif.: Stanford University Press, 1988).
7. Offen, 'Depopulation', p. 674.
8. On the problems of the origins, definition and spread of the words feminism and feminist, see Offen, 'Defining feminism', pp. 122–34, and 'Sur les origines des mots "féminisme" et "féministe"', *Revue d'histoire moderne et contemporaine*, vol. 34, no. 3 (July–September 1987).
9. See Offen, 'Depopulation', p. 662. See also Charles Maurras, 'Le Féminisme – la dépopulation', *Revue encyclopédique Larousse*, no. 191 (1 May 1897), pp. 353–7.
10. Eugénie Potonie-Pierre, speech at the September 1896 German women's congress, in *Der International Kongress dür Freuenwerke und Frauenbestrebungen. Berlin, 19–26 September 1896*, ed. Rosalie Schoenflies et al. (Berlin: Walther, 1897); Marya Chéliga, 'L'Evolution du féminisme', *Revue encyclopédique Larousse* (special issue, 'Les Femmes et les féministes'), no. 169 (28 November 1896), pp. 910–13. See Leopold Lacour, *Les Origines du féminisme contemporain. Trois Femmes de la Révolution: Olympe de Gouges, Thériogne de Méricourt, Rose Lacombe* (Paris: Plon-Nourrit, 1900), and Alfred Dessens, *Les Revendications des droits de la femme au point de vue politique, civil, économique, pendant la Révolution*. Thèse, Faculté de Droit, Toulouse. (Toulouse: Imprimerie de C. Marqués, 1905). A more extended discussion of these points is Karen Offen, 'Women's memory, women's history, women's political action: the French Revolution in retrospect, 1789–1889–1989', *Journal of Women's History*, vol. 1, no. 3 (winter 1990), pp. 212–30.

11 See the proceedings, *Congrès national des droits civils et du suffrage des femmes. Tenu les 26–28 juin 1908. Compte rendu in extenso, recueilli, mis en ordre et publié par les soins de Mme Oddo Deflou* (Paris: n.p., 1910). The best general account of feminist politics and organizing during the Third Republic, especially after 1889, is Laurence Klejman and Florence Rochefort, *L'Egalité en marche: le féminisme sous la Troisième République* (Paris: des femmes, 1989). On suffrage in particular, see Steven C. Hause, with Anne R. Kenney, *Women's Suffrage and Social Politics in the French Third Republic* (Princeton, NJ: Princeton University Press, 1984).

12 See Linda L. Clark, *Schooling the Daughters of Marianne: Textbooks and the Socialization of Girls in Modern French Primary Schools* (Albany, NY: State University of New York Press, 1984).

13 See, for example, the articles by Jacques Dupâquier and Jean-Pierre Bardet in 'Denatalité: l'anteriorité française, 1800–1914', special issue of *Communications*, no. 44 (1986). For my critique of the sexism of earlier French demographic history, see Offen, 'Depopulation', n. 3.

14 Paule Mink, 'Le Travail des femmes (1868)', as translated in *Women, the Family, and Freedom: The Debate in Documents*, ed. Susan Groag Bell and Karen Offen, Vol. I, 2 vols (Stanford, Calif.: Stanford University Press, 1983) p. 472.

15 The Radical Party programme is partially reproduced in *France: Empire and Republic, 1850–1940*, ed. David Thomson (New York: Harper & Row, 1968), p. 281.

16 For the socialist women's statement endorsing the suffrage struggle, see Bell and Offen, *Women, the Family, and Freedom*, Vol. II, pp. 231–2.

17 Henri Vedette, *L'Art de vaincre les Allemands: Protection de l'enfance et de la maternité, l'enfant et les éducateurs laïques; le soldat et les éducateurs militaires* (Auxerre: Laulanié, 1906), p. 35.

18 Jean de Valdor, *Le Vrai Féminisme* (Paris: Savaète, 1907), pp. 7, 219.

19 *Revue Hebdomadaire*, May–5 June 1909.

20 See Pinard's publications, among others (with Charles Richet) 'Rapport sur les causes physiologiques de la dimunition de la natalité en France', *Annales de gynécologie et d'obstetrique*, vol. 59 (January 1903), pp. 15–24.

21 Just Sicard de Plauzeoles, *La Maternité et la défense nationale contre la dépopulation* (Paris: Giard & Brière, 1909).

22 A. Vallin, *La Femme salariée et la maternité* doctoral thesis, Faculty of Law, University of Paris (Paris: A. Rousseau, 1911), pp. 3, 19, 23–4.

23 Fernand Boverat, *Patriotisme et paternité* (Paris: Grasset, 1913); quotations, ch. 9 subtitle and p. 361. See also Offen, 'Depopulation', pp. 668–70.

24 See Mary Lynn Stewart, *Women, Work, and the French State: Labour Protection and Social Patriarchy, 1879–1919* (Toronto: McGill-Queen's University Press, 1989). On Strauss's ideas, see especially Stewart, chap. 8, and Rachel Fuchs, *Poor and Pregnant in Paris: Strategies for Survival in the Nineteenth Century* (New Brunswick, NJ: Rutgers University Press, forthcoming), ch. 2.

25 See Hubert-Valleroux, 'Loi du 17 juin 1913 sur le repos des femmes en couches', *Annuaire de législation française, 1913*, vol. 33 (1914), pp. 83–91.

26 On Auclert and the radical party, see Steven C. Hause, *Hubertine Auclert: The French Suffragette* (New Haven, Conn.: Yale University Press, 1987), esp. pp. 190–200. On Pelletier, see her later publications, *L'Emancipation sexuelle de la femme* (Paris: Giard & Brière, 1912); and *Le Droit à l'avortement* (Paris: Edition du 'Malthusien', 1913).

27 Martin, 'Quantité ou qualité', *Journal des femmes*, no. 201 (December 1909). 'Tachons de faire de ceux que nous avons de bons et solides petits soldats capable, au besoin, de défendre leur patrie.'

28 Ida R. Sée, 'Féminisme et dépopulation', *La Revue philanthropique*, vol. 31, no. 181 (15 May 1912), pp. 23–6; quotations from pp. 23, 26.

29 Rapport de Mme le docteur Edwards-Pilliet, *Congrès international de la condition et des droits des femmes, Paris... 1900* (Paris, 1901), pp. 66–8; trans. in Bell and Offen, *Women, the Family, and Freedom*, Vol. 2, p. 145.

30 Blanche Edwards-Pilliet, 'Le Dépopulation; à propos de la loi d'assistance aux mères', *L'Action féminine: Bulletin officiel du Conseil National des Femmes Françaises*, no. 27 (April 1913), p. 480.

31 See the suffrage section report in *Conseil National des Femmes Françaises. Assemblée générale publique*, no. 4 (1907). See also Maria Vérone, *Appel à la justice adressé par le Conseil national des femmes françaises à la Chambre des Députés et au Sénat* (1909); see also Ferdinand Buisson, *Le Vote des femmes* (Paris: Denot & Pinat, 1911).

32 Abolition of Article 340 (recherche de paternité) figured prominently in the programme of Léon Richer and other women's rights activists during the early decades of the Third Republic. The issue was reinvigorated at the 1900 congress on women's condition and rights.

33 Marguerite Pichon-Landry, 'La Protection de l'enfant', *L'Action féminine*, no. 4 (1 August 1909), pp. 57–9.

34 *L'Action féminine*, no. 8 (March 1910), pp. 134–7. See also no. 11 (August 1910), pp. 172–4, which discussed the Senate debate on the paternity issue.

35 Brunschwicg to H. Auclert, s.d., in Bouglé collection, BHVP. Quoted by Anne Cova, 'Cécile Brunschvicg (1877–1946) et la protection de la maternité', *Colloque sur l'histoire de la sécurité sociale, Strasbourg, 1988* (Actes du 113e, Congrès national des Sociétés savantes) (Paris, 1989), p. 89.

36 On the so-called decriminalization of abortion, see Francis Ronsin, *La Grève des ventres* (Paris: Editions Aubier Montaigne, 1980), chap. 17. See also Angus McLaren, *Sexuality and Social Order: The Debate Over the Fertility of Women and Workers in France, 1770–1920* (New York: Holmes & Meier, 1983).

37 Ronsin, *Grève des ventres*, p. 159.

38 Jeanne Leroy-Allais, *Comment j'ai instruit mes filles des choses de la maternité* (Paris: Maloine, 1907); Leroy-Allais, *Une Campagne criminelle; avortement et néomalthusianisme* (Paris: Maloine, 1909).

39 'La dépopulation et les femmes', *L'Action féminine*, no. 25 (December 1912), p. 436.

40 Although he notes that quasi-official discussions about depopulation included references to contraception, abortion, free unions, divorce and the law against paternity searches, Alain Becchia scrupulously avoids any gender analysis of these issues in his article, 'Les Milieux Parlementaires et la dépopulation de 1900 à 1914', *Communications*, no. 44 (1986), esp. pp. 216–18.

41 Paul Strauss, 'Le Congrès de Paris', from *Le Progrès du Nord*, 10 June 1913; as reprinted in *L'Action féminine*, no. 28 (June 1913), p. 501.

42 *Annales, Ch.D., Débats'* session of 5 June 1913, pp. 512, 520.

43 See the official congress proceedings, *Dixième Congrès international des femmes. Oeuvres et Institutions féminines. Droits des femmes. 1913. Compte rendu des travaux par Mme Avril de Sainte-Croix, secrétaire générale du Congrès* (Paris: Giard & Brière, 1914).

44 *Annales, Ch.D., Débats*, 5 June 1913, pp. 512, 515, 520. Engerand (as Mornet before him) conveniently forgot the United States, which to this day has not enacted such measures.

45 Manifesto, *Union française pour le suffrage des femmes*, dated 12 August 1914. Bibliothèque Marguerite Durand, dossier UFSF.

46 Manifesto, *Conseil national des femmes françaises*, dated 25 August 1914. Bibliothèque Marguerite Durand, dossier 396 CON (CNFF 1901–14).

47 'Aux Femmes des Pays neutres et des Pays alliés' (joint declaration, CNFF and UFSF), in *La Française*, 24 April 1915. Cf. also the earlier communications from the CNFF in *L'Action féminine*, no. 37 (March 1915).

48 See Steven Hause, 'More Minerva than Mars: the French women's rights campaign and the First World War', in Margaret Higonnet *et al.* (eds), *Behind the Lines: Gender and the Two World Wars* (New Haven, Conn.: Yale University Press), pp. 99–113. On wartime pronatalist propaganda directed toward the soldiers, see Marie-Monique Huss, 'Pronatalism and the popular ideology of the child in wartime France: the evidence of the picture postcard', in Richard Wall and J. M. Winter (eds), *The Upheaval of War: Family, Work and Welfare in Europe, 1914–1918* (Cambridge: Cambridge University Press, 1989): pp. 329–67.

49 'Le Devoir particulier des femmes', *La Française*, 12 May 1917.

50 *La Française*, 16 June 1917.

51 See Offen, 'The Politics of Motherhood in France, 1920–1940', working paper no. 87/293, European University Institute (Florence, 1987).

16

Social defence and conservative regeneration: the national revival, 1900–14

Philip Nord

Invocations of a second French Renaissance, of a reawakening of the national spirit, punctuated the public discourse of pre-First World War France. Such declarations described a movement of opinion, conservative in hue, but not without appeal to maverick left-wingers. The chief political repercussion of the new, nationalist mood was Raymond Poincaré's elevation to the presidency in 1913. But it may fairly be argued that the phenomenon played itself out, not so much at the level of partisan as of interest-group politics. Poincaré's person provided a symbolic focus to the new nationalism, but the movement's principal base of operations lay in a network of interlocking voluntary associations.

The recrudescence of nationalist sentiment in the prewar years was in part a response to Germany sabre-rattling, but it also had a domestic dimension. Two arguments have been made in this connection: that the revival represented a reactionary reflex of social defence in the face of mounting labour unrest, and that it was orchestrated by Paris-based elites who represented little more than themselves.[1] It is not my intention to overturn these views but to modify them.

The revival's impact was both wider and deeper than is sometimes conceded. Wider in that it appealed to a multiplicity of constituencies: to Poincarist politicians, of course, but also to businessmen concerned to defend France's interests in a competitive world economy and to men of letters anxious to preserve the nation's cultural pre-eminence. And deeper in that traces of the revival crop up in unexpected places, in the assemblies of small as well as large businessmen, in artistic circles as well as in the corridors of the Ministry of Fine Arts, in the Paris Municipal Council as well as in the Chamber of Deputies. The revival was the handiwork of *minorités agissantes*, but the minorities in question were not fragments of marginal opinion but constituent elements of France's national elite.

No doubt, the national revival was fanned by defensive anxieties in the face of perceived foreign and social threats, but to interpret its project in negative terms alone would be mistaken. Elements on the right acknowledged that social defence, however necessary, was an inadequate response to the challenge of labour. Needed was an alternative, conservative vision of the future, sufficiently daring to capture the public imagination and undercut the left's reputation as standard-bearer of progress. Revival partisans at times spoke in the accents of reform. They called for a programme of economic rearmament, for the creation of a 'style Troisième République' modern in its pared-down look but also traditional in its respect for classical principles, and for an overhaul of the nation's parliamentary regime in the interests of sound administration and strong executive leadership. The revival, as conceived by reform-minded conservatives, was as much modernizing as reactionary in thrust.

ECONOMIC REARMAMENT

The *belle époque* witnessed an explosion of business unionism. The Union du Commerce et de l'Industrie pour la Défense Sociale had been founded in 1899 by Catholic businessmen. Despite its confessional origins, the organization soon passed into the hands of less religiously militant conservatives, Eugène Motte, Joseph Thierry and Paul Beauregard, all stalwarts of the rightist Fédération Républicaine. The political complexion of the Union des Intérêts Economiques (UIE), formed in 1909 by insurance and food-and-drink interests, was more moderate but just as clear-cut. UIE President Paul Forsans and Maurice Ajam, a member of the steering committee, were both deputies of the centrist Alliance Républicaine Démocratique (ARD).[2] The most powerful of the new employer unions, however, were interest-group formations with less formal links to party structures: the Union des Industries Métallurgiques et Minières (UIMM) (1900) directed by Robert Pinot; the Union des Syndicats Patronaux des Industries Textiles (1901) directed by Robert Carmichael; and André Lebon's Fédération des Industriels et des Commerçants Français (FICF) (1903), a formidable coalition of maritime, metals and textile concerns.[3]

The burgeoning of employer syndicalism brought to the fore a new generation of business militant. Nineteenth-century business organizations, such as the Comité des Forges, had been dominated by men of inherited fortune and social standing. But with the turn of the century, the older generation began to give way to a different breed of employer activist, men whose claim to power rested not on ascriptive attributes but on professional and bureaucratic skills. Leadership of the Comité des Forges became the virtual monopoly of engineers and École Centrale graduates. Academic experts in growing numbers made their way into the inner sancta of organized business. Lebon, Henry de Peyerimhoff, secretary general of the Comité des Forges, and Georges Blondel, a member of the FICF executive, were all or had once been professors at the École Libre

Nationalism and politics

des Sciences Politiques. It is striking, moreover, how many of the new men entered the business world via social policy institutes such as the Musée Social. This was the route Pinot took, serving a brief tenure as co-director of the museum (1894–6) before entering the industrial sector. The militants who presided over the business revival were not Malthusian dynasts but protobureaucrats risen through the ranks.[4]

But toward what end did such men deploy their organizational talents? There can be no doubt of the anti-labour bias of the prewar business mobilization. The UIMM and FICF jointly sponsored formation of a strike insurance fund to finance employer resistance to worker walk outs. Anti-collectivist employers channelled substantial sums to Catholic and 'yellow' (i.e. employer-run) trade unions as safe alternatives to the 'red' CGT.[5] Business response to radical-initiated social and fiscal reform was no less stiff-necked. In 1909, radical Minister of Commerce Alphonse Cochery raised the prospect of a state take over of the insurance and liquor industries. It was Cochery's pronouncement that prompted organization of the UIE which went on to conduct a well financed anti-nationalization campaign in the 1910 elections. The most bitter business opposition, however, was provoked by Caillaux's income tax bill, first mooted in 1907. Maurice Colrat, a one-time associate in Poincaré's law office, campaigned against the tax as a measure of socialist confiscation. To preserve the nation against the evils of collectivism and state socialism, he called for a vigorous *Mittelstandspolitik*, a Risorgimento of the middle classes.[6] The message galvanized small-business interests into forming an Association de Défense des Classes Moyennes (ADCM) presided over by Colrat himself. The groundswell of opposition to the Caillaux bill culminated in a pair of massive anti-tax rallies, co-sponsored by the ADCM and UIE, the first in 1910 and the second, whose keynote speaker was Poincaré, in 1913.[7]

The business revival's anti-labour, anti-reform posture was combined with a pronounced economic nationalism. Business circles discussed the institution of an all-French shopping day. At a minimum, consumers had to be persuaded not to buy German. It was a question of fostering a 'nationalist psychology', of making the nation's buying public aware that, in Lebon's words, 'no entente is possible between them [Germany] and us'. No entente on the exchange of commodities, and none on financial matters. Business militants raised a noisy clamour for 'financial protectionism', lobbying hard against the quotation of certain foreign securities on the Paris stock exchange. France dared not allow its financial life blood to be siphoned away, least of all by its hereditary enemy and 'possible adversary of tomorrow', Germany.[8]

Such defensive-mindedness, however, represented but one face of the business *ralliement*. Elements of the business community understood the need for a more aggressive strategy. A conservative economist Marcel Dubois addressed the FICF in 1912:

Commerce is war: only a phrasemaker profoundly out of touch could believe and proclaim that this form of warfare is not offensive. Today, a nation which has first conquered its rival economically will have but little difficulty finishing the job the day military hostilities are declared. We are in great danger; this is a question of national urgency.[9]

Preparation for modern economic warfare demanded first and foremost organization. Exhortations to organize glutted the business literature of the prewar years, from Francis Laur's massive *L'Accaparement* to lesser known texts by Paul de Rousiers, secretary general of the Syndicat des Armateurs, and Étienne Martin Saint-Léon, archivist at the Musée Social. Publicists evinced a particular enthusiasm for the industrial cartel and cited time and again the Comptoir de Longwy (founded in 1876 by Lorraine-based metals manufacturers) as a model. In place of the wasteful anarchy of the free market, their organization held out prospect of a more rational and efficient structuring of industry, of 'a regulated production'.[10] The export sector as well, it was felt, might profit from concentration. The exploitation of markets abroad entailed a collective effort: a network of foreign-based export houses to drum up business; a system of sales cartels to assemble bulk orders. In the name of 'order' and 'method', Lebon called on French businessmen to set aside an outmoded individualism and undertake the cooperative 'organization of exports'.[11]

Exhortations to modernize went hand in hand with exhortations to organize. France's transport sector in particular was targeted for overhaul. In 1907, Jules Siegfried submitted to the Chamber a bill providing for creation of local port authorities invested with autonomous decision-making and revenue-collecting powers. State officialdom was guaranteed minority representation on port boards, but the majority of seats were reserved for interested business parties – shippers, Chamber of Commerce representatives, and the like. The Siegfried project in effect empowered private interests to run France's port system, and business was expected to use its new powers to undertake a renovation of harbour facilities that the nation might 'sustain [its] struggle against foreign competition'. Despite endorsements from the FICF and Syndicat des Armateurs, the Siegfried bill made little headway in Parliament.[12]

More success was had soliciting public monies for the modernization of rail and canal facilities. It was in the state's interest, business reformers argued, to fund transport reform. Mobilization for war, after all, hinged on effective transportation. 'The improvement of our national plant,' the UIE reminded public officials, 'is another aspect of national defence.' In any event, investments in infrastructure paid for themselves over the long run. Modernization of France's *outillage économique* was bound to strengthen the nation's export posture and, as commerce expanded, so too would government tax revenues.[13] Such arguments carried sufficient weight to persuade the Viviani government in 1914 to float an fr.800 million bond issue earmarked for transportation improvements.

Similar arguments were marshalled to justify expansion of France's merchant marine. Shipping executive Maurice Rondet-Saint proposed the axiom: 'Economic activity follows maritime activity. Wherever a nation's fleet ceases to be active, there its business interests are jeopardized.' Alexandre Millerand elaborated on Rondet-Saint's axiom in a 1909 speech to Sciences Po graduates: 'If it is true that influence follows the fleet, it is also true that influence follows business.' Not only the prosperity but also 'the grandeur of France' required an expansion of the fleet, and it behoved public authorities to furnish cheap loans to interested shipbuilders.[14]

Reform of the nation's financial system constituted the final item on the business *ralliement*'s agenda. Business interests harboured long-standing grievances against France's great deposit banks. Centralized and internationalist, they functioned, in Lebon's phrase, as 'a kind of suction pump' sucking up France's accumulated savings and funnelling them into foreign development loans. Capital-hungry export interests agitated for a state-subsidized export bank, but the project came to nothing. Government proved more responsive to the complaints of domestic industry. In 1912, the Poincaré ministry proposed a banking reform act which provided for creation of a state-controlled and financed industrial development bank. The business community by and large welcomed the bill which the Chamber duly enacted in 1914.[15]

Business reformers understood that state assistance was critical to success of the economic offensive they envisioned. On the domestic front, the public treasury was called upon to subsidize transport modernization and banking reform. On the international front, employers' associations lobbied the Quai d'Orsay long and hard to establish a corps of foreign-based commercial consuls. The object was, in Paul Deschanel's telling phrase, to transform the Ministère des Affaires Étrangères into the 'Ministère des Affaires faites à l'étranger'. The Ministry of Finance too was in a position to help out. Business apologists wrote of 'the need to organize in a logical fashion the export of our capital'. No foreign loans should be floated without authorization of the Ministry of Finance, and the ministry ought not to render its decisions without first consulting the relevant business parties. Business did not want a passive or even protectionist state policy. It wanted, rather, active state backing in the prosecution of a programme of economic expansion, and more, it wanted an institutionalized role in the making and execution of economic policy.[16]

The business face of the national revival was two-sided. Economic elites conjured up the socialist bogey or the spectre of *étatisme* to justify measures of repression and self-defence. But at the same time they clamoured for a programme of reform articulated in neo-corporatist accents, a programme intended to rearm France's economy for the conquest of markets at home and abroad.

CULTURAL RENAISSANCE

Business activists worried about France's economic preparedness; at issue in cultural life was a reassertion of the nation's artistic and moral authority. Revival partisans never doubted such a reassertion was to be an elite-led affair. They spoke repeatedly of the necessity of elites, indeed, in Rousiers's case, of a 'super-elite'.[17] But just what kind of an elite did they have in mind? A staid patriciate schooled in the classics and devoted to the *bibelots* of yesteryear, to the picturesque streets of old Paris, to the unchanging countryside of *la vieille France*? At first glance, the answer appears to be 'yes'.

The fate of classical education did preoccupy conservative opinion in the prewar years. In 1902, the baccalaureate examination had been revamped. Hitherto, all candidates had sat the same exam, but under the new dispensation, four options were provided, including a science and modern languages option which permitted students to bypass the traditional Latin requirement. A chorus of protest greeted the measure. Academician Jean Richepin founded the Ligue pour la Culture Française in 1912 with the express purpose of winning repeal of the 1902 reform. Richepin execrated the reform's anti-Latin bias but also voiced a second, more serious complaint. The young cried out, not for a one-sided education, but for 'a general culture... which dreams of *cultivating*... the human plant, the French plant in particular'.[18] The new *bac* scheme, with its multiple options, constrained students to specialize prematurely, violating the classical ideal of 'the whole man'.

Classical education bred literate, rounded men, but perhaps its greatest virtue lay in the preparation it provided for practical life. Such was the vision of Edmond Demolins, a Le Playian social scientist and long-time admirer of Matthew Arnold, who indeed attempted a transplantation of Arnoldian values onto French soil. In 1899, Demolins founded the École des Roches, an all-male boarding academy in the Norman countryside closely modelled on the English public schools. The École offered a balanced curriculum which combined a grounding in the classics with a stress on modern languages and a full programme of physical education. The idea was to train an elite, 'strong in body' and 'habituated to the realities of life', destined to assume positions of responsibility in 'the vital professions' of commerce, industry and agriculture. Demolins vaunted general education as the best training for the active life which he defined in terms of the exercise of command in the private sector. Here was an interpretation of *la culture générale* to rejoice the businessman's heart.

Demolins was in fact invited to expound his views at FICF luncheons, and, shortly after his death in 1907, chairmanship of the école's administrative council passed to social-Catholic reformer and business militant Paul de Rousiers.[19]

But of all the partisans of *la culture générale*, none prosecuted the case with more verve than Agathon (Henri Massis and Alfred de Tarde) in a pair of national revival classics, *L'Esprit de la nouvelle Sorbonne* and *Les Jeunes Gens d'aujourd'hui*. Agathon accused prevailing pedagogical orthodoxy of a denatured intellectualism which was the very antithesis of the classical ideal. University mandarins preferred abstractions to the concrete 'realities of sentiment and of action'. They touted German-inspired methods of text verification to the neglect of 'high French culture' which taught principles of 'literary taste, finesse, *mesure* and sober synthesis'. The scientific bias of 'modern' education endangered the principle of literacy itself. Agathon wrote of a 'crise du français' and blamed it on a mechanistic fact-mongering which ran roughshod over the nuances of the French language.[20]

L'Esprit de la nouvelle Sorbonne and *Les Jeunes Gens* were assured a wide audience in elite milieux thanks to serialization in *L'Opinion*, a conservative weekly journal. The magazine boasted a talented staff of young professional men: Colrat (editor from 1910), Jacques Bardoux, André Lichtenberger, and Massis too. But it was at the same time well connected in senior circles of France's establishment. Owned by Paul Doumer and subsidized by members of the Comité des Forges, *L'Opinion* carved out for itself a reputation as a 'Poincarist journal' to which, it was said, Poincaré himself subscribed.[21]

Professions of classicism, of course, were not confined to pedagogical debate but overflowed into neighbouring arenas. The closest equivalent to an Agathon in the domain of arts policy was Joseph Paul-Boncour, a man of independent socialist views but also a devotee of the classical tradition and a lifelong friend of Colrat.[22] Paul-Boncour published *Art et démocratie* in 1912, which outlined a programme of cultural reform intended to restore a decadent France to artistic greatness. The classicizing thrust of Paul-Boncour's project is unmistakable. 'The peoples of the modern world,' he wrote, 'date their renaissance from the moment they renewed connection, after centuries of forgetfulness, with the unbroken thread of the Graeco-Latin tradition.' In practice, Paul-Boncour's commitment to tradition translated into a spirited preservationism. He saluted efforts to restore France's old regime heritage – Louis XIV's palace at Versailles, the renaissance château at Azay-le-Rideau. And he was a great *amateur* of antique furnishings. He did not wish, however, merely to preserve individual tables or chairs, but to restore period rooms, to arrange pieces in coherent ensembles to communicate a sense of the stylistic whole. Only thus, he believed, might the originality of France's decorative arts heritage be conserved to inspire a future generation of native artists to creative activity.[23]

Paul-Boncour's call for a 'renaissance of the decorative arts'[24] excited considerable interest in conservative circles. Here was a domain of traditional French pre-eminence and a source of enormous national pride, but it had fallen on hard times of late. There was talk of a 'crise des métiers'. Auguste Rodin attributed the crisis to an erosion of craft discipline and the decline of apprenticeship. It was believed possible, however, to breathe new life into France's ailing 'community of arts and crafts'.[25] The 1912 congress of the Association de Défense des Classes Moyennes (ADCM) was entirely devoted to a discussion of the apprenticeship question. Principal speakers included Colrat, Blondel and Léon Bérard, under secretary of fine arts, a Colrat friend from law school days and a man to whom Paul-Boncour had dedicated *Art et démocratie*. The ADCM at the same time organized an Exposition de l'Apprentissage. The collected *chefs-d'oeuvre* of recently promoted *compagnons* were displayed as an inspiration to others and as a signal that a 'renaissance of apprenticeship' was under way.[26]

The same kind of organicizing traditionalism tinctured the rhetoric of France's embryonic conservation movement. The turn of the century witnessed a redoubling of commitment to the preservation of France's urban and rural patrimony. The Club Alpin Français, the oldest of France's conservation-minded organizations (1874), expanded its operations and was joined in its endeavours by two newcomers: the Touring Club de France (TCF) founded in 1890 and the Société pour la Protection des Paysages de France (SPP) founded in 1901.

The protection of historic monuments, of course, constituted the principal focus of urban conservationist activity. But preservationists aspired to more than the simple rescue of individual buildings; they wanted to preserve a particular look. What imparted aesthetic value to a given site, what made it picturesque, was not just the individual monument but its peculiar fit into the tissue of surrounding buildings. Led by the SPP and TCF, conservationists lobbied hard to enshrine this principle in preservationist legislation. The outcome was a 1906 law providing for creation of departmental committees to designate landmark sites, supplemented in 1906 by a second bill which prohibited advertising in the vicinity of landmark locations.[27]

The organicist vision of the new urbanism also left a mark on widening efforts to conserve urban 'espaces libres'. The city, as any living organism, needed oxygen, and parklands provided the necessary breathing room. In 1903, pioneering urbanist Eugène Hénard proposed conversion of Paris's fortifications into a magnificent greenbelt of parks. Hénard's open spaces campaign received a welcome fillip from the Musée Social which, in 1908, created a special committee to study the parks question, staffed by, among others, Georges Risler, an urbanist and future director of the Musée Social. On the eve of the 1910 elections, it circulated a manifesto urging citizens to vote only for candidates pledged to urban conservation and park reform.[28]

It was not just the fate of urban France that hung in the balance; the countryside too stood in need of protection. Protection meant, of course, the preservation of picturesque sites but also reforestation and the setting aside of vast tracts of wilderness for recreational use. Both the SPP and TCF favoured creation of a great nature reserve on the model of Wyoming's Yellowstone Park. The object of such efforts was twofold: the out-of-doors cleansed the body and spirit, fostering a harmonious development of all the human faculties; and it taught lessons of patriotism – first-hand experience of France's natural glories instilled a love of country. The Club Alpin adopted 'Pour la patrie, par la montagne' as its motto and celebrated alpinism as a proving-ground of the will, which prepared the young for soldiering and citizenship.[29]

Preservation of rural France was a question of national hygiene, and so too was preservation of the regional cultures rooted in the French countryside. Two organizations competed for ascendancy in the nascent regionalist movement: the Fédération Régionaliste Française (1900), directed by Louis Marin, a professor at Sciences Po and soon-to-be chief of the Fédération Républicaine; and the Ligue de Représentation Professionnelle et d'Action Régionaliste, headed by Jean Hennessy, a deputy of the Catholic Action Libérale Populaire (ALP). A devotion to France's past, to 'her monuments or landscapes', to 'the picturesque quality of [her] old provinces, their customs, costumes, dialects', such, according to Joseph Charles-Brun, a Marin lieutenant and the movement's leading spokesman, was the abiding passion of the regionalist. But modern civilization threatened to flatten out local life; it posed a danger not only to the healthy body of the nation but to its very sense of self.[30]

The prewar cultural revival was constituted of multiple, overlapping strands: a crusade to preserve classical culture; an arts and crafts revival; the conservationist and regionalist movements. A web of institutional and personal connections linked these diverse currents, and a common vocabulary. The integrity of France's classical heritage, the virtues of the whole man and the artistic ensemble, the exaltation of energy and the active life and, withal, a fervent patriotism – such were the leitmotifs of the revival, whatever its particular incarnation.

But a nostalgic traditionalism represented but one face of the cultural revival. A reverence for the past was leavened with modernizing aspirations. Classical principle, for example, was as often cited to legitimate a novel stress on physical fitness as to defend traditions of Latinity. The Graeco-Roman ideal of *mens sana in corpore sano*, after all, prescribed cultivation of the body no less than of the mind. French youth, corrupted by a dry-as-dust pedagogy, might well profit from a purgative plunge into the strenuous life. Such was the lesson of Teddy Roosevelt's *La Vie intense*, a text cited with remarkable frequency by cultural revivalists.[31]

And for intensity of experience, there was no substitute for sport. The Baron de Coubertin, father of the Olympic movement, was a Le Play acolyte who, like Demolins, admired the muscular Christianity of England's public school system. Coubertin's vision of a 'physical and moral elite' was shared by Lt Georges Hébert, author of a celebrated text on scientific gymnastics. Hébert touted rational exercise as an instrument of regenerative national hygiene:

> We are stifling beneath a mountain of paper! Day by day, intellectualism gains in importance. We need above all men of action, of 'character'. And to educate such men, we must organize physical culture.[32]

The parallel efforts of Coubertin and Hébert fed into a public campaign to found a Collège d'athlètes, a so-called 'école de la renaissance physique', intended for the training of physical education instructors and future Olympians. The campaign, underwritten by the likes of Colrat, Richepin and Rodin, was launched in 1912 with publication of a manifesto couched in classical idiom.[33] The project came to fruition in April 1913 with the foundation of the first Collège d'Athlètes at Reims, to which Poincaré himself paid a much-publicized visit.[34]

The Reims facility was intended for adults, but sports enthusiasts were just as concerned with the physical and moral redemption of the young. Coubertin, André Chéradame, a nationalist publicist, and a certain Enseign Benoit founded the Éclaireurs de France in 1911. Scouting's appeal lay in its promise of spiritual revitalization through hard physical effort. Dressed in a simple and practical outfit 'which calls to mind the garb of Boers and cowboys', young tenderfoots plunged themselves into 'the primitive life'. Fortified by fresh air and exercise, they emerged 'vigorous, prepared to face life with a solid morality, and profoundly devoted to their *patrie*'.[35] Enthusiasm for the primitive life, however, did not preclude an admiration for the most advanced technology. The scouts' *comité de patronage* included president of the TCF Abel Ballif and the Vicomte de Vaulx, vice president of Aéro-club de France. The scouts of today were the sports car drivers and aviators of tomorrow.[36]

A true classicism trained *esprits d'élite*, equipped to succeed in a world of technology and sport. In the domain of arts policy too, cultural revivalists cast about for a trimmed-down aesthetic, for a classicism appropriate to the twentieth century. Art Deco is associated with the 1920s and 1930s, but its origins may be traced to an earlier period.[37] Already before the Great War, designers such as Louis Süe and Paul Fallot were experimenting in new forms of interior decoration. They eschewed the muted pastels and arabesques of art nouveau in favour of ensembles remarkable for clarity of line and brightness of colour. But Art Deco designers did not streamline to the point of a boxy asceticism. A well-made piece of furniture, it was felt, ought still to be comfortable and constructed for repose; and it ought still to be elegant, made of the finest materials and graceful in its contours. *L'Opinion* exalted the Art Deco aesthetic as the perfect marriage of tradition and modernity. The new style was celebrated (erroneously) as a home-grown, national product which, in its balanced refinement and sense of the whole, conformed to the fundamental principles of French tradition. Yet Art Deco was also a fresh and novel style 'with a generous solidity, a healthy, logical, simple strength'.[38]

A daring but elegant simplicity was the aesthetic ideal of cultural revivalists. It was attachment to this ideal that inspired their enthusiasm for Art Deco – and for parallel movements in the arts. For the painting of Maurice Denis in whose brightly coloured and decorative canvases Paul-Boncour detected a praiseworthy and 'almost superstitious emulation of the rich and noble forms of Raphael'. For the suave symmetry of Charles Plumet's and Mallet-Stevens's architecture. In all these forms, pursuit of an unadorned directness was coupled with a sense of refinement and luxury, a combination of profound appeal to reforming conservatives who hungered for a modern aesthetic which did not entail a rupture with tradition.[39]

Urbanists too dreamed of a reconciliation of past and present. Such was the vision of Georges Risler:

> A city... is an organism which grows unceasingly.... Just as we shape the growth of young trees... ought we not by the same token draw up plans for the expansion of our great cities, plans... to shape growth and make it profitable... all the while preserving the aesthetic beauties of our old urban stock?[40]

Various schemes for the redesign of Paris were floated in the prewar years, which, taken together, give a clear indication of how urbanists like Georges Risler planned to effect a marriage of beauty and growth. All agreed on the need to preserve and, via an extension of *espaces libres*, to embellish the city's old central core. But it was recognized at the same time that provision had to be made for growth. To accommodate increased volumes of traffic, Hénard called for construction of a network of ring-roads linked by a system of transverse and lateral arteries crisscrossing the city centre. To absorb the economic and demographic spillover consequent upon expansion, Risler projected a ring of satellite factory villages endowed with congenial tract housing and connected to Paris by rail.[41] Risler, for one, grasped that realization of such a complex package of changes hinged on long-range planning, and he urged Paris municipal authorities to draft just such a plan. Councillor Louis Dausset, a latter-day Déroulèdist turned real-estate booster, took up the project. A commission was formed which, counselled by Musée Social representatives, issued a declaration of guiding principles in 1913.[42] The urban reformers of the prewar years, however sensitive to the issue of preservation, did not conceive of the Paris of tomorrow as a museum, but as a happy and planned amalgam of old and new.

The same double commitment to old and new shaped the national revival's plans for rural France. Conservationists combined a back-to-the-land nostalgia with a clear-eyed determination to exploit the economic potential of the nation's rustic charms. In 1913, *Le Matin* organized a national conference, a so-called 'Estates-General of Tourism'. The conference divided into four working committees, one devoted to conservation and a second to regional issues. But a third took up the question of modern hotel management, and a fourth treated 'the relations between tourism and sport'.[43] How were conservation, sport, hotel-keeping and tourism linked? It took little business sense to spot the money-making possibilities in the development of picturesque sites and recreational areas. The careful husbanding of natural resources would promote 'the glorification of France', but conservation was no less an engine 'of general prosperity'.[44]

Nor were regionalists indifferent to the commercial possibilities of rural development. A region, Charles-Brun argued, was defined by climate, geology, local culture and, not least, productive capacities. A true regionalism then entailed a dual commitment: to preservation of local cultures but also to a rigorous *mise en valeur* of local economies. To organize development, both Marin and Hennessy envisioned a system of supra-departmental regional councils entrusted with wide authority on questions of economic policy. Lest council politics be infected with the kind of crass vote-mongering that poisoned departmental politics, regionalists proposed an electoral scheme designed to ensure a satisfactory *représentation aux compétences*. It was recommended that councils be elected by local corporate bodies – employers' syndicates, Chambers of Commerce, and so on.[45]

National revival partisans dreamed of a new elite: cultured and *sportif*; classical in its tastes but sympathetic to a simplification of form; respectful of the nation's natural patrimony, yet also development-minded. It seemed, as revival partisans looked at *les jeunes gens d'aujourd'hui*, that such an elite was in the making. One obstacle, however, remained to its triumph: the parliamentary constitution of the republic.

AN ELITIST REPUBLIC

Dissatisfaction with the institutions of the Third Republic was not new. The anti-parliamentary agitation of the *belle époque*, however, was distinctive in two respects: in its permeation of mainstream republican opinion and in its generation of an alternative constitutional vision – elitist, business-oriented and presidentialist.

The most notorious of the republic's prewar critics were Robert de Jouvenel and Gustave Le Bon. Jouvenel's *La République des camarades* (1914), was a full-blown indictment of the regime's political class, charged with cronyism and incompetence. Le Bon's diagnosis was harsher still. Universal suffrage had unleashed the masses into the public arena, a creature of irrational passions, which required resolute handling. The nation's natural authorities, however, had failed to show the requisite firmness, allowing destructive demagogues to step into the breach. But whether mediocrity or demagoguery were to blame, Jouvenel and Le Bon agreed that the parliamentary republic had brought France to a hazardous crossroads.[46]

Despite the radical tone of such criticism, Jouvenel and Le Bon were by no means marginal men. Jouvenel worked the lecture circuit for the regionalist movement. His brother Henri was one of Colrat's oldest friends, and indeed, *La République des camarades* was first excerpted in Colrat's *L'Opinion* before it appeared as a book. Le Bon was well known in elite circles thanks in no small part to a relentless self-promotion. From 1901, he hosted regular gatherings to which influential political and literary personalities were invited: Bardoux, Deschanel, Marin and, of course, Poincaré.[47] Jouvenel and Le Bon were welcome in elite milieux, and so too was the anti-parliamentarism they preached.

An item high on the conservative agenda was a change in electoral procedure from the *scrutin d'arrondissement* to proportional representation. Colrat endorsed the measure as an instrument to break the political stranglehold of what he called 'political committees without competence or mandate'. The current system, it was claimed by ARD deputy Étienne Flandin to an ADCM congress, favoured special interests to the detriment of 'the general interest'; proportional representation, on the other hand, would cause a purifying wind to cut through the corruption, giving voice to competent and principled minorities.[48]

Should electoral reform fail in its intended purpose, conservatives were prepared to tinker more substantially with the republic's constitution. As long as the Chamber was dominated by 'intellectuals', by 'lawyers, doctors, veterinarians, in a word *des incompétences*' (the phrase is Hennessy's), how could it be trusted to pursue sound fiscal policy? It made sense under the circumstances to circumscribe Parliament's initiative in fiscal matters.[49] Yet, if not by Parliament, how were social and fiscal policy to be made? Through negotiations between the executive and relevant interests came the answer. Poincaré himself was known to favour regular, if informal contacts between government and organized business, and more than one businessman talked of making such exchanges a matter of legal obligation.[50] Conservative reformers, ever anxious to contain democracy in the interest of competent elites, even entertained creation of a syndical senate. Elected by the organized professions, such a body would guarantee representation to the nation's productive elite which had proven its mettle in the practical affairs of commerce and industry.[51]

But the ultimate trump of an errant Chamber was a strong president, and on the question of presidential organization, reform-minded conservatives took a lead from the United States. National revival polemics were permeated with flattering asides to the principled character of America's leaders. In a laudatory preface to the French edition of Teddy Roosevelt's *American Ideal*, Rousiers praised Roosevelt as a 'Christian gentleman'. To *L'Opinion* he was a man of unflagging probity who had quit the republican party in 1910 to protest against 'republican bossism'. The ALP's preferences went to Wilson. It found in the Virginia-born democrat an *aristocrate à l'américaine*, a worthy heir of old south traditions of *noblesse oblige*. But Wilson's greatest asset was his strength of character, his determination as president to break an obdurate Congress to his will. If only France's president had the temerity to act with equal resolution. The ALP newspaper wrote apropos Poincaré's election to the presidency: 'It was not to be a rubber stamp manipulated by Parliament that public opinion designated M. Poincaré. M. W. Wilson has set the example: will he [Poincaré] follow it?'[52]

The United States owed its success, however, not just to great statesmanship but also to the soundness of its institutions. The US Constitution sanctioned the forceful exercise of executive authority, whereas in France sovereign power was vested in a Parliament that frittered away its energies in sterile debate. To rescue the nation from drift and chaos, a 'révolution de l'ordre' was called for. The moment had come for responsible elites 'to assume a clearly offensive posture'.[53] In 1911, *L'Opinion* published an article 'La Quatrième République' under the pseudonymous signature 'Cato', which projected the contents of an imagined presidential address to Parliament in the aftermath of the 1914 elections. The address insisted on the chief executive's right: to negotiate and ratify treaties; to address the Chamber at will; to reopen debate on ill-conceived legislation; to adjourn the Chamber for up to one month; and to dissolve it entirely in case of misbehaviour. Jules Roche, a Fédération Républicaine deputy, carried *L'Opinion*'s presidentialist fantasies one step further. An extension of executive privilege was pointless unless the president himself bore the legitimating stamp of universal suffrage. Roche advocated direct election of France's chief executive by popular ballot, citing the US system as a model.[54]

When the various political and administrative schemes advanced by revival partisans are added together, they constitute a constitutional ensemble as much reformative as reactionary in underlying thrust. The ideal republic of conservative fancy was governed by a president of forceful character, invested with extensive discretionary powers. It was expected that he would take vigorous action but only after due consultation with the relevant economic interests. As for the Chamber of Deputies, checked by a powerful executive and by a business-controlled corporate Senate, it would be reduced to minority status. The predilection for discretionary decision making and for energetic executive action, the stress on corporate representation and consultation, betray a hardened will to roll back public participation in government and a commensurate commitment to enhance the role of private interests. The democratic Third Republic had placed too many hurdles in the path of reforming elites. Not so the national revival's streamlined republic of the future.

National revival partisans dreamed of a new elite, high-minded and dynamic, suited to the task which lay before it: the moral and material rearmament of the nation for the test of survival in a competitive world. Such a vision represented a break with the defensive nationalism of the Dreyfus years. To be sure, the ranks of the national revival were sprinkled with anti-Dreyfusard veterans, and many anti-Dreyfusard themes echo in national revival rhetoric: anti-socialism, Germanophobia, resentment of academe. But in contrast to the *frondeur* radicalism of the anti-Dreyfusard leagues, prewar nationalism was a mainstream phenomenon anchored in France's economic, cultural and political elites. Nor was the revival a mere reflex of fear in the face of modernity. On the contrary, its votaries spoke less of decline and decadence than of reawakening and regeneration. At stake in conservative reform was preservation of elite rule through managed change, but more: the reaffirmation of French grandeur. Turn-of-the-century nationalism recoiled from the outside world with an inward-looking rancour. The nationalism of the prewar years did not eschew protective measures but conceived them as a prelude to offensive action. The stated aim was to enhance France's leverage in world affairs through aggressive economic, cultural and political initiatives, and in pursuit of this goal, conservative-minded reformers were prepared to draw on foreign models. Forward-looking and expansionist, the neo-nationalism of the *belle époque* attested to a signal recovery of self-confidence on the part of France's conservative elites.

The national revival set the conservative agenda for decades to come, and in this connection it is tempting to understand the *réveil* as a forerunner of Vichyism. Many Poincaré partisans became disillusioned with republican politics of the interwar years. Colrat converted to Maurrasism; Bardoux joined Ernest Mercier's Redressement Français. Bérard, Charles-Brun, Hennessy and Flandin were all one-time revivalists who subscribed, if momentarily, to Pétain's National Revolution. It is not only in matters of personnel that continuities can be discerned. Corporatism, middle-class defence, regionalism and anti-parliamentarianism were watchwords of the Vichy regime as of the *réveil national*.

Still, by no means all revival veterans succumbed to the Vichy temptation – Marin and Paul-Boncour, for example. And more than one son of the national revival chose the path of resistance instead. Such was the case of Charles de Gaulle, a 1912 graduate of Saint-Cyr, the very prototype of Agathon's *jeunes gens d'aujourd'hui*.[55] De Gaulle admired the writings of the revival's spiritual mentors, Bergson and Péguy. In the interwar years, he struck up friendships with Émile Mayer (from 1907 to 1914 military correspondent at *L'Opinion*) and with Paul-Boncour. He took an interest in Bardoux's critique of parliamentarianism, and on and off, over the course of a lifetime, flirted with regionalist schemes and the idea of a syndical representation. De Gaulle and Gaullism too may fairly be placed in the lineage of the neo-nationalism of the *belle époque*. From a certain angle, the Gaullist Fifth Republic bears more than a passing resemblance to the elitist regime imagined by national revival reformers. Pompidou's expansionist, pro-business policies, Malraux's refurbishment of Paris and regionalist experiments, Debré's presidential constitution, worked out in practice the unrealized schemes of Lebon, Paul-Boncour and Roche. Certainly, the Fifth Republic's welfare provisions and its sometime dirigiste proclivities would have given even the hardiest of national revival reformers pause, but the Gaullist pursuit of grandeur through a combination of elite rule and developmental policy might have struck many Poincarists as the consummation of their traditionalist/transformative aspirations.

The national revival constituted a seminal moment in the history of the modern French right. Its Janus-faced project foreshadowed Pétain's National Revolution but also, if more distantly, the birth of a new, Gaullist France. If de Gaulle married France to the twentieth century, the *réveil national*, it may be ventured, initiated the courtship.

NOTES

1 On the revival as a movement of social defence, see: Georges Michon, *Le Préparation à la guerre, la loi de trois ans (1910–1914)* (Paris: Rivière 1935), pp. 36–7, 113, 210; David Sumler, 'Domestic influence on the national revival in France, 1909–1914', *French Historical Studies*, vol. 6 (autumn 1970), pp. 517–37; and Henri Guillemin, *Nationalistes et 'nationaux' (1870–1940)* (Paris: Gallimard, 1974), p. 149. On the revival's impact on elites, see the discussion on Eugen Weber, *The Nationalist Revival in France, 1905–1914* (Berkeley, Calif.: University of California Press, 1968), pp. 6–8. While Weber argues for the importance of the elites in question, Jean-Jacques Becker is inclined to dismiss them as marginal to public life: *1914. Comment les français sont entrés dans la guerre* (Paris: Presses de la Fondation Nationale des Sciences Politiques, 1977), pp. 30ff.

2 'Union du commerce et de l'industrie pour la défense sociale', *La Croix*, 18 January 1898; Archives nationales (AN), Paris, F7 12720, 30 June and 6 July 1903; *Bulletin de l'union du commerce et de l'industrie pour la défense sociale* (hereafter cited as *Bulletin de l'UCIDF*), January 1908, front page; Georges Lefranc, *Les Organisations patronales en France du passé au présent* (Paris: Payot, 1976), pp. 64–5; 'Réunion du Conseil général de l'Union des intérêts économiques', *Le Réveil économique*,

no. 2 (July–August?) 1910; 'Réunion du 4e Conseil général de l'Union des intérêts économiques', ibid., 12 March 1913.

3 Lefranc, *Les Organisations patronales*, pp. 39–42; Michael Rust, 'Business and politics in the Third Republic: the Comité des forges and the French steel industry, 1896–1914', PhD thesis, Princeton University, Princeton, NJ, 1973, pp. 102–4; Bibliothèque de la Chambre de commerce de Paris, I 8–63, Fédérations, Confédérations, flier c. 1903.

4 Maurice Lévy-Leboyer, 'Le Patronat français a-t-il été malthusien?' *Le Mouvement social*, no. 88 (July–September 1974), pp. 26–8; Rust, 'Business', pp. 66ff., 461, 472; Sanford Elwitt, 'Social reform and social order in late nineteenth-century France: the Musée Social and its friends', *French Historical Studies*, vol. 11 (spring 1980), p. 448.

5 Jacques Expert-Bezançon, *Les Organisations de défense patronale* doctoral thesis, Faculty of Law, University of Paris, 1911, pp. 89–90; André-E. Sayous, *La Défense patronale* (Paris: Fédération des industriels et commerçants français, 1906), pp. 3, 16; T. B. Caldwell, 'The Syndicat des Employés du Commerce et de l'Industrie (1888–1919)', *International Review of Social History*, vol. 11 (1966), p. 245; AN F7 12793, 26 April 1905 and 18 August 1906.

6 Colrat, 'Vers l'équilibre social', *Les Études fiscales et sociales*, August–September 1909, pp. 6–7; and 'La Situation du petit commerce en France', *L'Opinion*, 10 June 1911, p. 732.

7 See Philip Nord, 'Le Mouvement des petits commerçants et la politique en France de 1888 à 1914', *Le Mouvement social*, no. 114 (January–March 1981), pp. 52–4.

8 Charles Grosclaude, 'Sincérité d'origine', *Bulletin de l'UCIDF*, March 1913, p. 15; Lebon cited in 'Pour la Défense des produits de notre sol et de notre industrie. Causerie de M. Marcel Dubois', *Bulletin de la Fédération des industriels et des commerçants français* (hereafter *Bulletin de la FICF*), January 1913, pp. 141–2; Lysis (Eugène Letailleur), *Oligarchie financière* (Paris, n.d.), p. 190; Sayous, 'Les Valeurs allemandes sur le marché de Paris', *Bulletin de la FICF*, June 1909, p. 399.

9 'Pour la Défense', p. 133.

10 Rousiers, *Les Syndicats industriels de producteurs en France et à l'étranger* (Paris: Colin, 1901), p. 274. See also Laur, *De l'accaparement*, 3 vols (Paris: Société anonyme des publications scientifiques et industriels, 1900), Martin Saint-Léon, *Cartels et trusts* (Paris: Lecoffre, 1903).

11 'La Fédération des industriels et des commerçants français. Son Programme, son oeuvre et ses espérances', *Bulletin de la FICF*, February 1905, p. 111.

12 'Assemblée générale du Congrès (20 avril 1906)', *Bulletin de la FICF*, May 1907, p. 556; Georges Hersent, 'Nouveau régime de nos ports de commerce', ibid., May 1908, pp. 308ff.

13 Georges de Nouvion, 'L'Emprunt', *Le Réveil économique*, 24 June 1914; Jacques Marc, 'Pour le développement des travaux publics,' ibid., 10 and 17 June 1914.

14 Rondet-Saint, '1 020 000 allemands contre 5 000 français', *L'Énergie française*, 16 November 1907, p. 726; Millerand cited in *Les Forces productives de la France* (Paris: Alcan, 1909), pp. 182–3; 'Les Causes principales de la décadence de notre marine marchande. Causerie de M. André Lebon', *Bulletin de la FICF*, April 1910, pp. 238–43; 'La Marine marchande', *Bulletin de l'UCIDF*, July 1905, p. 12.

15 Lebon cited in 'La Fédération des industriels et des commerçants français', *Bulletin de la FICF*, February 1905, p. 111; Octave Aubert, 'Le Crédit à l'exportation', *Le Réveil économique*, 14 and 28 January 1914; 'Crédit', *Bulletin mensuel de l'Institut international pour l'étude du problème des classes moyennes*, February 1913, pp. 71–5; 'Le Crédit au petit commerce et à la petite industrie', *Bulletin de la FICF*, January 1913, pp. 120ff.

16 Deschanel cited in *Les Forces productives*, p. 155; Henry Laporte, 'La Vrai Nationalisme financier', *Le Correspondant*, 25 March 1913, p. 1079; Sayous, 'Des Avantages à réclamer pour notre industrie ou notre agriculture nationale', *Bulletin de la FICF*, February 1909, pp. 163, 196.

17 Rousiers, *L'Élite dans la société moderne* (Paris: Colin, 1914), p. 147.

18 'Jean Richepin. Salut d'entrée à *L'Opinion*', *L'Opinion*, 6 July 1912, pp. 1–2; Richepin, 'La Ligue pour la culture française et les programmes de 1902', ibid., 5 and 12 July 1913, pp. 18–19, 49–50.

19 Demolins, *A Quoi tient la supériorité des Anglo-Saxons* (Paris: Firmin-Didot, 1897), p. 111; 'Les Groupes d'expansion commerciale. Causerie de M. Edmond Demolins', *Bulletin de la FICF*, February 1905, pp. 118–20; Louis-Modeste Leroy, *L'Education nationale au XXe siècle* (Paris: Vuibert, 1914), p. 307.

20 See the articles by Agathon in *L'Opinion*: 'Les Jeunes Gens d'aujourd'hui', 1 June 1912, p. 685; 'L'Esprit de la nouvelle Sorbonne', 23 July 1910, p. 97; 'La Sorbonne contre la culture classique', 13 August 1910, p. 208; 'La Domination primaire', 29 October 1910, p. 546.

21 Louis Guitard, *La Petite Histoire de la IIIe République* (Paris: Les Sept Couleurs, 1959), pp. 48–9, 56; Rust, 'Business', p. 439; Guillemin, *Nationalists*, p. 98; 'Ce qu'on dit', *L'Opinion*, 22 February 1913.

22 Guitard, *La Petite Histoire*, p. 27.

23 Paul-Boncour, *Art et démocratie* (Paris: Ollendorff, 1912), pp. 230–79.

24 ibid., p. 64.

25 See the interview with a crusty Rodin in 'La Crise des métiers', *L'Opinion*, 4 February 1911, pp. 143–4; Paul-Boncour, 'Vers un Réveil de l'art décoratif moderne', *Le Matin*, 23 October 1912.

26 Association de Défense des Classes Moyennes, 'Quatrième Congrès annuel, L'Apprentissage', *L'Opinion*, 16 November 1912 (supplement), pp. 66–8; Colrat, 'Pour l'Apprentissage', *Le Figaro*, 11 May 1912.

27 Paul-Boncour, *Art et démocratie*, pp. 215, 220–1; Georges Risler, 'Les Plans d'aménagement et d'extension des villes', *Musée social, Mémoires et documents* (1912), pp. 338–9. See also Eugène Hénard, *Études sur les transformations de Paris*, Vol. VI, (Paris: Librairies-imprimeries réunies, 1905), pp. 228–31; Robert de Souza, 'La Construction des villes', *L'Opinion*, 13 December 1913, p. 759.

28 Hénard, *Études*, Vol. III, p. 83, and (1904), Vol. IV, pp. 105–7; Peter Wolf, *Eugène Hénard and the Beginning of Urbanism in Paris, 1900–1914* (The Hague: International Federation for Housing and Planning, 1968), p. 77; Risler, 'Les Espaces libres', *Revue de Paris*, 15 September 1910, pp. 388–9; and Georges Bénoît-Lévy, *La Ville et son image* (Paris, 1910), p. 32.

29 Paul-Boncour, *Art et démocratie*, pp. 220–1; Formont, 'Les Oeuvres d'énergie. Le Touring Club de France', *L'Energie française*, 1 December 1906, p. 759; André Lichtenberger, 'La Lutte pour la race, espaces libres et terrains de jeux', *L'Opinion*, 24 Decenmber 1910, pp. 801–3; and Elizabeth Pulling, 'Regeneration through reform: conservation and the nationalist revival in France, 1900–1914' senior thesis, Princeton University, Princeton, NJ, 1985.

30 Charles-Brun cited in ibid., pp. 9, 82–5. See also Charles-Brun, *Le Régionalisme* (Paris: Bibliothèque régionaliste, 1911), pp. 46, 277–8; 'La Représentation professionnelle en France', *Bulletin mensuel de l'Institut international pour l'étude du problème des classes moyennes*, March–April 1914, p. 208.

31 For tributes to Teddy Roosevelt, see: Eugène Duthoit, *Les Idées du président Roosevelt* (Lille: Morel, 1903); Henri Moysset, '"La Vie intense" du président Roosevelt', *L'Association catholique*, 15 January 1903, pp. 7–15, and 15 February 1903, pp. 116–29; and Rousiers's translation of Roosevelt's *The American Ideal: L'Idéal américain* (Paris: Colin, 1910).

32 Lt Georges Hébert, 'Comment organiser l'éducation physique en France', *L'Opinion*, 28 June 1913, p. 802.

33 'Le Collège d'athlètes', *L'Opinion*, 19 October 1912, p. 485.

34 On Coubertin, see Weber, 'Pierre de Coubertin and the introduction of organised sport in France', *Journal of Contemporary History*, vol. 5 (1970), pp. 5–6. On the Collège d'athlètes, see: 'Il faut créer un collège d'athlètes', *L'Opinion*, 14 September 1912, pp. 335–6; Georges Rozet, 'La Grande Journée de Reims', ibid., 25 October 1913, p. 541.

35 J.-Raymond Guasco, 'Deux Jours de guerre avec les Boy-Scouts', *L'Opinion*, 29 March 1913, pp. 404–5; André Chéradame, *La Crise française* (Paris: Plon-Nourrit, 1912), pp. 394, 397.

36 Doumer and Marin also sat on the Éclaireurs' Comité de Patronage. 'XYZ', 'Méditation de rentrée', *L'Opinion*, 29 October 1910, p. 563.

37 For what follows, see the remarkable series of interviews conducted by F.-G. de Maigret and published under the title 'Une Renaissance décorative', in *L'Opinion*: 21 December 1912, pp. 790–1; 11 January 1913, pp. 54–5; 18 January 1913, pp. 85–6; 1 February 1913, p. 150; 8 March 1913, p. 309.

38 Alfred Richet, 'L'Evolution récente du mobilier', *La Revue*, 15 April 1914, p. 521.

39 Paul-Boncour, 'La Villa Médicis', *L'Opinion*, 16 March 1912, p. 324; Gabriel Mourey, 'Un Architecte: M. Charles Plumet', ibid., 2 November 1912, p. 555.

40 Risler, 'Les Espaces libres dans les grandes villes et les cités jardins', *Musée social, Mémoires et documents* (1910), p. 370.

41 For the principles underlying the new urbanism, see: Wolf, *Eugène Hénard, passim*; Hénard, *Études sur les transformations de Paris*, 6 vols (Paris, 1903–9) Bénoît-Lévy, *La Ville*, pp. 56–63; Risler, 'Les Espaces libres', pp. 376–404.

42 Anthony Sutcliffe, *Towards the Planned City. Germany, Britain, the United States and France, 1780–1914* (New York: St. Martin's Press, 1981), p. 159; Préfecture du Département de la Seine, *Commission d'extension de Paris. Aperçu historique et considérations techniques préliminaires (circulation, espaces libres)*, Vol. II (Paris: Préfecture de Département de la Seine, 1913), pp. 62–6.

43 Guasco, 'Les Etats-Généraux du tourisme', *L'Opinion*, 30 August 1913, pp. 259–60.

44 Formont, 'Les Oeuvres d'énergie. Le Touring Club de France', *L'Energie française*, 1 December 1906, p. 760.

45 Charles-Brun, *Le Régionalisme*, pp. 95, 100ff.; for Hennessy's views, see: 'La Profession représentée', p. 260; and 'Pour la Représentation professionnelle', *Le Réveil économique*, 2 April 1913.

46 For Jouvenel's views, see: 'La République des camarades', *L'Opinion*, 7, 14, and 21 March 1914, pp. 289–91, 321–3, 354–8; on Le Bon's, see: *La Psychologie politique et la défense sociale* (Paris: Flammarion, 1910), pp. 118–22, 148–52, 202–5, 330–47.

47 On Jouvenel's connections, see: 'Régionalisme et représentation professionnelle', *L'Action libérale populaire*, 15 November 1913, p. 342; Guitard, *La Petite Histoire*, p. 17. On Le Bon's, see Robert Nye, *The Origins of Crowd Psychology, Gustave Le Bon and the Crisis of Mass Democracy in the Third Republic* (London: Sage, 1975), pp. 84, 110, 113, 161, 177.

48 Colrat, 'Vers l'Équilibre social', *Les Études fiscales et sociales*, August-September 1909, p. 10; Flandin in 'Congrès des classes moyennes', ibid., November–December 1909, p. 63; Colrat, 'RP ou RC', *L'Opinion*, 3 February 1912, p. 135.

49 Hennessy as cited by A. Trépreau, 'A propos de la représentation professionnelle', *L'Idéal*, 15 October 1913; and 'Les Anciens Ministres du commerce, Jules Roche', *L'Ami des petits commerçants*, 15 October 1902. See also Rust, 'Business', p. 355.

50 'Congrès de la Confédération des groupes commerciaux et industriels', *Bulletin mensuel de l'Institut international*, March-April 1914, p. 184.

51 Martin Saint-Léon, *L'Organisation professionnelle de l'avenir* (Paris: Vitte, 1905), pp. 32–3; 'Pour la Représentation professionnelle', *Le Réveil économique*, 2 and 30 April 1913; Colrat, 'A la Confédération des groupes commerciaux', *L'Opinion*, 9 March 1912, p. 295; Paul-Boncour, *Le Fédéralisme économique* (Paris: Alcan, 1900).

52 On Roosevelt, see: Rousiers, *L'Idéal américain*, p. xv; and Georges Gaulis, 'Les Élections américaines', *L'Opinion*, 12 November 1910, p. 611. On Wilson, see *L'Action libérale populaire*: L.L. 'Le Nouveau Président des Etats-Unis', 15 November 1912, p. 339; and 'Les Deux Présidents', 15 April 1913, p. 117.

53 Jules Roche, 'La Révolution de l'ordre', *Les Études fiscales et sociales*, 15 March 1909, p. 6; Charles Prevet of the Fédération Républicaine as cited in 'La Situation politique générale', *Bulletin de l'UCIDF*, January 1912, p. 6.

54 Caton, 'La Quatrième République', *L'Opinion*, 4 November 1911, p. 580. For Roche's views (and more generally those of the Fédération Républicaine), see 'Élection et attributions du président de la république', *Bulletin de l'UCIDF*, March 1912, pp. 3–10.

55 For what follows, see: Jean Touchard, *Le Gaullisme 1940–1969* (Paris: Seuil, 1978), pp. 20, 126, 129, 235, 300; and Jean Lacouture, *De Gaulle*, Vol. I (Paris: Seuil, 1984), pp. 54, 137–8, 197.

PART 3
Policy in the era of nationalism

Introduction

David Stevenson

Nationalism is notoriously an elusive term. For that reason this introduction will begin with an essay in definition, before turning to the chapters reviewed here. As the title of this book suggests, nationalism is to be distinguished from nationhood, which is a feeling of belonging to, a sentiment of identification with, one's nation. As such it is the precondition for and taproot of nationalism itself, but the latter is more cerebral, more self-conscious, and entails a programme of political action. In Anthony D. Smith's careful definition, nationalism is 'an ideological movement for the attainment and maintenance of autonomy, cohesion and individuality for a social group deemed by some of its members to constitute an actual or potential nation'.[1] The nation should possess its own self-governing state, and this should be a cohesive and inclusive state, within whose boundaries as many members as possible of the nation are gathered. But in late nineteenth-century France, unlike much of Europe, these initial goals had already largely been accomplished. National independence was firmly established, at least juridically, and national cohesion substantially so, with the glaring exception of Alsace-Lorraine. From this point on then, what, apart from recovering the lost provinces, would form the agenda of a distinctively nationalist programme of policy?

The answer lay both within and without the state. Within, the task for nationalists was to raise the national consciousness, to stimulate the sense of nationhood, of their fellow citizens. D'Azeglio's remark, 'We have made Italy: now we must make Italians', has a wider applicability. The export of urban and metropolitan French culture to the rural fastnesses of the west and south has been retraced in Eugen Weber's *Peasants into Frenchmen: the Modernization of Rural France, 1870–1914* (Stanford, Calif.: University of California Press, 1976, esp. chaps 7 and 29). As he points out, there are similarities with the implantation of French culture in the overseas colonies, and this aspect of nationalist policy has some of the features of an internal imperialism. Yet the imposition of national identity from above – through universal conscription or the new primary schools, worked in conjunction with other social forces developing autonomously from below – the growth of long-distance trade and communications, the emergence of a national press, labour migration to the cities. For this reason it failed to generate strong movements of provincial separatism in reaction against metropolitan encroachments. The creation of a sense of nationhood can indeed be represented at one level as a form of cultural imperialism, but it is also more than that, and the question raised here is the deeper one of what constitutes the nation itself. The contrasting approaches to that question that were circulating in the nineteenth century emerge from the exchange of views in 1870 about the identity of Alsace between the German and French historians, Mommsen and Fustel de Coulanges. To Mommsen's objective criteria of national identity such as ethnic origin and language Fustel responded with the subjective one that 'The homeland is what one loves (La patrie, c'est ce qu'on aime).... Alsace may be German by race and language. But by nationality and sense of homeland it is French.' Or, to quote from Renan's celebrated lecture of 1882, 'The existence of a nation is... an eternal plebiscite.'[2] From these two starting points two approaches to the task of internal nationbuilding follow. The first is universalist and integrationist and entails the use of devices such as flags, anthems, military service and compulsory schooling to turn a latent or potential sense of nationhood into an actual one. This, to generalize, was the basis of French official policy before 1914. But an alternative, more xenophobic and exclusionist approach rests on the premise that certain elements in society – foreign immigrants, freemasons, Jews – are irretrievably anti-national and harmful and must be officially isolated and discriminated against. This second strand was already evident in the writing of some French nationalists in this period, and was ultimately to find expression in the Vichy government's *révolution nationale*.

The rest of this introduction and the four chapters here reviewed deal more with the external dimension of nationalism and policy. An ideologically consistent 'nationalist' foreign policy would entail promoting national self-determination and the establishment of nation-states not only within one's own borders but also everywhere else. There was a tradition of such nationalism in nineteenth-century France, especially among republicans and Bonapartists. But it was in conflict, especially after 1870, with a second and more defensive limited nationalism, which gave priority to the security and interests of the French nation-state itself. The Russian alliance concluded in 1891–4, with its implicit abandonment of the cause of Polish nationalism, is a case in point. In practice this second form of nationalism could and did slide over into imperialism: into a denial of the rights of self-determination and development to other nations and potential nations if these conflicted with the requirements of one's own. Outside Europe French nationalism had become imperialist long before 1914; inside Europe it had also been so in the earlier nineteenth century and became so once again, in the shape of French war aims in the Saar and Rhineland after the outbreak of the First World

War.³ It is difficult, however, to define a point at which a country's foreign policy becomes a distinctively nationalist one, and it is best here to think of a spectrum or continuum. What distinguishes a nationalist in external policy is the *priority*, the degree of importance, that he attributes to accomplishing national goals, and the extent to which he favours concentrating national energy and resources upon them. Among the indicators of the 'nationalism' of a country's external policy are the size of its defence budget, the proportion of its manpower undertaking military service, and the assertiveness and single-mindedness of its diplomacy. By implication, in the left/right political conflict over the distribution of power and wealth within the country, nationalists will tend to be opportunists, favouring one or other side according to their judgement of what is needed to attain external objectives. All nineteenth-century French regimes potentially therefore faced an undercurrent of nationalist opposition, as none was able to reverse the decisions of 1814–15 and 1870–1, though the Second Empire in the 1850s and the Third Republic in the 1870s and early 1880s and the last years before 1914 perhaps came closest to satisfying nationalist desires. Whereas under the monarchical regimes of the earlier nineteenth century this undercurrent was liable to express itself in support for Bonapartism or republicanism, under the Third Republic, when dissatisfaction resurfaced from the 1880s, it took on authoritarian, right-wing forms. The political evolution of Paul Déroulède epitomizes the trend.[4] Hence the apparent shift from left to right in the political centre of gravity of French nationalism in the later nineteenth century; although this is also to be accounted for by the separate movement of much of French radicalism and socialism towards a pacifist and internationalist position.

Of the chapters in Part 3, those of Jean-Charles Jauffret and John Keiger deal primarily with the sources of nationalist pressure on policy formulation; those of Gérard Canini and Jean-Claude Allain with policy itself. Jauffret and Keiger consider the influence of the military and of the diplomatic corps, and Jauffret generally downplays the significance of the former. Of the episodes he examines of rumoured or actual military subversion during the first two decades of the Third Republic, none appears to have seriously endangered the regime. He finds evidence of Bonapartist plotting in 1874 and royalist in 1877; and of nostalgia in the officer corps for the professional army that had predated the introduction of a qualified form of universal conscription in 1872. But here already lay a dilemma: a conscript army gave the advantage of numbers, and could be justified not only by democratic but also by strategic arguments, even if not all officers found such arguments persuasive. It was difficult to be radically alienated on patriotic grounds from a regime that, at least under the leadership of Adolphe Thiers in 1871–3, rebuilt French strength with considerable success. In any case, after decades of political instability, most officers owed loyalty to their profession and to *Notre Dame de France* rather than to any particular form of government, and they would support whoever had effective control. In the moments of crisis when that control was in doubt, they played a waiting game. Thus Jauffret finds little evidence of military disloyalty during the *seize mai* confrontation between republicans and royalists in 1877, partly because the authorities prudently avoided forcing the army to take sides. The same was true 10 years later, at the climax of the Boulanger Affair. Only a few careerist officers were prepared to dabble in politics, and they were kept under surveillance by the republican politicians. The apolitical preferences of the majority were encouraged by the system of promotion committees (*commissions de classement*), which until 1899 shielded appointments below the most senior level from ministerial interference.

Jauffret's account runs to the end of the 1880s, though it also helps to clarify the course of civil–military relations in the more turbulent succeeding phase. By the time of the next great crisis, in 1899, Maurice Larkin has found evidence that several corps commanders might have rallied to an anti-republican coup, but they were still reluctant to take the initiative themselves.[5] With the subsequent abolition of the promotion committees, the purging of the officer corps and the reduction in 1905 of military service to only two years, the army's worst fears about the republican regime might seem to be justified, but by now the civilians were firmly in command. Although in the last years before the First World War the army regained some of its institutional independence, a larger budget and the restoration of three-year service in 1913, this resulted from the 'nationalist revival' caused by the prewar international crises rather than from its own lobbying. The French armed forces failed, in other words, to act as a consistent nationalist influence on policy after the manner of their counterparts across the Rhine.[6]

Such an influence was constituted, however, by the officials of the French Foreign Ministry, as John Keiger, drawing on the more extended presentation in his recent book, successfully demonstrates.[7] Whereas the republicanization of the officer corps weakened its potential as a nationalist lobby, that of the Quai d'Orsay had the opposite effect. Keiger traces this to a series of reforms introduced from 1880 onwards that delegated greater authority to lower- and middle-ranking officials and made entry dependent on a rigorous competitive examination. An aristocratic pattern of recruitment was replaced by one dominated by the scions of the Parisian *grande bourgeoisie* who had graduated from the elite École Libre des Sciences Politiques. The distinction between those who stayed in foreign poostings and those who made their careers in Paris also became more sharply delineated. Policy formulation passed increasingly to men with little personal foreign experience to counteract their nationalist education. The Sciences Po graduates lacked a formal organization, and were no doubt divided by careerist rivalries amongst themselves, but they have similarities with the colonialist party analysed by C. M. Andrew and A. S. Kanya-Forstner as a pressure group embedded within the French administration.[8] Their influence was nationalist not only in its assertiveness towards and opposition to détente with France's Triple Alliance enemies but also in its hostility to the multinational Hapsburg and Ottoman Empires (in this perhaps harking back to the republican nationalism of an earlier generation). Keiger argues that the hotheads of the Quai d'Orsay bureaux were tamed by Raymond Poincaré after the latter took over as Prime and Foreign Minister in 1912, but Poincaré's own policies had much in common with theirs. Given the Foreign Ministry's generally unchallenged control over French diplomacy in this period,[9] we have here a much more striking example than the military one of the potential for an exaggerated and irresponsible nationalism to influence French policy.

The remaining chapters qualify the picture so far gained by stressing the limits to nationalist influence. Gérard Canini studies a failure: the attempt to give schoolchildren pre-conscription military training through the 'school battalions' (*bataillons scolaires*) of 1882–92. His material comes mainly from departmental archives in the east of France, which he selects as the region with the most favourable *prima facie* conditions for such an experiment. In fact, the results were disappointing even in the first few years, and from the Boulanger Affair to the suppression of the battalions the picture was one of unrelieved decline. To this outcome almost everything seems to have conspired: lack of money for transport, weapons and trainers; parental resistance to releasing the children from work in the fields and fear by the church of losing control over them at an impressionable age; and most of all the army's reluctance to see its own training mission supplanted or to grant exemption from service in the reserves as an inducement for instructors to volunteer. Although Canini questions whether the failure casts doubt on the strength of patriotism in the east, it certainly casts doubt on the strength of the priority given to national objectives that has been suggested above as the hallmark of nationalism in politics. It also indicates how France fell short of being a totally militarized society in these years.

Jean-Claude Allain's research on submarine cables points to a similar conclusion. At the turn of the century, when colonial friction with Britain reached its peak, France relied on British-owned cables for communication with all parts of its empire except North Africa. In the event of war it could send messages to its remaining overseas territories only by ship, in so far as the Royal Navy permitted. Under a programme beginning with laws passed in 1900 and 1901, this dependence had been significantly lessened by the eve of the First World War. Although more successful than the 'school battalions', however, this policy was from the outset much less ambitious than were nationalist aspirations. Parts of the empire – for

Policy in the era of nationalism

example, in the Pacific – were written off, and the immediate concern was for secure telegraphic links with West Africa and Indochina. Even here the policy was not a *tous azimuts* one of independence against all comers. Communication with Indochina was assured via Danish and Russian possessions; with West Africa through cooperation with Germany. Expense debarred France from emulating the 'all-red' objective of British cable strategy.[10] But there was also a more fundamental consideration. The developing entente with London after 1904 deprived an anti-British policy of much of its *raison d'être*, and it is significant that the new line to Indochina was not replaced when it broke in 1913. Of course, rivalry with Britain might later return, but as a power in relative decline with limited economic strength France had to select priorities and concentrate on the most dangerous enemies. Between the 1880s and 1904 colonial expansion complicated this requirement by diverting national energies into confrontations with Britain overseas rather than with Germany on the Vosges. Resources devoted to cable communications were resources that might be spent closer to home. The limited success of the cable programme, in other words, presumably reflects the shift in national priorities between 1900 and 1914.

This brief review has suggested that nationalism influenced French policy less through the army than through its impact on French diplomacy. It has also suggested that this diplomacy was more singlemindedly concentrated on national objectives than was national policy more broadly. It was not true of all Frenchmen, in other words, as it may have been of Clemenceau, that he was 'hypnotized, like all those who had seen the defeat of 1870, by . . . the question of the Rhine. There, for the men of his generation, was the real danger, the weak point *par excellence*; there we must concentrate all our resources, all our efforts, all our thoughts.'[11] This seems to coincide with a broader tendency in the recent literature to qualify the significance of nationalism in the Third Republic, exemplified in J. J. Becker's study of 1914.[12]

It is important, nonetheless, to take into account all aspects of policy, and to remember the view from the other side of the hill. In the prewar appraisals of the Prussian General Staff, France remained a formidable and highly militarized antagonist.[13] It called up and trained a much greater percentage of its population than did any other European power; its Parliament voted generously for military expenditure; its strategic railways to the frontier killing grounds had since the 1880s outnumbered those of Germany, and it could mobilize an army of near equivalent war strength in a shorter period of time. Nor did the Germans doubt that the pre-1914 'nationalist revival' was real. In 1914 the Chief of the General Staff, von Moltke, favoured an attack on France because its rifles and heavy artillery were inferior to Germany's, but also because the dislocation caused by the way in which the Three-Year Law was implemented had temporarily disorganized an inherently dangerous enemy. Similarly, France's apparent passivity in the crisis of July–August 1914 should not obscure the assertiveness of its prewar diplomacy in taking the initiative in Morocco, selling arms to Serbia and Montenegro, consolidating the 'encirclement' of Germany and promoting the Russian strategic buildup on the Reich's eastern frontiers. In the July crisis itself, as Poincaré reflected afterwards, the French leaders had a duty to urge moderation in St Petersburg but also not to endanger an alliance whose 'break-up... would leave us in isolation and at the mercy of our rivals'. And in addition they were bound 'to do our utmost to prevent a conflict, [yet] to do our utmost in order that, should it burst forth in spite of us, we should be prepared'.[14] On both counts, in the hour of decision, they made the nationalist choice.

NOTES

1 A. D. Smith (ed.), *Nationalist Movements* (London: Macmillan, 1976), p. 1.
2 Quotations from R. Girardet (ed.), *Le Nationalisme français, 1871–1914* (2nd edn, Paris: Seuil, 1976), pp. 63–6.
3 On which see D. Stevenson, *French War Aims against Germany, 1914–1919* (Oxford: Clarendon Press, 1982) and G-H. Soutou, *L'Or et le sang: les buts de guerre économiques de la Premiere Guèrre Mondiale* (Paris: Fayard, 1989).
4 Z. Sternhell, 'Paul Déroulède and the origins of modern French nationalism', *Journal of Contemporary History*, vol. 6, no. 4 (1971), pp. 46–70.
5 M. Larkin, '"La République en danger"? The pretenders, the army and Déroulède, 1898–1899', *English Historical Review*, vol. C, no. 394 (1985), pp. 85–105.
6 On this see further D. Porch, *The March to the Marne: the French Army, 1871–1914* (Cambridge: Cambridge University Press, 1981) and G. Krumeich, *Armaments and Politics in France on the Eve of the First World War: the Introduction of Three-Year Conscription, 1913–1914* (Engl. trans., Leamington Spa: Berg, 1984).
7 J. F. V. Keiger, *France and the Origins of the First World War* (London: Macmillan, 1983).
8 C. M. Andrew and A. S. Kanya-Forstner, 'The French "colonial party": its composition, aims, and influence, 1885–1914', *Historical Journal*, vol. 14, no. 1 (1971), pp. 99–128.
9 M. B. Hayne, 'The Quai d'Orsay and influences on the formulation of French foreign policy, 1898–1914', *French History*, vol. 2, no. 4 (1988), pp. 427–52.
10 P. M. Kennedy, 'Imperial cable communications and strategy, 1870–1914', *English Historical Review*, vol. 86, no. 341 (1971), pp. 728–52.
11 J. Mordacq, *Le Ministère Clemenceau: journal d'un témoin* (4 vols, Paris: Plon, 1930–1), vol. 3, p. 191.
12 J.-J. Becker, *1914: Comment les Français sont entrés dans la guerre* (Paris: Fondation Nationale des Sciences Politiques, 1977).
13 Many of these appraisals have been preserved at Munich in the Bayerische Hauptstaatsarchiv, Abteilung IV (Militärarchiv) Generalstab, 162–7. On railways, see the report by Von Wenninger to the Bavarian War Ministry of 25 April 1913 in ibid. Militärbevollmächtiger, Vol. I.
14 L. Albertini, *The Origins of the War of 1914*, Vol. II, 3 vols (London: Oxford University Press, 1957), p. 605.

17

The army and the appel au soldat, 1874–89

Jean-Charles Jauffret

In the early years of the Third Republic, *L'Appel au soldat* (title of a well-known novel by Maurice Barrès, published in 1900) was seen as the most radical solution by those who dreamt of overthrowing 'la Gueuse' – that 'slut' the republic. This wait for the 'grand soir' of a *coup d'état* was a feature of the years between 1870 and 1889, before the failure of Boulangism marked the definitive institution of the republican regime. Thus, for almost 20 years, while hope remained that the monarchy could be restored or that the ashes of the empire could be rekindled, conservative elements in the country continued to hope that a new General Monck would appear: this, in the words of Philippe Levillain, was 'le rêve du connétable'.[1]

Trying to discern the soldiers' response to these legitimist and Bonapartist siren-songs is no easy matter. An analysis of the political circumstances, combined with a study of the mentality of a social group bound by obedience and discretion, reveals various possible lines of research, rather than any final answer.

After the double defeat by Germany, of the army in 1870 and the nation in 1871, it was time for *recueillement* and national reconciliation over the smoking ashes of the Commune. Once social and colonial order had been reestablished, after the great Kabyle revolt had been crushed, France could tend its wounds and sharpen its sword once more.

In July 1872, despite Thiers's unconditional support for a professional army, Parliament adopted a system of conscription, which, though certainly still unequal, did impose compulsory personal military service for the first time.[2] Soon afterwards, in 1873, following the Prussian model, metropolitan France was divided into 18 military regions, each corresponding to an army corps which would absorb the reserves on mobilization. These basic reforms, completed by the laws of March 1875 on cadres and numbers, thrust aside the traditions of military organization built up by previous regimes. The aim of the legislature was simple: to muster on mobilization all available men. Despite criticism by those who exalted the merits of 'old soldiers', reserve units and then territorials began to be formed. It was in this context that a small group of Bonapartists, emboldened by the prince imperial's coming of age, and a few electoral successes, reestablished the Carbonarist tradition of plotting.

As George Gugliotta has shown,[3] it was following the victory won by Baron de Bourgoing, ex-equerry to Napoleon III, in a by-election in the Nièvre, that a splinter group of deputies of the Bonapartist Appel au Peuple group, the best organized in the National Assembly,[4] hatched a plot against the republic, with retired officers nostalgic for the empire. On 9 June 1874, a republican deputy close to Gambetta produced in the Chamber a circular from the Comité Central de *l'Appel au Peuple*. This stated that the committee intended to provide generously for retired officers in the territorial army once it was established, so as to be sure of support. This revelation caused a heated debate. Calm was eventually restored by General de Cissey, Minister of War, the merciless butcher of the Commune and peerless organizer of rearmament. He declared that there was no involvement of serving officers with the alleged plotters; but his statement implied that some retired officers, mindful of the privileges they had enjoyed under the empire, had allowed themselves to be drawn in.

The affair was left at that, a mere flash in the pan caused by a small number of troublemakers. To avert all risk of a pronunciamento, on 10 March 1875 Cissey sent a firmly worded circular to the corps commanders ordering the army to abide by the constitutional laws.[5] At the height of the Franco-German diplomatic crisis of 1875, he reiterated that the military should not concern themselves with political disputes. As William Serman emphasizes,[6] the soldier became a second-class citizen, since serving army officers were not eligible for political functions.

This does not, however, necessarily imply that 'la grande muette' was unshaken by the disturbances that racked the regime, at a time when the president of the republic was a marshal of France honoured by the empire. On the night of the second round of legislative elections in March 1876, the regime was swinging towards an increasingly marked republicanism. When control of power was assumed by republicans in 1879, the army was placed in the service of Jacobin patriotism. Until that time, it had been accustomed to serving a conservative state and, when confronted with the confusion of traditional values, a group of officers whose exact number is not known, closed ranks around the marshal-president. At Narbonne, a legitimist ex-officer of the 2nd Chasseurs d'Afrique, Laperrine d'Hautpoul, wrote a pamphlet entitled 'Tout pour et par l'Armée, le Salut de la France est là', dedicated to the memory of Bugeaud, in which he called for the reestablishment of a professional army in order to entrust the sword of national regeneration to Marshal de Mac Mahon. In the author's view, a France dedicated to revenge needed a strong government, capable of imposing the restoration of the monarchy and commanding an army totally devoted to it.

A similar analysis reveals a great deal about the action of General Ducrot, the Comte de Chambord's faithful vassal, and the centre of royalist plotting. Ducrot, in fact, represents only one tendency; the army as a whole was anxious and disoriented, and would not accept the white flag. This question was at the root of the political debate. By the time Thiers resigned, on 25 May 1873, the army was grateful to him for having reestablished order, by rearming and securing German evacuation of French territory, and it seemed to fear a monarchist restoration.[7] In the 1870s, as François Bédarida has shown,[8] despite the efforts of the *commissions de classement*, which slowed the advance of republican officers, the officer corps was not, in the majority, conservative. In the artillery and engineers, the spirit of Voltaire lived on, and not even the memories of imperial victories in Italy and the Crimea could overcome Orleanist sentiments developed during the conquest of Algeria, which had signalled the army's recovery following the disastrous end of the First Empire.

When the crisis of the *Seize Mai* arose, the great caution shown by General Berthaut, Minister of War, surely corresponded to the state of mind of both officers and men. The minister did not declare a state of siege so that the generals would not have to make political decisions, even if certain commanders were openly campaigning for the Marshal-President's candidates.[9] The high command waited on events when, in November 1877, the ministry led by General de Rochebouët was not recognized by the Chamber. Second-Lieutenant Regnault, who was then at the École d'Application de l'Artillerie et du Génie at Fontainebleau, recalled that

> After the parliamentary coup d'état of 16 May ... we wondered ... if Marshal de Mac-Mahon would try to impose a new military Government by a coup, against the constitution ... and many officers were wondering at that moment where their duty lay.[10]

During the political crisis, the army made a display of apoliticism, and no serious attempt reminiscent of 2 December 1851 could be attributed to it. The generals in Gambetta's sphere, Clinchant, Campenon, Farre, Lecointe and Galliffet, mounted a careful guard, and enjoyed the sympathy of the Duc d'Aumale, prestigious commander of the 7th Army Corps at Besançon. General Ducrot and the Marshal-President, who was too respectful of the constitutional law that he himself had put in place, did not dare to go into action following the widely known plot of 4 and 5 December 1877.

The army had passed its first real test of obedience to the republic, and the threat of the white flag was, by the same token, lifted. On 14 July 1880, in the symbolic tricolour marriage between the army and the republic, the regiments assembled at Longchamps received their new colours in the presence of Gambetta, the government and the President of the Republic, Jules Grévy. As France regained its rank as a major power by pursuing its colonial expansion, this aggressively nationalistic atmosphere 'd'en revenant de la revue' continued throughout the 1880s. But this ostentatious patriotism still did not create unanimity on the subject of the regime. General Galliffet, then leading light of the cavalry, interposed himself between Ducrot and Boulanger.

In 1884, a pamphlet entitled 'L'Armée Français en 1884 et le Général de Galliffet',[11] was published anonymously at Antwerp; the author could have been a staff officer, given his knowledge of German military studies. Galliffet, whom the author believed capable of restoring the professional army and the old military values, was portrayed as a providential figure, an established stereotype in French national history. This 'appeal to the soldier' was not a politician's appeal, however:

> in France, where the phrase on everyone's lips is 'What we need is a general' . . . it would be terrible for France if the fear of a chimerical Monk [sic] made people reject a Prince Eugene, if by chance one such existed in the ranks of the French army.[12]

At a time when, because of governmental instability, Ministers of War and Chiefs of the General Staff changed too frequently, the army desperately needed a leader. But he was wanted above all for patriotic reasons: he would have to ensure victory in the east, rather than think of overturning the republic.

This provides the key to Galliffet's attitude: the anonymous author was not alone in inviting him to head the troops, and he gave his unsigned reply by collaborating with the moderate republican deputy, Étienne Lamy in *L'Armée et la démocratie*, a now forgotten work but one which had two printings in the year it appeared, 1885, and several new editions before 1900. This reply of Galliffet's is indicative of a mentality. A complex and controversial character, the Marquis de Galliffet, Prince de Martigues, a late nineteenth-century Murat, was both one of the butchers of the Commune and a friend of Gambetta, at whose death-bed he sat. At heart he was a Bonapartist, but after the defeat of 1870 he became a republican, not out of self-interest but, like Thiers, because he felt the republic was the least bad regime and could assure the continuance of the nation; and yet he also personified the worries of the traditional military caste. Like other generals concerned at the projected reduction in military service to three years, Galliffet, in writing his book, was obeying an instinct for self-defence: the desire to preserve his speciality as a practitioner of military science.

Since the republicans had come to power, the army command had been faced with a freer society, as witness the laws passed between 1880 and 1884, ensuring freedom of association, the press, divorce and trade unions. Democratization seemed to be threatening discipline, traditions and hierarchy – in other words, everything that formed the confused sentiment of the military class. After the vote on the recruitment law of 1872, the high command could see only one advantage: numbers. It did not realize that the constant turnover of men (whose period of enlistment would vary between less than four years for the first portion of the contingent and six months to a year for the second portion) would start to create a truly national melting-pot. And while the rigid framework of traditional life for peasants and workers was starting to break down, the high command often continued to believe that there was a radical distinction between civil society and the army.

This feeling was strengthened by anti-militarism, which suddenly reappeared in 1880, less through the stylistic exercises of *Les Soirées de Médan*, with Zola and de Maupassant, than through the law of amnesty for the Commune. In 1880, a pamphlet appeared bearing the provocative title 'La République et l'armée.[13] The anonymous author, respectful of the Belleville programme, and using language similar to that of Rochefort, argued that the army was a threat to the republic because it was the traditional instrument of despotism and it 'carried within itself a dictatorship that was always ready to impose itself on the country'.[14] Three years later, Edouard Thiers, a former engineer officer who was elected as radical deputy for the Rhone in 1885, published *La Puissance de l'armée par la réduction du service*.[15] In it he called for the disappearance of any professional element within the army, saying that the intellectual and moral elements that directed civilian society should also rule the army.

Galliffet reacted strongly against these attacks. Although the original manuscript of *L'Armée et la démocratie* no longer exists, it can be attributed to him, particularly the last part which deals with the technical problems of recruitment. The attribution to Galliffet can be confirmed by his statement in 1885 before the Conseil Supérieur de la Guerre,[16] and by a direct allusion that neither Lamy nor Galliffet denied, on 6 June 1887, by Gaudin de Villaine in the Chamber.[17]

The first part of this polemical work demonstrates the incompatibility of the army with democracy, stating that compulsory service, the twin brother of universal suffrage, would result in poor quality soldiers, since the ideas of freedom and equality ran counter to the rigours of discipline and the sacrosanct 'military spirit'. The only solution was to re-establish a professional army, which would not be incompatible with a moderate republic. The second part of the work rejected any 'appel au soldat' in the form of a *coup d'état* hatched by a professional military elite: for the true enemy was encamped along the Vosges, and the theme of revenge rounded off the work, as in the pamphlet of the anonymous author who had called Galliffet to the head of the army:

The army and the appel au soldat

> The work of the greatest geniuses, of those who have laid down or restored the rules of war, has always been to conquer armed nations with professional troops.[18]

This expectant wait for an avenging Alexander had been a fashionable theme ever since the publication of the works by Ardant du Picq and von der Goltz,[19] and it condemned any imitator of Louis Napoleon Bonaparte to failure from the outset.

Boulangism was primarily a civilian movement. The high command was concerned only with the threat of war after the Schnaebelé incident in April 1887, and General Boulanger had been brought up to hate illegal mercenary violence. The fear that existed of a pronunciamento by an ambitious commander did not correspond to any existing 'army party'. Boulanger was a republican officer, and seems to have been isolated within the officer corps. The important observations of General Brugère, who during the crisis of May 1887 was head of the president of the republic's military staff and secretary-general of the presidency, show that fears of a military coup had no serious foundation. On behalf of Jules Grévy, Brugère met General Saussier, the powerful military governor of Paris, on 18 May. He asked him to take a number of measures to protect the Elysée against the 'saltimbanque' Boulanger. Saussier was optimistic, and was sure of all the cavalry division and the infantry regiments posted in and around Paris, but expressed some doubts about one professional unit: 'he cannot answer for the Garde Républicaine, the colonel of which is a rabid Boulangist'.[20] Saussier also believed that Boulanger had the support of only a few old classmates, and that the high command and the troops would not follow him. On his return to the Elysée, Brugère reassured Jules Grévy and confirmed that the soldiers of the elite Garde Républicaine would never march against the republic which privileged them. These observations appear in Brugère's diaries and were clearly made as events occurred; they differ from his memoirs, in which he expressed doubt, with hindsight, as to the loyalty of the infantry troops garrisoned in Paris.[21]

To those who felt quietly regretful that the army had not 'dared' in 1887, Lt-Col Péroz, a veteran marine, gave the following explanation: 'The political enfeeblement of the army took away a large part of its virility. When internal crisis arose, it followed the long training in inertia given by governments, and watched events taking place without becoming involved.'[22]

There followed Boulanger's purely political adventure, cut off from the realities of the army. When in January 1889, he did not march on the Elysée, the instinct to obey seemed finally to have won; after all, while Minister of War, on 1 February 1886, he had issued the following circular: 'The duty of the army is to remain outside politics. . . . There will be no political activity in the army; not by anyone.'[23]

There were several reasons for the army's political silence. The establishment of the 'armed nation' implies tight control of the high command by the civil power, for whom the temptation to transform the military, which should be a neutral instrument in the service of the state, into a docile servant of a regime and an ideology, may become irresistible. From just after the defeat of 1870 to the imperial sunset of the Algerian war, the still unwritten political history of the army was marked by successive purges intended to form a military clientele faithful to the regime. From 1871 to 1872, the famous Commission des Grades, presided over by the legitimist General Changarnier, inaugurated under the republic a process for inquiring into the public actions and private opinions of officers. The commission's main object was to rectify the career patterns of the officer corps, disrupted by the captivity of those of the imperial army, following Sedan and Metz, and by the recruitment of new officers by the Government of National Defence. The commission preferred officers returning from Germany over the new officers, who had obtained promotion to acting rank (*à titre auxiliaire*).[24] This reimposition of control, of which the republican and Protestant Denfert-Rochereau was one of the most famous victims,[25] took place in the context of 'le recueillement' – postwar self-examination – and 'ordre moral' conservatism, although the menace of a new war against Germany meant that the purge was, perhaps, less strict than it might have been. The case of General Carrey de Bellemare, who was removed from the active list for having expressed open hostility to any idea of monarchical restoration, should not be taken as representative.

In 1876, once the republicans had gained power, the desire to purge the army was more openly expressed. François Bédarida[26] has analysed the notebooks sent to Gambetta to inform him of the political opinions of the officers. Gugliotta provides a new element, the mania for keeping files, which started very early. Colonel Henri Iung occupied a position at the Ministry of War, as *sous-chef de cabinet du ministre*, with no officially defined function. In fact, he was responsible for a kind of political military police, the organization, ramifications (including the role of freemasonry) and power of which are not yet known. After Colonel Iung, General Farre took on the role of 'grand inquisitor'. More important than any results from this state-sponsored snooping, according to Gugliotta, is the fact that a number of senior officers knew both the names and the methods used by those unofficially charged with checking on them.[27] This was the source of a self-defensive reflex in military society.

Although the minister could manage the appointment of generals, and purge the high command, by removing General Ducrot and five other general officers from their commands in January 1879, he could not interfere with the progress of officers' careers, the management of which remained under the control of the Commissions de Classement, except

The army and the appel au soldat

by a legislative act (for example the forced resignation of the Orleans princes). It was not until 1899, on account of the Dreyfus Affair, that the minister, then General de Galliffet, first paralysed then destroyed the power of these commissions. Until then, strengthened by their long tenure of office, they had stood up to short-lived ministers and favoured the careers of conservative officers, particularly those from the military schools, to which royalist and Bonapartist families sent their sons, since they were effectively barred from administrative and diplomatic careers.

This opposition gave rise to a covert war in which political influence had an undue effect on the careers of ambitious officers, including General Brugère who was severely criticized for the rapidity of his promotion, and many others. It may also have been the case that this permanent need for protection stifled the officer corps's initiative, just as it restricted the 'grande muette' to the greatest prudence.

Apart from a minority of careerists, the officers of the republic's army as a whole felt the traditional detachment from political quarrels. Deprived of political rights, but comforted by corporate feeling, the soldier looked on, astonished by 'all the dissimulation that statesmen must employ'.[28] With the defence of the country as his primary duty, the officer performed his role conscientiously on meagre pay, and mistrusted those colleagues who schemed ambitiously with civilian politicians. In the nineteenth century, because of successive changes in the regime, the idea of loyalty to a ruling family or a republic became rather devalued. This can be seen in the statement of the highly conservative Jean-Marie du Temple de la Croix, deputy of Ille-et-Vilaine, on the symbolic date of 2 December 1874 before the Assemblée Nationale:

> For 80 years, we have lived in turmoil; the present calm results only from fatigue, and the army, tossed around from one regime to another, without God to sustain and guide it, no longer knows how or to whom it should be faithful.[29]

This heritage of successive vows of fidelity, added to the governmental instability of the Third Republic, explains the army's political passivity. As Serman has shown,[30] the army's apoliticism did not mean that the officers had no political opinions, but simply that they could not show them publicly, out of a discretion inherent in their duty as servants of the fatherland and guarantors of national sovereignty.

This innate caution accompanied the traditional respect for strong regimes. The army abhors a political vacuum, as Galliffet's memoirs[31] illustrate: in 1877, after the dissolution of the Chamber, Gambetta was worried by reports of another 2 December, and asked him the test question concerning legitimacy:

Policy in the era of nationalism

'General,' he said, 'you have firm control over your infantry division in Dijon. Are you prepared to take us in and defend us if necessary?' 'Monsieur,' I answered, 'It's simple. If the President of the Republic and the Senate come to Dijon, too bad for the Chamber of Deputies. If the President and the Chamber come to Dijon, too bad for the Senate. If the Senate and the Chamber come to Dijon, too bad for the President. I am for the majority in the government.[32]

For the Third Republic, this comment is of symbolic, and perhaps axiomatic, value. In the period of 'la Revanche', the *appel au soldat*, as far as the army was concerned, was based on nothing more than a few individual officers solicited by politicians. More important than the question of regime, as demonstrated by the behaviour of men like Galliffet and Lyautey, was the permanence, in the contemporary phrase, of 'Notre Dame de France'.

NOTES

1 Philippe Levillain, *Boulanger fossoyeur de la monarchie* (Paris: Flammarion, 1982), p. 166.
2 On the major debate leading to the 1872 law, see Jean-Charles Jauffret, *Parlement, gouvernement, commandement: l'armée de métier sous la IIIe République, 1871–1914*, Vol. I, 2 vols, (Paris: Service Historique de l'Armée, 1987), pp. 269–345.
3 Georges Gugliotta, 'Le Général de Cissey', PhD thesis, Université de Montpellier III, 1987, Vol. II, pp. 539–40.
4 On the groupings within the National Assembly, see Rainer Hudemann, *Fraktionsbildung im Französischen Parlament: Zur Entwicklung des Parteiensystems in der frühen Dritten Republik, 1871–1875* (Munich: Artemis, 1979).
5 Gugliotta, 'Cissey', p. 548.
6 William Serman, *Les Officiers français dans la nation, 1848–1914* (Paris: Aubier, 1982), pp. 72–3 and chap. 5 *passim*.
7 Gibert Bodinier *et al.*, *Histoire de l'officier français, des origines à nos jours* (Saint-Jean-d'Angély: Bordessoules, 1987), pp. 262–4.
8 F. Bédarida, 'L'Armée et la république: les opinions politiques des officiers français en 1876–1877', *Revue Historique*, 232 (1964), pp. 119–64. Of the 311 entries in the notebooks of information destined for Gambetta, 63 per cent of officers were classed as liberal or republican to 32 per cent conservative.
9 Jauffret, *Parlement*, p. 410.
10 Carton 1, 1 K 40, fonds général Regnault, Service Historique de l'Armée de Terre (SHAT). A Polytechnien and a gunner, he left a rich manuscript entitled 'Soixante Ans dans l'armée française, 1875–1933'.
11 (Antwerp: C. Legros, 1884).
12 ibid., p. 13.
13 (Paris: Dauvin, 1885).
14 ibid., pp. 6–7.
15 (Paris: Germain-Baillière, 1880).
16 Jauffret, *Parlement*, p. 406. The attribution of this work to Lamy and Galliffet is confirmed by Bédarida, 'L'Armée'.
17 Journal Officiel (JO), p. 1142, col. 1.
18 *L'Armée et la démocratie*, p. 220.
19 Ardant du Picq, *Études sur le combat* (Paris: Chapelot, 1880), pp. 380; Von der Goltz, *La Nation armée: organisation militaire et tactique moderne* (Paris: Hinrischen, 1884).

The latter work had a curious history, for the politicians only paid attention to its preface, which legitimized the professional army and the wait for a new Alexander. See Jauffret, *Parlement*, pp. 427–43, and Adm. E. Jurien de la Gravière, Vol. 1, *Les campagnes d'Alexandre: Le Drame macedonien* (Paris: Plon, 1885).
20 Agenda, p. 16, in carton 3, 1 K 160, fonds général Brugère, SHAT.
21 'Les Souvenirs du général Brugère' (MS), p. 2672, fonds général Brugère, SHAT.
22 *Par Vocation, vie et aventures d'un soldat de fortune, 1870–1895* (Paris: Calmann-Lévy, n.d.), p. 443.
23 Cabinet du ministre, 5 N 1, SHAT.
24 The file of the Commission des Grades at the Archives Nationales (141 C 2817) is empty. The final report gives no figures, annexe 1070, JO (30 March 1872), pp. 55–8. Jean Frédéric Grivaux, 'L'Armée et l'instauration de la IIIe République: une coexistance ambiguë (1870–1889)', doctoral thesis, Université de Paris II, 1984, p. 67, gives the figure of 11,600 cases examined by the commission (a little under half the total of serving officers at the end of 1871). Gugliotta, 'Cissey', pp. 386–91, describes the workings of the commission and concludes that its decisions were fairly moderate.
25 William Serman, 'Denfert-Rochereau et la discipline dans l'armée françaisé entre 1845 et 1874', *Revue d'Histoire Moderne et Contemporaine* (January–March 1973), pp. 95–103.
26 'L'Armée et la république'.
27 Gugliotta, 'Cissey', pp. 760–2.
28 Charles de Gaulle, *Le Fil de l'epée* (Paris: Berger-Levrault, 1932), p. 129.
29 First reading of the bill on army strength and cadres, JO, p. 7948, col. 1.
30 *Les Officiers français*, chap. 4.
31 Published in *Le Journal des Débats*, 19 July–8 August 1902. A solid testimony, although disappointing on the Commune; it was made up of fragments having survived a fire that destroyed most of the memoirs that Galliffet could never make up his mind to publish.
32 Number of 1 August 1902. In 1877, Galliffet commanded the 15th Infantry Division at Dijon, and since 1875 had also held the post of inspector of cavalry.

18

The school battalions in the east, 1882–92: reasons for failure

Gérard Canini

The school battalions created by decree of 6 July 1882 were brought into being through a combination of potent factors: a strong desire for the physical and civic regeneration of schoolchildren (in the words of General Chanzy, 'give us men, we will make soldiers of them'); to provide training from an early age to instil the ideas of defence and revenge and, later, premilitary instruction to prepare for the discipline of life in the barracks; and, most important, to fulfil republican ambitions to mould a nation of citizen-soldiers. In the east of France, marked since the defeat of 1870 by a revanchist nationalism, it was rather to be expected that this scheme would develop rapidly and successfully. Everything contributed to it: the region was conscious of being 'on the frontier', and gradually developed the feeling of having a national role that was out of the ordinary; there were many large garrisons, as the forts and entrenched camps of the Séré de Rivières lines were established; new barracks sprang up in the urban landscape, and social life was dominated by the military. All this led to the east of France (which formed the sixth and seventh military regions) making the institution of school battalions into a major pillar of premilitary training for children and adolescents. But although the start of this policy seemed very promising, it declined rapidly even before the Boulangist crisis. Surviving documentation, although incomplete, warrants careful study: not all departments show the same development of the school battalions, which sometimes existed only on paper.

A certain ambiguity in the intentions of the founders distorts the perspective of development from the outset. It is not that the patriotic feeling which should have supported and surrounded the idea of the school battalions was absent from the frontier areas, which were still scarred after the 1870–1 war, and its territorial consequences, but the exact object of the exercise was hard to discern.[1] It was sometimes felt that military training for young people was already available through shooting and gymnastics clubs;[2] on the other hand, some mayors were sceptical about the efficacy of this instruction for young people: 'Our school battalion won't help us scare the Prussians', one of them wrote to the prefect. Verdun is characteristic of this state of mind. While Séré de Rivières's fortified town concentrated troops and materials there, the prospect of creating a school battalion was accepted reluctantly; it was thought that the college with its 25 training rifles was quite enough.[3]

Reactions, however, were more favourable to the idea of integrating these school units into the first celebrations of the National Day. Typical in their response was the town of Gerardmer in the Vosges. In June 1883, it was anxious to have its battalion, complete with flag, take part in the 14 July parade 'to give rise, in our young pupils, to a legitimate pride, and stimulate the sacred love they already feel for the Republic'.[4] This desire to involve children in the republican celebration of the National Day, which was instituted immediately after 1880 around the celebration of army and flag, went beyond simple local display, and aspired to become a celebration of hope: it was therefore entirely appropriate for militarized youth to play a full part in it.[5] The mayor of Dompaire, in the Jura, protested vigorously when the prefect challenged his right, on 14 July 1884, to allow a non-regulation battalion to parade.[6] In the *arrondissement* of Neufchâteau in the Vosges, demography prevented the regulation force of 200 pupils from being assembled. The school inspector, by his own admission 'enamoured of the institution', did, however, manage to assemble and have inspected by the sub-prefect and town council 115 pupils on 13 July 1884: 'Each one equipped with a rifle and wearing a beret. The inspection was sufficiently impressive to win the acclaim of the public who, like the authorities, saw in it a spirit of order and discipline for the young.'[7]

Results were not always so encouraging. In this same area, which seemed so keen, the sub-prefect noted that the following year, all attempts to create a school battalion ended in failure.[8] In the Meuse department only the chief town, Bar-le-Duc, was up to establishing a battalion in 1883, thanks to boys already familiar with premilitary instruction from the *lycée*; in 1890, during the virtual disappearance of the institution, it was still the only one in the department, despite the proximity of Verdun, where the strong military element could have provided high-quality leadership. In 1887, the efforts of the chief school inspector to reinforce this single unit were vain.[9] In 1884, the prefect of Jura lamented the absence of any school battalion in his department.[10] In Vosges, it was not until July 1887 that three battalions were organized, at Épinal (264 pupils), Remiremont (240) and Saint-Dié (220). Just a few months previously, in April 1887, that of Saint-Dié was reported to be non-existent, despite a college with significant numbers and the willingness of the 10th Battalion of Chasseurs à Pied garrisoned there to provide instructors.[11]

Battalions, assembled quickly for reasons of circumstance, or because of the efforts of a single person determined to succeed, disappeared very quickly a few months into the summer holidays, as the need to work in the fields became pressing. At Épinal, in February 1885, the instructor attached to the college, a territorial army officer, was surprised to assemble only some 20 young people when he expected 83.[12] The overall picture was, therefore, far from encouraging. One should not assume the schoolchildren were not interested, for they regularly attended shooting clubs. The problems had various causes: the rural dispersion of the population, and cost, which posed serious obstacles to families, a factor not understood by the administration. A mayor from the Jura explained this firmly to the prefect: 'This would be too big a move for parents whose children, so far, have seemed disinclined to go to Rochefort' (the assembly point for rural school battalions in the canton). Another wrote to the same prefect: 'Is it obligatory to take children to Rochefort, because the parents are not at all inclined to let them go there, the journey is long, it involves some costs. Who is responsible for these? There are poor children with no resources.'[13] Almost all the primary school inspectors who were in touch with demographic realities speak of the difficulty of assembling the regulation 200 pupils since 'even in the most populated rural schools, there are not enough to form a company', as one of them notes, from Mirecourt in the Vosges, summing up the general opinion.[14] In fact, the real problems arose from the practical organization of the system, the shortage of instructors, a suspicion or even hostility on the part of the army itself, plus a curious failure to understand the psychological and pedagogical aspects of motivating and training children. Finally, the hostility of the Catholic church was significant in some cases.

Two circulars issued by General Billot, the Minister of War, specified that instructors chosen from volunteers of the reserve or territorial army should have the approval of local military and civil authorities. In practice, there were many problems. Political, religious and social dissent, regional traditions, the constraints of earning a living, which were all the more pressing since those concerned were former noncommissioned officers and ordinary soldiers with modest and sometimes even precarious livelihoods – all these factors conspired to restrict recruitment.[15] The volunteers who agreed to take part in the experiment demanded payment or, by way of compensation, exemption from the annual reservists' training period of 28 or 13 days. The municipal authorities were not inclined to pay the instructors, whose 'rate of pay' ranged between fr.20 and fr.100 per annum for 36 sessions; on the second demand, the army, although at first cautiously in favour of granting exemption, was not able to apply it generally, and abolished the practice completely from 1885. This was followed by a marked reduction in the number of men putting themselves forward for the role of instructor: from 414 possibles in Jura in 1883, the number fell to 124 the following year.[16] Throughout the period when the institution of the school battalions was maintained, it became clear that reservists from the frontier areas were not very enthusiastic about adding to their own military obligations by becoming Sunday instructors to the younger generation: in the words of one ex-dragoon, 'Five years service was enough for me'. When volunteers agreed to take part, their enthusiasm and competence were often doubted. Regular attendance was low, and the results mediocre. This extract from a letter, sent by the prefect of the Marne to his colleague from the Meuse on 13 August sums up the situation: 'Although we have appointed former NCOs to give this instruction in several schools, it has never been possible to teach the children adequate military drill.'[17]

The teachers, whose help was sought as a last resort, were no more enthusiastic. In addition, the departmental academic administration was divided. On the one hand it feared – although this may have been an excuse for not becoming involved – that the transfer of teachers between posts would disrupt military instruction, if they were made responsible for it.[18] On the other hand, it was under an obligation to apply faithfully any instructions it received. In September 1882, more than 300 teachers from the Jura were summoned to attend training courses at the teachers' training college at Lons-le-Saulnier. Included in the programme were military gymnastics, patriotic lectures and declamation of texts by Déroulède.[19] The school inspectors from the Saint-Claude and Dôle districts recommended giving 'a vigorous push to this aspect of the education of youth on the front line of the Jura frontiers',[20] but the teachers were less enthusiastic. Many excused themselves on the grounds that they had not performed active military service. Some prefects, particularly from the Meuse, envisaged stimulating their interest by financial incentives, but these were not sufficient.[21] The school inspector for Saint-Dié, in the Vosges, summed up the problem, in December 1883: 'The academic authority cannot reasonably demand that [school-masters] add to their already extensive responsibilities that of military instructor, for which generally they have little or no aptitude and knowledge.'[22]

The army never took the question of the school battalions seriously. In the specific case of the 6th and 7th Army Corps, its participation in the experiment was far less than was hoped and not at all in proportion to its resources. Keeping more strictly than the prefects to the letter of the regulations, the military authorities rarely authorized route marches or parades with arms for the school battalions, sometimes even forbidding them on the National Day, as at Bar-le-Duc in 1884.[23] The intervention of the army was, however, decisive in assessing pupils' training, and verifying that the regulation strength of 200 required to authorize a battalion had been reached. The officers were always very strict in their application of the regulations, and this was often a cause for complaint by the civilians, who were inclined to be more lenient.[24] Although the soldiers had, in principle, no greater say than the representatives of the academic administration, as the regional inspector for the Vosges noted despairingly in 1884, 'The school inspectors can do nothing on their own, and they lack the vital authority to give the instructors orders that will be put into effect'.[25] The same observations were made in 1887 by an inspector from the Doubs,[26] and many other similar examples can be found.

As for the Catholic church, this new brand of republican education could only inspire its hostility. Generally, it rejected the experiment by refusing to allow its pupils and teachers to take part. At Saint-Dié in 1885, the school run by an order of brothers with 538 pupils did not take part in the formation of the *arrondissement* battalion.[27] At Bar-le-Duc in 1882 an appeal to the church schools went unanswered. The commission, made up of the colonel commanding the 94th Infantry Regiment and the regional inspector, concluded: 'There is no point concerning ourselves with the Fénelon School, the pupils of which could not possibly join with those from the lycée, because of the undercurrent of hostility that exists between them and which would soon give rise to difficulties.' Parish priests protested if training for the school battalions took place on Sundays during mass.[28] Local elected representatives responded by refusing as instructors anyone too close to Catholic circles: in 1883 a mayor in the Jura rejected a candidate because 'he and his family have a clerical background'. He chose instead a former noncommissioned officer, whom he described as, 'patriotic, republican, intelligent and zealous'.[29] There are many similar examples.

The decline of the experiment started very early on. From 1885 to 1886, from the Vosges to the Jura, it was moribund. There were contradictory instructions on the weapons to be used (should they be dummies or not?); and elementary psychological mistakes, such as the army's stubborn refusal to allow uniforms too similar to those worn by real soldiers, further discouraged pupils and teachers who were not very keen to play at soldiers with wooden guns or sticks. Disaffection spread rapidly, with the numbers of candidates for examination falling sharply: in the Doubs in 1886, a third of those registered failed to turn up.[30] In the Vosges, town councils asked for their companies to be disbanded 'since the children are no longer assiduous at drill'.[31] In the Jura, in 1887, the school authorities reported mediocre results. In 1890, in the departments of the Jura and the Doubs (which resisted the general collapse to some degree), the examining commissions were severe in their judgement: 'It is apparent that the institution of the school battalions is less in favour than before'; 'There is no group of over fifty children here able to perform company drill'; 'Nor do I see any possibility of bringing together a sufficient number of children capable of forming a school battalion.'[32] From 1890, the official abolition of battalions in primary schools confined them to *lycées* and colleges, where they continued feebly for another two years. In 1891, it was reported that 'Each year the board has the disappointment of noting that the institution of school battalions is less and less in favour'.[33] This development in the east, at the frontier, in a region that was otherwise so prompt to react to nationalist phenomena, is an accurate portrayal of what was going on throughout France. A few rifles, stored away and forgotten in attics to be rediscovered many years later, bear witness to this abortive endeavour, which merited a different fate, if only because of the sincerity of the patriotic ideals of its founding fathers.[34]

The school battalions are generally thought to have been an experiment of little real interest. Marcel Spivak considers that 'navigating their way between Déroulède's declamatory prose and the gloomy humour of a Jules Renard, they were a phenomenon of collective psychological aberration'.[35] The *Histoire de l'enseignement et de l'éducation en France* contains no reference to them.[36] In contrast, Eugen Weber resituates this desire for military instruction within the context of patriotic regeneration after the defeat of 1870,[37] and the battalions are generally accorded a few lines in general histories of education.[38] In reality, the issue was far more complex. As the battalions were disappearing, there was a resurgence of interest in shooting and gymnastics clubs in the east, most of which were flourishing. If the known patriotism of the eastern marches failed to nourish the experiment of the school battalions,[39] lack of ardour is less to blame than weak organization, marked by hasty conception and poor direction, and a resultant incomprehension among the very people whose cooperation was needed.

NOTES

1 Archives Départementales (AD) des Vosges, 66 R 3, *liasse* 1.
2 AD Doubs, 1 T 159. This was the case of Besançon.
3 AD Meuse, 19 T 1, Rapports 1882.
4 AD Vosges, 66 R 3, *liasse* 1.
5 See Rosemonde Sanson, *Le 14 juillet: fête et conscience nationale. 1789–1975* (Paris: Flammarion, 1976), p. 69.
6 AD Jura, T 543.
7 AD Vosges, 66 R 3, *liasse* 1. But Neufchâteau was the exception in the department at this time.
8 AD Vosges, 66 R 1.
9 AD Meuse, 19 T 1.
10 AD Jura, T 923.
h811   AD Vosges, 66 R 3, *liasse* 1.
12 Letter to prefect, AD Vosges, 66 R 3, *liasse* 3.
13 AD Jura, T 543.
14 AD Vosges, 66 R 3, *liasse* 3.
15 AD Vosges, 66 R 3, *liasse* 5; AD Meuse, 19 T 1; AD Jura, T 923.
16 AD Jura, T 543.
17 AD Meuse, 19 T 1.
18 AD Jura, T 543.
19 AD Jura, T 889.
20 Letter to the *inspecteur d'académie*, 1884. AD Jura, T 543.
21 AD Meuse, 19 T 1. Sometimes comical excuses were given: in July 1884 the mayor of Morlaincourt (Meuse) asserted that their schoolmaster was 'too fat' to undertake military training.

253

Policy in the era of nationalism

22 AD Vosges, 66 R 1, and AD Doubs, 1 T 159. A report of the commission (11 May 1887) stated that 'military instructors are lacking.... The schoolmasters drill their pupils.... The results are mediocre if not nil in many communes'.
23 AD Vosges, 66 R 3, *liasse* 3, and AD Meuse, 19 T 1.
24 Archives du Service Historique de l'Armée de Terre (Vincennes), MR 2180. It is clear that the respective roles of civilians and soldiers within the commissions were badly defined by the decree of 6 July 1882.
25 AD Vosges, 66 R 3, *liasses* 2 and 3.
26 AD Doubs, 1 T 159.
27 AD Vosges, 66 R 3, *liasse* 3.
28 AD Meuse, 19 T 1.
29 Letter to prefect (31 March 1883), AD Jura, T 923.
30 AD Doubs, 1 T 159.
31 Minutes of municipal council of Fraize (21 February 1886), AD Vosges, 66 R 3.
32 Reports to the Academic Inspectorate (26 July 1887), AD Jura, T 923.
33 AD, Doubs, 1 T 159.
34 See G. Bernard, *Repertoire numérique de la série R (affaires militaires 1800–1939)* (Troyes: AD de l'Aube), pp. 15ff. and plates. In 1980, school battalion rifles were found in the attic of an old school building at Contrisson, and in that of the *mairie* of Rancourt-sur-Ornain (Meuse); they are now used for school theatre groups. See *Est républicain*, 19 August 1987.
35 See Marcel Spivak, 'Éducation physique, sport et nationalisme en France du Second Empire au Front Populaire: un aspect original de la défense nationale', doctoral thesis, Université de Paris I, 4 vols, 1985, p. 263.
36 Françoise Mayeur, *De la Révolution à l'école républicaine*, Vol. III of *L'Enseignement et l'éducation en France* (Paris: Nouvelle Librairie de France, 1981).
37 Eugen Weber, *Peasants into Frenchmen: The Modernization of Rural France 1870–1914* (London: Chatto & Windus, 1977), pp. 298–9, 332–6.
38 E.g. Maurice Crubellier, *L'Enfance et la jeunesse dans la société française 1800–1950* (Paris: Colin, 1979), p. 197. He quotes René Meunier's absolute dismissal: 'Outdated in conception, with an incompetent personnel, ignorant of children's mentalities, the battalions were an accumulation of errors.'
39 See Pierre Arnaud (ed.), *Les Athlètes de la république: gymnastique, sport et idéologie républicaine, 1870–1914* (Toulouse: Privat, 1987), esp. pp. 47ff.

19

Patriotism, politics and policy in the Foreign Ministry 1880–1914

John Keiger

From the 1880s to the outbreak of the First World War the French Foreign Ministry underwent a number of changes that were to affect not only its organization, but also the type of permanent official it employed and inevitably its politics. The result of this was greater pressure on French foreign policy by permanent officials in Paris to adopt a more aggressively nationalistic stance, particularly in dealings with Germany, which often ran contrary to the express wishes of its political masters. The long-term consequence of this was the struggle between official and unofficial foreign policy, between friendship and friction with Germany during the period 1907 to 1911 which culminated in the confused and contradictory negotiations during the Agadir crisis in 1911, and which in the long run contributed to making any serious détente with Germany unrealistic before 1914. It is not the intention of this chapter to discuss *how* the central administration at the Quai d'Orsay sought to infuse French foreign policy with a more nationalistic flavour,[1] but to discover *why* the French Foreign Ministry became more nationalistic from the 1880s to 1914.

In the 1870s the Third Republic existed more in name than reality. But from its early 'ugly duckling' status between monarchism and republicanism, by the beginning of the 1880s it had assumed the latter of the two forms. The seemingly paradoxical triumph of the republicans within the republic needed carrying from the political into the administrative arena. The old guard of public officials had to be purged, old administrative structures needed to be renovated, new ways of doing things had to be introduced. The French Foreign Ministry, with its reputation for being a bastion of aristocratic tradition and outdated working practices could not hope to escape republican renovation. From the early 1880s onwards the ministry was to be affected in two closely linked ways, by its reorganization and modernization, and by the particular nature of the individual it began to recruit. A desire for democratic reform and a new professionalism in keeping with the positivist ideas of the time led to a series of reforms of the administrative structure of the Quai d'Orsay and an increasing tendency to recruit from the newly created nursery for French public servants the École Libre des Sciences Politiques with consequences for foreign policy that its reformers had not intended.

The central administration of the ministry in 1870 was small in comparison to the other nine ministries of the period, which had in total some 3,000 employees, half of whom belonged to the Finance Ministry and its attendant institutions. With its 90 or so paid administrative employees, a figure which had remained virtually unchanged since 1845, the Quai d'Orsay retained an intimate 'almost family character'. And like traditional families it was very much governed from the top. It had a disproportionate share of upper-level permanent officials compared to the combined total of other ministries: 21 *directeurs, sous-directeurs* and *chefs de bureau* out of a total of 350 for the other ministries and in terms of only *directeurs* 4 out of 28.[2] This intimate and seemingly authoritarian structure, which was a throwback to the Second Empire, could not hope to escape for long the scrutiny of the new republicans.

In December 1879 President of the Council William Waddington resigned when the Chamber expressed its displeasure at his failure to purge the French administration in general, and the Foreign Ministry in particular, of its non-republican elements. His successor as premier and Foreign Minister, Charles Freycinet, attended to this matter with alacrity. The year 1880 was to be a watershed in changing the organization of the Foreign Ministry as well as the nature of its officials. Of course, the intention was to institute more efficient working practices in line with the call for greater professionalism in many European foreign ministries, necessitated by the general increase in workloads, itself brought about by the rapidly expanding activities of the European powers abroad in the commercial, financial and colonial fields. The old amateur policy making of a privileged few under the Second Empire could not cope with the new demands for monitoring and collating political, economic and social data. With unimpeachable logic Freycinet's first step was to create by decree of 23 January 1880 the Direction du Personnel, whose function was to republicanize the department.[3] Not surprisingly this *direction* was, from then onwards, of strategic importance, as shown by the way in which subsequent reforming ministers attempted to keep it under the control of their private office, the all important *cabinet du ministre*. A report by the republican diplomat Jules Herbette a week later on 31 January 1880 criticized the excessive concentration of power in the hands of senior officials in the central administration of the ministry and the 'insufficient number of intermediate grades'. The following day an *arrêté* reduced the number of senior posts and increased the lower ones.[4] This would be the trend for at least the next quarter century,[5] giving increased power to the younger recruits to the Foreign Ministry up to the Great War. In response to this demand for new skills and more middle management, by 1914 the number of permanent officials in the central administration of the ministry had reached 170, twice that of 1870 and one-and-a-half times that of 1880.[6] But whereas the total number of officials had dramatically increased, the number of higher officials from *chef de bureau* upwards had increased by only three.[7]

The dual need to republicanize and recruit more staff with better skills was also attended to by Freycinet in 1880. A decree of 10 July tightened up the rules for the competitive examination for recruiting attachés to the diplomatic and consular services, first introduced in 1877 and which had done away with the old patronage-dominated system of recruitment. It was slightly modified by the decree of Foreign Minister René Goblet which reaffirmed the conditions of Freycinet's July 1880 decree as being 'inspired by a democratic belief', while wishing to consolidate them 'by introducing only a few new provisions which respond to the growing importance of economic questions in international relations'.[8] The idea was to introduce into the *concours* a greater range of economic and financial subjects, while at the same time extending the range of qualifications which were a prerequisite for sitting the examination. These were to include economics, in particular the *diplôme de l'école des sciences politiques*. Soon this *diplôme* would become practically a prerequisite for passing the entrance examination to the Quai d'Orsay. The courses at the École Libre des Sciences Politiques perfectly dovetailed with the entry requirements to the diplomatic corps, which with characteristic Gallic thoroughness and juridical clarity were clearly set down in the 1880 and 1883 decrees. Article 14 stated that the subjects tested in the examination would cover: the constitutional, judicial, administrative and financial organization of France and the major foreign states; general principles of public and private international law; basic elements of civil, commercial and maritime law; diplomatic history since 1648; political and economic geography and related statistics; elements of political economy; and the English or German language.[9] Thus any Frenchman aged between 21 and 30 years with an accredited qualification could sit the annual entrance examination which in its thirty-eight sessions between 1881 and 1914 recruited 297 *attachés d'ambassade* and *consuls suppléants*.[10] This average annual recruitment of between six and seven candidates became the only source of recruitment for the ministry after 1890, when the rules were tightened up to exclude unpaid attachés from joining the service as trainees with the expectancy of being 'made up' to a paid post without taking the examination.[11] The number of candidates continued to increase so that in 1913 only five were successful out of a total of sixty-six. It was believed that this enlarged the field of recruitment and made 'diplomatic and consular careers more accessible to merit, without reference to wealth or background' in line with the objectives of Freycinet in 1880.[12] In reality this was not the case. The *concours* merely shifted the type of recruit from the aristocrat to a restricted group within the Parisian *grande bourgeoisie* : graduates of the private École Libre des Sciences Politiques.

A further reorganizational measure which was to have repercussions on the politics of the Foreign Ministry was the rigid separation between the central administration of the ministry in Paris and the foreign service in the embassies and consulates instituted by Alexandre Ribot. Hitherto a certain fluidity between the two services had existed,[13] but Article 12 now stipulated that 'Posts in the administration cannot be assimilated with those of the diplomatic and consular careers'.[14] It would still be possible for people from the foreign service to be seconded to the central administration, but this might now hinder their promotion. This measure was matched by an obligation on the part of members of the central administration to spend a number of years abroad in order to qualify for promotion.[15] These articles were intended as money saving measures to slow down the rapid rate of growth of the personnel of the central administration, which was outstripping the ministry's budget, and to curb the rapid rise of certain central administration officials.[16] But the reform was to have negative effects as the *rapporteur* for the 1912 Chamber budget report, Paul Deschanel, remarked:

> We wrote in 1906: 'in reality there are two careers, that of Paris and that of abroad. For those who spend most of their career in Paris, who live near to the heart of things, there is rapid promotion, and, the day they decide to be unfaithful to the charms of the capital, the coveted posts; for the others, for those whose health suffers in unhealthy climates, too often they are forgotten'.[17]

The result was a growing divide between the nationalistic outlook of the bureaux and the more sanguine, pragmatic outlook of the embassies, which was seriously to affect French diplomacy from 1907 to 1914.[18]

Budgetary restrictions on the Foreign Ministry were to force further reorganization with similar indirect consequences on the politics of the administration. Despite the ever increasing workload of the Foreign Ministry in 1904 its Minister Delcassé was forced to make cuts in his personnel. He introduced a decree which reorganized thhe distribution of work in the central administration and in the foreign service. Greater responsibility was handed to more junior officials by further reducing the number of higher posts and increasing the middle-ranking positions of second and first secretary. The 1907 reform of the central administration continued in the same vein, again reducing the number of *directeurs* and *sous-directeurs*, while doubling the number of *chefs de bureau* and tripling the *sous-chefs de bureau*.[19] The result of these reforms was that considerably more power was placed in the hands of middle-ranking functionaries, thereby reducing the capacity of their masters, both hierarchical and especially political, to control their activities. The following year Ambassador Jules Cambon wrote to his brother Paul commenting sarcastically on the 1907 reform. 'I am finding that the new organization of the Ministry is producing all its fruits. Louis [Political Director] is submerged, and these young wolves who are carving out for themselves whole regions in the Ministry are destroying all overall coherence.'[20] By April 1911 he was pleading with his brother to persuade Foreign Minister Cruppi to revert to the old organization and to tell him 'what you think of the impudence of all these presumptionus and ambitious youngsters... who have rifled everything'.[21] Another acute observer of French foreign office practices remarked in November 1911: 'We know that in Talleyrand's old firm there is no leadership anymore, that initiatives come from officials who are conveniently without responsibility.'[22] The result, as one Chamber Budget Commission member remarked, was 'the confusion that we witnessed during the 1911 incidents'.[23] That these young officials in the central administration had contributed to bringing about the Agadir crisis was a firmly held belief. There was little doubt that the succession of reforms since 1880 had given them power. But who were these officials and what views did they represent?

It is a commonplace, though insufficiently stressed in diplomatic history, that social and educational background play an important role in determining future political motives and actions. In the last quarter of the nineteenth century a certain kind of higher education had a considerable effect on the outlook and behaviour of permanent officials of the French Foreign Ministry, namely, that provided by the École Libre des Sciences Politiques. A rapidly increasing number of recruits to the Quai d'Orsay were graduates of the school so that from 1905 to 1927 of 192 men appointed to the diplomatic and consular services 153 were selected from its graduates.[24] But already by 1914 some 45 per cent of the key departments of the central administration were filled by 'Sciences Po' trained officials.[25] And that training was widely recognized to have heightened national sentiment. Whereas the British Foreign Office was stocked with an elite from the public schools and the universities of Oxford and Cambridge it was the affiliation to a certain social order not the content of the education which produced its cohesion and determined its modes of thinking. With 'Sciences Po' graduates the nature and aims of their education formed a new caste. The *école* was founded in Paris in 1872 by Emile Boutmy with the intention of dispensing an education based on the practical rather than the theoretical workings of the state, which would develop personal initiative, independence of mind and a spirit of leadership, thereby improving the calibre of French government and helping to prevent further national humiliation.[26] The positivist approach to education dovetailed with the growing nationalist feelings of the age to produce graduates whose national sentiment was heightened.

From the school's creation Boutmy had set his sights on filling the upper echelons of the French administration with its graduates. By 1874 the school had two sections, one preparing for administrative and financial careers, the second for diplomacy. By 1878 Boutmy had created classes in diplomatic history to prepare for the newly created entrance examination to the Foreign Ministry. Between 1877and 1889 the school had an 87 per cent success rate in preparing for the *concours* of the *grands corps* – Conseil d'État, Inspection des Finances, Cour des Comptes and Foreign Ministry. In that period, of the 32 'Sciences Po' graduates who sat the foreign affairs entrance examination 25 (78 per cent) were successful. The school's reputation for success pushed its numbers up from 230 in 1880 to 375 by 1889.[27] Because of the high fees (fr. 300 per annum) for the three-year course and the career prospects it offered, between 1885 and 1913 over 92 per cent of its students were from the upper bourgeoisie.[28] Its teaching staff were of a conservative political outlook: men like Taine, Boutmy, Albert Sorel, Albert Vandal, Paul Leroy-Beaulieu. Indeed, as one of the founding members, Taine had stated from the outset that the school's teaching would be scientific because science 'engenders prudence, and careful study diminishes the number of revolutionaries by diminishing the number of theoreticians'.[29]

For this reason many republicans looked on the school with increasing suspicion. The republican professor at the Faculty of Law in Paris, Emile Algave, wrote to Boutmy in February 1879: 'I have seen the liberal elements, few in number from the start, successively replaced by reactionary elements. . . . The situation can be summarised like this: since the founding of the School, only one teacher who accepts the Republic has been allowed in.'[30] There was also a well-founded fear that the school was producing a 'mandarinat administratif'.[31] Strangely, there was less concern about the content of the teaching. From the school's inception this focused on history, finance, taxation, political economy, demography, statistics, comparative law and public administration: just the subjects that the Foreign Ministry would choose to examine for entrance from 1877 onwards. Certainly, the teaching was liberal, Anglophile and patriotic by temperament. The view of history taught, was very much in the vein of Guizot and Tocqueville and heavily influenced by Taine, in stressing the continuities of the French national experience and French national interests. Albert Sorel, himself a former diplomat, emphasized the national aspects of French history in his lectures on French diplomatic history, the most popular course at the school. In this way Sorel profoundly influenced a whole generation of French foreign office officials between 1872 and 1906. Similarly, Boutmy's lectures on English and constitutional history between 1872 and 1886 stressed the importance of the national character,

Patriotism, politics and policy

of race, geography and language in the historical development of peoples. Albert Vandal's lectures on diplomatic history from 1882 to 1910 rehabilitated Napoleon I and stressed the national spirit.[32] This patriotic history had an important place in the teaching at the school. Little wonder then, as the examination for the Quai d'Orsay tended to test the same subjects as those taught at the school, that from 1890 the *concours* was modified to give greater prominence and weight to diplomatic history which comprised one of the only two written examinations in the *concours*.[33] Nor was it surprising that a growing number of Sciences Po graduates passed the entrance exam. From 1889 to 1914 of 185 candidates successful in the *concours* 104 were graduates of Sciences Politiques, a total of 56 per cent.[34] And the total number of graduates of the school employed by the Foreign Ministry continued to increase. The *Annuaire Diplomatique et Consulaire* lists 46 for 1898, 84 for 1904–5, and 152 for 1914.[35]

Patriotism within the *école* was strong. When after the first Moroccan crisis of 1905 nationalist sentiment was heightened, particularly among the Parisian youth of the *grande bourgeoisie*,[36] the École des Sciences Politiques was in the vanguard. A best-selling survey of French contemporary youth entitled *Les Jeunes Gens d'aujourd'hui*, compiled by two nationalist writers (one of whom was a graduate of the school) under the pseudonym of Agathon, explained that 'one can no longer find...in the *grandes écoles* students who profess antipatriotism.... In the Faculty of Law, in the Ecole des Sciences Politiques, national sentiment is extremely keen, almost irascible'.[37] It is not surprising that the practical, nationalistic spirit inculcated at the school should be carried through into the offices of the Quai d'Orsay. The diplomat Count de Saint Aulaire, a graduate of the school, acknowledged his debt and that of other Quai officials to his former professors, Albert Sorel, Louis Renault, Albert Vandal, Anatole Leroy-Beaulieu and Emile Boutmy: 'I am grateful to them most of all for having made my task easier...for the unity of doctrine and exclusively national character, without any party political considerations, that the "bureaux" of the Quai d'Orsay owed them.'[38]

A further point about the 'Sciences Po' contingent in the Foreign Ministry was its youth. Of the 152 graduates listed in the *Annuaire Diplomatique et Consulaire* for 1914 only 21 were born before 1870, in other words over 86 per cent were under 44 years of age. This compares with the 35.7 per cent aged between 31 and 50 for top civil servants in general in 1901.[39] Were these young nationalistic Sciences Politiques graduates not the 'presumptuous and ambitious youngsters' to whom Jules Cambon referred? He constantly bemoaned the Germanophobic nationalism of the bureaux of the Quai d'Orsay who constantly obstructed his policy of détente with Germany.[40] That policy was so dogged by this young element through leaks and obstruction that he was forced to send most

Policy in the era of nationalism

of his important dispatches under cover of personal correspondence direct to the minister. On 21 November 1909, wishing to explain certain sensitive issues taking place in Alsace-Lorraine, he wrote personally to Foreign Minister Stephen Pichon:

> I am sending you this dispatch under personal cover because the squall which is brewing in Alsace-Lorraine needs in my belief to be hidden with greater care than certain young people in the corridors of the Ministry would display if this dispatch was circulated too much in the 'bureaux'.[41]

Before and during the Agadir negotiations Cambon was constantly obstructed by these young patriots who wanted no truck with Germany. Indeed, he laid a good deal of the blame for Agadir at their feet. By July their power was such that he was contemplating resignation: 'My heart is full of bitterness – I don't know how it will all end. Whether it ends for good or for bad, I seriously feel like going. We can no longer serve with these young rascals who lead us.'[42]

But the Berlin embassy was not the only target. Camille Barrère, ambassador to Italy, who had developed a pro-Italian policy since the turn of the century, came constantly under attack from the young rebels in the bureaux who viewed any flirtation with Triple Alliance members as unpatriotic.[43] A prematurely retired consul general even published a pamphlet in the form of an open letter to the Foreign Minister Gaston Doumergue in 1913 criticizing what he called 'the irresistible upsurge of the young', which had been unleashed by the reforms in the ministry.[44] These young nationalistic elements, it asserted, also had policies of their own which they worked to implement, in particular in the cases of Austria-Hungary and the Ottoman Empire and which were based on national self-determination where again the influence of the school was clearly visible. The diplomat Robert de Billy confessed:

> I believed like many students from Sciences Po in the future of the Slav world which had been revealed to me by Vogüé, Louis Léger, Ernest Denis, Rambaud, Mackenzie-Wallace. Already we were building systems based on the finally autonomous Czechs and Yugoslavs. And then the division of the Ottoman Empire would enable the whole of Christian society to be satisfied.[45]

The Vicomte de Vogüé's romantic and nationalistic books on Russian history, Léger's prolific studies of Balkan nationalism and culture, Denis's works on central European nationalism and Rambaud's extremely popular editions on Vercingétorix, Napoleon and French civilization heightened national sentiment particularly among 'Sciences Po' graduates intent on a diplomatic career in which they could apply their views on the link between nationalism and culture. The effects of these beliefs, which became subversive policies when carried into the bureaux, were felt by ministers and ambassadors alike. They conflicted with France's 'official' foreign policy at the beginning of the twentieth century which was opposed to any modification of the status quo in the Near East which might lead to a disintegration of the Ottoman Empire and a collapse of France's privileged position in Syria and the Lebanon. From 1912 to 1914 Poincaré worked incessantly to maintain the integrity of the Ottoman Empire in the face of substantial opposition from the bureaux.[46] The 'Sciences Po' grouping in the ministry appears to have been behind the systematic obstruction of the Austrophile policy of the ambassador to Vienna, Philippe Crozier in the period up to 1912. The diplomat dispatched to Vienna to act as second in command at the embassy with strict instructions to tame Crozier's policy was the brilliant 'Sciences Po' graduate, Saint Aulaire. He constantly opposed his chief and worked successfully to bring about his downfall.[47] The seasoned ambassador in Constantinople, Maurice Bompard, who strongly favoured the maintenance of the integrity of the Ottoman Empire, was almost used to attacks from the bureaux. But in April 1911 during negotiations over the construction of railways in Turkey he was forced to complain bitterly to Paul Cambon and to ask him to intercede to stop their increasing subversive action: 'What is happening to me goes far beyond anything I have seen until now at the Quai d'Orsay.' He had already written to the Foreign Minister Jean Cruppi 'to complain of the spirit prevailing in his offices'.[48] But there was not much the ineffectual Cruppi could do to discipline the bureaux at a time when they were at their most powerful. A remark by Jules Cambon perfectly summed up the period from 1907 to 1911 in which the nationalistic bureaux of the Quai d'Orsay had become so powerful: 'All these wretched people are sabotaging foreign policy as they have sabotaged the organisation of the "firm"'.[49]

The Agadir crisis, which many believed was partly attributable to their Germanophobic tendencies, was the summit of their power, but it also signalled their decline. The narrowly nationalistic policy they had championed had contributed to bringing France to the brink of war. The government would soon be brought down over the ratification of the Franco-German treaty which had resulted from the incoherent negotiations during the summer of 1911. But the machinations of the bureaux had become too obvious. The press and Parliament were clamouring for a review of the Foreign Ministry and the role of the bureaux in the Agadir crisis. The Senate Commission for the ratification of the 4 November 1911 Franco-German treaty was to investigate these issues. Its *rapporteur* Raymond Poincaré became premier and Foreign Minister less than a month later. He attempted to reduce the power of the bureaux by selective reforms of the central administration of the Quai and by concentrating most of the decision making in his own hands. Though reasonably successful, Poincaré's policies would still feel the obstructiveness of the nationalistic elements in the central administration of the Foreign Ministry up to the outbreak of war.[50] They constantly worked for the break-up of the Ottoman and Austro-Hungarian Empires and continually sought to harass Germany, even when after 1913 Poincaré sought better relations with her, especially overseas. In the end the nationalistic influences within the Foreign Ministry, through their mischievous and unofficial action, seriously hampered the possibility of any improvement in Franco-German relations before 1914, and might be said therefore to have helped make the outbreak of war in 1914 more likely.

Between 1880 and 1914 the Foreign Ministry became increasingly affected by nationalistic influences from within its own walls. This chapter has attempted to explain why that was so and has pointed to two important reasons: first, the constant reorganizing of the ministry which resulted in power and decision making being passed down the hierarchy of the central administration to the middle-ranking officials whose numbers and ability to affect the formulation and execution of foreign policy increased substantially; and, second, the change in the nature of recruits away from the more amateur aristocratic diplomat of the Second Empire to a more professional, upper middle-class vocationally trained, technocratic mandarin of the 1880s and thereafter. That official was recruited increasingly from the nationalistic École Libre des Sciences Politiques which left its imprint on the political outlook and methods of the bureaux. Of course, it would be simplistic to attribute the nationalism of the French Foreign Ministry solely to these factors. The whole of this period was marked by a growth in nationalism which would have affected the ministry without the reforms and the influence of 'Sciences Po'. The Foreign Ministry in particular was perforce at the sharp end of and professionally sensitive to the image that Germany's foreign policy created. But there is little doubt that by giving great power to younger, less experienced, more idealistic officials, the Foreign Ministry was clearing a pathway that its new recruits (nearly all from the same institution which stressed in its teaching national values, personal initiative and drive), could soon begin to charge along, resulting in a heightened nationalistic outlook at the Foreign Ministry with inevitable consequences for French diplomacy. Ironically, then, the reforms to republicanize France's diplomatic machine merely replaced the old Second Empire aristocrat with a Parisian *grande bourgeoisie* technocrat – a trend that the École Nationale d'Administration might be said to have continued to this day.

NOTES

1. This has been done elsewhere. See J. F. V. Keiger, *France and the Origins of the First World War* (London: Macmillan 1983), and by the same author 'Jules Cambon and Franco-German détente 1907–1944', *Historical Journal*, vol. 26, no. 3 (1983), pp. 641–59.
2. J. Baillou (ed.), *Les Affaires étrangères et le corps diplomatique français*, Vol. II, *1870–1980* (Paris: CNRS (Centre National de la Recherche Scientifique), 1984), p. 106.
3. ibid., pp. 30, 51.
4. ibid., p. 107.
5. See the decrees of 1891, 1892, 1894, 1895, 1896 and 1907 which decreased the number of *sous-directeurs* and *chefs de bureau* but increased the number of *attachés payés* and *expéditionnaires*. ibid., p. 107.
6. ibid., p. 108. A substantial, though less dramatic increase for the central administration's permanent officials is recorded in J.-C. Allain and M. Auffret, 'Le Ministère français des affaires étrangères: crédits et effectifs pendant la III république', *Relations internationales*, no. 32 (1982), pp. 435–6.
7. Baillou, *Affaires étrangères*, Vol. II, p. 110.
8. Decree of 23 August 1888, *Annuaire diplomatique et consulaire*, 1889, p. 277.
9. ibid., pp. 278–80.
10. Baillou, *Affaires étrangères*, Vol. II, p. 155.
11. See Ribot, decree of 14 October 1890.
12. Baillou, *Affaires étrangères*, Vol. II, p. 155.
13. The decree of 21 February 1880 assimilated rank in the central administration and foreign services.
14. Ribot decree 12 May 1891.
15. Ribot decree of 17 January 1891.
16. ibid.
17. *Journal officiel, Chambre des Députés, Document Parlementaire annexe 1237*, p. 1245. At the beginning of the Third Republic one in four French diplomats worked in the central administration, by 1900 one in three. See Allain and Auffret, 'Ministère français des affaires étrangères,' p. 443.
18. See Keiger, *France and the Origins*, pp. 27–37 *et passim*.
19. Pichon decree 29 April 1907. For further details on the effects of the 1907 reform see Keiger, *France and the Origins*, pp. 26–7.
20. Jules Cambon to Paul Cambon, 8 February 1908, Ministère des Affaires Étrangères (MAE) Jules Cambon MSS, carton 25 Dos. 1908, p. 72.
21. Jules Cambon to Paul Cambon, 17 April 1911, ibid., p. 18. For further examples of the power of the younger officials see J. F. V. Keiger, 'Raymond Poincaré and French foreign policy 1912–14', unpublished PhD dissertation, Cambridge University (1980), pp. 15–21.
22. Lindenlaub (journalist with *Le Temps*) to A. Gérard (ambassador), 14 November 1911, Archives Nationales, Gérard MSS, 329 AP 19.
23. *Journal officiel, Chambre des Députés*, 10 March 1914, p. 1461.
24. W. R. Sharp, 'Public personnel management in France', in W. R. Sharp (ed.), *Civil Service Abroad*, New York, 1935, p. 105.
25. Keiger, *France and the Origins*, p. 30, and for a detailed breakdown of these figures per department see Keiger, 'Poincaré', p. 22.
26. See Thomas R. Osborne, *A 'Grande École' for the 'Grands Corps'. The Recruitment and Training of the French Administrative Elite in the Nineteenth Century*, (New York: Boulder Social Science Monographs 1983).
27. Guy Thuillier, *L'Éna avant l'Éna*, (Paris: Presses Universitaires de France, 1983), pp. 125–9, 165.
28. See C. Charle, *Les Élites de la république (1880–1900)* (Paris: Fayard, 1987), p. 50.
29. Quoted in Osborne, *A Grande École*, p. 91.
30. Quoted in Thuillier, *L'Éna avant l'Éna*, p. 149.
31. ibid., p. 157.

32 For a detailed development of this see, Osborne, *A Grande École*, pp. 92–3.
33 See *Annuaire Diplomatique et Consulaire* 1891, p. 281.
34 These figures are based on the 1914 *Annuaire*'s list of candidates successful in the *concours* cross-referenced with their qualifications in the *états de service*.
35 See *Annuaire* for 1898, 1904–5, 1914. Of course, many of the recruits also had a degree in Law. But students often enrolled in the Law faculties and rarely attended lectures, often doing an absolute minimum to obtain their degrees, thus its influence on them was minimal. Furthermore, the Law faculties certainly did not offer very vocational training, relying heavily on rote learning of Roman Law and the Civil Code. Indeed, because of the success of Sciences Politiques attempts were made to reform the degree and introduce study of more contemporary legislative practice in areas such as finance and commerce from 1889. Overall, Law did not create the 'esprit de corps' of Sciences Politiques graduates.
36 'Sciences Po' students were far more Parisian than those of other *grandes écoles*. See C. Charle, *Les Élites*, p, 51.
37 Agathon, *Les Jeunes Gens d'aujourd'hui* (Paris: Plon-Nourrit, 1913), pp. 28–9.
38 A. F. C. de Saint Aulaire, *Confessions d'un vieux diplomate* (Paris: Flammarion, 1953), p. 11.
39 For an analysis of the age structure of various elites in France at the time, see Charle, *Les Élites*, pp. 55–7.
40 See J. F. V. Keiger, 'Jules Cambon and Franco-German détente 1907–14.'
41 J. Cambon to Pichon, 21 November 1909, Institut de France, Pichon MSS, 4396, p. 55.
42 J. Cambon to Paul Cambon, 16 July 1911, MAE Jules Cambon MSS, carton 25, p. 192.
43 See Keiger, *France and the Origins* pp. 56–67.
44 See H. Pognon, *Lettre à M. Doumergue au sujet d'une réforme du ministère des affaires étrangères* (Paris: Figuière, 1913).
45 Robert de Billy, 'Souvenirs' (unpublished) in MAE de Billy MSS, Dos. 3, p. 6.
46 See Keiger, *France and the Origins*, pp. 121–3, 129–35 *et passim*.
47 ibid., pp. 81–6 *et passim*.
48 Bompard to Paul Cambon, 7 April 1911, MAE Paul Cambon MSS, vol. 12, p. 206.
49 Jules Cambon to Paul Cambon, 17 April 1911, MAE Jules Cambon MSS, carton 25, pp. 162–3.
50 See Keiger, *France and the Origins*, pp. 48–54 ff.

20

Strategic independence and security of communications: the undersea telegraph cables

Jean-Claude Allain

Political and popular nationalism draw their nourishment from military endeavours which provide ideals of glory and heroism. Patriotism and territorial defence, expansion and conquest all become part of the exaltation of power, symbolized by a flag, to be protected wherever it is raised by a professional fighting force, which in France was also responsible for instructing the coming generation in these ideals. National defence presupposed nationalism in its widest sense. Extreme nationalism, the aggressive, vain and exclusive glorification of the nation, could find in the theme of national defence a means of growth, even though it was often a damaging distortion of that national sentiment which is the necessary pillar of defensive organization and strategic planning, in which sentiment and interest come together to protect the sovereign territory against foreign ambitions.

This criterion of power had to be met by the state alone with its national resources. The ideal of strategic independence is to make the means of defence completely self-sufficient, an ideal that can be less and less easily achieved in the modern period, particularly for states whose territorial sovereignty is scattered outside the home country as a result of colonial expansion. Immediately prior to the First World War, France was in this position. It attempted to remedy this weakness by constructing a strategic system that functioned on several complementary levels, ranging from the alliance with Russia to a policy of seduction, so discreet as to be almost nonexistent in relation to Switzerland, but which with Great Britain took the form of an active *entente cordiale*.

Although the focus of the system was European, because of the possibility of war with Germany, the causes of conflict often came from outside Europe. Competitive colonial expansion during the last two decades of the previous century demonstrated this, particularly Franco-British rivalry which the agreement of 1904, while not ending, at least calmed and contained. At this global level, power was no longer solely linked to the capacity of arms or diplomacy to move into new areas and stay there; in order for it to be established, then administered, a means of communication had to be possible between the delegated authority far from the home country and the central political body, that took account of possible repercussions in Europe from unexpected conflict abroad. This traditional rule of political conduct was adapted to the technical improvements in communications: overseas, the ship remained the safest direct and national method, and in times of peace did not have to rely on the international hierarchy of warfleets, but it was slow compared with the electric telegraph which, by means of undersea cables, could link the continents together.[1] Whoever owned the cable controlled the information, and through having access to it and being able to pass it on, gained an increased ability to affect events.

The cable became an important factor in international power, but the states that were able to acquire the system and establish themselves as frontrunners were seemingly unaware of the potential until the turn of the century. France was among them, and attempted to provide itself with a national transmission network for communications outside Europe by laying undersea cables, thus guaranteeing confidentiality and the rapid transmission of information, both of which were essential for strategic independence.

In 1900, 'England is absolute mistress of all international undersea communications. She has patiently woven a huge net of cables that enfolds the whole world, and is therefore assured of a real commercial monopoly, as well as of tremendous strategic and diplomatic superiority.'[2] This imbalance was somewhat corrected by 1913, but its effects were still felt. While Great Britain no longer maintained the (absolute) monopoly she had enjoyed during the three decades that followed the laying of the first international cable (the Franco-British link between Calais and Dover in September 1851), she still in the early years of the twentieth century retained an incontestable leadership.

In quantitative terms, the world network was extended and diversified with the inevitable spread of undersea telegraph technology. The United States, France, the Netherlands, Denmark and Germany, once customers of British companies, became their competitors, albeit in a small way. In 1900, the British network represented 60 per cent of all undersea cabling, in 1913 Britain still owned just over half, and the gap between the British holding and that of the nearest competitor remained large: out of 539,000 km, Britain had 330,000 km; the United States, in second place, had 70,000 km and France, in third position, 46,000 km. British superiority was maintained by a comfortable margin and left plenty of room for manoeuvre.[3] Even if its hegemony was no longer total, it still represented the kind of superiority that the Admiralty might have dreamt of, since it was far greater than the ideal of the Two-Power Standard.

In qualitative terms, the British network had no competitor in the continuity and comprehensiveness of its layout, which really did 'enfold the whole world'. The length of the national networks, which determined ranking, did not take account of their positioning. Thus the eight Franco-British cables (representing a half, or 224 km, for each partner), the four cables linking Marseille and Algeria (3,800 km) or the two transatlantic cables from Brest to the United States (12,500 km), contributed to France's position and certainly indicate its telegraphic activity. But they also reveal the importance attached to a direct link with each of the countries mentioned rather than an attempt to construct a comprehensive and independent network. This is exactly what the British achieved, by working methodically and deliberately, the government acting as investor and user, and supporting certain large companies both financially and politically, depending on the areas covered. These were principally the Eastern Telegraph Company (1872) and its subsidiaries, such as the Eastern Extension Australasia and China Telegraph Company, and the Eastern and South Africa Telegraph Company.

Covering East and South-East Asia, the South Pacific, the Indian Ocean, the two coasts of Africa, and North and South America, generally following shipping routes, punctuated by island relay-stations (Malta, St Helena, Mauritius, Cocos, and so on), the ports of continental colonies (such as Aden) and stations in friendly countries (the Azores, the Cape Verde islands or São Tomé, owned by Portugal), this world network converged on London via the coastal stations, such as Valencia and Penzance. All international interests, governments and businesses used it for all or part of their overseas communications, since it provided an instant service and was cheaper than the installation of an equivalent national system. British companies, for their part, could become agents for foreign governments for the establishment and use of regional cables. They owned two thirds of the worldwide cabling fleet and could offer unequalled technical experience, beginning in 1865, when the *Great Eastern* laid the first transatlantic cable between Ireland and Newfoundland.

France also had recourse to help from the British. The same *Great Eastern* laid France's first transatlantic cable between Brest-Saint-Pierre and New York in 1868. It was replaced in 1879, again by the British for the Compagnie du Télégraph de Paris in New York, which was founded by the banker and ex-minister of Thiers, Pouyer-Quertier (hence the name 'cable PQ'). Similarly, the British laid the first German transatlantic relay between Emden and New York through the Azores. The second French cable between Brest and Cape Cod-New York, established in 1899, was made and laid by the French, and the Germans followed suit with their second link with North America, in 1905. Nonetheless, in 1900 the British had 11 cables connecting them with North America.

British companies were given the task in 1874 of laying and running the cable from Saigon to Haiphong in Indo-China (Eastern Extension), the Dakar/Saint-Louis/Tenerife link in 1883 (Spanish National Submarine Telegraph Company), and in 1885 the intercolony sections in black Africa, linking Senegal and Guinea Conakry, Ivory Coast and Dahomey, Dahomey and Gabon (West African Telegraph Company). French technology took off during the next decade with the reorganization of the industrial and commercial sectors encouraged by political support.

Between 1890 and 1892, an undersea link was established between Haiti, Martinique, Dutch Guiana, Venezuela and French Guiana, with an extension from there to Belem (Brazil). The Société Française des Télégraphes Sous-marins (1888), which owned this network, laid the cable between Haiti and New York in 1896, for the United States and Haiti Cable Company. Since the cable from Brest came ashore there, a North Atlantic and French Caribbean network was emerging, although continuity is not synonymous with security and homogeneity. New York, Haiti and Paramaribo were outside French sovereignty, and the connection in New York was American. Elsewhere, French initiatives were limited to connections between British networks: Madagascar-Mozambique, Djibouti-Perim (Aden), and New Caledonia-Australia. 'The half-measures so common in France were preferred, with small cables being placed at the four corners of the world, to link some of our colonies to the general telegraph network.'[4] Except with New York and North Africa, all French communications outside Europe depended to some degree on the British network, and therefore on the political power exerted from London. If a conflict arose with Britain, the whole of the colonial empire in Africa and Eastern Asia could be cut off from the home country, except for direct maritime contact. This basic vulnerability had a strategic significance: the cable network was 'a question of national defence',[5] which called for urgent reexamination.

The debate took this turn because of recent deterioration in Franco-British relations and the effect of war in the Transvaal on international communications. Although telegraphic transmission was carried out by private companies, who were supposed to pass on communications regardless of their contents, it was too closely linked to the exercise of political power to be entirely independent: the right to installation, landing rights in foreign countries, protection and security of lines and operating subsidies for official service all involved state intervention. The circulation of information had always preoccupied governments which, inside their own frontiers, frequently retained a monopoly over such operations: the post and telegraph services were run by the state in both France and Britain. At an international level, the British government could not give up the advantage provided by priority and initial exclusivity in the world telegraph network that it had helped to create. The convention of the Telegraphic Union of Saint Petersburg (1875, revised 1895) authorized member states to 'interrupt transmission of any private telegram that could threaten national security', and to 'suspend international service' passing through their territory, particularly in case of war. The schedule of conditions of the British companies authorized the government to requisition cables, stations and their employees on their sovereign territory or that placed under their protection. Station personnel had to be British.[6] Secrecy of communication was far from guaranteed since states were recognized to have the right to check the content of telegrams passing through their territories or transmitted by companies of their nationality. Britain made use of this right.

The tense circumstances of 1900 encouraged the recall of various British coups in this respect.[7] In 1870, France's declaration of war against Prussia, communicated by British cables to the French squadron in the China Sea, was also thought to have been passed on to German steamers which thus evaded capture. The fall of Langson (Tonkin) in 1885, which caused Ferry's government to resign, was known by the same means in London and by the British ambassador in France before Ferry himself was informed. This proved only a minor inconvenience, except to French pride, because the British were acting as intermediaries between Paris and Peking. There were more serious consequences in 1893, when the telegram communicating to Admiral Humann the text of the ultimatum to Siam was only passed on by the Eastern Telephone Company once it had been seen by the Foreign Office – Siam was an area in which French and British interests overlapped.

The problem of London having prior knowledge was even more serious in 1898, during the Fashoda crisis. Marchand could only communicate with Paris by sending his adjutant Baratier, and subsequently by going himself, to Cairo to telegraph, using a British cable, as did Kitchener, but directly from his camp, using military land lines. Having to rely on Britain for the use of cable removed secrecy of information and decision making from French diplomacy, and could also slow down the transmission of news. In 1894, the death of Hassan I, Sultan of Morocco, was not announced in Europe until the British minister in Tangiers allowed his foreign colleagues access to the telegraph station, some 36 hours after the event, after having decided the policy to be adopted with London. In 1895, the news that Tananarive had been taken by the French expedition was delayed by three days, 'the cable having broken at just the right moment', as it had between Tenerife and Dakar during the Fashoda crisis. 'Our colonies all know that, when the English cables suddenly go dead, they have to be on their guard.'[8] When a year later, in October 1899, London decided to censor private telegrams to southern Africa, then in November to forbid coded telegrams passing through Aden to the Indian Ocean (in this case for France from Madagascar and Réunion), the limits of tolerance were reached. The Boer War was not popular in

Policy in the era of nationalism

France because it was a British initiative, and because national opinion was still easily aroused after the Fashoda affair, developing into a feeling of real hostility towards the British.[9] The Parisian and provincial press made much of these interruptions of private transactions, which were judged to be arbitrary, arrogant and intolerable. Parliament took up the matter, on 27 November, at the request of the deputy Henrique, a member of the colonial group of advisers on external trade. Defence of the empire, nationalism and national strategy came together in this new attitude towards telegraphic dependence.[10]

In the context of this current of nationalist opinion, heightened still further by the Dreyfus Affair, and in this case Germanophobe, the cable issue, with its Anglophobe aspect, induced bad-tempered reactions but also government initiatives to try to calm them. Although these remained on a scale with the issue – just one element, though certainly an under-valued one – of general policy, they provided a new impetus to the policy relating to cables, which continued administratively and quietly for the next decade.

On 30 January 1900, Millerand, Minister of Commerce, Posts and Telegraphs, introduced a bill for the development of the colonial cable network, with a projected expenditure of over fr. 100 million over several financial years, but only fr. 17 million for the first.[11] This plan was supported by ardent colonialists and nationalists alike: the establishment of a 'complete system ... all ours and ours alone'.[12] There were lectures and articles (some referred to above) on the construction of such a network,[13] but the project submitted was very different. The limited effort it recommended was criticized less for its spirit than for its choice of routes. 'It would be rash to think of supplanting our neighbours now, or even equalling them,' wrote Millerand in 1900.[14] Maurice Ordinaire, who reported on the bill on behalf of the Colonies Commission, gave the cost of the programme as fr. 130 million, but altered its priorities in a way that was accepted by the Budget Commission.

All parties agreed to delay indefinitely the formation of a link with the Établissements Français d'Océanie, situated in an area whose future remained unclear.[15] Similarly, a national link to Madagascar and its neighbouring territories, Réunion and Comoros, while deemed highly desirable, was to be delayed until the completion of intermediate links. Two regions, however, came top of the list for disengagement from the British network, and received the necessary finance for this to be achieved, albeit as cheaply as possible: Indo-China and black Africa.

Communications with Saigon depended exclusively on the Eastern Extension, as they did in Indo-China, even between Saigon and Haiphong. Millerand and Ordinaire felt that the best method of changing this situation was to lay a cable between Hue and a point situated to the north of Hong Kong, either Vladivostock or Amoy (China), closer and therefore cheaper. The plan was to link up with the land-based network in Russia, a friendly ally. Amoy was the terminal of the continental and undersea network operated by the Danish Grande Compagnie des Télégraphes du Nord, which had been quoted on the Paris Bourse since 1874 and was linked to the state by convention for the Franco-Danish undersea link.[16] It was an added advantage that the company had the nationality of a small country and would therefore be less sensitive than the Eastern to political circumstances. 'The country's insignificant political role was a commercial advantage; the Danes viewed the international traffic as merely a business enterprise without any political goals.'[17] The Amoy/Vladivostock/Russian-network/Baltic/Denmark route was not, however, reliable: the Siberian open-air cable subjected the transmission to adverse climatic influences but, more importantly, Ordinaire noted that the financial independence of the company did not exclude technical agreements over service and use with the Eastern, which entailed the risk of dependence on Britain once again, albeit in an indirect and attenuated form. This imperfect route was still less costly than a direct cable to Vladivostock. In 1901, the cable ship *François Arago* laid the 1,700 km cable from Tourane to Amoy.

The ideal would have been a link between Indo-China and Madagascar, with a station at Java (controlled by the Netherlands), but first Madagascar itself had to be made independent of the East and South African network, and directly linked to the Congo, but that colony was not yet connected to the West African network. This long-term perspective was contained in the Franco-Dutch convention of 6 April 1904 (two days before the signing of the *entente cordiale*), the main object of which was to authorize the landing of a French cable between Saigon and Pontianak (Borneo).[18] The cable was laid in 1906, and this connection with the Dutch and even German-Dutch network opened the American route since, at Guam, it joined up with the cable of the Commercial Pacific Cable Company, which came ashore at San Francisco. From there, communication could continue along interior lines to Cape Cod, where it passed on to the French cable.[19]

The security of this convoluted route to avoid the Eastern – eccentric in every way – was by no means certain, but at least it ended total dependence on London. 'A multiplicity of lines crossing the territory of friendly powers would be a real guarantee of security,' concluded Ordinaire.[20] It was inconceivable that in the case of a conflict between Britain and France all the countries involved in transmission would be against France. The drawback was the increased cost of the telegraphic service, which limited its use and explains the fact that the cables in Amoy and Borneo were not replaced after breaking down in 1913. But on the other hand, all that had been required was an investment of 2,800 km of cable to provide a two-way link of 20,000 km. Telegraphic independence and budgetary prudence were both taken care of, and the

Policy in the era of nationalism

development of the West African network took this as a model in providing real independence.[21]

In 1900 there was discussion of the best route to link up with Dakar, 'telegraphic hub' and strategic site *par excellence*, since its situation made it the crossroads for communications between Paris, the colonies of Black Africa and South America. The most economical method was to link Oran with Tenerife via Tangiers: this solution would amount to a third of the cost (fr. 6 million as opposed to fr. 17 million) of laying a direct cable from Brest, although this would certainly be safer and more national. This was the solution advised by Millerand who, for the larger sum, could finance three other links (Dahomey–Congo; Reunion–Madagascar; Hue–Amoy). Another suggestion was to buy the cables used by the Spanish National between Tenerife, Saint-Louis and Dakar, but these were showing their age, the concession was soon to expire and the landing at Tenerife was no more safe than at Tangiers. This angle was, therefore, not pursued. The service to the colonies south of Dakar via West Africa was, however, in urgent need of reexamination.

Despite the Berlin conference on West Africa (1885), dependence on a British company had continued. But the British government, although certain of its power over the companies, was not satisfied with a mixing of lines and stations in foreign territories. They pressed for the formation of a strictly imperial network, and even greater independence of communication. 'As jingoist sentiments rose, it became increasingly galling to have British telegrams cross non-British territories. . . . The epitome of strategic cables was the "All Red Route", a scheme to gird the globe with a cable passing only through British territories.'[22] The line followed by the African Direct Telegraph Company resulted from this policy: from St Vincent (Cape Verde), it served Bathurst, Freetown, Accra, Lagos and Bonny; but its landfalls (Accra, for example) deprived the West African of its exclusivity, because it had conceded the right in contravention of its agreement with France. This was one of the points of contention with the West African which had not received the French subsidy for three years. The purchase of cables and, wherever necessary, disconnection from stations in British colonies appeared to be the solution.

It will be noted that the idea of cable nationalism originated in Britain and that it reflects, in its suspicious and exclusive character, a global, imperialist nationalism. It is not surprising, then, to note similar principles evoked in Maurice Ordinaire's report: the creation of entirely French lines, if not a complete network, with the least possible contact with foreign soil.

The options kept open for Africa were as follows: a cable from Brest to Dakar to be completed as soon as possible; the extension of the Marseille–Oran as far as Tangiers (completed at the end of 1901) because of the experience of 1894 and Moroccan politics; and the purchase of cables from the West African. A law of 25 July 1901 authorized this purchase at a cost of fr. 3.6 million.[23] When the Brest–Dakar link opened in 1905, it was connected with this colonial line made up of two separate sections: Dakar–Conakry and Ivory Coast–Dahomey–Gabon. The unification of the line by filling the gap between Guinea and Ivory Coast was achieved by an unlikely detour into South America.

On 25 July 1901, a second cable law was voted under the mysterious heading, 'Organisation of new undersea telegraphic communications'. No plan was shown for this line, the annual payment for which would amount to fr. 480,000, guaranteed by adding it to the PTT budget. The reporter made no mention of this and law was passed without debate.[24] Behind this enigma lay the purchase by the PTT of the South American Cable Company (SAC), previously British owned. Formed in 1891, this company used a cable linking Saint-Louis (Senegal) and Pernambuco (Brazil), where it had obtained a 25-year landing right. It competed with two cables owned by the Western Telegraph Company, from Lisbon and Western Africa through the station at St Vincent (Cape Verde). Its financial situation was less brilliant than Millerand implied to the Budget Commission, in his attempt to show that the state was benefiting both politically and commercially.[25] The purchase of the SAC would allow France to make a discreet yet direct entry into the South Atlantic and, once a link was established between Pernambuco and Pará with a French cable, a second network with the West Indies would be achieved or, in another sense, the circuit from Brest to the United States completed, as was undertaken in 1913. It also gave the government the landing right which, it was said, could not have been obtained from Brazil direct but which it acquired indirectly through the South American Cable. This explains the secrecy observed in Parliament, although the subterfuge was widely known in telegraphic circles. The adroit use of this right allowed the West African network to be united.

Imperial Germany was as anxious as France to free itself from British companies and from the Eastern, particularly in Africa. Its cable policy was led by the company Felton und Guilleaume Carlswerk, specialists in the field since 1853, who had mastered all the technology by 1900. Between Emden, the cable terminal, and the African colonies (Togo, Cameroon, South-West African) or Brazil, the best sites were held by the British (Azores, Cape Verde) or the French (Dakar). The terminal at Vigo (Spain) lay idle and the Spanish government determinedly refused, between 1907 and 1909, to allow it to be reused by laying an extension to Casablanca (either directly or via Tenerife), where Germany had obtained a landing right, during the conference at Algeçiras in 1906. In June 1907, Madrid was only prepared to accept the landing of a cable directly from Emden, with Cameroon as its destination. In August 1909, it had been laid as far as the Canaries, and thus rendered obsolete the route via Vigo or Casablanca, which would certainly have been more economical. To reach Lome and Douala, it passed through Monrovia, well situated for a connection with Brazil.[26] In 1908, Clemenceau's government failed to respond to German requests to grant them the right of installation at Pernambuco. A year later, Franco-German relations had changed: the time had come for economic and financial association, as set down in the agreement of 9 February 1909. In this climate of détente, Briand's government granted the requests: in 1910, two conventions authorized the landing of a German cable from Monrovia at Pernambuco, and another from Emden at Brest. These were to be followed by a cable covering the section Conakry/Monrovia/Grand Bassam (Ivory Coast), laid by Germany for French use.[27] A double circuit was thus created between Europe and Brazil, through Franco-German cooperation, avoiding British networks: Emden/Brest/Dakar, Emden/Tenerife/Monrovia. The joint venture provided for mutual assistance in using one of the lines if the other should fail. Germany thus provided, for fr. 500,000 francs, the French-owned West African network with unity and independence, between Dakar and Libreville (1912), and this was extended by the French in 1913 to Pointe Noire (Congo). Of the 5,400 km of cable laid, 18 per cent was French in origin, 22 per cent German, and the rest British. Security of national communication was thus achieved in relation to friendly Britain with the help of a potential enemy. The astonishment of the people of Brest can be imagined when, in October 1911, during the Agadir crisis when open conflict with Germany seemed possible, a German ship arrived: it was a cabler relaying between Brest and Emden the cable that had once linked Emden and Ireland, but which had been made obsolete by the duplication of the German transatlantic link, in 1905.

By 1913 France did not have an entirely independent cable network, although it ranked third in the world. Totalling 8.5 per cent of the world network, it would seem to be failing in comparison with the other criteria of international position: it was the second colonial power, and fifth commercial and maritime force. Its lack of independent communications capacity constituted a strategic failure, unnoticed by all but a few contemporary commentators,[28] because it concerned a subject that was still new to public opinion, unspectacular and, paradoxically for a means of communication, of little interest to the media.

After 1900, there was distinct, although unspectacular progress. Although not world-wide, the French network became homogeneous in a number of regions: in the Maghreb, West Africa, North America and the Caribbean. In Asia, the Pacific and the Indian Ocean, they were more dependent. These geographical parameters reflect the traditional international capacity of France: beyond Africa and the North Atlantic expansion tailed off and world ambition had to compensate with speeches and the imagination for the poverty of its resources, initiative and efforts. France may be described in this area as a medium power that saw itself as a major power. This middling position meant that the security of its undersea communications was limited. Such security as it had was acquired by political means, supported by national feeling, stimulated at the start of the century as much by internal affairs as by the contagious enthusiasms of externally directed nationalism. Nationalist fads lay in the background of cable policy, which they partially influenced. For the strategic implication of cables gave them an inherently national aspect, though this was not pushed to extremes.

The failure to achieve independence was practically inevitable, principally because of the cost of producing a complete 'nationalist' programme, but the new technology of wireless telegraphy made it possible to remedy matters. After 1904, the French sought to avoid open confrontation with Great Britain, since the two countries were politically friendly – hence the slow pace of French policy which was aimed at withdrawing quietly from British networks.[29] This tactic shows the plasticity of strategic systems. The stronger is as much envied as feared by the weaker, who is willing to make use of the potential enemy as an occasional support. Balance is therefore restored to power relationships by the tactical strengthening of the members' national capabilities; this also can be seen as a repercussion of nationalism.

NOTES

1 J.-H. Franklin, 'La Question des câbles sous-marins', *Questions diplomatiques et coloniales* (hereafter *QDC*), no. 70 (15 January 1900), p. 79. The victory in the America's Cup was wired in 30 seconds from New York to Brest (using an Anglo-American Telegraph Company cable), rewired 5 minutes later to Berlin and 7 minutes later to Balmoral.
2 Franklin, in *QDC* no. 67 (1 December 1899), p. 397.
3 *Nomenclature des câbles formant le réseau sous-marin du globe*, published by the Bureau de l'Union Internationale Télégraphique in Berne, known as the *Nomenclature de Berne*, supplement no. 4 (1 August 1914) to the 10th edition (August 1910).
4 J. Depelley, 'Les Câbles télégraphiques en temps de guerre', *Revue des Deux Mondes*, 1 January 1900, p. 197. He was manager of the Compagnie Française de Câbles Télégraphiques.
5 *QDC*, no. 67, p. 407.
6 Report by Maurice Ordinaire for the Commission des Colonies, 19 June 1900, *Journal Officiel de la République Française* (*JORF*), *Documents Parlementaires* (*DP*), 1900, annexe no. 1727, pp. 1327–33. See also n. 2 above.
7 Franklin, *QDC*, no. 67 (1 December 1899), p. 404. In the Reichstag, the same examples were given to justify the laying of the first Emden-New York cable. See Charles Lemire, *La Défense nationale: La France et les câbles sous-marins avec nos possessions et les pays étrangers* (Paris: n.p., 1900), p. 9.
8 'Proposition de loi Meyer *et al.*', 13 February 1900, annexe no. 1931, p. 4 Archives Nationales (*AN*), série C, carton 5671, dossier 2590.
9 See, for example, A. Barblan, 'A la recherche de soi-même: la France et Fachoda', *Relations Internationales*, no. 2 (November 1974), pp. 67–81.
10 Similar sentiments were expressed at the same time in Germany and the USA. *QDC*, no. 73 (1 March 1900), pp. 272–3, quotes notably from the *Deutsche Colonial Zeitung*

Policy in the era of nationalism

of February, urging a national link with West Africa and South America, 'where we have such great commercial interests', and also from President McKinley's message to Congress of 10 February (often quoted in other publications) stating as an objective the laying of a new cable, independent of the British, to the newly acquired Philippines.

11 *JORF, DP*, Chambre, 1900, annexe 1374, pp. 447–8.
12 Franklin, *QDC*, no. 70 (15 January 1900), p. 81. He deplored the fact that the first Franco-British link of 1851 had been built by the British with a French subvention, rather than by a French company: 'already at that date one finds proof of our blindness', ibid., p. 71.
13 See Depelley (n. 4 above), Lemire (n. 7), Meyer (n. 8), who presented a plan costing fr. 235 million, Franklin (in his articles in *QDC*), who was more modest, and M. P. Marcillac, in a lecture on 'Les Câbles sous-marins nationaux', published separately by the *Bulletin de la Société Scientifique Industrielle de Marseille* (first quarter, 1900), which examined access routes to Madagascar via the Mediterranean and West Africa.
14 'Rapport sur le fonctionnement de l'administration des PTT', *JORF* (12 May 1900), pp. 2296–7.
15 E.g. *QDC*, no. 73 (1 March 1900), p. 278.
16 *Annuaire des valeurs inscrites à la côté* (Paris, 1914), p. 1687.
17 Jorma Ahvenainen, 'Telegraphs, trade and policy: the role of the intercontinental telegraphs in the years 1870–1914', in W. Fischer, R. Marvin and J. Schneider (eds), *The Emergence of a World Economy, 1500–1914*, Vol. II (Wiesbaden: Steiner, 1986), pp. 511–12.
18 *JORF* (1905), p. 656, law of 17 January 1905 authorizing the ratification of the convention, and p. 1478, decree of application of 1 March 1905 (with text of convention).
19 Daniel Headrick, 'Câbles télégraphiques et rivalité franco-britannique, 1870–1914', paper presented at the conference on 'Télécommunications, espaces et innovations aux 19e–20e siècles' (January 1989), organized by the Association pour la Recherche Historique des Télécommunications, Paris.
20 See n. 6.
21 The section that follows is based on a paper entitled 'L'Indépendance câblière de la France au début du XXe siècle', given by me to the conference on telecommunications referred to in n. 19.
22 Daniel Headrick, *The Tools of Empire: Technology and European Imperialism in the Nineteenth Century* (Oxford: Oxford University Press, 1981), pp. 162–3.
23 *JORF* (28 July 1901), p. 4746. The cost was born by the 'dette flottante', with a corresponding emission of 3 per cent bonds over 9 years.
24 ibid., p. 4745; *Débats: Chambre*, pp. 1823–4; *Sénat*, p. 1206.
25 AN série C, carton 5629, 'premier registre de la commission du budget', 3 July 1901. The cost was fr. 9.6 million, met according to the same procedure as the West African (see n. 23). Charles Lesage, *La Rivalité anglo-germanique: les câbles sous-marins allemands* (Paris: Plon-Nourrit, 1915), pp. 139–43, is the best documented work, probably based on oral sources, concerning this affair, which surprised him and whose ulterior interest he failed to see.
26 Jean-Claude Allain, *Agadir 1911* (Paris: Publications de la Sorbonne, 1976), pp. 133–5.
27 Lesage, *La Rivalité*, pp. 156–8. The Tenerife cable reached Monrovia in 1911 and Douala in January 1913; the Brazilian link to Pernambuco was laid in March 1911.
28 Léon Jakob, 'Les Intérêts français et les relations télégraphiques internationales', *QDC*, no. 371 (1 August 1912), pp. 156–71.
29 The inauguration of the Brest–Dakar in 1905, for example, did not give rise to demonstrations similar to those that accompanied the opening of the cable from Constanza (Roumania) to Constantinople – 'a new success for German cable policy', according to the *Kölnische Zeitung*, quoted in *QDC*, no. 200 (16 June 1905), p. 782.

List of contributors

Jean-Claude Allain is Professor of Contemporary History at the Université de la Sorbonne Nouvelle (Paris III). He is the author of *Agadir 1911*, *Joseph Caillaux 1863–1944*, and numerous articles on many aspects of European international relations.

Christian Amalvi is a Conservator at the Bibliothèque Nationale and the author of *Une Icône républicaine: Rouget de Lisle chantant La Marseillaise par Isidore Pils* and *De l'Art et de la manière d'accomoder les héros de l'histoire de France*.

Pierre Arnaud is a professor at the Université de Lyon I Claude Bernard, and has published widely on the history of sport, including *Le Sportman, l'écolier, le gymnaste*.

Stéphane Audoin-Rouzeau is *maître de conférences* at the Université d'Amiens, and author of *14–18: Les Combattants des tranchées* and *1870: La France dans la guerre*.

Lenard R. Berlanstein is Professor of History at the University of Virginia. A specialist in modern French social and labour history, he is the author of *The Barristers of Toulouse in the Eighteenth Century* and *The Working People of Paris, 1871–1914*.

Michael Burns, Associate Professor of Modern European History at Mount Holyoke College, Massachusetts, is the author of *Rural Society and French Politics: Boulangism and the Dreyfus Affair*.

Gerard Canini teaches history at Verdun and is a specialist in military history. He is author or editor of numerous works including *La Lorraine dans la guerre de 14–18* and *Combattre à Verdun*.

William D. Irvine is Associate Professor of History at Glendon College of York University, Ontario. He is the author of *French Conservatism in Crisis* and *The Boulanger Affair Reconsidered* and is currently working on French fascism in the 1930s.

List of contributors

Jean-Charles Jauffret is *maître de conférences* at the military academy Saint-Cyr Coëtquidan, and a specialist in military history whose works include *Parlement, Gouvernement, Commandement: L'Armée de métier sous la 3e République 1871–1914*.

Bertrand Joly, former student at the École des Chartes, is a Conservator at the Archives Nationales. He is currently preparing a thesis on Paul Déroulède.

John F. V. Keiger is Senior Lecturer in French History and Politics at the University of Salford, author of *France and the Origins of the First World War* and a co-editor of *British Documents on Foreign Affairs: Reports and Papers from the Foreign Office Confidential Print*.

Gerd Krumeich is Professor of Modern and Contemporary History at the University of Freiburg, and author of *Armaments and Politics in France on the Eve of the First World War* and *Jeanne d'Arc in der Geschichte*.

Bernard Ménager is Professor of Contemporary History at the Université de Lille III Charles de Gaulle, and author of *La Vie politique dans le département du Nord de 1851 à 1877* and *Le Napoléon du peuple*.

Philip G. Nord is Associate Professor of History at Princeton University. He is the author of *Paris Shopkeepers and the Politics of Resentment* and is currently at work on a book on the republican revival in France, 1860–85.

Karen Offen is an independent scholar affiliated to the Institute for Research on Women and Gender at Stanford University. She has published many articles on French and European women's history, and is co-editor of *Victorian Women* and *Women, the Family and Freedom*.

William Serman is professor at the Université de Paris I Panthéon-Sorbonne. His books include *Les Origines des officiers français 1848–1870*, *Les Officiers français dans la nation 1848–1914* and *La Commune de Paris*.

Pierre Sorlin, professor at the Université de Paris III, has specialized in the study of audiovisual productions and images as sources for historians. His works on the topic include *Sociologie du cinéma: archives pour l'histoire de demain*, *The Film in History*, *Générique des années trente* and *European Cinemas, European Societies*.

Zeev Sternhell is the Léon Blum Professor of Political Science at the Hebrew University of Jerusalem, and author of many books and articles on nineteenth- and twentieth-century nationalist thought, including *Maurice Barrès et le nationalisme français*, *La Droite révolutionnaire 1885–1914: Les origines françaises du fascisme* and *Ni Droite ni gauche: l'idéologie fasciste en France*.

David Stevenson is Lecturer in International History at the London School of Economics and Political Science. His publications include *French War Aims against Germany, 1914–1919* and *The First World War and International Politics*.

Judith F. Stone is Associate Professor of History at Western Michigan University. She is the author of *The Search for Social Peace: Reform Legislation in France, 1890–1914*.

Robert Tombs is a Fellow of St John's College, Cambridge, the author of *The War Against Paris 1871* and co-author of *Thiers 1797–1877: A Political Life*.

Albert Vaiciulenas is currently carrying out research on Boulangist grassroots organization in Paris.

Eugen Weber is Joan Palevsky Professor of Modern European History at the University of California at Los Angeles, and the author of many books and articles on French history, including *The Nationalist Revival in France 1905–1914*, *Action Française: Royalism and Reaction in Twentieth-Century France*, *Peasants into Frenchmen: The Modernization of Rural France 1870–1914* and *France, Fin de Siècle*.

Index

abortion 202, 203, 206
Adam, Paul 124–5
Action Française 4, 19, 26, 28, 39, 42, 133, 136, 144–5, 155–6
Action Française 131
Action Libérale Populaire 144
Agadir crisis 255, 259, 262, 276
'Agathon' (pseud. H. Massis and A. de Tarde) 30, 216, 261
aircraft 81
'Alain' (pseud. Émile Chartier) 71
Algeria 16, 153, 238, 269
Allemane, Jean 25
Alliance Républicaine 121, 123
Alsace-Lorraine, lost provinces of 37, 45, 50–60, 112–13, 231–2, 262
anarchism 16, 41, 153
André, Gen. 178
antimilitarism 24
anti-Semitism 16, 18, 28–9, 32–3, 36, 56–7, 105, 125, 128–9, 130–1, 138, 140–1, 147–55, 171
Appel au Peuple 157
army 6, 25, 39, 46, 79, 81–2, 103, 108–9, 169, 233–4
 in 1914–18 war 89–99   passim
 and politics 238–47
 promotion in 244–5
 see also military service, military training, soldiers
art deco 219
Association de Défense des Classes Moyennes 212, 217, 222
Assumptionists 70, 130
Atget, Eugène 76
Aumale, duc d' 240
Auclert, Hubertine 201
Avenir Militaire 108–10

Balzac, Honoré de 11, 20
Barrère, Camille 262
Barrès, Maurice 5, 23–4, 26, 30, 32, 34, 36, 39, 43, 50, 57–8, 63, 78, 84, 91, 95, 124–5, 127–8, 133, 152, 168, 195, 238
Barruel, abbé 40
Bastille 42
Bert, Paul 16, 183

Berthaut, Gen. 240
Biétry, Pierre 144
birth rate 187, 198
 see also population
Bismarck, Otto von xii, 111, 113–16
Blanqui, Auguste 148
Blanquists 26, 104, 105, 156
Blum, Léon 58
Boers 155, 219
Boer War 81, 270–1
Bonaparte, Prince Napoleon-Jérome 137
Bonaparte, Prince Victor 136–40
Bonapartism xi–xii, 27, 29–30, 39, 136–45, 232–3, 238–9, 241
Boulainvilliers, Henri de 8, 11
Boulanger, Gen. Georges xiv, 16, 28, 52, 105, 108–9, 111–14, 116–17, 119n.31, 121, 125, 137, 162, 235, 241, 243
Boulangism xiii, xiv, 23, 26, 28–30, 66, 74, 79–80, 103–6, 108, 116, 123–7, 136, 142, 184–5, 234, 238, 243, 248
 organizations 123–7
Bourgeois, Léon 174
Bourget, Paul 34
Boutmy, Émile 259–61
boy scouts 219
brainwashing 91
Breteuil, marquis de 115–16
Briand, Aristide 276
Brugères, Gen. 243, 245
'Bruno' (pseud. Augustine Fouillée) 50–1
Buisson, Ferdinand 183
Burke, Edmund 30
business organizations 211–14

Cailly, Jacques (pseud. Louis Davout) 147–8, 152–3
Cambon, Jules 259, 261–2
Cambon, Paul 259, 263
Canard Enchaîné 24
Carnot, Lazare 40
Carnot, M. F. Sadi 41
Cassagnac, Paul de 136, 138, 140, 142–3
Catholic Church 4, 41, 103, 169, 186–8, 250, 252
Celts 42
Chambord, Henri comte de xiv, 240

Index

Chanzy, Gen. 248
Charles VII 64–5
Chéret, Jules 85
Cherfils, Gen. 46
cinema 76, 84–5
Cissey, Gen. de 239
class, lower middle 159–60, 164, 166
class conflict 3, 16
Clemenceau, Georges 16, 78, 108, 236, 276
Clovis 14, 40
Club Alpin Français 189, 217–18
colonialism 174–5, 236, 241, 267
Colrat, Maurice 212, 216–17, 219, 222, 224
Combes, Émile 169, 177–8
Commune of Paris (1871) 12, 238–9, 241–2
Confédération Général du Travail 24, 29, 160, 170, 212
Conseil National des Femmes Françaises 201–3, 205
conservationism 217–18, 221
Constant, Benjamin 6
contraception 206
Coppée, François 23, 26, 143
Corday, Charlotte 46–7
Coubertin, Pierre de 190, 219
coup d'état 105, 112, 117, 139–40, 143, 150, 153, 234, 238, 242–6
Courrier de l'Est 124, 128
Cri du Peuple 110, 123
Cruppi, Jean 259, 263

Danton, Georges 41
Daudet, Léon 50
decadence xiii, 32
Declaration of the Rights of Man 44, 60
Delcassé, Théophile 258
demography: *see* population
Demolins, Edmond 215, 219
Déroulède, Paul xiv, 4, 5, 14, 26, 36, 39, 43–5, 51–2, 104–5, 108–9, 111, 117, 123, 130, 136, 138–41, 143, 151, 153, 155, 159, 184–5, 195, 251, 253
Deschanel, Paul 214, 222, 258
Dillon, Arthur 114–15
diplomacy 237, 261–2
 see also foreign ministry
Doumer, Paul 174–5, 177, 216
Doumergue, Gaston 202
Dreyfus, Alfred 4, 5, 32, 52–60
Dreyfus Affair xiv, 23, 26, 27–8, 74, 80, 82, 105–6, 128, 130, 136, 138, 140, 145, 153, 159, 197, 245, 272
Dreyfus family 53–60
Driant, Émile 44–5, 132, 133
Drumont, Édouard 4, 18, 26, 30, 36, 41, 56, 105, 138, 141, 147, 152, 154, 159
Dubuc, Édouard 106, 147–58

Ducrot, Gen. 240–1, 244
Dufeuille, Eugène 111, 114
Dupanloup, bishop Félix 68–9
Durkheim, Émile 17
Duruy, Albert 44
Duruy, Georges 44–5

Echo de Paris 45–6
école des athlètes 191, 219
École des Roches 215
École Libre des Sciences Politiques 211–12, 218, 234, 256–62, 264
Edwards-Pilliet, Blanche 201
elections
 1885 121–2
 1889 125
 1893 137
 1898 128–9, 138
 1902 130, 155, 169
 1904 144, 177
 1906 131–2
 1910 217
 1911 133
electoral system 104–5
elites 223–4
England 10, 43, 47, 268
 see also Great Britain
English, the xi, 81
Étienne, Eugène 174, 177

Farre, Gen. 240, 244
fascism xiv, 7, 24, 156
Fashoda crisis 271–2
Fédération Gymnastique et Sportive des Patronages de France 185–8
Fédération des Industriels et des Commerçants Français 211–13, 216
Fédération Républicaine 211
feminism 195, 197, 203, 206
Ferry, Jules 16, 51–2, 104, 114, 182–3, 271
Flaubert, Gustave 11, 20
Floquet, Charles 111
foreign ministry 214, 234, 255–64 passim
 and nationalism 255–6, 258, 261–4
France, Anatole 74
Franks xi, 3, 8–19
Frederick, crown prince of Prussia 113
freemasonry 40–1, 43, 130, 178
Freycinet, Charles de 256–7
Fustel de Coulanges, Numa Denis 12, 58–9, 232

Gabriel, Alfred 122–7
Galliffet, Gen. de 240–2, 245–6
Gambetta, Léon xii, 50, 52, 182, 239, 241, 245
Gaulle, Charles de 47, 225
Gauls xi, 3, 8–19, 41

283

Index

Gautherot, Gustave 40
Germans 32, 95–6
Germany 14, 22, 31–2, 43, 210–12, 236–7, 255, 261, 264, 267, 275–6
Gervaize, Ludovic 128–30, 132, 152
Gobineau, Arthur de 32
Goblet, René 257
Great Britain 267–8, 270–7
Grévy, Jules 121, 240, 243
Grosjean, Georges 44–5
Guérin, Jules 36, 105–6, 128, 130, 147, 150, 152, 154
Guerre Sociale 24–5
Guizot, François 11, 260

Habert, Marcel 44, 128
Halévy, Daniel xiv, 56
'Hansi' (pseud. J. J. Waltz) 50, 52
Haussonville, Othenin d' 112
Hébert, Georges 219
Hénard, Eugène 217
Henner, Jean Jacques 50–1
Henri IV 47
Herder, J. G. 30
Herr, Lucien 56–7
Hervé, Gustave 16, 23–5
Hugo, Victor 67, 168
Hugues, Clovis 66
Humbert scandal 171–2, 175
Hume, David 10

imagery 75, 84–6
immigrant workers 121, 125
income tax 212
individualism 30
Iung, Col. 244

Jacobins 41, 44, 46
  tradition 103, 113, 117, 184
Jaurès, Jean 24, 46, 78
Jeunesse Antisémite et Nationaliste 147–56
Jews xi, 4, 18, 41, 43, 53
  see also anti-Semitism
Joan of Arc 4, 19, 40, 63–72, 81, 132, 144, 187–8
'Job' (pseud. J. Onfrey de Breville) 44, 48
Jouvenel, Robert de 222

Kahn, Zadoc 2, 51, 57

Laguerre, Georges 27, 105
Laisant, Charles 27, 66, 124
Lanessan, Antoine de 174–5, 177
Lasies, Joseph 138, 141
Lazare, Bernard 56
Le Bon, Gustave 34, 191, 222
Lebon, André 211, 225

legitimism 39, 238
Legoux, baron 138, 140
Lemaître, Jules 26, 34, 117, 143
Le Pen, Jean Marie 4, 19
Le Play, Frédéric 190, 219
Leroy-Beaulieu, Paul 260–1
Libre Parole 128, 152, 154, 156, 173
Ligue Antisémitique de France 105, 130, 147, 152–3
Ligue de la Patrie Française 106, 117, 129–31, 142–4, 155
Ligue de l'Enseignement 14, 189
Ligue des Droits de l'Homme 197
Ligue des Patriotes 4, 14, 26, 39, 43, 45–6, 104–5, 111, 136, 138–9, 142, 151, 185
Ligue pour la Culture Française 215
literacy 27
Lockroy, Édouard 174–7
Lonlay, Dick de 44
Lumière 82

Macé, Jean 14, 15
Mackau, Armand de 104, 113, 116
Mac Mahon, Marshal de 239
Mairet, L. 91
Marat, Jean-Paul 46–7
Marcère, Émile-Louis de 12, 17
Marconnet, Ferdinand 122
Margonnet, Henri 122
Marin, Louis 131–2, 218, 221–2, 225
Marr, Wilhelm 30, 36
Marseillaise 40, 43, 46, 47
Martimprey, Edmond de 43
Martin, Henri 4, 14, 63, 65
Marx, Karl 13
materialism xiii, 30, 36–7
Maurras, Charles 3, 4, 26, 28, 30, 34, 39, 41–2, 47, 74, 103, 106
Méliès, Georges 81–2
'Mermeix' (pseud. Gabriel Terrail) 104
Méry, Gaston 41
Messager de Toulouse 110
Mézeray, François de 66
Michelet, Jules xi, xii, 4, 30–2, 42, 51, 63–4, 67, 168
Michon, Jules de 112
military service 238, 242
military training 182–4, 188, 248–53
Millerand, Alexandre 272, 274–5
Ministère des Affaires Étrangères: see foreign ministry
Mommsen, Theodor 36, 232
Monck, Gen. 238, 241
Montlosier, François de 9–10
Morès, marquis de 147, 152
Morocco 237, 261, 271
Mun, Albert de 45, 111, 116

Index

Musée Social 212–3, 217, 220
Mussolini, Benito 36

Napoleon I 9, 47, 261
Napoleon III xii
Naquet, Alfred 27
nationalism
   concepts xi, xiii, xiv, 3, 5, 6, 17, 22–3, 26–7, 30–7, 39–47 passim, 74, 77–8, 82–3, 86–7, 106, 117, 231–3, 261–3, 267
   and conservatives xiv, 106, 108–18 passim, 130–3
   and culture 210, 215–21
   movement xiv, 4, 23, 25–9, 103, 106, 121, 144
   'revival' 196, 210, 223–4, 234, 236
   support for 122–4, 126–8, 130–1, 149–51, 156, 159, 164–6
   and women 196–8, 206–7
'National Revolution' (1940) 224–5, 232
national socialism 25, 58
nationhood
   concepts xi, 3, 5–6, 31–2, 86–7
   sentiment 3, 5–6, 50–60 passim, 94, 97–9, 168, 267
navy 81–2, 169–70, 174–8
nobles 8, 9, 41

office workers 160–2, 165–6
Olympic Games 190–2, 219
Opinion 216, 220, 223
Ordinaire 272–3
Orleanism 39, 238, 240
Ornano, Cunéo d' 138–40
Ossian 9

Panama scandal 103, 137
Paris, comte de 112–14
Parisian Gas Co. 160–5
parliament, criticism of 222–3
Pasquier, Étienne 8, 66
Paul-Boncour, Joseph 216–17, 220, 225
Péguy, Charles 53, 56
Pelletan, Camille 168–78
Pelletier, Madeleine 201–2
Pétain, Marshal 24, 224–5
Petit, Gabrielle 202
Petit Caporal 138–40
Petit Palais 47
photography 75–7
Picquart, Col. 56
Piou, Jacques 116
Poincaré, Raymond 71, 106, 144, 210, 212, 214, 219, 222–5, 237, 263–4
Polignac, prince de 124–5
population
   concern with 196, 198–200, 203–4, 206

   legal measures 206
   women and 199–200, 203–4, 206
postcards 75, 77–8, 85
posters 75, 77–8, 85
Précurseur 150–3
press: *see* individual titles
Pressensé, Francis de 23, 170, 173
protectionism 212
protestantism 8, 40, 43
Prussia 43, 47

Quai d'Orsay: *see* foreign ministry
Quicherat, Jules 63, 65, 67, 70
Quinet, Edgar xii, 15

race
   concepts 22, 31, 32–4
   conflict 4, 16
radicalism 16, 168, 170
radicals 27, 168–9, 178
Ranke, Leopold von 36
regionalism 218, 221
Régis, Max 154
Renan, Ernest 30, 32–7, 40, 74, 232
republicanization 162, 255–6
revanche 52, 55, 112, 182, 246
revolution
   fear of 109–10, 112, 118
   of 1789 xi, 4, 9, 27, 30, 39–47, 60, 133, 168
revolutionary situation 5, 29
Richepin, Jean 215, 219
Risler, Georges 217, 220
Robespierre, Maximilien 40
Rochebouët, Gen. de 240
Rochefort, Henri 23, 26, 56, 108–9, 117
Rodin, Auguste 217, 219
Roosevelt, Theodore 218, 223
Rouget de Lisle, Claude 40
Roussel, Nelly 202
royalism xiii, 39, 108–18
Rude, François 11, 43
Russia 232, 237
Russians 32

Saint Aulaire, A.F.C. de 261
Saint-Simon, Henri de 13, 18
Sandherr, Col. 56
Saussier, Gen. 243
Scheurer-Kestner, Auguste 57, 148
Schnaebelé incident 43, 111, 243
schools 14–15, 183
   school battalions 109, 184, 235, 248–53
Scott, Walter 10, 20
Section Française de l'Internationale Ouvrière 24–5
Seeberger, Jules 76–7, 81–2
seize mai (1877) 240

Index

'Séverine' (pseud. Caroline Rémy) 104, 123
Siegfried, Jules 213
Sismondi, Léonard de 11, 63–4
socialism 16, 24–5, 29, 103, 127–8, 130, 186, 212
Societé pour la Protection des Paysages de France 217
soldiers
   brainwashing of 91–2
   in 1914–18 war 89–99
   and nationalism 94, 97–9
   writings of 91–3
Sorel, Albert 260–1
sport 182–93
Stöcker, Adolf 30
Sue, Eugène 11, 16
Syveton, Gabriel 23

Taine, Hippolyte 30, 33–4, 44, 260
Taxil, Léo (pseud. Gabriel Jogand-Pagés) 70–1
telegraph 235–6, 267–77
Thalamas Affair 71, 144, 146 n.59
Thierry, Augustin 10–13, 15, 18, 20, 63–4
Thiers, Adolphe xi, xiv, 233, 238, 240–1, 269
Tocqueville, Alexis de xi, 260
Tour de la France par deux enfants, Le, 50, 54
Touring Club de France 217, 219
Toussenel, Alphonse 18
Treitschke, Heinrich von 30, 36
tricolour flag 39, 43, 45–6, 79, 188, 240
Turinaz, bishop 125, 130, 132

Union des Industries Métallurgiques et Minières 211–12
Union des Sociétés Françaises de Sports Athlétiques 183, 186, 189–91
Union des Sociétés de Gymnastique de France 182, 184, 188
Union Française pour le Suffrage des Femmes 202, 205
unionization 163
urbanism 217, 220

Vacher de Lapouge, G. 34
Valois, Georges 47
Vandal, Albert 260–1
Vendée rising 40, 47
Vercingétorix 4, 14, 262
Vichy regime 206, 224, 232
Viviani, René 214
vocabulary 74–80, 82–3, 86, 93

Wales, Prince of 115
Wallon, Henri 68–9
war xii, 109–10, 112, 118
   and women 204–6
   economic 213
   revolutionary and Napoleonic xi, 43–6
   1870 xii, 23, 35, 182–3, 238, 248, 271
   1914–18 23, 89–99, 232, 264; preparations for 236–7
   1940 36–7
Wilson, Woodrow 223
Wilson scandal 121
women 47, 70, 85–6, 195–207 passim
   and childbirth 199, 201
   and employment 161, 198, 201
   and law 202, 206
   and nation 196–8, 206–7
   organizations 197, 201, 203
   suffrage 203, 205, 206

Zevaes, Alexandre 25
Zola, Émile 23, 74, 138, 242